Terry,

1/00

Please Return!!

Griots and Griottes

Griots and Griottes

Masters of Words and Music

Thomas A. Hale

Indiana University Press

Bloomington and Indianapolis

This book is a publication of

Indiana University Press
601 North Morton Street
Bloomington, Indiana
47404–3797 USA

www.indiana.edu/~iupress

Telephone orders 800–842–6796
Fax orders 812–855–7931
Orders by e-mail iuporder@indiana.edu

LIBRARY OF CONGRESS CATALOGING-IN-PUBLICATION DATA

Hale, Thomas A.
Griots and griottes : masters of words and music / Thomas A. Hale.
p.   cm.
Includes bibliographical references and index.
ISBN 0-253-33458-6 (cl : alk. paper)
1. Griots—Africa—History.   2. Oral tradition—Africa—History.   3.
Storytelling—Africa—History.   4. Laudatory poetry, African—History.   5.
Folklore—Africa—Performance.   I. Title.
GR350.H275   1998
398'.092'26—dc21   98-31798

1 2 3 4 5   03 02 01 00 99 98

"A siin de mé"

To the people of Niger and to their griots,
whose warmth and generosity during my first stay there
from 1964 to 1966 inspired me to take the path of learning about the
oral tradition. In the words of the late Nouhou Malio, *jeseredunka*
or master griot, that path has no end—

"a siin de mé."

❊ Contents ❊

❊ Illustrations ❊

❈ Maps ❈

✖ Acknowledgments ✖

This book in many ways is the result of my first encounters with griots during a two-year stint as a United States Peace Corps volunteer in Niger in 1964–66. Subsequent stays in Niger during the academic year 1980–81 for research on the oral epic while serving as a Fulbright lecturer at the University of Niamey and in 1987 and 1989 for followup fieldwork while serving as director of the Penn State–University of Niamey Affiliation Program supported by the United States Information Agency, enabled me to collect additional information, especially from griottes.

For a book of this scope, there are more people to thank than there is space available. They range from the scores of griots who consented to tell me about their lives during interviews from Banjul to Timbuktu, to scholars, local officials, and friends who helped to arrange these visits, and other people who provided access to archives and libraries, or who forwarded items of information from sources that I would not otherwise have consulted. Several, however, deserve special mention: in Niger, Dioulde Laya, director of the Centre for the Study of Linguistics and History by Oral Traditions, as well as Ousmane Tandina and Fatima Mounkaila of the Modern Literature Department at the University of Niamey; in Mali, Mahmoud Zouber, former director of the Ahmed Baba Research Center in Timbuktu, Mamadou Gueye, Tanhoulé Keita, Mamadou Soumaré, and Dramane Dembelé from the Ecole Normale Supérieure in Bamako; in Senegal, Bassirou Dieng, Lilyan Kesteloot, and Mahady Diallo; in The Gambia, Bakari Sidibe, Papa Bunka Susso, and Jali Madi Kanuteh.

Many of my colleagues have offered valuable comments on part or all of an earlier version of this study: Stephen Belcher, Eric Charry, David Conrad, Lucy Durán, Barbara Hoffman, John Johnson, George Joseph, Roderic Knight, and Christopher Miller.

I want to thank the institutions that supported my research. The National Endowment for the Humanities provided a fellowship that was the key to enabling me to carry out much of the fieldwork for this book in 1991–92; The Pennsylvania State University offered additional support so that I could devote the entire year to the project. Penn State also granted me two one-semester sabbatical leaves in 1989 and 1996 that contributed both to the early stages of this project and to its completion; the Institute for the Arts and Humanistic Studies and the Comparative Literature Department funded research in Senegal and The Gambia in 1991; the American Philosophical Society, the French Department, the Liberal Arts Research and Graduate Studies Office, and the Office of the Vice President for Research supported work in Mali in 1992; the College of the Liberal Arts Research and Graduate Studies Office and the Institute for the Arts and Humanistic Studies funded the production of the maps and other visual documentation for this book. The staff of the Deasy GeoGraphics Laboratory at Penn State, in particular David Barnes, created the maps.

I also want to thank my students at Penn State who enrolled in a graduate seminar on West African griots in fall 1994. Their curiosity and questions, as well as their research, contributed to greater understanding of the subject for all of us.

I thank the following people and organizations for permission to reproduce photos and sketches: the Société de Géographie in Paris for two 19th-century photos of griots; the British Library for permission to reproduce the figure of an Egyptian woman playing a lute from MSS 29851, 257–60; Susan Gunn Pevar for permission to reproduce her sketches of a *kora* that appeared also in *Sing Out!*, vol. 25, no. 6, 1977; Roderic Knight for his sketch of the *kora* bridge.

Finally I thank John Gallman, director of Indiana University Press, whose vision and interest in African subjects has contributed greatly to the development not only of this book but of many others.

❉ A Note ❉
on Orthography and
Measurement of Distance

Most of the names and places cited in this study bear the mark of French spelling, for example Ségou instead of Segu, a city in Mali, or Nouhou Malio, instead of Nuhu, the name of a griot in Niger. The reason for the French orthography is that, with few exceptions, the information for this book comes from Francophone West Africa. To avoid confusion for readers who may want to do further research on griots, I have maintained the French spelling throughout this study for Francophone names and places but followed English when the subject came from Anglophone Africa. The one notable exception to the rule is Timbuktu, spelled in French as Tombouctou. The name of that city entered the English language long ago as a synonym for a distant place, and for that reason I have chosen to keep the anglicized form.

The reader will also notice variations in spelling within a given area: Balla Fasseke and Bala Diabaté for two griots from the Mande heartland, one from seven centuries ago, one from the 20th century, and Nakoyo Suso and Papa Susso, two cousins from The Gambia. These differences reflect changing usage within a region, within a family, and over time.

Distances in Francophone West Africa are measured in kilometers, not miles. For this reason, I have listed all distances in kilometers. But on the maps, the reader will find a scale that lists both kilometers and miles.

Griots and Griottes

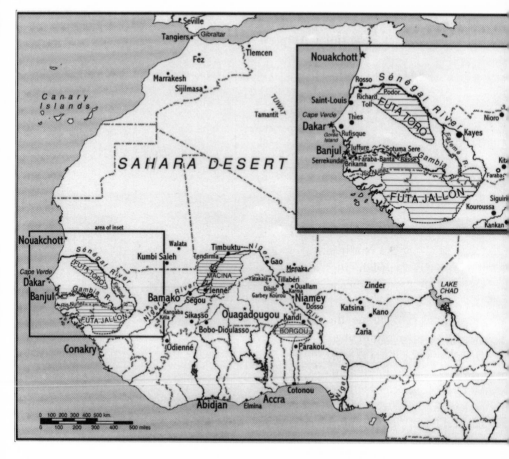

Map 1. Regions, cities, towns, and villages cited, both current and ancient.

❈ Introduction ❈
Ibn Battuta, Alex Haley, and the Diffusion of Knowledge about Griots

On July 28, 1352, a North African traveler from Fez, Morocco, arrived in the capital of the Mali empire, in the region known today as the border between northern Guinea and southwestern Mali. There, at the court of Mansa Sulayman (reigned 1341–60), he encountered griots.

After returning home, the traveler narrated a description that includes the first written portrait of griots, the West African artisans of the word (see Hamdun and King, 1975, pp. 34–45). Although his brief sketch was only a small part of Ibn Battuta's narrative about people of the Mali empire, the picture of the fourteenth-century griots is especially important today because it provides evidence that the oral tradition maintained by these bards is at least seven centuries old. In fact, their verbal art quite likely is as old as the most ancient cities of West Africa, such as Jenne-Jeno, which archaeologists now tell us antedates the time of Christ.

At a time when most North Africans had only a vague idea of where Mali was located, Ibn Battuta traveled there and to many other countries for a variety of reasons rooted in his own intellectual curiosity. He had heard extraordinary tales about the gold of Mali, stories stemming from a pilgrimage to Mecca in 1324–25 by an earlier ruler of Mali, Mansa Musa.

Over 600 years later, on May 17, 1967, another traveler, the American writer Alex Haley, went to Juffure, a village in The Gambia on what was once the western fringe of the Mali empire. There he encountered a man of griot, or *jali*, origin who recounted what Haley reported to be a narrative about Haley's family roots in Africa. For the American, the words of this man provided a link between his American ancestors and an African heritage nearly erased by the slave trade. Haley's trip to The Gambia was motivated not simply by intellectual curiosity but also by a desire to reconstruct the past.

The publication in 1976 of *Roots*, the fictional and factual blend that Haley called "faction," created an extraordinary interest in genealogy in the United States and other parts of the world. A video series based on the book drew the largest audience in the history of U.S. television. In *Roots II*, a sequel that told how Haley went about his research for the book, many viewers saw for the first time a Mandinka griot, or *jali*, from The Gambia, Alhaji Bai Konte, who plays the role of the man who told Haley the story about his ancestor Kunta Kinte.

Although griots had performed outside West Africa decades before *Roots*, Haley's visit to Juffure generated an enormous increase in interest in these wordsmiths around the world. Since 1976, thanks to the continuing impact of *Roots*, West African griots have dramatically expanded their performance contexts. They have appeared on the stages of university auditoriums, in churches, and in television and recording studios in Paris, London, New York, and Tokyo.

In Search of a Term

The term *griot* now occurs in a wide range of contexts that goes far beyond the scholarly community. The online Lexis-Nexis database, which covers thousands of publications around the world, contains over 1,500 references to the word *griot* in performances, organizations, and the media. Here I will mention a few examples that I have come across during the past two decades.

Dance. "Griot New York," a dance performance about urban life for African Americans, was created by choreographer Garth Fagan in collaboration with the trumpeter and composer Wynton Marsalis and the sculptor Martin Puryear. It premiered in New York on December 4, 1991, and was televised nationally by the Public Broadcasting System on February 10, 1995.

Music. In newspapers and magazines, African American musicians are sometimes referred to as griots. A story about the drummer Arthur Taylor appeared in the *New York Times* under the headline "A Jazz Griot with a Sense of Civility" (Sherman, 1994), while the singer Abbey Lincoln was described in *Newsweek* as "a culture bearer" who, like Paul Robeson, acted as a griot (Leland, 1992).

Cultural Organizations. The Griot Organization, the Griots' Palaver, L'Association des Griots de la Martinique, and the Roxbury Griots are organizations that work in one way or another with the oral tradition. Brenda Givens, executive director of the Griot Organization, offered a storytelling session, advertised as "Griot: African and African-American Folktales and Biographies," at the South Hill Library in Puyallup, Washington, in 1994. L'Association des Griots de la Martinique, led by Georges Fitte-Duval, organizes poetry and story readings in schools, makes audio and video cassettes, and attempts to familiarize Martinican students with their national literature (Anon., 1994). The Griots' Palaver in Toronto held evenings of literary readings by authors of African descent during the annual meeting of the African Studies Association at Toronto, November 3–5, 1994. The Griots of Roxbury, a project of the Oral History Center in Boston, helps young people learn about their history and how to interview members of the community in order to preserve and disseminate their culture (Capaccio, 1993; Freydberg, 1993).

Magazines and Newsletters. The range of publications that have adopted the term *griot* is unusually diverse. *Les Griots* was founded in 1938 by a group of Haitian intellectuals whose goal was to promote black consciousness. Today *The Literary Griot* carries scholarly studies of African and African American literature in the United States. *Le Griot*, a mimeographed newsletter, informs the U.S. Embassy community in Mali of current events, while another publication by the same name in Senegal is distributed free to Dakarois interested in upcoming concerts, sports events, films, and other forms of entertainment. *The Griot* functions as a forum for friends of Mali in the United States. *Le Griot des Antilles*, a glossy bimonthly magazine, serves the Caribbean community in Paris, while *Griot*, a newsletter produced by the Communications Workshop of the African-American Cultural Program at the University of Illinois, reaches out to African American students there.

Books. Publishers have adopted the term *griot* to designate textual and visual material linked to or aimed at the African diaspora. *Le Scribe et le Griot* is the title of a series of instructional materials produced by the Canadian publishing house La Littérature de l'Oreille for students in Africa who want to learn to read and write French with the aid of texts and cassettes drawn from African resources. In the United States, the Quality Paperback Book Club listed its African American writers in a fall 1994 mailing under the heading "Griot Editions: A special QPB library, celebrating the voices of the African diaspora." One publisher has adopted the term as a company name — Griots Publishing in Lancaster, California.

Griot also appears in a variety of titles of books about Africa or related in some way to the continent. Jean Rouch, a French ethnographer and filmmaker, is compared to a griot in the title of two volumes, *Jean Rouch: un griot gaulois* (Prédal, 1982) and *The Cinematic Griot: The Ethnography of Jean Rouch* (Stoller, 1992). *Scribe, Griot, and Novelist: Narrative Interpreters of the Songhay Empire* (1990a), my own comparative study of the way chroniclers, a griot, and a novelist recount the history of the Songhay empire, offers insights into *jeserey*, griots from the Songhay-speaking world, and provides the text of *The Epic of Askia Mohammed. Jeliya: Etre griot et musicien aujourd'hui* (1992) is a book-length combination of narrative and interview focusing on Adama Dramé, a Burkinabe *jeli*; it is co-authored by Dramé and Arlette Senn-Borloz. *Jeliya* is a particularly significant book because the reader finds in it a griot's view of the world.

Cultural Identity. In the United States, African Americans have identified with griots in a variety of ways, from cuisine to poetry to history. *The Griots' Cookbook: Rare and Well-Done* (1985), by three African American women from Baltimore—Alice McGill, Mary Carter Smith, and Elmira M. Washington—provides recipes from the African diaspora. Smith, who is also a storyteller, is the official griot for the city of Baltimore (1996). The poet Amiri Baraka assumes the role of griot in his collection of poetry *Wise Why's Y's* (1995). By including variant spellings in the subtitle (*The Griot's Song: Djeli Ya*) and in the listing of the author (Amiri Baraka, Djali), he embraces a large swath of the vast Mande world, because *djeli ya* refers to the profession of griot (*jeliya*), *griot* is spelled *jali* in the western region (the Mandinka and Khassonké areas of The Gambia and western Mali), and it is heard as *jeli* in the Bamana and Maninka regions of central Mali. In the introduction, Baraka states: "Why's/Wise is a long poem in the tradition of Djali (Griots) but this is about African American (American) History" (3).

African Americans are adopting the term *griot* as a sign of respect for those who know about the past, are artists in various media, or are simply high achievers. Elders in Harlem were described as griots in a letter to the *New York Times* from a local member of the New York State Assembly. Responding to a question in a news article about the origin of the term *Big Apple* to describe New York City, the Assembly member, Geraldine Daniels, explained in 1990 that "according to Harlem griots (oral historians), the clue to the mystery is Harlem. It is my understanding that Alain Locke, professor of philosophy at Howard University, originated the term during the Harlem Renaissance of the 1920's." In a review of Sara Lawrence-Lightfoot's collection of case studies about successful African Americans, *I've Known Rivers: Lives of Loss and Liberation*, Linda Quillian (1996) described the subjects as modern-day griots who convey lessons on how to survive racism in the United States. These twentieth-century griots included a filmmaker, a professor, and a university dean.

Questions in Search of Answers

The growing use of the term in the media and in particular its appearance in a two-page *Time* essay by Lance Morrow on September 21, 1992 ("television . . . is the griot of American transience") prompted readers to ask for a definition. The *Time* editors obliged with a response at the end of the letters section on October 19 that gave a brief and partial glimpse of what griots do: "an African historian or village storyteller" (Anon., 1992a).

The queries by *Time* readers and the partial definition offered by the editors reveal both the current interest in the term and the great gap between its growing use and the public's understanding of griots. For those readers, as much as for Ibn Battuta many centuries earlier and most scholars in African studies today, griots are mysterious and complex people who inspire a variety of questions. Are they simply storytellers and historians, or do they have other functions? What are the origins of their profession? What is the difference between *griot* and other terms such as *jali*? What kinds of verbal art do griots create? What is the nature of their music and how does it relate to the words they speak, chant, or sing? How does one become a griot? Where do griots fit into their own societies? Are they all male or do women play a role in the profession? If griots are keepers of the ancient oral tradition, how are they managing to survive in the era of print and electronic media? What kinds of rewards do they receive for their services? And what is their future in Africa and the rest of the world?

The answers to these questions are not hidden behind some veil of secrecy maintained by griots. Although these artisans of the word do not reveal everything they know to all audiences, the lack of information about their profession is due more generally to the fact that relatively little research has been done on them by either African or non-African scholars. What is available appears most often in specialist publications not easily accessible to the general public. Except for the occasional Africanist who has devoted years to studying a particular culture, few people outside the region where griots live know the languages spoken by these wordsmiths and musicians—Wolof, Soninké, Mandinka, Maninka, Bamana, Songhay, and Hausa, for example. Furthermore, much of the research on griots appeared originally in French because most of these performers live in French-speaking parts of West Africa, where many ancient empires, kingdoms, and states once flourished (see map 2).

The purpose of this book is to bring to readers interested in Africa a synthesis of information from my own work and that of other scholars. The book is based on contacts with griots from 1964 to the present and includes

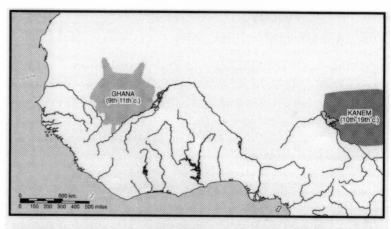

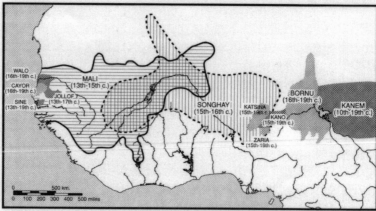

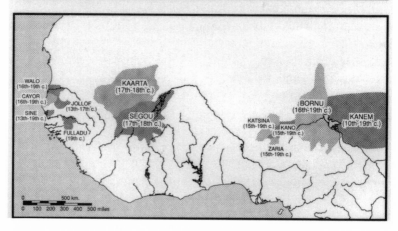

Map 2. Empires, kingdoms, and states in the Sahel and Savanna regions of West Africa, ninth through nineteenth century.

research in Niger, Mali, Senegal, and The Gambia as well as in archives and libraries in Europe and North America. Accounts by travelers, explorers, and colonial administrators, as well as recent anthropological and historical reports by scholars and my own interviews with more than a hundred griots on three continents, create a diverse mosaic of information on a profession that is central to understanding many West African societies.

The data collected for this study are extensive but often highly specialized — for example, the information on the tuning systems for instruments played by griots and the many theories for the etymology of the term *griot*. Because of space limitations and the need to present this diverse material in as clear a fashion as possible, I have adopted two strategies that will enable the reader interested in a particular aspect of the subject to dig further while allowing the narrative flow to continue without too many digressions. First, references to sources are indicated in the text rather than in notes at the bottom of the page, the end of the chapter, or the end of the book; complete details can be found in the bibliography. Second, information that is too detailed for inclusion in the narrative is provided in one of seven appendices. These appendices include a discussion of the many theories about the origin of the word *griot* and a list of the many ethno-specific terms for griots. The reader will also find information in short form that will be immediately useful for a variety of purposes: the names and addresses of griots working in the United States, sources of films and videos about griots, lists of English translations of epics narrated by griots and of their recorded music, and a short bibliographic essay on books about African music that include sections on griots.

My hope is that this book will be of value to the widest possible range of readers, from those interested in Africa because of their own roots on the continent to researchers in a variety of disciplines — history, music, anthropology, linguistics, and literature.

Origins, Geography, and Usage

Before embarking on this study, it is useful to deal with questions about the origins of the term *griot*, about the geography of the griot world, and about which word to use, *griot* or a more ethno-specific word.

Origins

Although appendix G contains a detailed study of the various theories for the origin of the term *griot*, it is important to include in this introduction a brief discussion of the term's origins. The reason for raising this issue at the outset is that the term itself is one of the most controversial features of the profession. Some West Africans feel that the word can be insulting, and say it should not be used because it does not appear in any African language. But for many African Americans, *griot* constitutes an invaluable and highly symbolic link with their cultural traditions.

There are enough theories for the origins of *griot* to fill a book. I describe them in greater detail not only in appendix G but also in "From the Griot of *Roots* to the Roots of Griot" (Hale, 1997). Although no one has uncovered enough evidence to prove a particular theory, I have advanced one of my own that points to both African and European influences in the creation of the term.

The most common theory is that *griot* comes from the French *guiriot*, ancestor of griot, which first appeared in 1637. Other views hold that *griot* comes from the Wolof term *guewel*, Fulbe *gawlo*, Mande *jeli, jali*, Portuguese *criado, grito, gritalhao*, or the Portuguese term for Jew, *judeu* (creole *djidiu*), Spanish *guirigay*, Catalan *guirigaray*, Berber and Hassaniya Arabic *iggio, egeum*, and Arabic *qawal* via *guewel*.

My own theory—and it is in many ways no better than the others—takes the question back as far as the Ghana empire by way of the slave trade through Berber to Spanish and then French: *Ghana-agenaou-guineo-guiriot-griot*. Such a long itinerary, seven centuries old, requires a lengthy and digressive explanation, one that may interest researchers more than the generalist reader, and for this reason I have included it in appendix G. But to summarize, slaves from Ghana imported to Marrakesh, Morocco, from the eleventh century onward passed through a still-standing city gate called the Bab Agenaou, or Gate of the People from Ghana. Some of them eventually reached Spain, where they were called *guineos*. When French ships, following in the path of the earlier Spanish and Portuguese fleets, arrived on the coast of Senegal in the early sixteenth century, probably manned at least in part by Spanish sailors who knew the coast, the captains may have asked their most experienced crewmembers about the noisy musicians and praise-singers who announced visits by local rulers. The answer, I speculate, was that these highly audible Africans were "just a group of guineos"—or Africans—a term that evolved into *guiriots* and later *griots*. If true, this theory makes griot a term that has both African and Western roots. Map 3 traces the linguistic itinerary I have proposed for griot.

Even though *griot* may be of African origin, it serves only to open the door to a world of wordsmiths that is far more complex than anyone, from

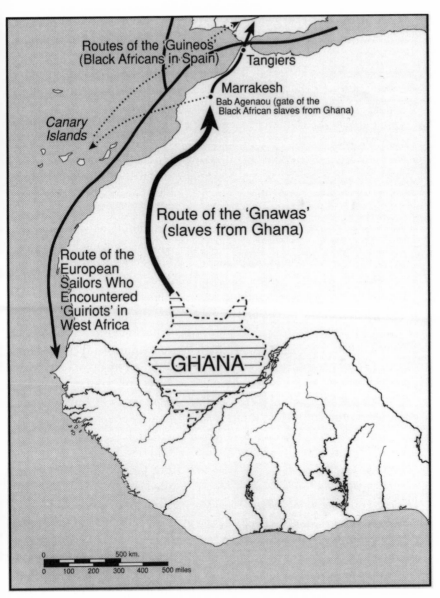

Map 3. Proposed itinerary for the term *griot* in the Ghana empire.

Ibn Battuta to Alex Haley, ever imagined. Here I give a brief list of some other terms for griot. A longer and more detailed discussion of these ethno-specific terms appears in appendix G. I list them by language.

Wolof. In this language, spoken in Senegal and The Gambia, the griot is called *gewel*, sometimes spelled *guewel*, and is part of a group of artisans known by the general term *nyeenyo*, also spelled *ñeeño*.

Mandinka of the western Mande in the Senegambian region. Here the term is *jali*, with *jalimuso* for women and *jali ke* for men. The plural of *jali* is *jalolu*. *Jaliya* is the profession or activity of griots.

Bamana and Maninka of central Mande: *Jeli*, with *jeliw* as plural. For a woman the equivalent is *jelimuso* and *jelimusow*. The master singer, male or female, is known as *nara* or *ngara*.

Khassonké, western frontier of Mali. *Laada-jalolu* are griots who are attached to a particular family; *naa* are newcomers, or itinerant griots. A chief griot was a *jali-kuntigo* (Cissoko, 1986, pp. 160–61) or *jalikuntio* (Lucy Durán, personal communiction, 1996).

Soninké, western Mali, southern Mauritania. The term here is *geseré* (plural *geserun*), sometimes spelled *gessere*. Also used is *dyare* or, in other spellings, *jaare*.

Songhay, western Niger, eastern Mali: *Jeseré* (plural *jeserey*) is the term here, with *jeseré-dunka* used for master griot and *timmé* for descendants of master griots.

Bariba, northern Benin. *Gesere*, with *gesere-bà* for chief griot.

Fulbe, scattered across West Africa from Senegal to Cameroon. *Gawlo*, *mabo*, *farba* (master griot), but with much variation in meaning across the region.

Moor, Mauritania. *Iggiw* or *iggio* (plural *iggawen*); female *tiggiwit* (plural *tiggawaten*).

Mossi, Burkina Faso. *Bendere, bendere naba* for chief griot.

Dogon, eastern Mali. *Genene.*

Hausa, northern Nigeria, western Niger: *Marok'a*, with *marok'i* (masculine singular) and *marok'iya* (feminine singular).

Dagbamba, northern Ghana: *Lunsi*, drummers who carry out some of the functions of griots.

Tuareg, northern Mali and Niger, southern Algeria. *Enad* (singular *inadan*), blacksmiths who perform many of the functions of griots.

Geography

From many references to particular peoples, a map of the griot world is beginning to emerge (see map 4). If the vast Mande region stands at the

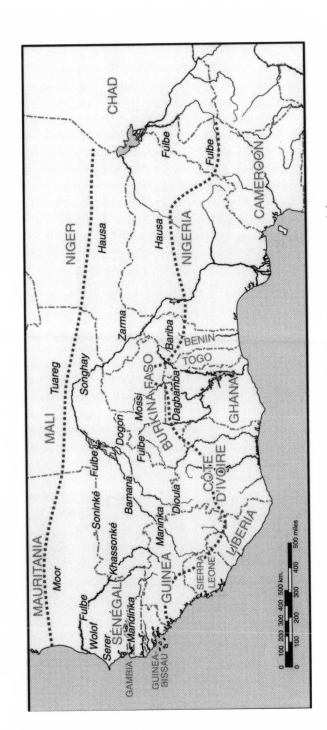

Map 4. Approximate outline of the griot world in West Africa. Broken line indicates great permeability of the frontier between regions that have griots and areas where they may travel or migrate.

center and includes Senegal, The Gambia, and southern Mali, the fringes extend northward well into Mauritania, northern central Mali, and central Niger. The southern frontier extends as far south as Guinea, northern Sierra Leone, northern Liberia, northern Côte d'Ivoire, part of Burkina Faso, northern Ghana, northern Benin, and northern Nigeria. In these areas of the Sahel and Savanna regions (see map 5), one finds both peoples who do not have griots — the Diola of southern Senegal — and societies that have long maintained hereditary professional wordsmiths who carry out a variety of other functions.

Although one may find counterparts along the southern coast of West Africa, the griots of this inland band that stretches from Senegal to Lake Chad share a common tradition of social function and verbal art that distinguishes them from those farther south. This is not to say, however, that one will not encounter griots in the southernmost areas.

Within the Mande region, the area of West Africa that is richest in the griot tradition both verbally and musically, lies the heartland of the Mali empire in northern Guinea and southwestern Mali. The spread of the empire during the European Middle Ages and its resulting cultural influence suggest that the dynamic griot tradition that we know today may have come from this region and diffused to the Senegambian area many centuries ago. Activities such as the playing of the *kora*, the most complex instrument in the world of the griots, and the chanting of the longest narratives that celebrate the past are common to this region which includes southern Mali, northern Guinea, and most of Senegal and The Gambia as well as Guinea-Bissau.

To the east and north the picture changes. The farther one travels from the northern Guinea–southwestern Mali heartland, the fewer the common features. For example, griots can be found in eastern Mali, in the area around the northern bend of the Niger river, but at the extreme northern end, around Timbuktu, those still practicing do not normally chant long epics. Downriver from Timbuktu, in western Niger, Songhay griots do not play the *kora*, and the long narratives they recount tend to be shorter than those of their Malian counterparts. Farther east, Hausa *marok'a* sing praises, poems, and songs. But there is comparatively little recorded evidence for long epics about the past (Muhammed, 1981; Tandina, 1997).

Information about the Kanem and Bornu region around Lake Chad is extremely sketchy. Denham, Clapperton, and Oudney, who visited the Sultan of Bornu in the early nineteenth century, described both a "declaimer shouting praises" of the ruler and a trumpeter (cited in Brenner 1973, p. 22). In the twentieth century, there are indicators of the existence

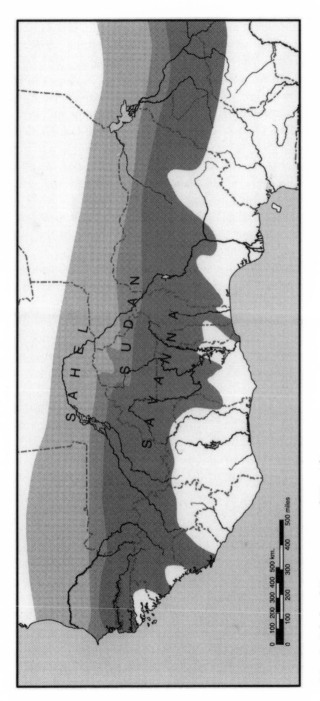

Map 5. Sahel and Savanna zones of West Africa.

of a fading class of court musicians (Palmer, 1936, pp. 110–11) and a more active tradition of female singers (Mariko, 1989; Schultze, 1968 [1913], p. 173). In 1989, during the tour of the Africa Oyé group of musicians from all over Africa, a musician named Chetima Ganga, who was listed in the program as a Kanouri griot from eastern Niger, led a quartet that performed a war anthem for the Sultan of Bornu. Further research in the cultures of the Lake Chad area may reveal a professionally maintained oral tradition similar to that of the Hausa.

Why the relative uniformity to the west but changes to the east in what is often called the western Sudanic region? Certainly the western area was heartland not only of the Mali empire, but also of a region that represented in many ways the center of the Sahelian civilization of the Middle Ages: elements of the Ghana empire migrated southeast to this and other regions, carrying with them a rich cultural heritage. The same Mali heartland fell under Songhay influence from the east for several centuries. The Niger River served as a cultural conduit in both directions. But farther eastward in what is described as the central Sudanic region the cultural thrust of the civilization represented by Ghana, Mali, and Songhay seems to undergo a slight shift as we enter another zone of influence. Northern Nigeria, eastern Niger, Chad, and northern Cameroon all were far more influenced by Kanem and Bornu of the Lake Chad region.

The one cultural strand that spans these two zones of influence is that of the Fulbe, who migrated eastward for centuries, bearing a cultural heritage that goes back to Ghana and earlier and absorbing other influences along the way. The relative unity of a profession anchored in verbal art, service to noble families, and the symbiotic relationship of word and music is a common trait of griots that spans this vast region.

Usage

If the map of this world is relatively clear, the question of which word to use—one of the many terms encountered among the diverse peoples or simply *griot*—offers no easy answer. Mamadou Diawara and many other scholars, African and non-African, do not like *griot* because of its ambiguity. It certainly does not do justice to such an ancient and varied profession.

One might simply replace it with *bard* or some other term and that is what the government of Niger tried to do in 1980. On December 18, 1979, the president of Niger, Seyni Kountché, complained in his annual address to the nation about what he saw as economic waste occasioned by griots. He felt that people were devoting too many of their resources to gifts for griots at weddings and naming ceremonies. The result of his speech was an unsuccessful attempt to "sanitize" the profession. A study commissioned by the government of Niger recommended that the word *griot* be replaced with *artist, musician,* and *singer.* The authors of the report, respected scholars, also proposed the establishment of a professional association, a school to train griots, and the awarding of medals to the most talented of them (Hale, 1990a, 42–43). In spite of this effort at linguistic change, the term *griot,* like the profession it designates, survives in Niger today.

Such a negative view of griots is not new. Early travel accounts portray them as a social plague. This notion is held today in many cities. When a naming ceremony is announced on the radio, the event can attract scores of griots and griottes eager to help the parents celebrate the occasion — and to collect rewards from the many relatives who attend and become the subjects of praises. Offshoots of the word — *griottage, griotique,* and *griottism* — have also taken on negative meanings in France, where, as in West Africa, they often signify empty praise or praise for pay.

Another reason for the negative meaning attached to *griot* is the dominance of the Mande cultures in West Africa. They cover an area of nearly 1,500 kilometers from west to east and almost 1,000 kilometers from north to south. Not all peoples in this area are Mande, but the Mande influence is the most prevalent. For this reason there is a tendency on the part of the comparatively large number of scholars interested in these interrelated peoples to take a Mandecentric view of the profession and call for the exclusive use of the Mande terms, *jeli* and *jali.* This usage stems from both a desire for greater precision and the fact that the profession of griots is largely populated by Mande *jeliw* and *jalolu* from the region. But this ethnocentric view of the griot world also comes from a general lack of information about non-Mande griots in surrounding countries, such as Mauritania, Niger, and Benin, as well as among non-Mande groups scattered throughout the region — for example, the Fulbe.

For two reasons, it seems inevitable that *griot* will continue to serve as the generic term for these wordsmiths. First, *griot* has spread into many parts of the African diaspora, in particular the Caribbean and the United States, taking on extremely positive connotations for those who see the profession as a link to their ancestors. It has entered the vocabulary of African Americans to such an extent that it would be impossible to try to suppress it. And like griots themselves who travel so widely, the term *griot* is now recognized around the world.

Second, the regional nature of the term *griot* and its female counterpart *griotte* in West Africa underscores the fact that the profession carries out some of the oldest and most important cultural activities linking many diverse peoples, including those that are not related to the Mande. The words are useful reminders of what Paul Stoller has identified as deep Sahelian and Savanna civilization (Hale and Stoller, 1985). Like so many other cross-culturally generated words in the Sahel, *griot* has come to serve the needs of West Africans who must communicate with each other across numerous linguistic frontiers within Africa as well as with peoples outside the continent, African and non-African. As with many regional words embedded in West African languages, *griot* has traveled across much of the continent and found a home in the modern French and, to a lesser extent, English spoken by West African peoples. The fact that only a minority of the populations in these countries speaks these European languages does not affect the griot's role in them.

How, then, can one reconcile the ambiguity of *griot*, a term with probable African roots, and the specificity of such ethnically linked words as *jeli?* The answer is that by using both *griot* and *griotte* as well as the more precise words, scholars can more effectively bridge the gap in knowledge about the oral tradition for persons outside West Africa. At the same time, the adoption of both *griot* and *griotte* signals to those who are unaware of the existence of *jelimusow* and their sisters in neighboring West African cultures that women play an active role in the profession. Although *jeli* can refer to both sexes (a woman may say that she is *jeli—ni ye jeli ye*; Barbara Hoffman, personal communication, 1996), the central Mande *jeliw* distinguish when necessary between *jeli ke* and *jelimuso*—man and woman griot. Given the lack of information about women griots, it is useful to maintain the gender distinction in the regional terminology by pairing *griotte* with *griot*.

Use of both kinds of terms, the general and the specific, provides the regional framework into which discussions of different kinds of griots—past and present, from diverse ethnic groups, carrying out different functions—can be conducted. This solution allows the varied audiences for griots to hold on to what they value, as long as each understands more clearly the reasons for the different connotations attached to the various words that designate these keepers of the oral tradition.

Griots remain enigmatic figures in part because they have no equivalent outside the continent. In this study, in addition to both *griot* and the more culturally specific terms such as *jali*, I shall occasionally employ partial synonyms such as *bard*, *wordsmith*, and *artisan of the word*. There are three reasons for using these partial synonyms. First, simply to avoid repeating the same word more than once in the same sentence, it is useful to have a synonym or partial synonym. Second, and perhaps more important, the primary function of griots is verbal art. Music is a closely related but secondary activity, hence the validity of the term *wordsmith*. Finally, griots are part of a larger group of artisans who hold a professional monopoly on the working of certain materials—for example, blacksmiths and metal. The expression *artisan of the word* reflects clearly the griots' link with this group of craftspeople.

But none of these partial synonyms conveys the full range of the profession. During the six centuries from Ibn Battuta's landmark description of griots in his *Travels* to the late Alex Haley's popularization of the profession in *Roots*, one of the most difficult concepts to grasp for those who have not been raised in a society that supports griots is the multifunctional role these artisans of the word play for their people. They are far more than the storytellers and village historians cited by the editors of *Time*. In the chapter that follows, a description of the extraordinarily diverse range of activities carried out by griots will answer the fundamental question of just what it is that they do.

✻ 1 ✻
A Job Description for Griots

Because the terms *historian* and *storyteller* reveal only part of the story of *griot*, translators and scholars have often adopted another word from the list of griot activities to describe the profession: *praise-singer* (Laye, 1954; Kourouma, 1981; Irwin, 1981; Ebron, 1993). The choice of such a term to designate what griots do comes from the fact that the praise-singing function is by far the most obvious and audible manifestation of their profession.

Scores of accounts by travelers from the fourteenth to the nineteenth century reveal that the foreigners' first encounter with griots generates much praise-singing, both for the patron of these wordsmiths and for the visitors. But it also stems from some of the local terminology for griots. Among the Hausa, the most common term is *marok'i*, often defined as both professional beggar and singer, from the verb *roka*, "to beg, to ask, to request" (Newman and Newman, 1979). But the many other functions of griots that one finds in the wide swath of the Sahelian and Savanna zones become apparent only when framed in a broader and longer-term perspective.

The goal here is to identify and describe all the functions griots carry out in this region, even though their roles may be limited to certain areas or time periods. In light of information from a variety of places, it will be apparent that *praise-singer* is far too limited a descriptor for the profession when viewed in the regional context. In fact, what we call praise-singing is an activity somewhat more complex than this compound term suggests.

Most of the griots' functions involve words, but many—for example, advising, diplomacy, and instrumental music—do not require poetry. Other roles produce forms of verbal art—songs, tales, epics. A few textual examples of some of these poetic functions are included in this chapter, but the subject of verbal art requires a more detailed discussion, reserved for chapter 3, while an analysis of the different kinds of music performed by griots is the focus of chapter 4. Here I will touch on all of the functions but dwell to a greater extent on the relatively lesser-known roles, such as the advising and ceremonial duties. The purpose here, then, is to provide an overview of all of these social functions—recounting history, providing advice, serving as spokesperson, representing a ruler as a diplomat, mediating conflicts, interpreting the words of others into different languages, playing music, composing songs and tunes, teaching students, exhorting participants in wars and sports, reporting news, overseeing, witnessing or contributing to important life ceremonies, and praise-singing. Seen from a functional perspective, the descriptions of these activities contribute to a portrait of an extremely dynamic profession that enables societies to cohere.

The evidence for these functions ranges from narratives by griots themselves to accounts by visitors to Africa and fictional portraits by African writers. The descriptions by these writers, based on intimate knowledge of the cultures in which they grew up, are not a substitute for the many other kinds of data, but they provide depth and texture to the picture of the profession.

Genealogist

The list of griot functions is long, but the best known outside Africa, thanks to *Roots*, is that of the genealogist. The individual who hears his or her genealogy recounted at a ceremony or in an epic is transformed from a member of the audience to the living product of those who went before. The genealogy is important not only to the individual but also to others— for example, prospective marriage partners and their families. When a griot conveys a proposal to the family of the prospective bride, the presentation may focus at least as much on the family history as on the personal qualities of the man who is proposing.

The genealogy can represent both a virtue and a challenge to the individual in the present. To understand and appreciate the full measure of someone today, what he or she represents to other members of society, one must place the individual into a long-term perspective that includes the ancestors. The individual is part of a lineage and can win a permanent or higher-profile place in it by his or her actions in the present. But that lineage is also one of many others.

In a sense, there are many layers of human context for the genealogy.

But from the perspective of a male adolescent, the first competitor is his father. This kind of rivalry is one dimension of a cultural value known as *fadenya* in the Mande world and by other terms elsewhere. Charles S. Bird and Martha B. Kendall (1980) describe *fadenya* as "father-child-ness" (15). They point out that "this conception of patrilineage as competitor is captured in the proverb *i fa y'i faden folo de ye* (your father is your first faden)" (14). Without a distinguishing act or deed, the individual may be dropped or relegated to a minor mention in the roll call of the family genealogy. Worse, without many such distinguished descendants, a line may become less visible and less important in a given society.

A genealogy recounted at a naming ceremony or in an epic is more than a listing of ancestors. Whether or not the genealogies are accurate, they are of immense significance for understanding the way people in the present view the past. John William Johnson, referring to *The Epic of Son-Jara*, notes that "the genealogies recited in these epics function in part to establish a culture hero's inheritance of occult power" (1986, p. 4).

Genealogies hold great meaning for people on both ends of the list—those in the past who are still remembered today and those in the present who must measure themselves against the past recounted in the deeds of ancestors. The yardstick of measurement may change, but the basic notion of distinction does not diminish. Whereas an ancestor made his name in war, a descendant today may acquire a similar level of renown by traveling from the Sahel or Savanna regions to the coast to find a job and eventually returning to distribute some of the wealth he has accumulated, or by going off to Europe to earn an advanced degree and then returning to assume a position as a civil servant, doctor, or lawyer who is able to help support an extended family.

The human link between past and present, the griot or the griotte, may depend also on genealogy to establish his or her own credentials before the audience. Here the benchmark or starting point for all parties is a basic tie between a noble clan and a griot clan. For example, the Kouyaté griots serve the Keita nobles in a relationship that goes back at least as far as the father of Sundiata Keita (founder of the Mali empire) and the father of Sundiata's griot. In addition to the clan link, however, the griot may want to emphasize at the beginning of the epic his own genealogy.

Jeli Mamadou Kouyaté, principal source of *Sundiata: An Epic of Old Mali* (Niane, 1960), cites his ancestors and reminds listeners of the ancient bond between the Kouyaté *jeliw* and the Keita nobles who founded the empire. It is this linkage over time that serves as the basis for the *jeli*'s claim to provide only the most accurate interpretation of the past: "My word is pure and free of all untruth; it is the word of my father; it is the word of my father's father . . . royal griots do not know how to lie" (Niane, 1965, p. 1). It is a statement that he reiterates at midpoint in the narration to remind his listeners of his own pedigree before recounting the most gripping episode:

> I, Djeli Mamadou Kouyaté, am the result of a long tradition. For generations we have passed on the history of kings from father to son. The narrative was passed on to me without alteration and I deliver it without alteration, for I received it free from all untruth. (40–41)

References by the *jeli*-narrator to a *jeli*-ancestor are instances of "self-referentiality" in these narratives (Bowles and Hale, 1996), a trait that gives authority and life to the history being recounted.

Other genealogies within a text may link the audience to the events. One example that involves a listener of griot origin occurs in *The Epic of Son-Jara*, a linear version of the Sundiata epic recounted by Fa-Digi Sisòkò in Kita, a major center for *jeliya* in Mali. Recorded on March 9, 1968, by Bird and translated by Johnson along with a team of Malian scholars, this 3,083-line narrative clearly reveals the verbal artistry of the *jeli* in a performance that took four hours. One of the Malians who helped Bird with arrangements for the recording session was Massa Makan Diabaté, a descendant of a well-known *jeli* family who decided to make his career as a writer and scholar.

About a fourth of the way into the narrative, *jeli* Fa-Digi Sisòkò seamlessly shifts to a brief recounting of the origin and genealogy of Massa Makan Diabaté's clan, known in English as Jobarteh, in French as Diabaté, in Bamana as Jabattè, and in Maninka as the Jebagatè. In the midst of the story of the killing of a wild buffalo by two brothers of the Tarawèrè clan (known in French as Traoré), Dan Mansa Wulanba, the elder, generously praises his younger brother, who succeeded in bringing the animal down. The younger brother replies.

749   "Should you become a bard,

    "One who could refuse you won't be found."   (That's the truth)
    And from him thus descended Sangoyi, the Long Bow   (Indeed)
    Sangoyi, the Long Bow, he begat Tuba Katè,   (Indeed)
    And begat Mònsòn Katè,   (Indeed)
    And begat Fatiyan Katè,   (Indeed)
    And begat Sagaburu Katè, the Tall   (Indeed)
    These are the six clans of Jebagatè bards.   (That's true)

    . . . .

769   Mansa Magan begat Sigiya,   (Indeed)
        And Sigiya's son is this one right here.   (Mmm, that's true)

                                (Johnson & Sisòkò, p. 41, 1992)

The reference to Massa Makan Diabaté's father in the last line validates the expertise of the narrator for the audience and underscores the spread of *jeli* influence into literature, the modern equivalent of narration.

The griot's merit depends not only on how well he knows the genealogy of others and of his own family but also on a clear understanding of the complex relations between clans and the identity of their particular symbols. Sory Camara lists over fifty clans in his study of *jeliw* (1976, p. 30). One can understand why the griot's task is hardly an easy one.

In *Les Soleils des indépendances* (1968; *The Suns of Independence*, 1981), Ahmadou Kourouma dramatizes what happens when a griot slips up. Commenting on the late arrival of the protagonist, a noble named Fama Dumbuya who has fallen on hard times, the *jeli* observes:

> "That he is late, does not matter; the customary rights of noble families have been respected; the Dumbuya have not been forgotten. The princes of Horodugu have been put with the Keita."
> Fama asked the griot to repeat what he had just said. The man hesitated. Those who are not Malinké may not know it; in the circumstances this was a deliberate insult, enough to make your eyeballs explode with rage. Who had lumped Dumbuya and Keita together? The latter are kings of Wasulu, and their totem is the hippopotamus, not the panther. . . . Bastard of a griot. There are no real griots left; the real ones died with the great masters of war. (6–7; I have modified the translation of Adrian Adams)

Thorough knowledge of genealogy and clan relations is the essential component of any griot's historical baggage. Without it, the griot cannot advance beyond a backup role in a chorus of singers. The recounting of someone's genealogy in the course of a ceremony or in the narration of an epic constitutes not only the recreation of the past but also a legitimization of those in the present, including the griot.

Historian

The portrayal of a past that depends on genealogies for its foundation would not, from a traditional Western perspective, pass for history; it is undocumented or not documented by methods that are usually acceptable in the West. From a West African perspective, however, the genealogy gives credibility to a story. Extraordinary events in an epic are reported to have been accomplished by real people whose genealogy is well known. For this reason, the events take on a reality that is as difficult to refute as religious belief. Historian Bogumil Jewsiewicki has argued for recognition "that belief is social fact, not a false consciousness" (1987, p. 20). In the case of long narratives by griots, belief in the existence of heroes from the past may also be viewed as "social fact" for West African listeners.

In the Western cultural tradition, epics fall into the category of literature, though there is often a link with an historical event—the fall of Troy or Charlemagne's wars in Spain. But African audiences listening to *The Epic of Son-Jara, The Epic of Askia Mohammed,* or *The Epic of Samory Touré* may not make such a neat distinction between fiction and fact. When a griot recounts for several hours the story of one of these heroes in a multigeneric narrative that includes genealogies, praises, songs, etymologies, incantations, oaths, and proverbs (Johnson 1986, 57), he is recounting the past—the history—of a people. The Western-trained historian or folklorist, however, may understand history as a documented phenomenon that differs from epic, legend, and saga.

If one places the notions of history and literature into one category broadly defined as interpretations of the past, the griot as historian emerges as a "time-binder," a person who links past to present and serves as a witness to events in the present, which he or she may convey to persons living in the future. In this sense, the griot's role as historian is somewhat more dynamic and interactive than what we have in the Western tradition—the scholar who spends years in libraries going through archival sources.

We know from comparisons between written and oral sources that griots are not interested in wasting their voices on persons who did nothing (Hale, 1990a). These comparisons also reveal that griots' notions of time are different from what we might expect. What Joseph C. Miller describes as the hourglass effect (1990, 37) occurs often in these narratives: birth and death are much more important than what happens in between.

In their narratives, griots provide deep insights into the values of a people and their social structure. The text of the griot is less a representation of the past than a contemporary reading of that past (Johnson, 1989). By studying their "texts," one can learn much about the way people view their past and draw a variety of insights about the nature of society today. We cannot, however, confirm the accuracy of the events described in epics on the basis of knowledge currently available. This does not mean, however, that these texts cannot tell us anything about the past. The names and places cited in the narrative are in some ways the equivalent in historical terms of dates. Archaeologists, for example, often study oral traditions as well as other sources in order to make decisions on where to dig. That was the case when Roderick and Susan McIntosh excavated the ancient city of Jenne-Jeno in Mali (1981, p. 9) during the late 1970s and made discoveries that revolutionized our understanding of West African history.

To appreciate griots as oral historians, we need to take a culturally relative view of history, one that accepts other people's notions of what constitutes the past. Their view of history cannot be dismissed just because it does not contain dates and because it is oral rather than written. One may, however, ask what this distinction means for students of African history.

Two examples from recent history offer some insights. If one's goal is to learn the date of the fall of the Songhay empire in the sixteenth century, the best source is the Timbuktu chronicles written in Arabic by Muslim scribes in the sixteenth and seventeenth centuries, the *Tarîkh es-Soudan* (Es-Sa'di, 1898–1900) and the *Tarîkh el-Fettâch* (Kâti, 1913). But, as I have argued in *Scribe, Griot and Novelist*, if one wants to understand the deeper meanings of the event, the researcher should read in *The Epic of Askia Mohammed* how the descendants of the Songhay ruler weakened their society by violating some of its most basic rules. By the same token, in the modern context, if one wants to know on what day in 1968 the Modibo Keita regime in Mali was overthrown, one need only turn to an encyclopedia. But to discern the way clan relations—in this case a clan conflict seven centuries old—contributed to the coup d'état that brought Colonel Moussa Traoré to power, one could read or listen to a version of the Sundiata epic that describes how Tira Maghan Traoré came into conflict with his leader, Sundiata Keita, after the founding of the Mali empire. One could also note the change in sign-on music on Radio Mali the day of the event (Bird, 1978). The praise-song for Sundiata Keita was abruptly replaced with the praise-song for Tira Maghan Traoré.

It is evident that the griot's role as historian is far more than simply the retelling of events. It is a reading of the past for audiences in the present, an interpretation that reflects a complex blend of both past and present values. I will return to this function in more detail in chapter 8.

Adviser

Griots offer advice to a variety of clients—rulers, patrons, and other members of society. The form of this advice can vary considerably depending on the context. Some scholars suggest that the extent of the advice has sometimes been exaggerated by griots (Innes, 1974, p. 7; Conrad, 1990, p.

21), and it appears that this role is not as significant as it was in the past (Sylla, 1978, p. 122).

The narrators of the *Tarîkh el-Fettâch* cite one example of this powerful advisory role. After Askia Moussa overthrew his father, Askia Mohammed, in 1528 to take the Songhay throne at Gao, 424 kilometers downriver from Timbuktu in eastern Mali, he planned to kill off all his rival brothers. Many of them fled to Tendirma, ninety kilometers upstream from Timbuktu, to seek protection from another brother, Otsmân Youbâbo, who was the governor of the western provinces and the second-highest administrator in the Songhay empire. After receiving several letters from Askia Moussa requesting him to return to Gao to demonstrate his loyalty to the new ruler, Otsmân Youbâbo reluctantly decided to travel to the port on the Niger River where he could embark for the trip downstream to Gao. The narrators of the *Tarîkh es-Sudan* report that Otsmân Youbâbo's "singer," or *jeseré*, shouted, "Have the boats unloaded, everything in the boats. By my head, the one who speaks to you will never place dust on his head for anyone" (Es-Sa'di, 1898–1900, p. 136; Hale, 1990a, p. 40). In this case, the *jeseré*'s deep knowledge of human relations in general and of the character of particular members of the royal family served as the basis for advice that probably saved the life of his patron, a descendant of Askia Mohammed.

David Conrad (1990, pp. 21–22) observes in *The Epic of Bamana Segu* that "in some of the dialogue between the powerful Faama Da and his bard Tinyètigiba Danté . . . and between Chief Samanyana Basi and his griot . . . the narrator [Tayiru Banbera] moves beyond subjectivity of ordinary description and provides some rare views of the vital partnership of *mansa* [ruler] and bard as it may have been two centuries ago." He finds that the 7,942-line epic from which these examples are taken is "somewhat more balanced than usual" in the portraits of the griot as adviser.

In the following dialogue from this epic, Danté replies to Da's military plans:

3870   Da said, "I want to start with Samanyana.
      I want to capture Basi at Samanyana."
      Danté said, "If somebody wants to fight against his rival brother,
      Would you provoke him simply because he is said to be a brave man?"
      Da said, "Eh, why not?"
3875   Danté said, "Eh, that would not be right.
      When one noble wants to fight against another,
      He must have a good reason.
      Would you attack just because you are a faama?
      With no head or root to your reason?

3880   Will we go to war against Basi just because he is a man?
        That would not be right."
        Da said to the bard, "Oho, do you yourself have a motive we
        can use for going against Samanyana?" (199)

Danté then offers his master both a reason for going to war and a detailed battle plan.

One finds similar cautions in the short *Epic of Kelefa Saane*, the story of a nineteenth-century Mandinka prince in the Kaabu region of The Gambia narrated by *jali* Bamba Susso. The hero listens to advice from Jali Maadi, who warns that his patron will lose his followers if he is not more restrained in his public behavior and his dealings with others. Having just escaped from capture, Kelefa Saane is seeking to restore his reputation. But Jali Maadi declares:

211   Prince, I am afraid of treachery
        For treachery is not good;
        A person for whom things go well—many followers
        A person for whom things go wrong—no followers
        Prince, do not treat treachery lightly
        Treachery is not good. (Innes, 1978, p. 41)

Sometimes the advice of griots was given in such a direct and critical fashion that the listener had no choice but to follow it. During the wars that marked the end of Samory Touré's regime in the late nineteenth century, a French officer, Captain Quiquandon, was assigned to act as head of a liaison group traveling with Tiéba, ruler of Sikasso in southern Mali and an enemy of Touré. The captain's report, based on ten months' close observation of combat in the region, included a description of the power of the advice of a griot over Ba-Bemba, a brother of Tiéba and one of his closest lieutenants. Substituting for Tiéba, who was ill, Ba-Bemba led an attack on a large town with fortified sites and achieved a preliminary victory over part of it. He accepted the submission of one group of the defeated in exchange for their cattle and thirty hostages. But coming on the heels of a much bloodier victory by Tiéba's chief general, Nienigalé, Ba-Bemba's decision to accept a submission over one group rather than push forward to achieve total victory was perceived as a sign of weakness by Tiéba's griots. Quiquandon reports that the griots insulted Ba-Bemba by asking him to turn over the command either to a captive or to another general called the Crazy One, the eldest son of Tiéba who was known to suffer from a mental imbalance. Faced with this criticism of his actions, Ba-Bemba reversed his decision and attacked the remaining defenders the next day rather than accept their submission (Quiquandon, 1892, pp. 427–28).

In times of peace, the advice of griots appears to have been made in a somewhat subtler fashion, as suggested by two examples from the same period. In a report from *commandant de cercle* Lavallière, a French administrator for Siguiri, a town in Upper Guinea at the turn of the century, there is a description of the griot as adviser that underscores the importance of this function. Lavallière observed that in addition to their traditional role as wordsmiths, griots in the Upper Guinea region had other functions that included managing the current affairs of the chief. Griots became so valued that they were not allowed to leave the chief's side, "especially during discussions, trials, and deliberations, in order to support his criticisms and to approve his decisions." In particular, Lavallière added, "They demonstrate their value by taking the risk sometimes of giving advice that contains common sense or by saying just the right word" (1911, p. 277).

Gordon Innes (1976) offers a fascinating example of a subtle form of advice reported to him by someone who had observed a griot at the court of the son of Musa Molo, a nineteenth-century ruler: "When Musa Molo's son Cherno Bande was Seyfu (chief) of Fulladu West District in The Gambia, a griot would play softly in the background while Cherno discussed matters with the elders. When some proposal was made which the griot supported, he would play loud and fast for a minute or two" (6).

Visual evidence of the closeness of the griot to the ruler appears in a nineteenth-century photograph from one of Galliéni's campaigns in West Africa. One sees the ruler Bassé flanked on his right by his griot and on his left by his marabout (figure 1).

Rulers are not the only ones who benefit from the advice of griots and griottes. For example, in *Al Haji Bai Konte*, a documentary film made by Marc Pevar and Oliver Franklin (1979) about *jali* Al Haji Bai Konte from Brikama, the narrative read by the African American musician Taj Mahal emphasizes the fact that the late Gambian bard was often visited by other persons who sought his advice on sensitive matters.

Advice can also be given in a public context such as a ceremony. Ibn Battuta offered an example of a royal *jali* giving advice to the king of Mali during a ceremony (Hamdun and King, 1975, p. 42). At weddings across the Sahel, griottes give advice in the form of songs to the bride and her family. In the video *Griottes of the Sahel*, Weybi Karma, one of the most sought-after *jeserey weyborey* (female Songhay griots) in Niger, offered this wedding song:

1. The ruler Bassé with his griot at his right. From Galliéni. (Société de Géographie, Paris).

Stop crying, bride,
Stop crying, and listen to me.
If your mother-in-law abuses you,
Just cry, but don't say anything.
If your sisters or brothers-in-law abuse you,
Just cry but don't say anything.
If your husband's mother abuses you,
Just cry, but don't say anything.
But leaving your house is not a crime. (Hale, 1990b)

Counsel can be offered in many forms: communicated by music as described by Innes, quietly conveyed by one who sits close to the ruler as suggested by the Galliéni expedition photograph and Lavallière's description of griots in Siguiri, or shouted in commanding fashion as in the incident with one of Askia Mohammed's sons.

Advice for a ruler may be presented in the context not simply of what is good for a prince but also, in a broader sense, of what society expects from their leader. Such advice can be carefully framed in praises that reveal both a personal and a collective link between the subject and those who are inescapably bound to him or her for political and social reasons. Gitu Sagado, one of the *jeserey weyborey* of Yatakala whom I interviewed in 1989, chanted for me a typical praise-song for a canton chief which revealed this interdependence.

> Father of the poor people
> Husband of beautiful ladies
> At whose absence the city is not interesting
> At whose absence people are not happy . . . .
> Be our mother
> Be our father
> Provide us with clothing
> Be the salt we need for our gravy
> Be the oil we need for our porridge . . . .
> You are our eyes
> You are our mirror
> You are our hands and legs
> That we use to walk. (Hale, 1990b)

On one level, the *jeserey weyborey* may appear to be seeking rewards for themselves from a new leader. But in a deeper sense they speak for society when they remind the noble of his responsibility. A prince who does not serve as the "hands" and "legs" of a people simply does not measure up to the ideal as articulated by the griottes and is therefore, by implication, less of a prince.

The griot appears also as an adviser in an informational sense. What the prince does not understand the griot can explain, because he or she is more attuned to the world around. Kourouma illustrates this role in *Les Soleils des indépendances* (1968, 1981) when Fama Dumbuya returns to his home village, Togobala, after a long stay in the capital of a neighboring country. His griot, Jamuru, warns him about the political changes that are coming.

> On Monday morning Jamuru had drawn him aside and leaned over to spit the secret into his ear. The village and committee president (his name was Babu) and all the other committee members were going to question Fama; not for a joke, either, nor to honour him! There would be a one-party system in the sauce, and *sous-préfet* and counter-revolution, with still more things Jamuru had forgotten. (90)

Many plays about nineteenth-century heroes illustrate the role of griots as important advisers to kings at critical points in the history of a kingdom. In Cheik Ndao's play *L'Exil d'Albouri* (1967), a dramatization of the retreat of the ruler of the Jollof state from his kingdom in the interior of Senegal in 1890, the *guewel* Samba intervenes throughout the play but has two especially important advisory roles. The first is to explain why the half-brother of the king has decided to collaborate with the French. When asked by Albouri how he knows so much, Samba replies: "Well, King, you forget that Samba is forewarned of everything. He has signed a pact with the wind." When Albouri asks Samba why his own brother has betrayed him to the French, the *guewel* replies with answers that reflect his fundamental understanding of human nature: "Power! Power!" Samba then prepares the king to make an announcement that he will lead his people into exile. The preparation involves the repetition after the *guewel* of ancient incantations that will endow the king's words with power. Samba concludes by declaring, "Albouri, like your ancestors, be the Fire, the Wind, the Rain. Speak to the people, they will listen to you. Samba will loan you his tongue which will plunge into the heart of men in spite of themselves" (Ndao, pp. 77–78; my translation).

In Djibril Tamsir Niane's play *Sikasso* (1971), about the resistance of Ba-Bemba against the French, his former allies who attacked his fortress in southern Mali in 1898, Djéliba (the name means great griot) contributes along with other advisers to the discussion about strategy (53), reports later to his patron on the progress of the defense of Sikasso (62), then warns him of the impending fall of the fortress: "O Prince! Let's not try to fool ourselves; around me I have seen so many men fall, young and valiant! ...We cannot stop the advance of our enemies. Prince, this is the end" (63; my translation). Ba-Bemba takes the warning of the *jeli* to heart, then makes plans to die defending the fortress while sending Djéliba with instructions to the remainder of the army to flee to the south (64).

These fictional depictions support the impression conveyed by other kinds of evidence—chronicles, reports, and recently recorded visual material—that griots did in fact play significant roles as advisers.

Although many observers have pointed out quite correctly that the griot's advisory role has changed today with the decline or disappearance of traditional rulers and the need to find new patrons both at home and abroad, one incident reveals how a griot can still be part of the political picture. After The Gambia underwent a popular military coup by Captain Yahya Jammeh in July 1994, the governing junta invited a griot, Al Haji

Papa Bunka Susso, to serve in the cabinet as minister of youth, sports, and culture. Although he declined, the fact that he was offered the position suggests that under some circumstances there may be a role for griots in contemporary governments. The invitation, however, seems to be an exception. The advisory role of griots has changed since the days when a king never traveled without his marabout and his griot, and it is not likely again to be as significant as it was in the past.

Spokesperson

Many travel accounts by both North African and European travelers portray the griot as spokesperson. The chief or ruler expresses himself in a low voice that is appropriate for someone of his rank. The griot repeats and embellishes these words, much as a spokesperson for a leader or agency might do today in Washington or Paris. There are two differences here, however, from the Western notion of spokesperson.

First, as Lilyan Kesteloot points out, "this process is part of protocol, and it contributes to the consecration or *sacralisation* ('to make sacred' but also 'to separate') of the royal person. At the same time it increases the importance of the griot" (1991, p. 20). She offers examples of the power stemming from this special role, then concludes quite perceptively that these spokespersons "are instruments of power, but they also influence the way it is exercised" (21).

One reason for the accumulation of the power inherent in the griot's role as spokesperson is that he or she in many cases speaks for both the ruler and for those who come to him for redress or other matters. This function of representing others takes on both individual and collective overtones.

In Camara Laye's autobiographical *L'Enfant noir* (1953; *The Dark Child*, 1954), the woman who wants Laye's father to make her some gold earrings hires a *jeli* to plead her case. The purpose is quite specific and personal. In other cases, the wishes of an entire family or clan are repre-sented by a griot—for example, in the presentation of a marriage proposal. At the level of those who rule, however, when the griot conveys a request from an individual to the chief, the griot may, in a sense, be speaking for many people, depending on the nature of the request. Finally, as seen in the praises of the Songhay *jeseré weyboro* for a canton chief, the words of the singer contain a clear social warning: the welfare of the people depends on the presence of the ruler.

Diplomat

The role of spokesperson takes on greater significance when the griot becomes an ambassador, conveying messages for a ruler in a much broader context than the ruler's palace.

Sory Camara sums up the most striking examples from the era of Samory Touré, last of the great nineteenth-century resisters of French imperialism. In the course of a brief truce between French colonial forces and Touré in 1886 near Bamako, the two sides exchanged delegations. Touré's delegation was led by a griot named Oumar Diali, or Oumar Griot. In his summary of the accounts by Galliéni and Peroz, Camara explains that this initial exchange was a failure for the French because Touré was convinced of the weakness of France in comparison with Britain.

The French leaders then persuaded Touré to send a diplomatic mission to France, the unstated goal being to impress on the African ruler the notion that France was as powerful as Britain. Touré agreed to send Oumar Diali to France with his own son, Karamoko, and another griot—a *fina*, or Islamic griot named Nassikha Mahdi, who turned out to be a spy for the French (Camara, 1976, pp. 209–10).

The delegation landed at Bordeaux on August 9, 1886, then went on to Paris, where it was received with much pomp and circumstance. The results of this trip were not significant in terms of treaties or agreements, and the visit did not keep the war between Touré and the French from continuing for nearly a decade thereafter. But the French achieved their goal of impressing Touré's third and favorite son with their military power. This impression was conveyed by the two griots, one an envoy, the other a spy, who returned home with the delegation in late September to report to Touré on what they had seen.

The diplomat as spy is hardly new to the world of modern international politics, and griots are no exception. David Conrad recounts several versions of the story of an unnamed griot who was caught spying on the Tukulor in Ségou for Bamana patrons at some point in the 1860s and was eventually executed (1981, pp. 20–32).

Farther east and nearly a century later, the spying took on a different form. In 1943, the Sultan of Zinder, the second largest city in Niger, assigned his most talented *marok'i*, or Hausa griot, Mazo dan Alalo, to serve as his diplomat and spy for relations with a newly arrived French adminis-trator for the region, Jean Boudot. Although he remained in Zinder for only eleven months, Boudot left an indelible imprint on the memory and the language of the Hausa-speaking peoples in the region because of Mazo dan Alalo's role as diplomat and spy. Peter Chilson explains:

> Mazo dan Alalo would ride behind the commandant, beating his drum and singing with a troop of singers, a half-dozen men backing him up on foot with voices and drums, singing as the commandant and his *tirailleurs* [riflemen] marched men out of villages at gunpoint; as he ordered a man to be beaten for taking a rest from his job crushing laterite on the road; or as he handed a cash reward—five francs—to the man whose work particularly pleased him. (1994, pp. 179–80)

Here is one of Mazo dan Alalo's songs about Boudot:

> He came to see if the people were working
> And he beat those who were not. For Bodo
> Everything was work . . . .
> Even the marabouts and the roosters
> who wake them for the prayer call went
> to work. (180–81)

Chilson (181) explains that "subversion lies in Mazo's work, as if he were a spy, which he was, reporting what he saw and heard to the Sultan . . . making a musical caricature of him—Bodo who sends the roosters and lepers 'and even the Sultan' to work. He did it to sabotage . . . playing the image maker's double game. . . . The words . . . contain something of the implied insult, a suggestion of absurdity and mockery, falling deaf on the ears of the unwary white man who spoke no Hausa. 'Who but Bodo . . .'"

Mazo dan Alalo's role as the the sultan's public shadow for Boudot led to the insertion of the term *Bodo* into the Hausa language to mean someone who does much hard work and forces others to do the same. Fifty years after Boudot was reassigned elsewhere, his memory and his *marok'i* survive in the music as well as in a mimeographed booklet in Hausa produced by Niger's Adult Literacy Service.

Mediator

The difference between the mediator function and the roles of adviser, spokesperson, and diplomat may appear to be small, but in the context of the hierarchical societies of the Sahel and Savanna, it can be very significant.

Sory Camara explains that in Malinké society there is a complex and subtle system of mediation of disputes within a family. But there are limits to this system. When the family cannot solve the problem internally, *jeliw* may be called in to help. They have the advantage, Camara notes, of maintaining joking relationships with all members of society. And, he adds, "they have special means of persuasion: the art of speech" (1976, p. 229). Because of the hierarchical nature of Malinké society—"caste hierarchy, gender hierarchy, age hierarchy"—as well as other kinds of hierarchy based on success in war, business, or marriage, "social cohesion faces clear danger. How then to preserve dialogue and communication while maintaining hierarchy and authority?" (230)

Camara gives examples of conflicts that can arise within a family, between families, and at the court of the ruler. In most cases, "thanks to the joking relationship that he maintains with everyone, [the *jeli*] is always able to lighten the atmosphere" with his word and his service as mediator, one who serves as go-between for the two parties. In face-to-face dealings, such as those between members of a ruling council, "this phenomenon of mediated communication allows the control and suppression of aggressive manifestations that can surge forth. . . . The fact of having to speak to a person who is not the actual interlocutor, of receiving a response from that person by a third person, places the individual in an inauthentic situation. This artifice considerably tempers passions by shielding in some manner their true object" (235).

Camara adds, however, that this kind of mediation can become dysfunctional when the use of a *jeli* creates too much distance between the two parties. Camara's conclusion, one that is valid for other societies, is that "mediation is an important means of communication and dialogue for the Malinké, and the *jeli* is the agent par excellence of this function" because he is the "specialist of the word" (235).

Barbara Hoffman describes in her Ph.D. dissertation (1990a) a massive project of mediation by griots. When an extremely bitter dispute arose between the Tunkara and Jabaté clans of *jeliw* about which clan would assume the leadership of bards in Kita, an important center of *jeliya*, the *jeliw* of Siguiri in Guinea and Kéla in Mali eventually intervened to mediate the difference. The resolution of what had become a war of words and magic turned into an event that eventually involved thousands of bards, coverage on television, and a novelized recreation of the dispute, *L'Assemblée des djinns* (1985) by a writer of *jeli* origin, Massa Makan Diabaté (1985).

Interpreter and Translator

If the griot is the ideal mediator between people who speak the same language but have different views, these wordsmiths are also the most likely candidates for the job of interpreter, the most literal kind of mediation. Not all interpreters are griots, and not all griots serve as interpreters. But for a variety of reasons including the griots' facility with language, their past travels to learn the profession, and their desire to interact with people, these artisans of the word are likely to have learned most of the languages of the multicultural areas in which they live.

In The Gambia, it is not unusual to find griots who know both Mandinka and Wolof, Mandinka and Pular, all three of these languages, or other tongues of the region. At the installation of the chief in Faraba-Banta that I attended on October 2, 1992, *jali* Fabala Kanuteh interpreted in several languages a speech given on the occasion by the president of The Gambia, Dauda Diawara. Diawara spoke in English and Mandinka and Kanute translated into Wolof and Fulbe.

In the case of Songhay griots, the interpreter role emerged from the occult language known as Silantché or Silance, which they employed originally to maintain their oral tradition. Songhay griots claim roots in the Soninké oral tradition. Hence, in recounting an epic they traditionally spoke a line of Soninké followed by a line of Songhay translation. Today the archaic Soninké that appears in Songhay epics occurs much less frequently and is far more difficult to understand than it might have been a century or two ago. In many cases, the *jeserey* themselves have only a vague understanding of many of the words. One result is that epics from the region cannot be entirely explained. But Silance persists in those parts of epics that appear to be the oldest, the genealogies. In *The Epic of Askia Mohammed, jeseré* Nouhou Malio often starts a line with "A saara" (he fathered, in Soninké) followed by "A hay," the same phrase in Songhay. The running translation is a way of reminding listeners of the deep roots of Songhay culture—roots in this case that stretch back a thousand years to the Soninké people of the Ghana empire.

The narrow function of the griot as interpreter from other languages needs to be placed in the broader context of interpreting knowledge. The boundary between subject and form, events and the languages used to convey them, is blurred in the griot's larger role as interpreter of what is known about the past and what is happening in the present. The griot must interpret not simply the words but also the meaning behind the words. The language of origin for this meaning is merely the starting point for a complex and delicate process of exegesis, clarification, and embellishment.

Only the most culturally literate persons can understand what is being interpreted to them. Even then it is hardly surprising that much of what a griot recounts often contains obscure words and references that no one can understand, even, in some cases, another griot. Hoffman (1995a, p. 41) notes that "in my attempts to discover what it is about praise genres that is so powerful, I found that most nobles could not decipher the referential content of *jelikan* [the speech of *jeliw*]; even more surprising, a large proportion of any individual griot's repertory of phrases is empty of referential content to him/her as well."

Musician

Griots are best known outside Africa for their musical performances. They sing songs about people and events and many of them play instruments. Not all griots play, however, and not all griots recount epics. But many do accompany themselves on an instrument and consider this accompaniment to be essential to their total performance.

The songs, both words and sound, contribute in an indefinable way to the events they celebrate and thus cannot always be viewed as mere entertainment. No one has captured this picture better than Camara Laye (1953, 1954) with his description of the *jeli*'s role in the task of fabricating earrings.

> For the *jeli* participated in a curious way—I should say rather that it was direct and effective—in the work. He too was drunk with the joy of creation. He shouted his joy, he plucked his kora like a man inspired. He sweated as if he were the artisan himself, as if he were my father, as if the jewelry were created by his own hands. He was no longer the hired flatterer, a man whose services anyone could rent. He was a man who created his song out of some deep inner necessity. And when my father, after having soldered the large grain of gold which crowned the summit, held out his work to be admired, the griot would not be able to contain himself. He would begin to intone the "douga," the great chant which is sung only for famous men, which is only danced by them alone. (38–39; I have modified the translation of James Kirkup and Ernest Jones)

The creation of the earrings, a delicate task that involves not simply the working of gold but also protection from *nyama*, or the occult power generated by that precious material, becomes in this scene a process involving far more than metallurgy. The griot and the smith, who share a common appellation and identity as *nyamakala*, those endowed with and able to deal with *nyama*, participate in this activity in ways that are not evident on the surface. The music the griot produces is in some ways the external manifestation of a highly complex and synergistic process surrounded by mystery.

Composer

In *Sundiata*, Balla Fasséké composes "Niama" near the end of the narrative to celebrate the victory of his patron. The song becomes both an original composition and a marker of an event: "It was amid such joy that Balla Fasséké composed the great hymn 'Niama' which the griots still sing: 'Niama, Niama, Niama / You, you serve as a shelter for all, / All come to seek refuge under you'" (Niane, 1965, p. 75).

An echo of that period is heard seven centuries later when another Mande griot composes a song for the Senegalese national hero Lat Dior just as he is about to go into battle. After hearing the boasts of the warriors on the eve of the conflict, Samba Koumba Kalado "played on his *xalam* the tune *lagya*, while seated on the ground, and composed that day this song: 'Niani refuses to be subjected'" (Dieng, 1993, lines 401–403, also in Johnson, Hale, and Belcher, 1997, p. 218).

In the latter case, the song was composed for a living person but with a distant and legendary referent, the capital of the Mali empire. Both songs have become part of the collective verbal heritage accessible to all listeners.

A newly composed song can also contribute significantly to the individual's sense of identity and reputation. In one legendary case, a ruler not only claimed to own a song but also wanted to control who could hear it. The result nearly caused the death of one of his wives.

In *The Epic of Hambodedio and Saïgalare*, about a late-eighteenth- and early-nineteenth-century Fulbe ruler in the Macina region of Mali, the hero, Hambodedio, known as Hammadi, hears for the first time a song being played by a genie one evening in the entrance hall to his palace. He assembles all of the griots of his kingdom the next day and sends them off in search of the tune. Only Ko Biraïma Ko is successful in persuading a genie who lives in a termite mound to teach him the tune known as "Saïgalare." When the griot returns and performs, he is richly rewarded by the ruler. But Hammadi imposes one condition: the tune must be played only in his presence. If Ko plays for anyone else, he will be killed.

After Hammadi goes off to rustle some cattle, one of his wives, Fadia, demands to hear the new tune. A servant has told her that Fadia will not be the preferred wife if she has not heard the tune. Fadia offers Ko a large reward to play the tune, enough to prompt him to break his vow to Hammadi. He starts to play for Fadia, but Hammadi returns early from cattle rustling, hears the tune, and threatens to kill Ko. But his wife intercedes and declares, "Heavens, really, Hammadi! It is not proper for [the blow] to fall on Ko, for he is your griot. It must fall on me, yes, on me. It's on me, your wife, that it must fall" (Seydou, 1997, p. 160). She accepts willingly two spear strikes to her bared thighs while the griot continues to play "Saïgalare." The newly composed tune appears, then, as a key to the status not only of the griot but also of his master and one of his wives.

The matter of composition for the living versus the dead raises delicate political issues, especially in the modern context. The late Ban Zoumana Cissoko, one of the greatest *jeliw* in modern Mali, composed many songs about heroes of the past, though he refused to do the same for the living because he felt that the last great men had died during the colonial conquest. But most griots compose songs for the living.

During a visit to Penn State in 1987, Papa Bunka Susso met with the dean of the College of the Liberal Arts, Hart Nelsen, who had helped sponsor the two-day residency. To mark the event as well as to thank the dean for his contribution, the *jali* composed a praise-song and sang it in his office. Two years later, during a public performance that highlighted the *jali*'s return to Penn State, Susso was asked by a member of the audience if he ever composed new songs. He quickly answered that he had created one for the dean two years earlier, then proceeded to sing the song. Once created, a song is not forgotten.

Teacher

In the past, each prince had his own griot who taught him about life and where his family fit into society. Mamadou Kouyaté gives Niane a good example of this role in the person of Balla Fasséké, tutor of Sundiata. Balla Faséké "gave the child education and instruction according to Mandingo rules of conduct. Whether in town or at the hunt, he missed no opportunity of instructing his pupil. . . . Sogolon Djata also listened to the history of the kings which Balla Fasséké told him" (Niane, 1965, p. 25).

Western-style schools have assumed the role of education today, and what few princes are left may be sent off to Europe to complete an education that will enable them to deal with the demands of a new and rather different world. But contemporary artists—novelists and filmmakers—have not forgotten the value of the griot as an educator. Two portrayals of griots as teachers, one in a novel, the other in film, suggest what may be lost in the shift from traditional forms of education to Western ways.

In *L'Appel des arènes* (The call of the arenas), a novel by the Senegalese writer Aminata Sow Fall (1982), Nalla, a child who lives in the city, enjoys hearing about the past and his heritage from both the wrestlers he encounters and Mapaté, the family griot, who visits the house often. "One day," Sow Fall writes, "after having told Nalla about the tragic end of one of his uncles who had submitted willingly to the saber of the enemy in order to express his allegiance to his prince who had fallen in battle," Mapaté explains to Mame Fari, the boy's grandmother, that his goal is "to teach him about life" (106; my translation). But Nalla's mother, Diattou, is more interested in contemporary concerns—school attendance and getting ahead.

> One day, no longer able to restrain herself, she said to him: "Why don't you griots look for work instead of living like parasites at the expense of others. The genealogical histories that you recount for a banknote, they are out of style!"
>
> The face of Mapaté was transformed by a mask of anger that Nalla had never seen before. . . . He rolled into a ball the thousand-franc [$4.] bill he had just received from Ndiogou . . . and replied: "I don't come here for this money. My ancestors swore allegiance to the fathers of Ndiogou. The oath was sealed in blood. On the fields of battle we were in the first rank, we were the shields. That is why I come. You are not the worthy daughter of your mother. The baobab has produced a thorn. Good-bye." (107–8; my translation)

A more recent portrayal of the griot as teacher in the urban context dominates *Keita: L'Héritage du Griot* (Keita: the heritage of the griot) by the Burkinabè filmmaker Dani Kouyaté (1995), who is of griot origin. Viewers discover a *jeli* named Kouyaté from a rural area who moves into the home of a family named Keita in order to teach the son about the past. The echoes of the past in the film are immediately evident to local audiences, because Sundiata was of the Keita clan and his griot Balla was a Kouyaté. As in *L'Appel des arènes*, the new tutor's presence is met with different reactions on the part of the mother and the father. The mother comes to see the *jeli* as a disruptive and alien influence who endangers the child's success in school, while the father appears to understand the importance of learning about the past. Each day the *jeli* recounts episodes of the epic of Sundiata. The director skillfully intercuts scenes of the epic with the narrative of life in the city, becoming, in a sense, a meta-*jeli*. In other words, a griot filmmaker tells a story about a griot who tells about the past. As this story-within-a-story or frame tale unfolds, the child loses interest in school and begins to tell his classmates about Sundiata. In the end, the family and the school can no longer tolerate the presence of the griot, and he is forced to leave.

These examples from two different media suggest several conclusions. First, one gets the impression that the two systems of education are incompatible. A child who hears stories about the past from griots and other members of society appears in these two fictional portrayals to lose interest in the Western-style school he or she attends. What is more likely is that children who attend these schools simply do not have time to listen to griots and griottes. In *L'Appel des arènes*, the loss of interest in school seems to be rooted more deeply in the personality problems of the parents, especially the mother. Second, in both the novel by a woman and the film by a man, urban women appear as the enemies of tradition while the husbands seem to be more tolerant. This image of urban women as more cut off from their roots than men may be interpreted many ways, but the most likely explanation is that the focus on the past—heroic deeds, genealogy, etc.—is a more male-centered activity. Finally, the telling of the story in both media serves the dual purpose of portraying the difficulties arising from the shift to Western education and of recounting numerous episodes from the past. The creators of these two narratives have chosen to tell a griot's story in media that reach out to new audiences. The instructional context has thus shifted from the courtyard of the nobility to the movie theater, the television screen, and the book.

Exhorters

Griots prompt people to immediate action by their words. This is particularly significant in the context of war, as seen earlier in the *Sundiata* recounted by Mamadou Kouyaté to Niane (1965). Sundiata arranges a special review "so that Balla Fasséké, by his words, should strengthen the hearts of his sofas [soldiers]. . . . To the king of Tabon, [Balla] said: 'You whose iron arm can split ten skulls at a time . . . can you show me what you are capable of before the great battle is joined.' The griot's words made Fran Kamara leap up . . ." (58). Turning to another king, he asks, "'But what will I have to relate of you to future generations?' Before Balla had finished speaking, the king of Sibi, shouting his war cry, started his fiery charger off at full gallop" (59) to pierce a wide tunnel in a mountain with his sword.

The power of the griot's words to inspire men about to go into action has, of course, a negative side. Lavallière (1911) describes how griots can drive men and armies to their destruction by their words and deeds. The impact can work on both sides in a conflict. Bassirou Dieng offers several examples of "the war of mouths" that precedes actual conflict (1993, pp. 17–19). In the Bamana epic of Da Monzon, the griot of the ruler of Kaarta attempts to provoke the ruler of Segou with words. He asks the enemy the meaning of his name by a series of word-play questions on the meaning of Da.

My master has requested that I ask you the exact meaning of your
   name Da.
Is it Da Guinea hemp
Is it Da clay pot?
Is it Da the syphilis?
Is it Da the mouth?
Is it Da the door?
Is is Da do you sleep there?
If you are a pot, Kaarta Tiéma will break you.
If you are Guinea worms he will harvest you in order to give you to
   his fishermen who will make nets of you.
If you are syphilis, he will treat you with a red hot iron.
If you are a mouth, he will rip you open to your ears.
If you are a door, he will close you for good and you will never
   serve for any pathway.
If you are sleeping there, he will stand you up like a house at the top
   of a hill.
That's what my master put in my mouth with the order to spit right
   into your face. (Kesteloot, Traoré, Traoré, and Bâ, 1992, vol. 2, p. 131)

Sometimes the mere sound of griot music is enough to communicate
the prospect of war. In a reprint of an anonymous chronicle of the
seventeenth-century Walo kingdom in Senegal, one reads a description of
an attack by the thirty-sixth Brak, Yérim Mbagnik, against the town of
Rosso, 150 kilometers up the Senegal River from Saint-Louis. Before
attacking, the ruler ordered his griots to beat the drums of war and then sing
of the glories of the past. The defending ruler, Béthio Malikhoury, "hearing all this noise was taken by fear. He moved out of Rosso and went to
Thiagar, from which he left again at the approach of the Brak." Eventually
he was caught and killed (Anon., 1944; my translation). In this brief note
from the past, we see how the griots constitute a form of psychological
warfare—they announce the impending conflict and, by the sound of their
music and chants, instill fear and therefore weakness in the hearts of the
enemy. The result is a cost-free victory for the attackers.

Two examples illustrate the way griots can contribute to wars in the
modern era. Aldonía Gomes and Fernanda Cavacos report that during the
war of independence of Guinea-Bissau in the 1970s, the *djidius* (the
Portuguese creole term for *griots*) played key roles in mobilizing the
populace and maintaining support for the war efforts in the liberated zones
(1993, p. 93). In December 1985, the government of Mali attempted to
achieve the same goal on a national level during a conflict with Burkina

Faso. During this time, the government played the songs of Ban Zoumana Cissoko on the radio. The songs prompted people in Bamako to take to the streets to show their support for the conflict, according to Barbara Hoffman (in Arnoldi, 1995, p. 92).

In another example involving radio, the words of griots both incite conflicts and serve as a substitute for guns in the resolution of differences. On the northern edge of the griot world, where sub-Saharan meets Saharan Africa, one finds an extraordinary encounter between two poetic traditions, one rooted in local, Arabic, and even Spanish written and oral forms, the other in black African verbal art conveyed by griots. The result is sometimes a blend of both and a great variety of meters, rhythms, and modes. What is fascinating about this poetry is not simply the variety of forms it takes but also its power and its use in lieu of combat. Michel Guignard writes:

> Formerly, the countless quarrels between peoples included a veritable war of poetry involving both great epic works of the *thaydina* genre as well as little poems of the more popular type. . . . The importance that the Moors attach to these verbal combats can be very surprising. Even today, certain epic poems are forbidden on the radio because of the fear that they will arouse old inter-clan quarrels and damage national unity. . . . Griots are . . . the spokesmen of the honor of a people and its chiefs, and it is not surprising that rivalries develop: a people tries to prove that they possess a better musician than another group, and instead of launching a war, they fight by the intermediary of griots. (1975, pp. 38, 43; my translation)

If there are fewer wars in the Sahel and Savanna today, griots in many parts of the region are still busy in another hortatory role at sports events, especially wrestling, the national sport of Senegal and highly popular in many other countries across the continent. Sigrid Paul points out that griots once announced matches and summoned the participants, though today the events are advertised in newspapers (1987, p. 25). But the role of the griots is somewhat more complex than this brief mention. Isabelle Leymarie explains that

> as famous wrestlers obtain wealth and prestige and symbolize power, some griots join their entourage and follow them from arena to arena, acting as their counsellors and chaperones outside the competitions. At matches, the griots' role consists in playing the rhythm pattern of each fighter on their drums while they enter the arena. During the match itself . . . the griots stand on the side of the ring and play drums between bouts. (1978, p. 152)

Some of the best descriptions of griots at wrestling matches in Senegal appear in Geoffrey Gorer's dated but still useful book *Africa Dances*. Based on research done during the summer of 1934 in West Africa, it was first published in 1935, then rediscovered in 1962. Gorer reports:

> If a young man wishes to enter for the wrestling championship he will be accompanied everywhere by his griot who will look after his comfort and morale, help him with his grigris [protective charms], act as his boaster in the arena, play the drum which will announce his entrance and collect the greater part of the money and gifts, which, should he be successful or popular, will be showered on him. . . . The griots take up their positions in the corner of the arena, playing for their patron regardless of the rival griots by them, shouting their patron's glory, occasionally turning somersaults and handsprings to make people laugh, and before the fight doing the necessary grigri with their patrons . . . and making spells to avert ill luck. (1962, pp. 49–50)

In this context, the griot serves not only as spokesperson but also as the one who can save the wrestler from disaster. Gorer cites one example of a young wrestler who challenged a far more experienced competitor, Babacar Thiaw, much to the surprise of the audience and the family of the junior competitor. Faced with certain defeat, the challenger's family, friends, and griot persuaded him to withdraw before the match started. Gorer writes: "After a long argument, in which everyone joined, his griot withdrew the challenge and the young man left the arena in tears" (51).

The incident heightened the popularity of Babacar Thiaw, who was "smothered in gifts which he handed to his griot." But not long thereafter, Massemba, the local champion, arrived. The narrator describes him as "a great butchery gladiator of a man, with an absolutely enormous retinue of griots, dancers and followers." When Thiaw won the match against Massemba, Gorer explains, the event made wrestling history, not only because of its length, but also because of the gifts. As the winner was escorted to his patron's home for a feast, his griot, Gorer adds, "was staggering under the gifts" (51–52).

In the Wolof sporting context, then, the griot is more than an exhorter. He appears to combine the roles of cheerleader for his patron, manager of the competitor's financial and spiritual affairs, spokesman, and adviser.

One example of how important the griot can be in the eyes of the audience and the wrestler appears in a fictional portrait of a match in Sow Fall's *L'Appel des arènes*. Nalla's tutor, Mr. Niang, explains the parallel between the griot's role at wrestling matches and the traditional role of griots to inspire soldiers on the field of battle. He then describes an extraordinary match he witnessed whose outcome turns on a challenge by a griot to his patron Pathé, the smaller of the two combatants.

> One could see a man with a long red hat, a black gabardine coat, and a large talisman on his right ankle. . . . It was the griot of Pathé. He was called Birima. He approached the wrestling area, unsheathed his knife, pointed it at his heart, and shouted: "Pathé, if you fall, know that you will also have to bury your griot, and that your shame, you will carry it all alone on your two shoulders. . . ." He repeated his warning three times. . . . Pathé spun like a top . . . drove like an arrow into the legs of the giant, and knocked him down. He then raised his two arms in the air, in the arena that had become a boiling volcano, and, turning to Birima, roared, "The humiliation of the fall is more degrading that the pain of blows. . . . I was not born yesterday." (Sow Fall, 1982, pp. 83–84)

Here the wrestler's success is more intimately linked to the words and deeds of the griot than one might expect by mere cheerleading. From a Western perspective, it is as if the warning by the griot, combined with the threat of suicide and the indelible stain on family honor, acts directly upon the adrenaline of the wrestler, prompting what appears to be a superhuman response. From an African point of view, however, no scientific explanation is needed: the words of the griot contain a mystical and transcendent power.

Leymarie states in her discussion of griots and wrestling that these multifunctional exhorters have begun to play music for other sports, such as football (known in the United States as soccer). The difference, she points out, is that the griots are not attached to particular players, though she predicts that this may occur if the athletes "acquire enough prestige in the eyes of the traditionalist masses" (1978, p. 153).

Boxing is another sport that may attract the encouragement of griots. Attihirou has described the activities of a Hausa singer who was recruited to encourage a champion boxer:

> 'Dan Anace's most famous songs were in praise of the famous boxer, Muhammadu Shago . . . [who] boxed for 60 years, had 1,115 bouts and was never beaten. . . . His relationship with 'Dan Anace started off unpromisingly. Shago kept beating all the boxers whom 'Dan Anace had been supporting and 'Dan Anace refused to switch allegiance to him. Shago, having decided he wanted 'Dan Anace as his singer, was forced to enlist the help of 'Dan Anace's father to put pressure on him to agree. When finally 'Dan Anace did agree they became inseparable, going everywhere together. (Attihiru; cited in Furniss, 1996, p. 166)

The words of the griots, whether before battle or before some other challenge, force the listeners to look inward briefly with some intensity, to question whether they are up to the challenge on the horizon, and, in so doing, to raise their sights before embarking on a new venture. The impact of the words is hard to measure, but it is clear that the hortatory speech of griots is endowed with considerable power to move people in ways that may surprise them.

Warriors

Griots are sometimes perceived as eager to inspire others to go into battle, unwilling to fight themselves, and quick to switch loyalties to the other side (Sory Camara, 1976, p. 334). This widespread view veils a more complex relationship rooted in the division of labor between those who actually engage in combat and those who lead. The role of griots in battle falls somewhere in between and might be likened to that of a noncommissioned officer. In other words, it is the griots' knowledge of the psychology of people that suits them to the task of assisting the leaders of armies.

While on a military campaign near Ségou with Ahmadou, son of El Hadj Omar, in the 1860s, the Frenchman Mage noted that at nightfall, "griots on horseback rode through the camp, calling for silence and advising that horses be tied up" (1980, p. 191). The next morning they awakened the army with the sound of music at 5:30, much like reveille. Griots, it seems in this case, not only inspired men about to go into war, but also served in a broader capacity as supervisors, what one today might call sergeants, who were responsible to some extent for the maintenance of a degree of order in armies on the march.

But evidence also suggests that griots held other roles such as generals and as combatants. Adama Dramé, the griot narrator of *Jeliya*, one of the few books ever to be published by a griot, includes the voice of his female cousin Fatim, who offers examples from their family history of *jeliw* who fought alongside their patrons. Fatim cites her grandfather M'Paran Kouyaté, who fought side by side with Dagali, a ruler of the kingdom of Nioro, and was awarded a griotte for his services (Dramé and Senn-Borloz, 1992, p. 22). She explains that some griots attempt to demonstrate their fidelity to their patrons by participating in wars, while others do not engage in war, simply because of the division of labor in a society that reserves combat for warriors. Some of Samory Touré's most trusted generals were griots. Morifing Dian was not only Touré's closest and most trusted collaborator but also the only combatant to accompany him into exile.

The role of griots on the front lines reflected the reality that they could not inspire warriors very effectively if they were not out in front themselves. In the early twentieth century Lavallière (1911) explained that when the armies go into action, the griots

> go out front, flattering the pride of the warriors. . . . Shame on those who bend, when a griot without any concern at all marches at the head of an army and shows heroism. People often say, following examples of this temerity, that many are the griots who cause the loss of more than one army by remaining completely exposed to firing from a much stronger enemy. In spite of many wounds, they persist in exciting the combatants who, in order not to be unworthy of their ancestors, race off to a certain death rather than give way.

Literary portraits echo this image of the griot as warrior. In the passage cited earlier from Sow Fall's novel *L'Appel des arènes*, the griot Mapaté declared to Nalla's mother that "on the fields of battle we were in the first rank, we were the shields" (107–8).

Griots, leatherworkers, and metalsmiths all had their special roles to contribute in any war effort. It is reasonable to include griots in the category of warriors, even though their functions on the battlefield may have varied widely from exhorter to combatant to officer, depending on the circumstances.

Twentieth-century armies may have no need for griots, but in one case a griot's presence on the battlefield was reassuring to other soldiers. Richard Warms (1992) conducted a lengthy interview with Zoumana Kouyaté, a man of griot origin from Yanfolila, Mali. He was drafted in 1951 into the French army and served as a combatant in both Indochina and Algeria during a six-year enlistment covering one of the most difficult periods the French army faced in the postwar era. Kouyaté explained that until around 1950, when the French recruited soldiers, chiefs never allowed griots to be taken because they were considered to be part of the royal entourage. The chief would send people of captive origin instead, a practice that, paradoxically, led to the creation of new families of griots. Zoumana Kouyaté explained that one might have the name of Traoré or Koné, but if one was sent off to the army as the "substitute" for a Kouyaté, one was forced to assume the name Kouyaté. But when recruiting increased in the early 1950s to meet the growing manpower needs of France, recruiting officers simply took people without consulting chiefs.

Once Kouyaté was in the army and became known at roll calls, other Africans recognized his professional identity by his clan name, and began to treat him with special care, offering gifts and other considerations. Even though he did not have a musical instrument and carried out no functions of a griot, by his presence he was a much-appreciated symbol of home for other African soldiers from the Sahel in a situation that was highly alienating.

Witness

The griot is a witness to events in many senses of the term. Treaties and agreements may be witnessed by a griot, whose description of what happens may then be conveyed to subsequent generations in what we might call an oral document.

One finds numerous references to oaths sworn in the past. In the Mamadou Kouyaté version of *Sundiata* collected by Niane, the *jeli* declares at the very beginning that "when a quarrel breaks out between tribes it is we who settle the difference, for we are the depositories of oaths which the ancestors swore" (Niane, 1965, p. 1). In the same way, when two families are united by the marriage of their children, griots serve as witnesses to the event.

That is true even in the modern context. Rosa De Jorio (1995) has reported that griots now serve as witnesses, in the Western sense of the term, at civil ceremonies in much the way that a best man and maid of honor function as witnesses in a wedding in the European tradition. The griot, she writes, marks the official document with a cross or a thumbprint at the end of the ceremony.

This role of witness reflects the broader tradition of the griot as the "official" representative of a town, clan, or family at a major event—one who sees and then announces the news. If an event is important, it cannot be completed, it seems, without the presence of a griot.

Praise-singer

Praise-singing is one of the most widespread verbal phenomena in Africa. In West Africa, it is also one of the most complex functions carried out by griots, because the praise-singer serves as a means of social control, of balancing social functions.

On the surface, one might assume that the griot is simply seeking rewards, and in many contexts that may be the case. But there is much more to these praises. The praises represent the nexus of an exchange of power between nobles and other members of society. The singer of praises elevates the subject of these songs and chants.

As flattering as such a situation may seem, it is charged with potential difficulties because those who are praised must fulfill their responsibilities and conduct themselves in the manner expected by society. These responsibilities may range from effective leadership of a people in times of war and peace to providing for the basic needs of citizens in times of disaster.

Praise constitutes, then, an announcement not simply of qualities but also of duties and responsibilities. The few moments of joy at being the subject of praise may fade quickly before the lifetime of burdens such a position entails. These duties are owed not simply to the praise-singer but to all members of society who may rightly expect some degree of help or support from the noble.

Where the outsider sees abject flattery, insiders observe a complex drama that highlights the roles of different members of society. The question that remains at the end of the drama is not who holds the power, the nobles with their wealth and status or the praise-singers who can undo their patrons with a torrent of insults, but what kinds of power each has and how they are wielded (Barbara Hoffman, personal communication, 1996). This power can be exercised through praises in a variety of contexts, ranging from the home of a noble to a battlefield, a wrestling arena, or a political rally.

At least three problems arise in any analysis of praise-singing. First, much of what is known about this function comes primarily from those who are praised. We rarely hear the griot's explanation of the significance of praises. Second, there is also much generic overlapping. George Joseph, in a study of a praise-song by a griotte for the Wolof noblewoman Sému Coro Wende, who died in the early 1960s, discovered that the 155-line song was really a poetic genealogy that covered four centuries and included more than a hundred names (in Priebe and Hale, 1979, pp. 31–48). Third, much praise-singing fits into the stereotype of praise-for-pay and contributes to the negative reputation of griots as people who will praise anyone at any time if the reward is sufficient.

Donald R. Wright cites an example of this kind of praise-singing in The Gambia during the Second World War. Surrounded by a French colony in the hands of authorities controlled by the puppet Vichy regime in France, British officials were concerned about the loyalty of the Gambian people. They used a variety of propaganda devices, including griots, to "insure the correct direction of their sympathies." At a competition for griots organized by the British, the bards were primed "with rude things to sing about Vichy and the Germans, and the opposite about the British Empire" (Wright,

1997, p. 204). Chapter 3 will include a variety of examples of praise-singing that give a clearer sense of this ubiquitous and diverse verbal form.

Ceremony Participant

Griots often participate in ceremonies that mark major life events—naming of a child, initiation, marriage, installation of a chief, and, in some cases, funerals. The particular role varies from society to society and from one kind of griot to another. In some cases the griot is the master of ceremonies, in others merely one of the participants. In nearly every situation, however, it is hard to imagine the event going on without some involvement by these artisans of the word, because they bring people together with their speech.

Namings

The Soninké, known also as Sarakollé in southern Mauritania, hold a ceremony that is largely Islamic in nature, presided over by an imam, or religious leader. But as Gerteiny (1967) notes, a woman "from the bards' or musicians' caste" known as a "nyamakhala" announces the festivities surrounding the ceremony at sunset of the seventh day after the birth. She is accompanied by music and dances. After the announcement of the child's saint's name by the imam and his or her first name by his mother, followed by the family name called out by the father, "the nyamakhala then whispers the names into the baby's ear—three times for a boy and four times for a girl—and carries the child to the alimam and then to the council of the elders to be blessed" (99).

The Malinké *jeliw* and *jelimusow* announce the naming ceremony to the friends, neighbors, and relatives of the child's family. Sory Camara explains that on the morning of the naming ceremony, a *jeli* calls the assembled crowd to silence.

> The first name is whispered into the ear of the griot: standing in the middle of the compound, the griot turns toward the assembled men and announces loudly for the first time "The child will be called so-and-so, like his grandfather," for example. Then, with an epic declamation, he recounts the facts and deeds of the man whose first name the child bears. This done, he turns toward the women and proclaims the first name of the child . . . it is at this time that the men will present their gifts. The griot will stand to the right of each man who makes a speech. He will sometimes repeat each of the phrases of the speaker.

"I am not rich," one of them will say, for example; and the griot will repeat it to the audience as "I, So and So, it is not simply to make a gift that I have come before you, for I and everything I possess belong to [the child]." (1976, p. 198)

Camara goes on to explain that the interaction between *jeli* and speaker reveals something about the relationship of the newborn to the donor. If the speaker is eloquent, the *jeli* simply repeats his words. If the gift is large, the *jeli* normally keeps a small part of it.

For a Mandinka naming ceremony in Serrekunda, The Gambia, described by Mark Hudson (1989, p. 117), the newborn was carried out of the house by a *jalimuso*, followed by a group of singers. When the singing stopped, a *jali ke*, or male griot, announced the name of the child, who was then blessed by a group of marabouts, Muslim religious leaders. The other male griots then approached male members of the naming ceremony party to recount their family histories.

Initiation

Initiation ceremonies, in particular circumcisions, are often carried out by blacksmiths. But griots also play a role, because these events, in the broader context, represent a highly significant moment in the education of young men. Sory Camara (1976, p. 199) points out that for the Malinké, the *jeliw* provide music for dances during the week prior to the initiation, then serve as witnesses to the actual circumcision. Afterward, they report the results and "are not afraid to reveal any instances of cowardliness."

Bouillagui Fadiga (1934) describes the griots' diverse roles in an initiation ceremony for a Marka group, a people who were once thought to be part of the Soninké diaspora but who today are identified more in terms of their activities as traders. A master griot is designated by a wealthy Marka noble to visit the 127 young men destined to go through the ceremony. His task: to keep up their spirits and to educate them. A crowd assembles for a celebration that will last until dawn. The noble presides over the ceremony and sits next to the musicians. "By the voice of his griot, Diely Diatourou, sparkling with joy on this day of generosity, he thanks all the guests for coming in such large numbers . . . ." A dance begins, interrupted from time to time by the griot, who announces the gifts given by the guests. "The donor is applauded and the dance starts up again as his name and his genealogy are proclaimed and take on, at this occasion, their full meaning."

In this example, the griot serves as educator of the young initiates, spokesman for the sponsor of the ceremony, and praiser for the guests. It is the function of educator of the young initiates that Alex Haley chose to feature in Chapter 24 of *Roots* (1976). He describes the kingdoms of the past, emphasizing the richness of Mali for his readers and the fact that Africans possessed forms of education that predate the arrival of colonialism (117–18).

Courtship

Sory Camara (1976) describes the role of *jeliw* in Malinké courtship by explaining that once a young man has shown an interest in a young woman, a *jeli* is sent to the father of the woman to give him ten kola nuts. On subsequent visits, he offers more valuable gifts. During a period of weeks or months, these visits by the *jeli* obtain no clear response from the family of the woman. At the same time, the young man visits the future spouse often, always accompanied by his *jeli*, who presents the gifts and asks both the woman and members of her family about her feelings toward the man. His goal is to find out who is holding back and who needs to be persuaded. Finally, during a ceremony called *wòròté* (breaking the kola nut), the family gives its response to the *jeli* (200). Throughout this courtship, it is the *jeli* who is the principal intermediary. He serves in a sense as a human cushion in a risky and delicate negotiation. If the family replies negatively, the suitor can blame his *jeli* rather than himself for not making his case in the most effective manner.

The late Senegalese author Mariama Bâ illustrated the roles of griots and griottes in courtship in each of her two novels. In *Un chant écarlate* (1981; *Scarlet Song*, 1986), a Senegalese student named Ousmane returns home from France with a French wife. His former girl friend Ouleymatou decides to undo the alliance. She prepares a sumptuous dinner for Oussou and some of her friends. When it draws to a close, she heightens the seductive atmosphere of the evening by calling upon a griot whose name means his profession in both Fulbe and Mandinka.

Gradually, the other guests slipped away. When they were alone Ouleymatou drew the curtain. Then Mabo Diali began strumming on his Khalam. As he plucked at the strings, his voice rose up in a warm cadence.

Oussou, prince of culture!
But before you were a prince of culture
You were and are a Lebu prince.
A White woman forsook her country to follow you
But the Black girl is more suitable for you

Than the White woman.
Look, look at Ouleymatou, your sister by her blood and by her skin.
She is the one you need.

He was lulled by the harmonious plucking of the strings. How many inflexible wills, how many heroic resolutions have been overcome by the notes of the Khalam!

"Trouble, trouble, Diali!" sang the young Black woman. "Trouble his senses, trouble his heart, Mabo Diali. Help me to seduce him. I advance towards him. Neither a knife at my throat nor a wall of flame can stop me." . . . And he melted like a lump of karite [butter] on hot coals. . . . He drew Ouleymatou unresisting toward him. Diali put on his slippers and discreetly disappeared. He had already pocketed on his arrival a thousand-franc note [$4.] to pay for his services. (1986, 118–19; I have slightly modified Dorothy Blair's translation.)

In Bâ's first and most widely read novel, *Une si longue lettre* (1980; *So Long a Letter*, 1981), the reader encounters a sharply contrasting description of a griotte's role in a long-dead courtship. The courtship has been revived by a marriage proposal from Daouda Dieng, a former suitor to the main character, Ramatoulaye, who has just been widowed in middle age after thirty years of marriage to another man. When Dieng makes his second proposal, he adds that he will return the next day for an answer. Farmata, Ramatoulaye's lifelong griotte, appears to report that a wealthy man has just given her 5,000 francs ($20).

Before leaving, Farmata, the griotte woman of the cowries, had declared, "Your mother was right. Daouda is wonderful. What *guer* [noble] gives five thousand francs today! Daouda has neither exchanged his wife nor abandoned his children; if he has come back looking for you, you, an old woman burdened with a family, it is because he loves you; he can look after you and your family. Think about it. Accept." (67)

Ramatoulaye decides to refuse the offer and sends Farmata with a warm but firmly negative written message to Daouda Dieng. But she finds herself uncomfortable not only in having to turn down Dieng but also in relying on Farmata, who cannot read and has entirely different expectations.

For the first time I was turning to Farmata for help, and this embarrassed me. She was happy, having dreamed of this role right from our youth. But I always acted alone; she was never a participant in my problems, only informed—just like any "vulgar acquaintance," she would complain. She was thrilled, ignorant of the cruel message she was carrying.

When the griotte returns to report Daouda Dieng's troubled reaction to the letter of rejection, she excoriates her patron with the most penetrating and painful insults she can utter:

> What was it you dared to write and make me messenger of? You have killed a man. . . . God will punish you for not having followed the path towards peace. . . . You shall live in mud. . . . I wish you another Modou [her disloyal late husband] to make you shed tears of blood. Who do you take yourself for? . . . You, so withered, you want to choose a husband like an eighteen-year-old. (69)

The outburst of the griotte reflects her disappointment as well as her privileged role as a servant of the family who can express her view directly to her patrons, much the way the griot of a king is allowed to speak directly and candidly to his master. The decision of Ramatoulaye to reject the offer and her admission that she had always kept her griotte at some distance from her own personal decisions reflect in microcosm one of the larger themes of the novel—the Westernization of the main character and her frequent inability to respond to social problems and customs in ways that meet expectations of those more deeply rooted in traditional ways.

Marriages

If a courtship is successful, the wedding itself in many parts of West Africa, as in other parts of the world, becomes a joining of two families, not simply two people. In many areas, the wedding is not an event for a single day; it constitutes a week-long affair during which the griots and griottes continue to provide entertainment.

For the Malinké, Sory Camara (1976) explains that on the day of the wedding, a *jeli*, at the head of a group of brothers of the groom and friends from his age group, goes to look for the bride. A *jelimuso* dresses the bride. "Then a *jeli* carries her on his back across the threshold of the new home. . . . When the bride rejoins her husband, a *jelimuso* remains not far from the home. When the union is consummated, she will come to take the sheet bearing the proof of the virginity; the next day, she will carry this sheet in a beautiful calabash on her head; she will present it to all the elder women in the village" (200). Camara adds that the *jelimuso* can serve as a witness in the event of problems during the night—impotence or the discovery that the woman is not a virgin. She may even, he notes, participate in a plan to use chicken blood to hide the fact that the bride is not a virgin (211).

That is what occurs in Ousmane Sembène's novel *Xala* when the main character, El Hadji Abdou Kader Baye, fails to consummate his marriage to his third wife. The young woman's aunt arrives the next morning with a griotte carrying a rooster for sacrifice between the legs of the bride, both as an offering and to ensure that there is blood on the sheets. The news of El Hadji's failure stops the sacrifice, and word of the event quickly leaks out, presumably via the female griot (Sembène, 1973, pp. 44–45).

Again in Senegal, Nafissatou Diallo describes the wedding of her cousin in her autobiography about growing up in Dakar, *De Tilène au Plateau: Une enfance dakaroise* (1975). "All day long griots sang the genealogy of the family, not without some mocking words for those unwed mothers who had not had the patience to 'wait'" (69; my translation). The next day, after the wedding night, the family of the groom arrives with three suitcases of gifts. They are led by a griot singing the praises of the family. "All these items were exhibited, spread out, and counted by the family griot, who offered special comments on each along with praises for my cousin and her family" (71). The young narrator discovers, however, that all of these gifts are distributed among relatives, friends, and griots, with little left for the bride.

At weddings, griots and griottes also sing the praises of the arriving guests. A vivid example of the atmosphere that can prevail in an urban context is the wedding scene from *Xala*, the film version of Sembène's novel. Although the context is highly Westernized, with a local orchestra playing European instruments, the arrival of a multitiered wedding cake, and many guests wearing suits, the sounds of the griottes announcing the guests with praises and ululations offer a striking reminder of the main character's African roots.

Installations

Rarer than weddings and naming ceremonies, installations of chiefs normally draw much larger crowds and, inevitably, more griots. These events are marked by the participation of delegations of chiefs from the surrounding area. Each may make an entrance, preceded by griots and griottes who sing their praises and announce their arrival. Once the chiefs have arrived and installed themselves in homes or around an open area where the event will take place, griots may stroll around, seeking to find out who else is there—especially who else they may be able to recognize and praise. During the installation, which may involve the placing of a hat or turban on the new ruler, griots may intone special chants or recount the history of the chief's family. The event may take a day or many days, depending on the office—village chief, canton or district chief, province chief, or traditional regional ruler.

Two descriptions of installations of chiefs, one brief and from the distant past, the other much longer and from the present, give hints of the diversity of the griot's role.

According to a legend about the founding of the Ama Siga dynasty of the Serer people in Senegal in the early eighteenth century, the ruler is conducted in the morning to the public square by Fara N'Doucane, chamberlain and supplier for the king, and Fara Lambe, chief of the griots. Three small piles of sand are lined up there in a row. Fara N'Doucane, after having sacrificed a white rooster on each pile of sand, orders: "Powerful king, sit on the middle pile of sand, facing the east." The king does so. Fara Lambe places a gray cotton hat on his head. Then, with the help of a small band of white and black cotton, he wraps up the headgear tightly in the form of a turban (Diouf, 1944, p. 182; my translation). Here the griot is central to the installation process.

At an installation I attended, that of Bakari Sanya, a regional chief, in Faraba-Banta, The Gambia, on Oct. 2, 1991, the role of the griots was more diffuse but also, in some ways, more pervasive. During the morning, neighboring chiefs, accompanied by griots, arrived to salute the new chief. A *jelimuso* from Kita, Mali, greeted each arriving chief. A group of *balafon* players performed through the morning on the porch of the chief's home, while other *jalolu* strolled through the growing crowd, singing and playing instruments. In midafternoon everyone walked from the chief's home down to the center of the village, where a covered stage and hundreds of chairs were set up on both sides of it as well as across the street. The sounds of griots and other performers increased as the crowd grew and as new groups of performers arrived, ranging from a small jazz band to acrobats and a man on stilts. *Jalimusow* walked slowly past the rows of people seated on either side of the stage, calling out praises for people they recognized.

At 3:30 that afternoon, President Dauda Jawara arrived. After a welcoming speech by the minister of the interior, the new chief was invited to step forward. President Jawara read a proclamation in English, which the new chief repeated while holding his hand on a copy of the Qur'an. He then signed a document.

During all the speeches, Fabala Kanuteh, the *jali* who most often accompanied the president on trips, interpreted into Wolof or Fulbe, depending on the language of the person speaking. Throughout the speeches, each time a name was mentioned, scores of *jalimusow*, massed across the street from the stage, would sing praises.

From the foregoing, one can sense the way griots dominate such events. An installation ceremony is a day for them to shine, to deploy their verbal talents to the maximum, and to reap the rewards that they expect. It is also an event that reminds the audience about the past and the intimate—though fading—relationship between rulers and their griots.

Funerals

For many Sahelian and Savanna peoples who are Muslim, their religious leaders, the imam and the marabout, conduct funerals. Many griots I interviewed said that they did not perform at funerals because of the solemnity of these events. Lynne Jessup (1983, p. 31) reports that in the Mandinka area where she conducted research, the *balafon* is not played at the death of a person. But Bala Diabaté, who was the chief griot in Kéla, Mali, told me in 1992 that at a funeral he walks around the body intoning the clan name of the deceased, reminding the mourners what the ancestors of the person did and also what the person who died accomplished. Sory Camara reports that the task of griots is to announce a death (1976, p. 201), a report that matches information contained in Alexis de Saint-Lô's 1637 account and in many other sources. In his *Relation du voyage du Cap-Verd*, Saint-Lô describes how these "guiriots . . . ran through the villages with I don't know what kind of drums strung around their necks and beating their hands on them, shouting that the wife of the chief was dead and adding to these announcements a great deal of praise in honor of the deceased" (71; my translation). Later, at the burial, four marabouts carried the bier, "preceded by some Guiriots, making much noise with their drums" (77).

Louis Diène Faye, in describing the burial on March 8, 1969, of Maye Koor Juuf, a Serer king in the Sine region of Senegal, states that the ruler was buried along with the drum of his chief griot. His other drums were played for the last time before being placed on the ground and pointed toward the east. Griots then sang songs marked by sadness and praise (1983, pp. 33–39).

From this limited evidence it seems that griots may once have had a significant role at funerals, but their function has been supplanted by Islamic religious representatives. One of the paradoxes of this change is that in some parts of West Africa, especially Senegal, the muezzins who call worshipers to prayer at the mosque are often of griot origin because of their natural talents (Villalón, 57–58).

✂ ✂

It is evident that many of the functions of griots of the past are less important today, while others have taken on a more significant role as social and performance contexts change. Fewer wars are being fought in

Africa and there are fewer chiefs to serve. But the demand for musical performances by griots is increasing worldwide.

The list of functions described in this chapter—genealogist, historian, adviser, spokesperson, diplomat, mediator, interpreter and translator, musician, composer, teacher, exhorter, warrior, witness, praise-singer, and master or participant in a variety of ceremonies—is both extraordinary and incomplete. Occasional references to griots as bonesetters, executioners, and diviners hint at other functions that may be localized or simply ephemeral, occurring during a particular period in the past. John William Johnson told me that Ban Zoumana Cissoko, the blind Malian *jeli*, read cowries by feel. Johnson (1996a) notes that divination among *jeliw* was widespread, though not all diviners were bards, nor all bards diviners. The conflict between clans in Kita cited by Hoffman (1990a) included much casting of spells by parties on both sides of the issue, though it is usually the case that sorcerers, not griots, specialize in this activity.

The evidence from the functions I have described suggests three conclusions. First, one cannot attach a single label such as praise-singer or storyteller to a profession with so many roles to play in society. Not all of the griots' past functions are as significant as they once were, and in both past and present, few griots carried out all of these roles. But it is clear that they have adapted many of these activities—especially those that focus on recounting the events of the past and performing music—to new contexts in an effort to maintain their position as key members of society.

Second, the functions described here suggest that griots constitute in many ways a group that serves collectively as the social glue in society. By their efforts to inspire people, mediate conflicts, and facilitate important life ceremonies, they seem to operate as secular guides to human behavior and as social arbiters. At events related to birth, initiation, marriage, family history, sports, music, and government, griots and griottes are there to witness the occason, to enliven it, to facilitate it, and to convey what happened to others. No other profession in any other part of the world is charged with such wide-ranging and intimate involvement in the lives of people.

Finally, the griotcentric world view—that society cannot survive without griots—appears somewhat less exaggerated after seeing the evidence presented in this chapter. It is true that societies in the Sahel and Savanna are undergoing considerable change as the result of external influence and that griots may become less significant for these peoples over time. But the multiplicity of roles seen in this chapter fits well with the public image of the indispensable wordsmith that we find in both verbal and visual sources, from oral epics to the nineteenth-century photograph (figure 1) of the griot seated at the right hand of the chief from Bassé.

If their contributions to society are clearly so diverse and so important, one can only wonder how they managed to become so indispensable to so many people around them, from ordinary citizens to chiefs. The answer to that question lies in the complex and lengthy history of griots, the subject of the next chapter.

❄ 2 ❄
The Origin of Griots

The wide range of functions that griots carry out suggests that these specialists of the spoken word must have extraordinary origins. The evidence certainly supports this view. But just as the stories of heroes from the past are constantly reinterpreted to reflect changing values in the present, so too the history of griots has evolved over time as the result of new influences on West African societies, from Islam to European colonialism. There are many narrative strands in the story of griots. They include origin tales as well as accounts by travelers to West Africa. In this chapter, I bring together several strands of this rather long and complex history—origin tales of griots from the oral tradition, written descriptions by Africans that date back nearly a thousand years, and more recent accounts by Europeans from the seventeenth century to the present.

Oral Narratives

How a society interprets its own cultural heritage reveals as much about the past as it does about the present. Oral accounts that describe griots—by griots and by others in society—offer the most appropriate starting point, because these narratives are widely diffused over time and space. Often they contain many variations on the same theme, an indication of contemporary cultural diversity and also of the probability that the basic story in question is rather old.

Blood and Taboo

Nearly all stories about the origins of griots, that is, etiological tales, focus on an extraordinary act involving blood—spilling it, consuming it, or participating in a blood crime. Much of the current discussion on the subject comes from twenty-seven Maninka tales collected in the 1960s in northern Côte d'Ivoire by Hugo Zemp. His initial analysis of them in 1968, followed by a reexamination of the same evidence in 1969 by Laura Makarius and a further review in 1976 by Sory Camara, constitutes the most extensive treatment of origin tales about griots.

The focus in these studies is on one of several peoples who share a common cultural and linguistic heritage referred to as Mande. There are many Mande languages and dialects, including Soninké, Khassonké, Bamana, Mandinka, Maninka, and Dioula. The peoples who speak these languages trace some or all of their roots to the Mali empire, in particular the town of Kangaba in contemporary southwestern Mali, and to the thirteenth-century founder of the empire, Sundiata Keita.

For these peoples, as well as for many others throughout the Sahel and Savanna, oral narratives and other evidence collected by ethnographers suggest that blood is a highly dangerous substance. Makarius notes that its spread or handling in some contexts, especially within a family, may be a violation of deeply rooted traditions governing its treatment. This kind of violation is only one of many different sorts of behavior that place griots in a distinct social category (1968, pp. 627–28). According to Makarius, "because he violates a taboo that is the foundation of social order, the magic violator of taboos is depicted in mythologies as an anti-social person, like the rebel who defies authority, whether it is social or religious. He is often the adversary of divinities and their earthly representatives" (629; my translation).

Blood appears at the center of the most common origin tale, about the two brothers. In 1916, Hamet Sow Télémaque, an assistant teacher at the Thiong Street School in Dakar, contributed this Wolof version to an article about the origin of griots published in a West African journal for school-teachers:

> Blacks says that griots and "guers," freemen, are descended originally from two men who had the same mother and the same father. These two brothers were traveling together. The trip was long and their food ran out. They went for two days without eating. The elder took pity on his younger brother, and said to him: "Wait for me, I have my gun and I know how to hunt." He disappeared. A few instants later, a gunshot was heard and he returned carrying a piece of meat which he took care to cook himself. He offered it to his brother. "I have eaten my share, here is yours." The younger brother ate and gave thanks to God and to his elder brother. When he felt better, he asked him how he had been able to find game in this barren region! In effect, the elder had never found any. The gunshot in the air was a trick to make the younger brother believe that the elder

had killed some game in order to feed him without guessing that the meat had been cut from his elder brother. He didn't want to give his younger brother any kind of disturbing explanation, but the secret did not remain hidden very long, for after three days of walking, the wound became infected, and the older brother could not stand up. It was then that he confessed to his younger brother the great dedication of the act that he had done to save his life. The younger brother was surprised by this moving tale. In spite of the apparent horror and the feeling of distaste that it left in him, for the younger brother this act remained at bottom a magnificent demonstration of the highest conception of fraternal love and of the great responsibility that nature imposes on older siblings toward the younger in difficult circumstances.

When the two brothers arrived at their destination, the younger composed in honor of his elder brother praises in which he vaunted the courage and nobility of his character. The elder was very happy and showered the younger with gifts.

Thus, according to indigenous tradition, began the origin of griots, descendants of the younger brother who, by his own act, made himself socially inferior to his elder brother. (Télémaque, 1916, 277; my translation)

Roland Colin, who summarized this story for a study of the tale in West Africa, added that in an unidentified Mande variant the elder brother gives the younger his blood to drink. He suggests that this might explain the origin of the term *jeli* or *djeli*, the central Mande term for griot. Colin explains that the blood tie among the Mande, *senenku*, is similar to other kinds of blood links that bind groups in society (1957, p. 65).

Sory Camara expresses skepticism about claims that the Malinké terms for griot and blood are anything more than coincidence. Aware from his own observations of how nimbly griots embroider on a particular word and how the Malinké make nouns out of verbs, he proposes an equally tantalizing tie between *jali*, a common word that does not mean blood, and *jiyali*, from the verb *jiya*, "to house a person." *Jiyali* would mean the action of housing or the noun housing. The origin of the link would come from the fact that patrons normally housed their griots (1976, p. 101). But Camara concludes that both *jeli*/blood and *jiyali*/housing are no more than unverifiable hypotheses. Other peoples in the region with matching origin tales give different names to their griots—for example, the Fulbe *mabo* (145). Camara concludes that the origin of these terms must remain, at least for the moment, ambiguous (102).

The story raises one other question: are griots cannibals? The answer is clearly no. The consumption of flesh and blood can only be viewed as an extraordinary response to a life-threatening situation, a phenomenon that has occurred among other peoples around the world at times of starvation and disaster or in symbolic religious contexts. It is the unusual nature of the incident here that marks indelibly the origin of griots, not their social functions.

Aside from the importance of blood and the appearance of the anachronistic gun, two significant features emerge from this story. The first is that it has diffused throughout the Sahel and Savanna region and is therefore probably rather old. There is no way of knowing exactly how old, but one might speculate that this etiological tale about griots is at least several centuries old. Zemp reports a Fulani version published by Mamby Sidibé in 1959 and adds that Claude Meillassoux collected a Soninké version embedded in the Wagadou legend that describes the fall of the Ghana empire (Meillassoux, 1964).

The second remarkable trait in the story appears in the basic change that occurs in the younger brother. The consumption of the elder's flesh and blood creates a special bond between the two. But it also marks the younger as someone who must now be seen as different from other men because of the violation of a basic social custom. Charles Monteil explains that among the Soninké "it sometimes happens that a freeman, someone not of 'casted' origin, declares himself to be the *geseré* (one of several Soninké words for griot) of another man to whom he wants to demonstrate his thanks, his submission, or his desire to link himself to that man's fortune. In the latter case, it is not unusual for there to be a solemn and ceremonial exchange of blood between the two men to seal the relationship. In all cases, the *geseré* becomes a member of a professional group of artisans, often called 'casted,' as do his descendants" (Monteil, 1953, p. 364, n. 2; cited in Zemp, 7). This fundamental shift in social identity is far more complicated than the hierarchical change that it suggests.

Although the story of the two brothers seems to be the most widely diffused etiological tale about griots, other tales have been collected. They also involve blood, but here the consequences lead to death. In the same 1916 article by Télémaque that contained the story of the two brothers, Ahmadou Mapaté Diagne recounted this story of the killing of a brother as the origin of griots:

> A long time ago, two brothers were sent by their mother to look for firewood. They fought over a branch that each wanted, and the elder unfortunately killed the younger. Not knowing what to do, he picked up the corpse and carried it toward home. At the moment he was about to enter his mother's house, he was spotted by his parents, who chased him away, saying, "Go wherever you want

with this dead person; we don't need it, we have no idea what should be done with it."

The brother killer sat down behind the house in the shade of a large tree. At mealtimes, he called and was brought his share. When the wind blew very hard, his voice was not loud enough. To remedy the situation, he obtained two sticks that he struck against each other.

One night, one of his sticks was hollowed out by termites. The next day, the unhappy brother killer noticed that this stick was louder than the other. Profiting from this discovery, he obtained a hollow log on which he struck his two sticks to produce melodious sounds.

On the seventh day of his exile, two crows who were fighting landed on his head. He stepped back without touching them. One had killed the other, and then scraped out a hole in the ground with his claws and buried the corpse.

The brother killer imitated him—an event seen as the origin of burials—and returned to the house with the hollow tree trunk and the stick that he would never part with. The neighbors came to see them, asking him to make sounds from them, and gave him various items to reward him.

Since then, they have forgotten his accidental crime and think only of his drumming. (275–76; my translation)

Although the result in this version is the opposite of what happens in the first version and the focus is more on the musical rather than the praise-singing function, the underlying theme of spilling blood under extraordinary circumstances serves to mark the griot and all of his descendants as people who are somehow different from others.

A version even more widely distributed, at least outside Africa, also involves death in the family. In 1909, the German ethnographer Leo Frobenius collected a Soninké story in which seven children die for no good reason before the protagonist succeeds in becoming a griot. It appeared in German in 1921 and in English in 1937, under the title *African Genesis* (reprinted as *Gassire's Lute* [Jablow, 1971]). It is an epic about a young prince who is advised to become a griot because his old father does not appear ready to step down soon from his post as king. After having a lute constructed by a blacksmith, Gassire is unable to draw any sound out of it until the blood of his children is spilled on it. After losing seven sons in a senseless war and spilling their blood on his lute as he carries each one back from battle, Gassire and his family abandon their home only to discover one night the sound of the lute. Only then does his father die, and Wagadou, the capital of the Ghana empire, disappears for the first of four times.

Laura Makarius sees in the spilling of blood here an example of the magical power of this liquid in the context of a violation of a taboo, the sacrifice of one's children to obtain a given result. An equally significant feature of this tale is the noble origin of the griot. When a noble takes up activities of a griot, whether he is the cousin of Askia Mohammed in *The Epic of Askia Mohammed* or the modern singer Salif Keita, he crosses a major barrier separating his own people from others in society.

Another origin tale involving the spilling of blood was collected by Zemp from a Malinké griot in northern Côte d'Ivoire. The narrator tells of a slave who, when ordered to kill one of the wives of a great chief, makes a mistake and brings the head of the wrong one to his patron. Scheduled to die for his error, the servant takes the advice of a marabout and begins to sing the praises of the chief. The chief then gives him a horse and orders him to remain always at his side to sing his praises. The narrator concludes: "thus the slave became a griot. He was the first griot in the world" (Zemp, 637).

These two stories illustrate the ambiguity about the status of griots. In one the griot is of noble origin. In the other he is of slave origin. In fact, as will be seen later, griots do not normally come from either of these groups.

Beheaded victims appear in another tale, although the griot is not the source of the act. A Malinké griot from the Koné clan in Man, western Côte d'Ivoire, reported to Zemp that

> the first griots accompanied their chiefs into combat. When the great warriors killed their enemies, the griots cut off the heads of the corpses. They loaded the heads on their shoulders and carried them to the village as proof of the heroic exploits of the warriors. The blood of the heads flowed onto their bodies, and that is why they were called *jeli*. (Zemp, 637)

Blood, then, appears as a common feature of all of these stories of origin and reinforces the close association between the griot and a significant social taboo.

Islamic Reinterpretations

Islam arrived in sub-Saharan West Africa in the eleventh century by a variety of means, peaceful and violent: trade, migration because of changes in the environment, wars between those who had adopted the religion and those who resisted it, and invasion by forces from across the Sahara. Some peoples, especially those farther inland from the west coast, including the Bamana and the Dogon, put up varying degrees of resistance to Islam. Others, especially those such as the Fulbe and the Soninké, who had much earlier contact with the religion, accepted the new system of belief more readily. However it arrived, the values, traditions, images, and great figures conveyed by Islam impacted societies in a variety of ways.

In the case of the etiological tales about griots, the characters become Muslim but the violation of taboo remains. Makarius sees in Muslim versions of griot etiological tales a perfect fit with the earlier violations: "It is not surprising that in almost all of the Islamicized tales collected by Zemp, the ancestor of the griots appears as the enemy of Mohammed" (629).

Zemp argues that these tales are rooted in Arabic stories about one of Mohammed's enemies, a man named Suraqa ben Malik ben Ju'shum. Three of Mohammed's contemporaries reported Suraqa's adventures, and they were written down not long after the events.

In a version of this story first published in 1907 by André Arcin, Sourakata, son of a slave, fathered two branches of griots, the Yéli, or Diali, and the Gaolo. The mothers of these two branches produced forty children each. Sourakata refused to submit to Mohammed's demand that he convert, and attempted to kill the Prophet. He succeeded only in injuring him and drinking blood from the wound. He and the children of the first branch were condemned by Mohammed to wander for eternity. The members of the second branch, the Gaolo, converted to Islam because their captive mother had been abandoned by Sourakata. They became the "caste" of musicians and praise-singers. The first branch, the Yéli or Diali, were more serious and became orators and advisers; they even gave orders to chiefs (Zemp, 615–16).

Zemp retells another version of the story as published by Frobenius in 1925 in which Sourakata never manages to touch Mohammed because the Prophet can make himself disappear temporarily. Impressed by this magic, Sourakata agrees to convert and serve Mohammed. A third version, collected by Zemp in Côte d'Ivoire, reveals a Sourakata who screams when he is tortured for refusing to pray. Mohammed, impressed with the unbeliever's voice, declares that he should not be killed but be condemned instead to the role of griot for the rest of his life, serving as an arbiter in disputes.

Another variant, from a griot of the Doumaya clan from Biankouma in the Dan region of northern Côte d'Ivoire, 250 kilometers south of Odienné, gives us a portrait of Sourakata planning to kill Mohammed while en route from Mecca to Medina. The Prophet makes Sourakata sink into the earth three times so that he can do no harm. Sourakata proclaims his fidelity to Allah and Mohammed, then accompanies the religious leader on all of his trips, singing his praises to all who will listen. In subsequent wars, he carries

Mohammed's gun and the Prophet gives him a *kora* to play. That version partially matches another recounted to me by Lamine Kouyaté, a man of dual Soninké and Maninka origin whom I interviewed in Bamako (1992). In his version, Ibn Malik, an Arab, goes to see the Prophet, who is speaking to the earth. When Ibn Malik arrives, he is swallowed up by the earth. When he asks the Prophet to save him, Mohammed asks what Ibn Malik will do in return. "Ibn Malik said he would be his griot," Kouyaté related. "When he got out of the ground he became a griot, but without a guitar. If the Prophet was planning to travel, he would announce his visit."

Zemp recorded another in which the griot who wanted to kill Mohammed finally sings the Prophet's praises after being released from the grip of the earth:

> Hamidali Mohamadi
> It is a great good fortune
> Ibi nuruli Mohamadi
> Mohamed is not the messenger of a man
> Na bina Mohamada
> He is the messenger of God!

The griot concludes his story by explaining that "each time Mohammed gave advice to men, Sourakata repeated his words loudly and explained them so that everyone would understand. That is how he became a griot" (Zemp, 619).

The intrusion of Islam into the origin tales of griots constitutes just one part of a far larger and more complex case of cultural diffusion that occurred during the past millennium. David Conrad explains how information about the Prophet was conveyed over the centuries not only by pilgrims from Mali who brought stories back from Mecca but also by Islamic scholars in West Africa and, more recently, by narrators on the radio (1981, 1985). One result is that the link with Islam is longer and more detailed in versions that Conrad collected a decade after Zemp's research.

In both kinds of tales, those marked by Islam and those that appear to predate Islamic influence, Makarius sees a pattern of traits perfectly matching the information on griots that ethnographers have collected today. She lists them as follows: frequent contact with blood, bleeding flesh, and the bloody soiling of things; violations of taboos (murders, especially within a family, transporting of bodies), followed by magical results; characterization of ancestors of griots under a veneer of conformity to Islam, as adversaries of God, the Islamic religion, and the Prophet; nonviolence and the role of arbiter in disputes; ritual "pillage" in the form of collecting gifts that cannot be refused.

Conrad (1985) interprets the references to blood as, at the very least, a possible indication of the sealing of a relationship between the griots and Mohammed and, with more certainty, as an echo of traditional Mande customs of dripping blood onto an altar (*boli*) "as part of a ritual process of communicating with the spirit world" (41). He suggests that "this might reflect an ambivalence toward Islam with which the bards have apparently struggled since the introduction of that religion . . . . As oral traditionists, their duties included the guardianship of ancient religious lore, while at the same time they participated in the maintenance and celebration of more recently introduced Islamic beliefs and practices" (41–42).

Makarius sees all these traits as interdependent, part of a whole that characterizes griots. They are members of a larger social group commonly referred to as "casted" that includes blacksmiths, butchers, and other craftspeople called *nyamakala* (possessors of occult power) in the Mande world. Their innate "impurity" allows them to carry out tasks that no other members of society would ever do because they involve the violation of a taboo: recoat the mud walls of the home of a menstruating women, for instance, or bury a woman who died in childbirth. It is as if they were infected by a disease that was "inherent, unerasable, and contagious. . . . Sexual contact, or the simple suspicion of some form of intimacy suffices to render someone a griot" (633).

Social Status

The differences between griots and others in society lead to the question of hierarchy: where do griots stand on the social scale? There is considerable debate about this issue (see chapter 6) and the roots of the question are found in the origin tales in which one person pledges fealty to another.

Camara discerned a hierarchical relationship developing between the two parties in the origin tales: "The consumption of the flesh of the elder by the younger brother who is incapable of surviving by himself . . . symbolizes the fundamental impotence of the griot by instituting forever inequality between the two parties" (1976, p. 147). Such an interpretation from the basic elements of so many of the etiological tales, both Islamic and non-Islamic, seems at first to be unavoidable, and in fact appears to influence the popular attitude toward griots. But the evidence is rather ambiguous. In some origin tales the ancestor of these wordsmiths is of high status, while in others, he is of low status.

For example, in the article by Télémaque cited earlier, Ahmadou Mapaté Diagne reports a Wolof tale that gives a princely origin for griots.

> The ancestor of griots was supposed to have been the son of a king. After the death of the father, the son traveled throughout the country to demand payment of the *galague*, the tax that subjects paid each year to the ruler. But each time that he presented himself to an individual, the person refused to pay him anything, saying, "You don't know me at all. Therefore I have nothing to give you." To counter this response, the young prince repeated the genealogy of each inhabitant of his kingdom: "You are the son of so-and-so, the grandson of so-and-so. My father received such an object from yours; your grandfather gave such an animal to mine. You must offer me such a thing; otherwise you will be inferior to your ancestors."
>
> Since then, the griot, son or grandson of this prince, continues to ask for gifts and demand them as payment for a debt. (Télémaque, 1916, p. 276; my translation)

Another prince who becomes a griot appears in the Songhay version of *The Epic of Askia Mohammed* recounted for me by Nouhou Malio in Saga, Niger, in 1980. In the narrative, Askia Mohammed, the Songhay ruler known among his people as Mamar Kassaye, is the nephew of an earlier Songhay ruler, Sonni Ali Ber, known as Si and identified as the brother of Mamar's mother, Kassaye. After Mamar kills his uncle Si at the beginning of a Muslim ceremony and claims the throne, the son of Si, who would normally fight for his own right to the throne, submits to the evident power of his cousin.

200   That is how Mamar took the chieftaincy.
       When they finished praying
       He mounted his horse, and the people followed him
       Then the son of his uncle says to him, "Son of Kassaye, you did it all by
          yourself" . . .
       Kassaye glanced in back of herself to see her nephew, the son of her
          brother.
       She said, "You want to shame yourself.
       You who are the son of the man, you want to beg for the son of the
          woman."
       He said, "Me, I sing his praises.
       I follow him, I become a griot, I follow him."
       That is why we are griots. . . .
       "I put my share in his share throughout the Songhay area, and I'll take
          whatever I am given."

A griot has thus been created.
218   There's how the profession of griot begins. (Hale, 1990a, p. 197)

A third example of noble origin for griots comes from the same region. Fati Diado Sékou, a *jeseré weyboro*, or female griot, from Niamey, Niger, reported a story to Aïssata Sidikou from her late father, Diado Sékou, about the ruler of Karma, a Songhay principality forty kilometers up the Niger River from Niamey. When the ruler was visiting a neighboring village, the drumming that normally announces the arrival of a distinguished visitor fell silent because of rain. A cousin of the king decided to make up for the lack of an appropriate reception by chanting the praises of the ruler. "The king decided that day that his cousin would be his *jeseré* because he knew how to praise and he had such a wonderful voice. That is why we are *jeseré*. We descended from that person" (Sidikou, 1997, p. 142).

The association of the origin of Songhay griots with a great historical event or a prince ennobles the profession and enhances the reputation of the person recounting the epic. The high status of these first griots may be a reflection of the deep sense of fear or fealty that one man can inspire in others in a society that is based on a feudal social structure. But it may also reveal more recent efforts to raise the status of griots in the eyes of a public that does not consider them to be the social equals of people of noble or free origin. Camara suggests that today, with the disappearance of the captive class, griots, who traditionally served as an intermediate group between nobles and those taken in battle, have dropped to the bottom of the social ladder (1976, p. 25, n. 17). One might therefore conclude that griots are going to greater lengths to raise themselves in the eyes of their audiences. But the relationship of griots to nobles or free people reflects a somewhat more complex social reality (see chaper 6). In fact, there are cases of nobles who attempt to work as griots in order to make money. For now, all one can say with any assurance is that these stories of noble origin for griots simply heighten the sense of ambiguity that characterizes the profession's place in society.

Although the sixteenth- and seventeenth-century chronicles describing the empires of the Sahel support the notion that royal griots held high status, some origin tales framed in broader perspectives—for example, a creation myth for an entire society—may offer less positive views. Roland Colin published a short origin tale that apparently comes from the Fulbe of the Fouta Djallon region. It explains why griots always come second to those of higher birth:

When god distributed wealth and destiny to men, says the oral tradition, the ancestor of the griots was absent. He arrived too late, so there was nothing left for him. That is why God assigned him to another family who, from then on, was designated to support him. (1957, pp. 64–65, my translation)

In *The Epic of Askia Mohammed* we encounter another reason for the lower status of griots. The narrator reports that when Askia Mohammed went to Mecca on a pilgrimage, an event that happened in 1497–98, his only two companions on the final leg of the trip, the crossing of the Red Sea to the Arabian Peninsula, were a marabout specialized in divination and a griot. From the epic text we can discern the closeness of the griot to his patron, an apparent sign of high status. But the scribes and griots maintained what might be called an uneasy relationship, each competing for the attention of the ruler.

After arriving in Mecca, Askia Mohammed descends into the tomb of the Prophet, then emerges with both hands full of onion shoots. He gives some to each companion.

337   Modi Baja [the marabout] brought his from Mecca all the way home,
            he sold it.
        None of Modi Baja's people suffered.
        From that day to the present, Our Lord did not make their lives hard.
        Our ancestor ate his.
        He left, and he left us in suffering.
        Since that day until the present, no descendant of Modi Baja has
            suffered.
        They didn't tire from a hard life, they didn't seek to work hard in life.
        They sup well, they lunch well, they dress well. (Hale, 1990a, p. 205)

One can interpret in many ways the griot's decision to consume immediately the green plants found in Mohammed's tomb: failure to appreciate the sacred nature of the plants, desire for instant communion with the Prophet, unwillingness to seek profit from the plants. Whatever the reason, the narrator's revelation conveys a clear sense of envy for religious men, who seem to lead a rather leisurely life. By profiting from this highly valued souvenir of the Prophet's tomb, the marabout ensured that his descendants would not suffer, in contrast to those of the griot. The difference both illustrates the griot's view of why Muslim religious leaders seem to live in relative comfort (they are shown to benefit materially from Islam) and gives an explanation of the second-class status of griots (they tend to live for the present).

That view is echoed today in the explanations of other griots from the same culture. Djeliba Badié, a well-known *jeseré* in Niamey, Niger, reports that his father told him that a griot who praised Mohammed was once rewarded with some of the Prophet's hairs. He traded the hairs to a businessman in exchange for ten donkeyloads of gold. The businessman then made a fortune curing people with a bucket of water into which one of the hairs had fallen. The griot, in the meantime, spent his money and was rebuked by the Prophet for his shortsightedness (Anon., SCOA, 1984b, p. 13; my translation).

This notion of the griot as somehow inferior to others in society appears also in a creation story published by Germaine Dieterlen in 1956 and analyzed by Camara (1976, pp. 151–58). In it, the ancestor of griots, Sourakata, and a blacksmith appear as the products of the blood of Faro, the first person in the world to be sacrificed to God. On earth, each tries to generate rain, the griot by drumming on the skull of Faro, the blacksmith by striking a rock with his hammer. Only the blacksmith succeeds in producing rain. Camara interprets the comparison between the two as an indication of the congenital inability of griots to contribute to the material life of society.

Camara asks rhetorically what talents or virtues compensate for this impotence. The answer appears in the remaining sections of the myth, in which Faro, a spirit, is reincarnated as a human being and attempts to establish order on earth. He is accompanied by four men, one of whom is designated to reveal a series of sacred words while ringing a small iron bell. The griot repeats these words while playing the *tama* drum. Camara sees in this myth the origin of two basic traits of the griot—music and repetition of words. The power of the griot lies in the mysterious, occult, and mythic nature of these words. The full nature of the power emanating from them is not at all clear from this one example.

The social status of griots emerging from these different tales and the interpretations of them by scholars appear to be highly ambiguous, a reflection of social ambivalence about griots in general. The tales also suggest several themes for examination.

First, it seems as though griots in the distant past were different, or voluntarily became in some way different, from others, either because of an original violation of a taboo or because of some other behavior that was not seen as normal. The portrayal of the blood relationship between griot and patron provides clues to the complex relationship between these bards and those they serve. These clues help explain a striking reversal in the behavior of some nobles who become griots today in order to survive in hard times.

Second, it is evident that the tie that links griot to patron goes far beyond the matter of material rewards. The reward is a symbol of the relationship, not the source.

Third, some of the texts suggest that the griot must be viewed in the context of other artisans who work with materials. The difference is that the griots produce sounds—vocal and instrumental—conveying complex meanings.

Fourth, if many of these tales reflect ethnic and regional versions of the origin of griots, there remains an aspect of the origin of griots that calls for further research: the origin of special relationships between clans. For example, the Kouyaté griots have traditionally served the Keita clan associated with Sundiata Keita and the founding of the Mali empire. But many other clans of griots have established special ties rooted in some legendary event. Further research on the origin of this link, as on the origin of griots themselves, may help us to understand more clearly the power of their verbal art.

Written Descriptions

Oral narratives offer tantalizing clues to how griots of the past are viewed today. But in these tales, we cannot distinguish clearly between the present interpretation of the past and what actually occurred centuries ago. Written descriptions are more firmly rooted in the period in which they were composed, though they too are subject to change over time as the result of editing, translation, and other influences. Chronicles by Africans as well as reports, travel accounts, and narratives from the eleventh to the nineteenth century written in Arabic, Portuguese, French, Spanish, and English, offer an extraordinarily rich and diverse panorama of information about griots. The descriptions conveyed by these accounts, however, are often limited or biased by the perspective of the narrator and the second- or thirdhand nature of the information.

Writers did not often understand the language of their hosts or what the griots were saying or singing. Even when the authors were part of the culture portrayed, biases sometimes blurred or skewed the image of griots. The narrators from Timbuktu and other cities along the Niger who wrote in Arabic the landmark chronicles known as the *Tarîkh el-Fettâch* and the *Tarîkh es-Sudan* were very much part of the multicultural Songhay world they described. But inevitably their portrayals reflect a Muslim bias that tended to downgrade certain non-Islamic customs as well as those responsible for them, including griots. By the same token, a nineteenth-century Senegalese priest drew on his Christian and European-style training to sketch an extremely negative view of griots.

In many ways these written narratives reveal as much about the authors and their cultures as about the griots they describe. Travelers from outside the region who carried the baggage of a contemporary Western world view thought that griots were clowns or wandering minstrels. Early Portuguese explorers drew upon the long tradition of discrimination against Jews to arrive at the conclusion that griots were Jews. That is why, five centuries later, these professionals of the spoken word are still called Jews in Guinea-Bissau, a Portuguese-speaking, or Lusophone, country on the western edge of Africa. Furthermore, some seventeenth- and early-eighteenth-century travelers from Europe assumed that griots were a species of sorcerer.

By the end of the eighteenth century, explorers, soldiers, and administrators had began to understand more clearly the roles of griots. This awareness stemmed from frequent contact with them in the course of negotiations with African chiefs. The evidence appears not only in written accounts but eventually in photographs that often include a griot and sometimes a griotte as important personages in the retinue of a local ruler. In one extraordinary case, a shipwrecked European traveler was able to save his own life because of what he had learned about griots.

Earliest Accounts by Arabs and Africans

The earliest descriptions are quite sketchy because they are based on secondhand information. Al-Bakri, the Arab author who lived in Cordova, Spain, mentions in 1068 in his *Kitāb al masālik wa-'l-mamālik* (The book of routes and realms) that the King of Ghana has interpreters and that audiences are announced by the beating of a special drum made of a hollow log (Levtzion and Hopkins, 1981, pp. 52–87). In 1154, Al-Idrīssī, a North African geographer who studied in Spain and traveled in Europe, Africa, and Asia, described drummers in the Kingdom of Ghana (*Nuzhat al-mushtāq fī ikhtirāq al āfāq* [The pleasure of him who longs to cross the horizons], Levtzion and Hopkins, 104–31). It may be that the drummer for the King of Ghana was a Soninké *geseré*, or *jaare* (griot).

In 1337–38, Al-'Umāri, a Syrian scholar and administrator who lived in Cairo for many years, described the court poets of the Kingdom of Mali in *Masālik al-absār fī mamālik al amsār*. Drawing on interviews with Egyptians who had witnessed the visit of the Malian ruler Mansa Musa to Cairo in 1324 while en route to Mecca, Al-'Umāri described men who acted as intermediaries between the people and the king and as musicians who preceded the king on his return from trips. The references here are without doubt to the ruler's griots, or *jeliw* (Levtzion and Hopkins, 252–53 and 412, n. 46).

IBN BATTUTA

In 1352, less than two decades after Al-'Umāri's reference to griots, Ibn Battuta encountered griots at the court in Mali and later dictated the first eyewitness description of them. Although historians are quite familiar with Ibn Battuta, few nonscholars know who he was. Given his importance for the task of tracing the roots of our understanding of griots, it is essential to explain how he happened to visit the court of Mansa Sulayman, the ruler of Mali.

Ibn Battuta ranks with Marco Polo as one of the world's great travelers. Unlike the authors just cited, he was of Berber origin and therefore descended from Africans rather than Arabs. This is an important distinction today for many North Africans, some of whom now prefer the term *amazigh* to Berber, although the cultural mixing in the region since the Arab invasion over a millennium ago makes it sometimes difficult to separate one people from another.

Born in 1304 in Tangiers, Morocco, Ibn Battuta set off in 1325 on an odyssey to visit the peoples of the Muslim world. By midcentury this vagabond had traveled through what we know today as Algeria, Tunisia, Egypt, Israel, Lebanon, Syria, Jordan, Arabia, Iraq, Iran, Somalia, Tanzania, Asia Minor, the Crimea, the Balkans, southern Russia, Afghanistan, Pakistan, India, the Maldives, Ceylon, Bangladesh, Malaysia, Indonesia, China, and Spain.

No one knows why Ibn Battuta went to Mali, but there are plausible reasons: it was the one part of the Muslim world he had not yet visited and Morocco had a long history of trade with Mali. Ross Dunn suggests another reason that may have piqued the traveler's interest:

When Ibn Battuta visited Cairo in 1326 on his way to his first *hajj*, the population was undoubtedly still talking about the extraordinary pilgrim who had passed through the city two years earlier. Mansa Musa, ruler of the West African empire of Mali, had arrived at the Nile in the summer of 1324 after having crossed the Sahara Desert with a retinue of officials, wives, soldiers, and slaves numbering in the thousands and a train of one hundred camels loaded with unworked gold. (1986, p. 290)

Among the extraordinary consequences of Mansa Musa's visit was a drop in the value of gold in Cairo. Another reason for Ibn Battuta's trip to Mali may have been a desire on the part of the Sultan of Morocco for more inside information about the land, though Dunn suggests that there is no evidence to support the belief that the traveler was either an official or unofficial envoy.

Whatever the motivation, Ibn Battuta set off in fall 1351 from Fez to Mali by way of Sijilmasa, a Moroccan commercial center on the northern edge of the Sahara near the present-day Algerian border (see map 6 for his itinerary). There he joined a caravan in February 1352 and headed south across 1,500 kilometers of desert in the direction of Mali. When he reached Walata, a northern outpost of the Mali empire in present-day southern Mauritania approximately 225 kilometers north of the current border with Mali, he rested for a few weeks. Then, sometime during the spring, he journeyed farther south to an unidentified town on the Niger River. Dunn suggests that it could have been either Niani in upper Guinea or a site farther north.

Ibn Battuta arrived in the capital of the Mali empire on July 28, 1352, Dunn reports, and stayed for eight months. He left on February 27, 1353, traveled approximately 1,500 kilometers downriver to Timbuktu and Gao, in present-day eastern Mali, then headed home in early January 1354

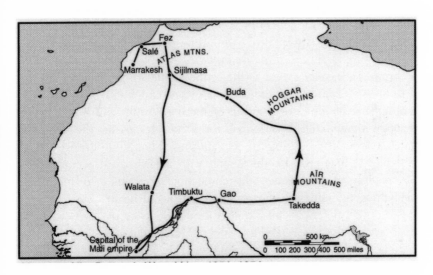

Map 6. Itinerary of Ibn Battuta in West Africa, 1351–1354.

(Dunn, 290–309). Sultan Abu Inan, who ruled Morocco from 1348 to 1358, asked him to dictate his tale to a scribe. Ibn Battuta did so, then disappeared into relative obscurity and died in 1368 or 1369.

The path that Ibn Battuta's account took from the fourteenth century to the present is as extraordinary as the itinerary of his voyage. The ambiguity and the great precision that scholars find in his descriptions of griots at the court of Mali remind us of our dependence on subsequent interpretations to understand what he has to report. One of the most surprising features of Ibn Battuta's account is the accuracy of his transcription of a Mande term for griot. Given the early date and great detail of Ibn Battuta's account, it is important, then, to understand just how his observations survived for readers today, six centuries following the traveler's return to Tangiers.

The unknown scribe's Arabic transcription of Ibn Battuta's tale was edited by Ibn Juzayy, a scholar from Spain who died in 1356 or 1358. The process of copying and editing inevitably led to modifications and adaptations. But Ibn Juzayy was careful to give details on the pronunciation of strange names and sounds by marking for vowels (Hamdun and King, 1975, p. 7). In Arabic, vowels are indicated by a mark above, below, or after a consonant, but in normal script these markers are omitted, so there is always room for interpretation when dealing with new words.

Ibn Juzayy's revision of the scribe's manuscript was subsequently copied by hand and examples eventually ended up in Europe. The French scholars C. Defrémery and B. R. Sanguinetti drew upon a variety of these copies to produce the first printed edition of the account in Arabic, along with the first translation into a Western language (Batoutah, 1854). The title was simply *Voyages d'Ibn Batoutah*.

From the traveler's voice to the scribe's handwriting, Juzayy's editing, the copyists' reproduction of the editor's work, and, finally, the French re-editing, translation, and printing of Battuta's *Voyages*, this text passed through many hands. It is difficult for us now to measure the losses and gains that occurred during the six centuries of handling. But we are left with a text that provides the reader with a fairly clear record of the observations of an outsider who could not be expected to understand everything he witnessed. For example, the word he first used for griot means "interpreter" because that is the function he observed when he encountered the chief *jali* of the ruler of Mali. He praises "the interpreter Dugha, a noble black and leader of theirs. He sent me a bull" (Hamdun and King, p. 36).

In spite of this example of great generosity on the part of Dugha, Ibn Battuta depended for his own welfare on the local Muslim community, which was largely North African. After four months, he still had not had a chance to speak at any length with the ruler, Mansa Sulayman. Finally, he reports, "I had a word with Dugha, the interpreter. He said, 'Speak before him and I will express on your behalf what is necessary'" (36). The result of the meeting and Dugha's service as spokesman for the traveler was that Mansa Sulayman gave Ibn Battuta gold and a house.

Dugha, then, was both interpreter and spokesman for the ruler, functions that griots still carry out today. But as Ibn Battuta discovered, on audience days Dugha also served as master of ceremonies, entertainer, musician, and praise-singer.

> The interpreter Dugha stands at the door of the audience chamber wearing splendid robes of zardkhana [probably a kind of embroidered silk, Hamdun explains] . . . . On his head is a turban which has fringes, they have a superb way of tying a turban. He is girt with a sword whose sheath is of gold, on his feet are light boots and spurs. And nobody wears boots that day except he. In his hands there are two small spears, one of gold and one of silver with points of iron. . . . He who wants to speak to the sultan speaks to Dugha. Dugha speaks to the man who is standing, and he speaks to the sultan. (37–38)

On a Muslim holy day, there are special sessions in late afternoon with all officers of the court present. Ibn Battuta explains:

> The interpreter Dugha brings his four wives and his concubines, who are about a hundred in number. On them are fine clothes and on their heads they have bands of silver and gold with silver and gold apples as pendants. A chair is set there for Dugha to sit on and he beats an instrument which is made of reeds with tiny calabashes below it, praising the sultan, recalling in his song his expeditions and deeds. The wives and the concubines sing with him and they play with bows. (41–42)

Following some acrobatics with swords by both the *jali* and what Hamdun and King describe as Dugha's "pages,"

> the Sultan orders that a gift be given him, they bring him a purse of two hundred mithkals of gold dust. An announcement is made to him over the heads of the people. The commanders get up and twang their bows, thanking the sultan. On the following day every one of them makes a gift to Dugha according to his means. Every Friday after the *asr* prayer Dugha performs ceremonies like those which we have recounted. (42)

There is a clear hierarchy here among the griots. Not all are held in such high esteem as Dugha. The "pages" are common court griots who, along with the wives and the other children, are part of Dugha's vast retinue

(Camara, 1976, p. 208). It is not clear which languages Dugha translates from or into but presumably he is interpreting common tongues of the area—Fulbe and other Mande languages. Dugha may also know Arabic.

It is clear that Dugha is wealthy. The number of wives he has, his richly adorned weapons and clothing, his proximity to the ruler, and the 200 mithkals of gold he receives all indicate that he is at the top of the griot hierarchy. At a rate of 4.7 grams per mithkal, the gold amounts to approximately two pounds of the precious metal, $10,000 in today's metals market and certainly an extraordinary reward, but no more so than some of the most elaborate gifts now given to griots in different contexts: automobiles, homes, and performance contracts.

The most important function to emerge from this portrayal of griots at the court of Mali appears under a mockingly titled subheading, "An Account of the Laughable Manner in Which Their Poets Hold a Recitation."

> When it is a festival day and Dugha has completed his play, the poets called the *jula* (and the singular is *jali*) come. Each one of them has got inside a costume of feathers to look like a thrush with a wooden head made for it and a red beak as if it were the head of a bird. They stand before the sultan in that ridiculous attire and recite their poetry. It was mentioned to me that their poetry is a kind of preaching. In it they tell the sultan that this *banbi* [a kind of dais] on which he is, such and such of the kings of Malli sat on it, and such and such were the good deeds of one, and such and such another's. "So do good, that good will be recounted after you." Then the Archpoet mounts the steps of the *banbi* and places his head on the sultan's lap. Then he climbs to the top of the *banbi* and places it on his right shoulder, then on the left, meanwhile speaking in their tongue; thereupon he comes down. I was informed that this performance is old amongst them; they continued it from before Islam. (42–43)

Ibn Battuta distinguishes between Dugha and the other griots. Dugha appears to us clearly as the chief *jali* because of his status, his role as spokesman and singer, and his playing on what appears to be a *balafon*, a xylophone-type instrument (Charry, 1992, p. 316). The "archpoets," a seemingly separate group whose functions are to recount the past in poetic form, dress distinctively and appear to have a slightly different function, that of offering both praise and advice to the ruler. The term given by the scribe and the editor Juzayy for the court poet, *jali*, matches the modern spelling for griot among the Mandinka, a Mande people who migrated from the area described by Ibn Battuta westward to The Gambia in several waves during the past few centuries.

The narrator's report that the ceremony he witnessed predates the coming of Islam in the area several centuries earlier underscores the likelihood that the griot profession, at least in Mali, is indeed very old. Ibn Battuta confirms what the earlier writers reported from secondary sources. We may assume that the profession goes back many hundreds of years before 1352, at least to the origins of the Ghana empire late in the first millennium. It is probable from this preliminary evidence that griots have been practicing their art in West Africa for at least a thousand years.

It is clear also from Ibn Battuta's account that the rulers of Mali included griots among their closest aides. These men and women served a variety of functions. They were interpreters, spokespersons, intermediaries, musicians, praise-singers, historians, and entertainers. But one other function emerges from both Al-'Umāri's brief reference and Ibn Battuta's longer description: that of representative of the people. Although the *jali* is evidently in the service of the ruler, his words contain not-so-subtle warnings to the king. Mansa Sulayman must "do good" so that he too will be remembered as a great ruler. The social compact embodied in these two words reflects a sense of expectation on the part of the people that is articulated most appropriately to the ruler by the *jali*. It also echoes the Mande value of *fadenya*, or father-child-ness. Members of the younger generation compete not only among themselves for fame but also with their ancestors' reputations for a prominent place on the living tree of family history.

Ibn Battuta's description of griots at the court of Mali serves in many ways as a benchmark against which may be measured other portrayals by writers who appeared in the centuries after the North African completed his travels. But the number of texts from this period is very small and the references to griots rare. Between Ibn Battuta's fourteenth-century account and reports by French travelers in the seventeenth century, one finds only a handful of brief references to griots by Portuguese seafarers and a few more detailed descriptions in the two Timbuktu chronicles.

TARÎKH EL-FETTÂCH AND TARÎKH ES-SUDAN

Before discussing the Portuguese, whose accounts appeared earlier, it is helpful to turn to the two African texts, which I have termed the Timbuktu chronicles because their authors were from that ancient city or lived there at some point. Like Ibn Battuta's narrative, these texts have traveled rather remarkable itineraries. Inevitably it was sometimes difficult to ascertain the meaning or even the sound associated with an African word that had been transcribed into Arabic, recopied many times, then translated by

European Arabists unfamiliar with African languages. (For more information on the history of the Timbuktu chronicles, see Hale, 1990a, chapter 3.)

The African authors of these texts were Muslims who seem to have been little interested in telling readers about their fellow artisans of the word, griots. One reason might be that the griots were probably not as fervent followers of Islam as the scribes. But perhaps a more significant factor is that the griots competed directly with the chroniclers for the attention of the rulers. The scribes view the griots as sources about the past or as eyewitnesses, but more than once they hint at the need to corroborate information from their competitors by speaking with other people. In describing the misfortunes that befell Askia Ishaq II, the Songhay ruler who presided over the fall of the empire at the hands of the Moroccans in 1591, the narrator concludes: "I report these details from the *guissiridonké* [chief griot] Boukâri, who gave me the account of these events; others in whom I have complete confidence have also told me the same story" (Kâti, 1913, p. 276).

In spite of what might be interpreted as reticence about accepting the word of the griot, the narrators of the chronicles do not hesitate on several occasions to give credit to the extraordinary verbal power of griots. In *Tarîkh es-Soudan*, for example, when Askia Ismâïl (reigned 1537–39) comes to the throne of the Songhay empire, the French translators describe as a *chanteur* a man who proclaims the importance of the event in such glowing terms that the ruler suffers from a sudden, violent emotion and begins to bleed from the anus. John Hunwick, who has made the first English translation of this important text, believes that the *chanteur* here is a griot (Hale, 1990a, p. 39).

Another example of the same dramatic effect of a griot's words on an individual occurs during the reign of Askia Daoud (1549–1582/83), the most respected and effective ruler among the descendants of Askia Mohammed. En route home after a victory over the ruler of Mali at a place called Dibikarala, Askia Daoud stops to visit one of his predecessors, Askia Mohammed Benkan (1531–37), also known as Bounkan and Bunkan, who had settled in Sama, a town somewhere upriver from Jenne near the end of Daoud's reign over the Songhay empire. Benkan has already been described by the scribes as both an avid warrior and a patron of the arts who liked ceremony and introduced new musical instruments into the empire. In Hunwick's translation, the visiting ruler "ordered all the musicians to greet Askia Muhammad Bunkan by playing their instruments. When he heard the sounds the veins in his heart were severed and he died instantly"

(Hale, 1990a, p. 39). The power of griots here to stir deep emotions in the individual who is the focus of their words and music fits closely with what is known of their verbal art today.

The narrators of the chronicles confirm Ibn Battuta's portrait of a hierarchy among griots, with each ruler served by a chief griot. Askia Daoud's chief griot is the *guissiridonké* Dako, a man who understands his patron so well that, ironically, it is he, the keeper of the oral tradition, who reveals to a Muslim scribe the extent of the ruler's knowledge of the Qur'an (Kâti, 176–77; Hale, 1990a, p. 40). The relationship is so close between ruler and chief griot, according to the narrators of *Tarîkh el Fettâch*, that only *guissiridonké* Dako has the right to address Askia Daoud by his first name (Kâti, 14; Hale 1990a, p. 40).

There are more references to griots in the 800 pages of the French translations of these Arabic chronicles (Kâti, 1913, and es-Sa'di, 1898–90), some of which will appear in later chapters. For now it is evident that the scribes valued these bards mainly as sources who had close access to the rulers and their activities, not as fellow wordsmiths whose service should merit much attention. These two different artisans of the word were in many senses rivals, with different functions, values, and goals. But in spite of these contrasts, the portraits of griots that the scribes penned in the Timbuktu chronicles confirm what Ibn Battuta reported several centuries earlier and nearly a thousand kilometers away: griots, whether *jali, guissiri,* or *jeseré*, were professionals who played many significant and visible roles in society.

Early Accounts by Europeans

SIXTEENTH CENTURY

If it seems as though the African and Arab descriptions cited so far are a bit limited in what they tell us about griots, the earliest European narratives appear even less useful because the authors—explorers, missionaries, administrators, and, in the earliest case, an editor who never visited Africa—viewed the continent as a land almost as foreign as the moon. Nevertheless, if they did not always understand what they saw or read about, some of them produced documents of considerable value when placed in the context of more recent information.

Valentim Fernandes, the first European to describe griots, offers a brief secondhand sketch written in Portuguese in 1506–7 that is based on both oral and written accounts (Fernandes, 1938, 1951). A German printer, publisher, author, and courtisan from Moravia, he collected a wide range of reports on Africa, many of which were assembled and published posthumously.

> In this country and in Mandingo there are Jews who are called Gaul and they
> are black like the other people of the country. But they don't have synagogues
> and they don't hold the same ceremonies as other Jews. They don't live with the
> other Blacks, they live by themselves in their own areas. These Gauls are often
> buffoons and play the viol and the cavacos [stringed instruments], and are
> singers. And because they don't dare to live in the villages they live behind the
> homes of the noble and sing his praises at dawn until he orders that they be
> given a ration of millet, and then they leave. And when the noble leaves his
> house then the Jews go out ahead of him and sing and shout their buffooneries.
> They are also treated like dogs by the Blacks and don't dare enter into their
> houses except for that of the chief, and if they appear in the village people hit
> them with sticks. (Fernandes, 1951, p. 15; my translation.)

Fernandes rightly observes that the griots are perceived as quite different from other members of society. But the sharp contrast between the royal griots seen in the Arabic-language accounts and those that appear here leaves the reader perplexed, and illustrates once again the great paradox in the griots' social status. The travelers whose accounts inspired Fernandes apparently encountered a class of griots known today as *gawlo*, a Fulbe term that has diffused to several ethnic groups in West Africa. The status of the *gawlo* varies depending on the ethnic group. The assimilation of the *gawlo* to Jews reflects a complex set of European and North African attitudes, beliefs, and traditions, most if not all of which influenced Fernandes and the people who reported to him about Africa.

As a European, Fernandes was certainly familiar with the mistreatment of Jews, who had been expelled from Spain in 1492. The separation of *gawlos* from the rest of society may have appeared to observers he cited as a parallel kind of discrimination. But the discrimination occurred on both sides of the Mediterranean basin. In 1467 there was an anti-Jewish riot in Tlemcen, a city on the Algerian-Moroccan border close to the Mediterranean (Hunwick, 1985, p. 33). A native of that city, Muhammad al-Maghīlī, a Muslim theologian of Berber origin, is cited as one who contributed to massacres of Jews elsewhere in the region. After moving to the town of Tamantit in the Tuwat oasis region of central Algeria at some point in the 1460s or early 1470s, he offered seven mithkals (one ounce) of gold to anyone who killed a Jew, a reward that apparently helped incite the massacre of members of the minority in the 1480s (Hunwick, 33–39; Hale, 1990a, p. 149). Jews lived in many other cities of the Maghreb but were barred from spending the night in some of them. For example, they had to live forty kilometers from Marrakesh in southern Morocco and could not spend the night in this city until the end of the sixteenth century (Chouraqui, 1985, p. 157).

Fernandes reported that there was a Jewish community in Walata, an important trading city in southern Mauritania 1,000 kilometers from the Atlantic coast. These Jews were "very rich but greatly oppressed, some of them wandering merchants, others goldsmiths or jewellers" (quoted in Bovill, 1995, p. 50). He may have heard about the common belief among Moors that griots and other craftspeople were of Jewish origin.

Attilio Gaudio, in describing griots from the western Sahara north of Mauritania, explains that "the popular tradition claims that griots have no ancestors and that their patron saint is David" (1993, p. 276). H. T. Norris offers additional evidence for this belief from Mauritania in a praise poem written by *īggīw* (Moor griot) Isalmu wuld Bāba wuld Hamma wuld Nafar that had come down for several generations from another *īggīw* named Awlīl. When referring to a day of rest to repair the hero's gun, the bard plays on the word *tahwiid* in Hassaniya Arabic. Norris explains in a note that "*tahwiid* means also 'judaizing': the poet connects the act of repairing the arms with the current legend that the artisans and smiths were Jews in origin" (1968, p. 86).

Although there is much debate over the validity of this belief, it appears to be quite widespread in legends from the region (al-Idrīssī, 1154; C. Monteil, 1951a; Chouraqui, 1985, pp. 275–76; Cuoq, 1985, pp. 146–47). In fact, there is legendary and archaeological evidence to suggest that a Jewish community lived in Tendirma, near Timbuktu, many centuries ago (Hale, 1990a, pp. 149–50). Although some scholars see the existence of such a group that close to the Niger River as a figment of popular imagination (Tamari, 1987, pp. 283–294), no one has effectively refuted the archaeological evidence unearthed by Bonnel de Mézières in 1913.

It is quite possible that the Portuguese were aware of these communities and their activities and therefore based their description of griots as Jews on more than simply observation of apparent social discrimination against them by other members of society. But in spite of these references to a Jewish presence in West Africa and the contemporary use of the term *Jew* for griot in Guinea-Bissau, it seems unlikely that there is a link. Conrad suggests (personal communication, 1996) that the Portuguese association of griots with Jews may well have been the result of confusion with a term similar to *Juddy*, a rendering of *jeli* that appears in the writings of Richard Jobson.

By the late sixteenth century, Portuguese travelers had increased their contacts with local rulers and begun to understand more about griots. In 1594, André Alvares d'Almada described briefly their role as itinerant musicians, going from ruler to ruler like Gypsies and playing their drums to announce wars or fires (Charry, 1992, p. 318).

SEVENTEENTH CENTURY

By the early seventeenth century, griots were appearing more frequently and in much more detail in the writings of merchants and missionaries. The Jesuit Manuel Alvares, writing of what he saw in Senegal in 1616, comments on their art and ability to inspire soldiers:

> Nobody does this better than the Judeus. . . . They are a people of much art and grace. . . . The women dress in different kinds of clothing that the kings give them. They are troubadours, singers, and serve as inciters in time of war. ("Etiopia Menor")

At about the same time, Richard Jobson, a British trader who traveled up the Gambia River, offered a much more detailed, though somewhat distant, description of the activities of griots in his book *The Golden Trade* (1623). Among other matters, he discussed their burial practices. He remained puzzled by the fact that

> howsoever the people affect musicke, yet so basely doe they esteeme of the player, that when any of them die, they doe not vouchsafe them buriall, as other people have; but set his dead corps upright in a hollow tree, where hee is left to consume. Whenever one of the foreigners would play a musical instrument, the Africans would in a manner of scorn say hee that played was a Juddy. (133–77; Charry, 1992, p. 319)

A decade later, the Capuchin missionary Saint-Lô provided European readers with the first description of griots in French. His *Relation du voyage du Cap-Verd* (1637) was based on travels by ship from Rufisque, a town on the coast of Senegal thirty kilometers below Dakar, southward to other trading centers, including Portudal in January and February 1635. Saint-Lô's report predates by half a century the better-known and more detailed narrative of La Courbe from the same region.

In Saint-Lô's report one finds for the first time the use of the term *griot* in its seventeenth-century form, *guiriot*, which gives the impression, as yet undocumented, that it is of French origin. Of immediate value in Saint-Lô's two descriptions of griots are the earliest glimpses of the roles they play at funerals and harvest celebrations, as well as some hints about both the diversity of their instrumental talents and their tenacity in seeking rewards.

He observes that

> everybody assembled at a large square to dance, having no other instruments than the drums that their guiriots struck rather roughly, maintaining nevertheless some rhythm. They chanted at the top of their lungs and repeated often the same thing. They have on their arms and knees little pieces of flat metal with lots of rings that they call casquabelles; they make a little sound like cymbals. (85–86; my translation)

Saint-Lô adds a remark that confirms the great ambiguity surrounding the social status of griots, reporting that "the guiriots who make them dance are an ignominy among the ordinary people, and when a Frenchman wants to anger a black, he calls him guiriot" (87).

One reason for the negative image that griots suffer is their tendency, Saint-Lô observes, to demand rewards from everyone they meet.

> Even if they have not met a person, they accost him and they sing all kinds of praises. . . . When they die, they are not viewed as worthy of normal burial, so they are placed upright in a hollow of a large tree. I saw the body of one of them in this sort of sepulcher. (87)

For Saint-Lô, griots were drummers. But he also describes what is either a *kora* player or a *simbin* player at Port de Iovalles, without identifying him as a griot.

> An old black man arrived; he had a certain instrument that was shaped something like a harp, and he played it without stopping, which pleased the ears. But instead of asking for something for his services, at the end he showed himself to be so assiduous and so eager to sing and to play that I would have liked Sir Domingue to give him something to shut him up. (181–82)

Saint-Lô's descriptions fit in some ways with what we know of griots today. He does not tell us the origin of the word *griot,* but he distinguishes clearly between Jews and griots. He notes that there are two wealthy families of Jews in Rufisque, and three or four more in Portudal.

Saint-Lô's contacts with griots apparently were quite limited, and for this reason his observations amount to little more than a peek at their profession. But his usage of *guiriot* does constitute a historical marker for the introduction of the word into French.

Half a century later, another Frenchman who lived for several years in Senegal wrote the most fascinating and detailed descriptions of griots up to that time. They stem from a variety of contacts with chiefs while the author was carrying out his duties as a director of the Compagnie du Sénégal for three separate periods: 1685, 1688 to 1690, and 1709 to 1710.

Michel Jajolet de La Courbe's *Premier voyage du Sieur de La Courbe fait à la Coste d'Afrique en 1685* did not appear in published form until 1913. But the manuscript served as a source for at least one writer on Africa in the early eighteenth century, according to Sory Camara (1976, pp. 98–99). The Reverend Father Labat borrowed considerably from it, sometimes word for word, then attributed it to another man, André Brüe. One feature of the account is that the term *griot* appears in its modern form, apparently for the first time (La Courbe, 1913, p. 116). But this spelling occurs only once in several dozen references to these artisans. Without having consulted the original manuscript, it is hard for me to determine if this appearance of the word *griot* is an editing mistake or a variant used by La Courbe. The 1913 publication normally spells the word *guiriot*, but also once varies it with *guyriot* (118).

La Courbe's portraits of griots are of particular interest and value for several reasons. First, they are the most detailed available from this early period. Second, his travels straddled the frontier between two people with different but related professional traditions: the Moors, who live for the most part north of the Senegal River, and the Wolof, who tend to settle to the south of this frontier. Third, his service as administrator placed him in a position to witness a variety of ceremonies. Finally, he is the first traveler from outside the region to devote any attention to griottes. Given the wide variety of information contained in his account, I shall give much consideration to what he had to report. All citations in English from La Courbe are my translations from the 1913 French edition.

Before proceeding with La Courbe, however, it is useful to explain briefly just what the French were doing in the Senegambian region at the time. In 1626 a private company of merchants from Rouen decided to explore the coast between the Senegal and the Gambia Rivers, a 300-kilometer stretch that included Cape Verde, the western tip of Africa. In 1638, the French traders set up their first fixed base of operations at the mouth of the Senegal River and eventually established a permanent settlement on the island of Ndar, where the city of Saint-Louis, the early capital of the colony, is located today. By the time La Courbe was sent to the area, there was considerable contact between Europeans—French, Spanish, and Portuguese traders as well as Jews exiled from Spain—and their African suppliers of ivory, ostrich feathers, ambergris, acacia-tree gum, and slaves.

Part of La Courbe's job as chief administrator for the French company included travels up the Senegal River to towns and villages where he negotiated trading rights with local chiefs and exchanged European goods for African products. His book-length account of his experiences includes numerous descriptions of griots in a variety of contexts: at plantings, weddings, circumcisions, Islamic holidays, and ceremonial visits of rulers to the French headquarters or trading vessels. La Courbe describes both Wolof and Moor griots but does not use the terms for griot in these languages—*guewel* in Wolof and *iggiw* or *egeum* in Hassaniya Arabic.

The griots and griottes appear as praise-singers and entertainers who are usually part of the ruler's entourage. They sing the praises of both their patrons and La Courbe. Any celebration, whether at the home of an African ruler or friend or at the habitation, the house of the French traders, inevitably involves griots who announce or animate the occasion with their music and serve as witnesses.

One of the most important events was the circumcision of young men of fifteen or sixteen years, a ceremony that was part of their initiation into adulthood. La Courbe describes a circumcision celebration attended by 2,000 people that begins with the entrance of the candidates preceded by a corps of griots beating their drums to announce the forthcoming event (116).

The virginity of a bride is also a matter of public significance, La Courbe explains. Her condition is announced by the groom, who parades through the village with a bloody cloth on the end of a spear. Griots follow the husband, chanting the praises of the bride so that all will know that she has met one of the highest social standards required of women (31).

The collective planting of crops brings people together in an activity that has a direct impact on the survival of society. On a visit to the island home of Jean Bare, a retired African river pilot named by the French for his knowledge of the shifting sandbar at the mouth of the Senegal River, La Courbe found the man directing a group of sixty villagers clearing a field, "all to the sound and to the cadence of a wild music produced by six guiriots with their drums and their voices; it was a pleasure to see them working like possessed men, and they increased or diminished their work depending on whether the drums beat more or less loudly" (52–53). After an apparent interruption of work for the usual exchange of greetings, La Courbe asked Jean Bare if he could watch this unusual blend of work and sound again. But, La Courbe added, "it was necessary to give something to the guiriots who, because they liked me so much, had employed every effort of their symphony and of their shouts to excite the others to work with even greater fury" (52).

Griottes contributed to public events in a variety of ways. In the village of Bouscar, forty-five kilometers upriver from the French headquarters, La

Courbe came upon a feast marking the end of the Muslim fast month of Ramadan. The local women were led by a "guiriotte who sang something concerning the feast that evoked a choral response from all of the women" (92). The distinction between the role of the *guiriotte* and the other women in the village disappears as the event shifts from food to sports: "They then walk around the feast area several times while singing, after which a fire is lit and the young men of the village come out for a wrestling match." The women "encouraged them and sang praises for the winners, marking the cadence by clapping their hands, after which they began to dance to the sound of several drums" (92–93).

The role of the griot as entertainer occurs often and not simply at the homes of Africans. On the visit to Jean Bare's home to attend the circumcision celebration, La Courbe spent the night and was treated royally. Jean Bare arranged for a large fire to be built in the village square in front of his house to lower the humidity, chase away the mosquitoes, and provide warmth. La Courbe and his men lay down on mats and were surrounded by young girls who fanned them to drive away mosquitoes. In this relaxed atmosphere, the local griots came by to "give a symphony with their drums, each made out of a section of hollowed-out tree trunk, some six feet long, others shorter, and they play them by hand and with a stick with much skill; it is with the sound of these instruments that girls and boys, after supper, relax from their work, dancing far into the night" (77).

La Courbe was aware that he had to organize some events himself, both to keep up the morale of his French employees and to reciprocate the hospitality that he received at every stop on his trips around the region. To the Christian Feast of the Epiphany on January 5, 1686, which occurred only a few days after the circumcision ceremony he attended, he invited local leaders. They, of course, traveled only with an entourage that included their griots. Short on French wine, La Courbe ordered 400 pints of palm wine for his 200 guests. The success of his party, however, depended as much on the griots as it did on the palm wine: "The guyriots [*sic*] who had been at the preceding celebration [the circumcision ceremony] made sure that they did not miss this one, and people danced all day and all the following night" (118).

The role of the griots is more than that of entertainer. When La Courbe meets with local rulers to negotiate trading rights, the griots carry out a significant and multifaceted function. Their praises serve to impress upon the Frenchman the importance of their patron. But they also sing the praises of La Courbe as a way of thanking him for his generosity to their patron and as a means of obtaining gifts for themselves. The griots' music and chants appear to change the atmosphere of the event, raising tension at first, then releasing it at the end. The griots also serve as essential witnesses to the meeting, in the legal, journalistic, and historical senses of the term. It is they who report the event to the world, both in the present and in the future. For this reason, it is rare for a leader to leave home without a griot. Two incidents underscore this point.

When a regional governor of the Wolof kingdom of Walo, on the left bank of the river, wanted to meet the new head of the French outpost, he first sent interpreters to find out if such a visit would be appropriate. Then, with a large entourage, the governor, called "Little Brac," crossed the river to the home of La Courbe. But when he entered the building, he left most of his followers outside. Only two of his lieutenants and two griots entered with him to meet La Courbe (40).

Later, after La Courbe had settled into his new position, he traveled to meet another ruler with a similar title, "Brac," who governed all of the Walo region. The Brac had come to a town 120 kilometers upriver to negotiate the annual payment to him by the French for permission to trade in the region. There La Courbe anchored his little fleet of three vessels in midstream near the port town of Désert, today Diekten. He sent a small boat ashore in the evening to pick up the Brac, who had just arrived with an entourage of thirty people. There was much hubbub as all the members of the ruler's party tried to crowd onto the small craft. But the Brac's *alquier*, or prime minister, who had traveled upriver with La Courbe, warned his patron that La Courbe would receive only six people on his vessel. The ruler then boarded the launch and designated three other chiefs, his river toll collector, and his griot to accompany him on this important mission (138–39). The composition of the delegation reinforces the notion that no event of significance could be consummated without the chief griot.

According to La Courbe's highly detailed narrative, the griots are keenly aware that they must not only praise their own patron but also recognize the positive contributions to the negotiations on the part of the French. When La Courbe learned that a local ruler in the region where the French headquarters was located happened to be visiting in a nearby village, the Frenchman sailed to meet him. The ruler boarded La Courbe's boat and the two men, with their lieutenants, exchanged greetings. La Courbe marked the event by giving a variety of gifts to the visitor. The French administrator recalled clearly the hyperbole of the griots, who

shouted themselves hoarse from chanting my praises, accompanying their voices with their three-stringed instrument, on the end of which were attached rattles. They were saying that they could clearly see that I was an important person because of the gifts I had given to their king, that no chief administrator before me had been so generous, and that they hoped that I would be equally generous to them. The other griots, who had remained on the shore, made a frightening noise with a dozen drums and screamed at the top of their lungs while calling me Samba Bourguaye, which means master of the sea. (73)

After the first meeting with the leader, named Malo, La Courbe offered wine and the guests brought out their pipes. At this point the griots began to

sing my praises and those of their master, accompanying their voices with a small lute strung with three horsehair strings, which was not disagreeable to hear; their songs are martial, saying as they name you that you are of a great race, what they call in bad French *grands gens*, that you overcome all of your enemies, that you are generous, and other things of this nature, finally concluding with a request that you give them something. (43)

La Courbe was quick to adapt to the local customs and seemed to understand the social function of the griots as highly visible members of a ruler's entourage. But if he appreciated certain aspects of griot music, there were times when the sound became too much for him. At Jean Bare's home the night before the circumcision, La Courbe awakened at dawn to the sound of twenty griots, who saluted him "and made around our house such a racket and devil's sabbath. I thought that the way to shut them up was to give them something, but instead of that, they began anew by demonstrating their thanks and appreciation; this lasted until eight o'clock." Later, during a trip down the coast to Bissau, the capital of the Portuguese colony south of Senegal, to settle an incident involving three deaths and damage to French-owned property, La Courbe was well treated, but he and his French host were unable to stop flute players from performing all night around their house.

La Courbe's encounter with griottes stemmed not from commerce or diplomacy but from their curiosity about him. During his stay at Désert he was visited by several groups of women, each accompanied by at least one griotte or griot. Two women of noble origin, daughters of the previous king of Walo, came to see him on board his boat, each accompanied by her own griotte. After chatting with him, these noblewomen sang a song that was popular at the time at the court of their ruler, then had one of the griottes dance. La Courbe avowed, however, that "I tired soon of the dance; she made so many lascivious moves, even shamelessly hugging me around the neck, that I asked them to have her stop" (144).

The visit of the princesses with their griottes was only a prelude to a later and more formal meeting with the Brac's wife, on April 10, 1686. Accompanied by her ladies-in-waiting, servants, valets, and two griots, the queen wanted to know more about royal life in France. While they were visiting with La Courbe in the cabin of his boat, the griots, who remained outside, sang the praises of both the women and La Courbe (161).

Another woman, this time a queen mother whose son was the Moor king Leydy, came to visit La Courbe on May 5, 1686, with a large entourage that included a griotte. After chatting, the queen mother had her griotte perform. La Courbe observed that

> she held a kind of twelve-stringed harp whose body was made of a calabash covered with leather which she played rather nicely. She began therefore to sing a fairly melodious Arab song, but rather languid, a little in the style of the Spanish or the Portuguese, accompanying it with her harp with much restraint. But what was most agreeable was that she really threw herself into the performance by making all kinds of movements and gestures of her head, which made her *gris-gris* [talismans] and pendants shake, showing the most beautiful teeth in the world; the only thing I can find to criticize is that her words seemed extremely rough and as if pronounced from deep in the throat. (172)

The woman was undoubtedly a *tiggiwit*, or Moor griotte, and she played an *ardin*, an eleven- to fourteen-stringed instrument held in a position opposite to that of the *kora*, with the strings facing outward, the neck toward the performer, and the smaller calabash sounding board in the lap (see chapter 4).

La Courbe seems not to have observed or noticed many other roles of the griot, especially genealogist and historian. But he did come away from Senegal with a clear understanding of the symbiotic relationship between a ruler and his griot, as well as an awareness of some of the ceremonial roles of these wordsmiths. There was no doubt in his mind that griottes were integral members of the profession. Because of the details and the numerous references to griots and griottes, La Courbe's narrative serves as our most valuable source of information from the seventeenth century.

Other travelers from the late seventeenth century described griots in some of their other functions. John Barbot, general agent for the Royal Company of Africa and the Islands of America, traveled to the Senegambian region in 1681–82. In a narrative written in French but first published a century later in an English translation (1792), he describes griots in several important functions. A new husband carries the blood-stained bedsheet "in publick thro' the village, attended by some *Guiriots*, who sing aloud the praises of the woman, and the happiness of the man" (Barbot, 35–36). At funerals *guiriots* sing the praises of the deceased, "extolling his virtues, actions, and qualities" (52). At wrestling matches, "the great satisfaction they [the men] have in throwing their antagonists consists in the guiriots extolling their valour with a loud voice and encouraging them to gain many more such victories" (53). But the definition Barbot gives of *griot* reflects the deep sense of cultural superiority shown by most travelers from Europe:

> The name of *Guiriot*, in their tongue, properly signifies a buffoon, and they are a sort of sycophants. The kings and great men of their country, keep each of them two, three, or more of these *Guiriots*, to divert them, and entertain foreigners upon occasion. These men are so much despised by all other *Blacks*, that they not only account them infamous, but will scarce allow them a grave when they die; believing the earth would never produce any fruit or plants, should it be defiled with the dead carcasses, nor will they throw their corps into ponds or rivers, for fear of killing the fish, and therefore they only thrust them into the hollow trunks or stumps of trees. . . . The usual cant of these buffoons, either in speaking or singing upon the like occasions, as I was informed by the interpreter, is no more than this: He is a great man, or a great lord; he is rich, he is powerful, he's generous, he has given Sangana a brandy; and much more such wretched stuff, often repeated, with such sorry voices, bawling, and impertinent gestures and grimaces, that it must tire any but a *Black*: nay sometimes it is in a manner intolerable, and yet must not be found fault with, but rather applauded as if extraordinarily pleasing. Among many such expressions as above-mentioned, which *Condé's Guiriots* used toward me, they oftenest repeated, *that I was the king's chief slave*; thinking they did me a might honour. (55)

In Barbot's contemptuous comments, we see confirmation of two traits noted earlier. The first is that griots are fundamentally different from other people — almost a different race — and cannot therefore, for example, share the same burial grounds. Second, in the brief reference to the power of griots to defame someone appears some sense of the nature of their power over others.

The contrast between the observations of La Courbe and the comments of Barbot reflects a fundamental personality difference shaped by different cultural experiences. We find similar differences among other travelers. Some are hostile and contemptuous, like Barbot, while others manifest a greater sense of curiosity and equality.

A contemporary of those two men, Father Jean-Baptiste Gaby, whose work appeared shortly after he came back from Africa, took a more balanced view of the griots he saw. In his *Relation de la Nigritie* (1689), Gaby described the role of griots in sports and war in the Senegambian region.

> On the afternoon of Frougar [defined in a marginal note as an unidentified local holiday], five or six of their Guiriots [defined in a marginal note as buffoons and clowns] come to the central square of the village, dragging on their left side their drums with a leather strap. They begin to sing and beat the drums in order to get everyone to come; and having assembled them, the leader of the band of Guiriots announces that Frougar will begin with a wrestling match, warning that only strong and robust men need present themselves, so that the Frougar will be more enjoyable and entertaining. Then the symphony begins with seven or eight drums of different sizes, some large, some small. At the same time, men and boys who want to wrestle enter into the Frougar circle, naked to the belly button, stripped of clothing that might encumber them or be torn during the match. They dance in a slow manner, so that each can choose his equal, whom he takes by the head or embraces by the middle of the body, trying always to make him fall. When one of the two has beaten his man by throwing him to the ground, all the Guiriots, as well as his friends, congratulate him and sometimes give him some Couscous or Sangle [types of food]. This done, he returns to the circle and wrestles as if nothing has happened until he becomes tired. The dance of the warriors follows this game. After this exercise of weapons, the girls step forward and into the square, two or three at a time, dressed in their most beautiful clothes; and no sooner arrived in the middle of the square than they dance in a violent manner, lowering successively their shoulders, raising their arms into the air, moving their jaws and lips, smiling, opening and closing their eyes until the Guiriots approach, who redouble their symphony the closer they get, adding throaty yells that animate the girls and make them walk and dance with great agility. The Guiriots, seeing that the girls are beginning to become very hot, return to their earlier rhythm of music in order to get the girls to stop. But because it is only right that each one should live from his profession, at the end of the dance the Guiriots stop and want to be paid, which is not refused to them, each person giving them a vassade or verot [untranslated terms that do not appear in seventeenth-century French dictionaries], and those that have none leave something in its place which does not remain long in their hands, especially when they have lovers. (Gaby, 1689, pp. 43–46; my translation)

From this lengthy sketch it is clear that the griots are more than simply strolling musicians. They serve several roles here: producers of the entire event, promoters who attract the crowd, masters of ceremony who control the timing of each phase, musicians who match the music to each event, exhorters who lead the celebrations for the victors, and collectors of performance rewards from those who attend. The subtlety of Gaby's description seems to clash with the note defining griots as buffoons at the beginning of the narrative. One wonders whether it was added by the publisher to explain a word that readers might not understand.

In his description of griots as part of armies heading off to war, Gaby makes what appear to be, in contrast to Barbot, strikingly positive comparisons with European cultures.

> To arouse these peoples to combat, they have Guiriots who carry drums four or five feet long, with which they amuse and entertain soldiers during marches, like our fifes and drums, our kettledrums and trumpets; but there is something special about them: to incite better the soldiers they compose songs in which the simple naming of an ancestor is equal to their greatest praise: like the Romans who never stopped shouting "Caesar, Caesar, Caesar," and as in our last campaigns when soldiers proclaimed nothing else but "Long live the great Louis, long live Louis the Great." By these kinds of rustic chants they say in a gay and assured manner that they will not fail to match the valor of their ancestors, and that on the contrary they will surpass them in bravery, and that they know as their ancestors did how to attack, to beat, and to throw down their enemies, but don't know how to turn and run. (60–61)

Several features emerge from Gaby's description. First, as seen earlier, the allusive references to ancestors insert the individual into the most important historical context, that of his family. Second, although there is much evidence of griots playing central roles as inciters of troops about to go into combat, here for the first time a narrator gives a hint of their function of providing musical accompaniment for soldiers on the march. Third, the comparisons with the armies of Caesar and Louis XIV reveal a sense of historical and cultural relativity that is rare among European travelers to West Africa.

Saint-Lô, La Courbe, Barbot, and Gaby describe griots as something of a social novelty. That all of these observers used the same term suggests that the word *guiriot* or *griot* had, by the end of the seventeenth century, taken on a regional life of its own, either as the product of a French adaptation of some other local term or as the result of the interaction of French, Portuguese, and some other language. But the spelling of the term still varied from one traveler to another. For example, Le Maire, in *Les Voyages du Sieur Le Maire aux Isles Canaries, Cap-Verd, Senegal, et Gambie* (1695) calls them *Guiriotz* in his brief and rather negative description, which focuses primarily on the music they produce and the rewards they seek (cited in Charry, 1992, 326).

EIGHTEENTH CENTURY

In the eighteenth century, contact between Europe and Africa expanded considerably, and the accounts of travelers reflect a growing understanding of griots by identifying new functions, offering insights on their social status, and describing the role of griottes. Francis Moore, author of *Travels into the Inland Parts of Africa* (1740), even hires a griot to cheer up the men of his entourage (189; cited in Charry, 1992, 329).

A book written by De Lajaille, a French naval officer sent to explore the coast of West Africa in 1784–85, and edited by P. Labarthe, who also updated De Lajaille's letters, offers an example of the greater detail that includes a description of the role of women griots at a wedding. In a letter from Gorée, the island slave depot just off Dakar, De Lajaille describes the complex social status of griots and griottes. His use of the feminine spelling as well as his reference to men and women provides another indication of the importance of women griots.

> Griottes, men and women, are reputed to be infamous and are deprived of a burial after their death: their buffooneries are gross and indecent; each village has its own. They are well treated during their life, in order to avoid insults that they vomit against those for whom they have complaints. The fear that they inspire procures them a kind of consideration, but it is only apparent, for it creates revenge after their death. Their body is normally attached to a tree branch. In Senegal, they are buried like other people. (De Lajaille, 1802, p. 163; this and subsequent translations mine)

De Lajaille's description of griots' participation in wedding ceremonies matches those encountered earlier. But here the griottes not only proclaim the woman's virginity but also carry the blood-stained sheet.

> The griottes, a kind of charlatan, wait at the door for the marriage to be consummated, in order to then proclaim the success of the victor. These griottes carry into the street the proof of the triumph, that is to say a white cotton sheet. They sing of the efforts, the combats, the victory of the hero of the fête, which ends with a great dinner given to the family. (163–64)

M. Lamiral, author of *l'Affrique et le peuple affriquain* (1789) and a slave trader in Senegal from 1779 to 1789 who then changed his views on slavery after the French Revolution, describes griots in the Senegambian region, in this case among the Moors, as privileged members of a ruler's entourage (99–100). His portrayal echoes the descriptions of earlier travelers but adds a note on the hereditary nature of the griot profession. He points out the paradox inherent in their reputation. Nobody wants to marry them, but "everybody seeks them out, everybody gives to them; the rich always have one of them at their homes; kings never travel without several of them in their entourage to sing their praises" (269). He offers one of the first clues to explain this paradox: griots have freedom to do certain things that are normally forbidden to others.

From his encounters with black populations south of the Senegal River frontier, he describes how both male and female griots amuse people at organized entertainments with

> dances and the most lascivious gestures. They pantomime all the caresses and the ecstasy of love. The griottes approach the spectators, and seem to provoke them to amorous combat. Girls provide vocal accompaniment and speak the same kinds of words to the subjects. . . . Sometimes the girls take the place of the griottes in order to demonstrate their agility and attract the love of the young men who watch them; they demonstrate more grace and skill than the griottes; when they have completed two or three turns, they throw themselves into the arms of their friends, hiding their faces as if they were ashamed of what they had done. (266–67; my translation)

By the end of the century, the European image of griots had become even more nuanced. Mungo Park, the Scottish explorer, reports (1799 [1903], p. 301) that the caravan of merchants and slaves he joined during the return from his first trip in April 1796 included six "Jillikeas," or singing men. *Jeli ke* is the term for male griot in the heartland of the Mande world. It is not clear from the narrative if these griots were simply fellow travelers who joined the caravan for reasons of safety or if they were included because of their talents. In any event, Park explains that they were quite useful to the travelers because "their musical talents were frequently exerted either to divert our fatigue, or obtain us a welcome from strangers."

Park's observations are significant for three reasons. First, he seems to understand more clearly than his predecessors the importance of griots in the societies through which he travels. Second, he is one of the first travelers to draw a parallel between griots as poets and their counterparts of Europe. Finally, he is also the first to discern a difference between the *jeli*, what we know as a griot from the central Mande area, and the *funé*, often called Islamic praise-singers or griots.

> With the love of music is naturally connected a taste for poetry; and fortunately for the poets of Africa, they are in a great measure exempted from the neglect and indigence which, in more polished countries, commonly attend the votaries of the Muses. They consist of two classes; the most numerous are the *singing men* call *Jilli kea*, mentioned in a former part of my narrative. One or

more of these may be found in every town. They sing extempore songs, in honour of their chief men, or any other persons who are willing to give "solid pudding for empty praise." But a nobler part of their office is to recite the historical events of their country; hence, in war, they accompany soldiers to the field, in order, by reciting the great actions of their ancestors, to awaken in them a spirit of glorious emulation. The other class are devotees of the Mohamedan faith, who travel about the country, singing devout hymns and performing religious ceremonies, to conciliate the favor of the Almighty, either in averting calamity, or insuring success to any enterprize. Both descriptions of these itinerant bards are much employed and respected by the people, and very liberal contributions are made for them. (213–14; cited in Charry, 1992)

Park's ranking of different aspects of the profession into nobler and, by implication, less noble functions reflects both the reality of a hierarchy among griots and an inevitable misunderstanding of the complex relationship between patron and *jeli*.

By the end of the eighteenth century, the griot was a well-known member of West African societies to many European administrators and traders, who came in contact with them in the course of their negotiations with local rulers. One administrator, M. de Brisson, had seen enough of griots to imitate one of them. This unusual talent turned out to be the key to his survival after a shipwreck in 1785 (Brisson, 1984).

On a trip from France to Senegal, the cargo vessel *Sainte Catherine* on which he was traveling went aground near Cape Timiris on the Mauritanian coast just after midnight on July 10. It was approximately 360 kilometers north of its destination, Saint-Louis, Senegal. Brisson knew from the experience of other shipwrecked Europeans on a coast where Christians were not welcome that his fate would depend on the whims of his captors—he might encounter death or enslavement or, with luck, he might return to France in exchange for a ransom.

Captured by a group of Moors who fought over their human booty, Brisson and twelve other passengers were led off into the interior on a trip that lasted many weeks. Half of them were apparently shipped north to Morocco, where they were immediately freed by the sultan. Others died of their wounds and mistreatment or, like Brisson, became slaves traded from one owner to another.

Brisson reported in his account of the trip that he believed he could avoid some of the worst forms of mistreatment by telling his captors that he had been visited once in Senegal by a Moor ruler, Prince Allicoury, his wife, and their entourage. To substantiate his claim, he demonstrated the behavior of the king's griots, known as *egeums*, a form of the Moor term for griot mentioned earlier, *iggiw*. His ability to imitate a griot not only provided immediate rewards but also saved him from capture by rival Moors.

> I faked these clowns that are called Egeums. This kind of farce had pleased my master so much that he used to have me repeat it whenever he found it appropriate. He used this little strategy skillfully to divert the attention of those whom he thought might pillage his own goods. No sooner had he realized my talent for imitation of Egeums than I was surrounded by men, women, and children who repeated to me "*ganne*," "sing on." As soon as I finished, they made me start all over again, and I was obliged to do it as much to amuse them as to obtain for myself (why shouldn't I admit it) a few drops of camel milk, the reward for this bad clowning. (36)

After several months and different masters, Brisson eventually managed to reach Morocco, where he met the sultan and was returned to French authorities. It is not clear from Brisson's account if he had actually met the Moor ruler with the entourage in Senegal or had simply observed them during their visit to the colony. It seems quite likely, in any case, that his knowledge of griots saved him from the possibility of death in captivity. From his experience as a captive, however, one should not draw the conclusion that griots were slaves, a misconception that continues to appear in print even today (Conway, 1995, p. 27).

NINETEENTH CENTURY

By the early nineteenth century, European travelers, adventurers, missionaries, explorers, soldiers, and administrators were arriving on the coast of West Africa in growing numbers, either to serve expanding settlements or to learn more about the region inland from the coast. Typical of their experiences with griots was the account given by Silvestre Meinrad Xavier Golberry, a captain in the French army engineers who was sent to be an aide to the governor of Senegal. He became chief engineer for the colony with the assignment to explore every part of the Senegambian region. His account, originally published in French in 1802 as *Fragmens* [sic] *d'un voyage en Afrique*, was translated into English by William Mudford in 1808 as *Travels in Africa*. Mudford, in his preface, cites many faults in Golberry's encyclopedic account.

Perhaps more than most writers of the period, Golberry reveals a deep disdain for his subjects, Wolof or perhaps Mandinka, particularly in his discussion of *griots* and "*griotes*." But in his description of their roles in society he gives a clue to the functions of griottes, and in particular their role in recounting the past.

> The griotes are the female jesters; they are very numerous, and are not so amiable as the Almehs of Egypt; like them, however, they sing histories, dance, narrate amusing adventures, make astrological calculations, and they are likewise the agents of concupiscent love.
>
> These griots and griotes are equally bad musicians and poets. They may always be seen in crowds at the courts of negro kings and princes, and among the great and rich; they lavish on them the most exaggerated eulogies, and they praise them with the most abject flattery, which are well received and well recompensed. (Golberry, 1802 [1808], pp. 297–98)

Amid the ethnocentrism of Golberry's comments, the reference to "*griotes*" as singers of histories raises a significant question: do female griots narrate epics? Most researchers today as well as their male sources insist that only men recount long poetic narratives about the past. Is Golberry's comment simply another generalization, the kind that prompted his translator (on an unnumbered page) to declare that in his narrative the author "mars its general excellence by the introduction of false and idle theories"? Or does his remark provide evidence that women in some West African societies have always shared the stage with men when recounting the past? (For further discussion of these questions, see chapter 7.)

During the nineteenth century, Europe's fascination with Africa led to a series of missions into the interior to learn more about the people and geography. At each stage of these journeys, the expedition leaders needed to negotiate with local rulers. Explorers on military missions, such as Major William Gray (*Travels in Western Africa, in the Years 1818, 19, 20, and 21, from the River Gambia, through Woolli, Bondoo, Galam, Kasson, Kaarta, and Foolidoo, to the River Niger*), described the way these meetings were conducted and the role griots played in them.

> The proceedings commenced by a griot or bard proclaiming in a loud voice the object of their meeting, and desiring that all those who had any thing to say on the subject should do so. . . . One person only presumed to speak at a time, and that in a low voice, and the person never received any interruption before he announced his having finished, which, as well as all that each had said, was repeated in a loud and distinct voice by the respective bards, or griots of the chiefs. (Gray, 1825, pp. 282–84; in Charry, 1992, 336)

The importance of the griots in meetings such as the one described by Gray is echoed by Major Alexander Gordon Laing (*Travels in the Timannee, Kooranko, and Soolima Countries, in Western Africa*), who ranks the "jellē, or minstrel . . . high in the scale of society and . . . possessed of great privileges. They travel throughout the country unmolested, even in war; and strangers, if of the sable hue, are always safe under their protection" (Laing, 1825, p. 132; cited in Charry, 1992, 337). The notion that the griots can provide protection and are themselves protected by a certain social immunity underscores the paradox of their social rank.

The accounts of travelers such as Golberry and these military explorers stimulated even more curiosity about Africa and contributed to a new wave of adventurers eager to be the first to reach parts of Africa that no European had ever seen. One of the most famous of these nineteenth-century travelers was René Caillié, a Frenchman who was the first European to reach Timbuktu and return to Europe, where he claimed a prize of 10,000 French francs. He reported the results of his journey in a 750-page book, *Journal d'un voyage à Tombouctou et à Jenné, précédé d'observations faites chez les Maures, Braknas, les Nalous et autres peuples, pendants les années 1824, 1825, 1826, 1827, 1828*. In addition to giving us a much more intimate view of African life than was given by earlier travelers, he provides descriptions of griots that add to our understanding of the profession from a different perspective, 1,500 kilometers east of the Senegambian coast.

Caillié arrived in Senegal for the first time in 1816. But it was not until a return trip in 1824 that he began to train himself for his voyage to Timbuktu by spending many months with Moors north of the Senegal River. North of Podor, 450 kilometers upstream, he learned how to live as a nomad as well as how to imitate the ways of Muslims. During a month with the Brakna ruler Hamet-Dou, he discovered griots at the northern fringe of their vast world. Caillié's description gives us valuable geographical and historical insights.

> Hamet-Dou is almost always surrounded by "guéhués" or professional itinerant singers. There are many of them among the Moors. They follow the princes from whom they obtain everything they want by employing at times the lowest forms of adulation, at other times menaces. Each prince has one of them attached to his entourage. That of Hamet-Dou follows him wherever he goes. Often, seated in his tent, he sings his praises and comes out with the most outrageous flattery. One has to be an African king to hear them without blushing; the praise-singer's wife and children accompany him normally, and repeat in chorus all the idiocies that he has just sung. This sect of parasites has found the means of making themselves feared as much as they are despised by the Moors. They possess to the highest degree the talent of persuasion. And although the guéhués are known as impostors and destined by public opinion to the eternal fires of hell, their calumnies are so skillful that they always

influence the reputation of those against whom they are directed. The
marabouts are those who despise them the most, but they receive them well
when they go to their houses, for fear that they will inspire them to false reports
that they would be capable of making against those who do not treat them
properly.

The guéhués have two kinds of instruments with which they accompany
themselves when they sing. One, made in the form of a guitar, is nothing more
than a small oval calabash covered with a well-prepared goatskin; a stick one
foot long crosses it horizontally near the edges, and serves to attach the cords of
the instrument, which are five made of several pieces of mane twisted together.
This instrument is touched and gives very agreeable sounds. The second is a
sort of harp with fourteen strings from sheep gut mounted on a stick two feet
long placed obliquely in a much larger calabash. A leather cord, stretched
horizontally on the skin that covers the calabash, serves to attach the cords at
the bottom. Sometimes it is a piece of wood placed across to which they are
attached. At the bottom of the calabash and under this cord is a flat, oval-shaped
piece of metal five inches long, decorated with little rings of iron. When one
plays the harp, they make a clicking sound that is fairly harmonious. These
musicians never forget to ask for something from the princes whose praises they
sing, and since they are rarely refused, they all have large herds and good
mounts. Often they give gifts to the marabouts to obtain their friendship. The
marabouts accept the gifts but still despise them (Caillié, 1830, vol. 1, pp. 104–
5; my translation)

The term Caillié uses here to describe griots, *guéhué*, appears to be a
transcription of the Wolof word for griot, *guewel*, which differs from the
usual Moor words for griot, *egeum* and *iggiw*. The difference here, however, probably stems from the fact that the people he is with live not far
north of the southern frontier of Moor territory, an area where the griot
tradition is dominated by black Africans.

Caillié's passage is particularly rich in the description of the *ardin*, the
instrument most commonly found among performers in Moor territory.
But it also underscores two important features of the profession that will be
discussed in more detail later: first, that talented griots, especially those
who serve the most highly ranked members of the artistocracy, are well-
rewarded, and second, that those rewards come not simply from the
connection with the wealthy but also from other members of society,
including marabouts, who fear and respect the power of the griot's words.

Caillié's portrait of the griots who serve the Moors contrasts with what he
discovered farther south en route to Timbuktu several years later. Dis-
guised as an Arab going home to Egypt after being captured by Christians,
Caillié joined a small caravan and headed east on April 19, 1827, from

Kakondy, a French town at the mouth of the Rio Nunez, about 600 kilometers south of Saint-Louis, just across the border of what we know today as Guinea. A year later and somewhat the worse for wear after traveling nearly 4,500 kilometers, he arrived at the home of the French consul in Tangiers with the news that he had reached Timbuktu.

As he traveled inland toward Timbuktu, he encountered griots on several occasions. In Bacodouda, en route to the city of Kankan in upper Guinea, he viewed a demonstration of war dancing, drumming, and chanting to incite the warriors to conquer their enemies (vol. 1, pp. 288–89). After reaching Kankan, Caillié watched a griot repeat the words of a speech by the local ruler, Mamadi-Sanici, to the citizens of the town on the Muslim holiday of "salam," either Ramadan or Tabaski (vol. 1, p. 313).

But the most interesting comments on griots that we find in Caillié's report concern music performed by both men and women, often in mixed groups. At Diécoura in Malinké country, somewhere in the vicinity of the Guinea-Mali border, on July 17, 1827, Caillié was greeted by people who performed a kind of music he had never heard before. They had a group of

> twenty musicians, many with instruments made out of hollow pieces of wood covered with sheepskin . . . the instrument produces very harmonious sounds. Then they have a large box, and a tambourine made of a little calabash covered with sheepskin, with iron rings all around that make an agreeable clicking sound. Two little well-dressed negroes, with feathers on their heads, jump in time and accompany the music by striking two pieces of iron against each other. . . . The chief of the musicians . . . rhythmically shook a round calabash that had a six-inch handle and was covered with a net containing large beans which, in spite of the racket that they made, accompanied the music very well. The musicians followed in file, playing and walking while keeping time; the women and the boys followed, dancing and clapping their hands. I enjoyed very much watching them; there was nothing indecent in their dance. . . . Since my departure from the coast, I had not seen anything that pleased me so much; I could never tire of listening to their music, which seemed harmonious to me, although it does have something savage about it; it is worth the attention of the traveler. (vol. 1, pp. 336–37)

When he reached Bangoro, a small walled town on the route north toward Jenne in present-day Mali, he encountered other musicians who reminded him of the "griotes" that he had seen in Senegal. The difference here was that these performers seemed to relate to their audiences in a way that varied from what other travelers had encountered on the coast.

In the evening, women came to the market square, 100 of them. . . . Several held tambourines made out of a calabash covered with tanned sheepskin; these drums were decorated with rings of iron that made a pleasant sound. They sang savage tunes with a deep voice and jumped together in cadence while shaking their drums. . . . I saw several men who were carrying large boxes that they struck and other women who had a drum hanging from their necks on the end of which was a little piece of wood covered with little bells and pieces of metal that shook and sounded at each movement; this produced a fairly nice effect. I thought that all of these musicians were what are called in Senegal *griotes* or itinerant singers, who make a profession of celebrating the praises of those who pay them. I found these ones fairly reserved, for I never saw any of them, as is the case in Senegal, harass anyone in order to obtain a gift. (vol. 2, p. 77)

Caillié never mentions griots in Senegal. But from what we have seen in the earlier descriptions by La Courbe as well as in Caillié's portrait of griots among the Moors, we have a clear sense of what he means. However, we can only wonder whether the less demanding behavior of the local musicians reflects the fact that they have not been corrupted by the external influences on the coast, whether their customs are simply different because the musicians come from a different ethnic group, or whether they are not professional musicians. It is unlikely, in any event, that there would be no professional griots among the group that performed for him.

Caillié's detailed descriptions came from extended contact with Africans during a long voyage inland. Other Europeans had settled on the coast for generations as part of the colonial enterprise. In some cases they had intermarried with Africans and produced a significant population of mixed heritage. Their children could identify with either the European or the African view of their cultures—or both. One of the most famous of these offspring was Abbé David Boilat, the son of a *signare*, a woman of mixed African and European heritage, and a French father. In 1853, Boilat published *Esquisses sénégalaises*, a detailed study of the peoples of Senegal. Born in Saint-Louis and speaking both Wolof and Serer as well as French, Boilat viewed the people he knew not simply from an external perspective, as is evident in his description of griots, but from the eyes of a Christian priest who condemned the customs of his own ancestors.

That is evident in his descriptions of griots, which begins: "We arrive now at the basest class of people in Wolof society, and which richly merits the distrust and horror of all people. These griots believe that God created them for earthly pleasures" (Boilat, 1853, p. 313). After criticizing what he presents as the happy-go-lucky lifestyle of griots, he adds that "one would search in vain to discover the slightest poetry in their loud chatter, yet they praise the spirits of the Wolof and make them sometimes shed tears by praising the courage and the pretended virtues of their ancestors. The Negroes can't resist giving them cloth, gold, silver, and sometimes part of their own clothing." Boilat is particularly incensed that they approach Christians at major holidays, making "an infernal racket with their songs and drumming." He adds that "the women of these species of poet-musicians are covered with all kinds of glass beads and gold jewelry. . . . It is from these griottes that young girls learn those lascivious postures that they know how to do so well in their dances" (314). Finally, he condemns the alcoholism of this "shameless and disgusting caste" (314–15). For Abbé Boilat, griots carried in their profession nearly all of the evils Christians sought to suppress in Africa.

Another French traveler wrote a description of his trip to the West African coast. Like Caillié and Abbé Boilat, he too describes women. Anne Raffenel reports on a trip to the Senegambia region in 1843 and 1844. He makes the usual comparison between griots and the bards and minstrels of the European Middle Ages. What interests the reader here is not the comparison, which contributes to the distorted image of griots today, but Raffenel's insistence on a kind of professional equality between men and women.

> Among the Negroes, griots and griottes exercise a kind of profession, primarily for the most important chiefs, that is almost exactly like that of . . . bards and minstrels. Griots, both men and women, amuse chiefs and the general public by their vulgar buffoonery, and they improvise bombastic praises to sing for all those who pay them . . . this profession, also followed by their women, becomes an inherited family tradition. (Raffenel, 1846, vol. 1, p. 16; my translation)

Raffenel underscores this equality between the sexes with detailed color sketches of griots and griottes (figures 2 and 3), part of a series of finely drawn images included in an atlas that accompanies the narrative of his trip.

Raffenel's contribution to European awareness of griots includes one other notable feature. He was the first to attempt to record a version of an African epic (Samba Galadieghi) and publish it (in volume 2 of the account of his second voyage). Stephen Belcher, who has conducted the most thorough search of early reports about African epics, views him as the first reporter of this genre (personal communication, 1997).

By the second half of the nineteenth century, as the result of these various explorations, the colonial powers had taken many steps to divide up Africa. Even before the 1884–85 Congress of Berlin, the pace was quicken-

Griot du pays de Galam
Jouant du tam-tam.

2. Sketch of male griot. From Raffenel, 1846.

3. Sketch of female griot. From Raffenel, 1846.

ing for Europeans to survey what lands were left and lay claim to them through wars, treaties, roads, and railways. The process led not only to new information about inland Africa but also to a clearer sense of the importance of griots in the local context. The evidence comes not only from reports but also from engravings, maps, and photos.

Eugène Mage was sent by Governor Faidherbe into the interior for three years, from 1863 to 1866, on a mission to find out more about the possibility of extending the French colonial presence and, in particular, to learn more about the empire of El Hadj Omar. Like Raffenel, Mage took note of both griots and griottes in his travels, offering what appear to be balanced portrayals. His awareness of their power and influence is reflected in his written accounts and in illustrations of them and their homes.

Mage even had a sketch done of a Malinké griot named Sambou in Niantanso, in the Bambuk region of what is today eastern Senegal and western Mali (Mage, 1868, p. 33). This portrait, which bears the name of the artist, Emile Bayard, and presumably that of the engravers, Gauchard and Brunier, is without doubt the most widely circulated image of a griot today (figure 4). It appeared not only in the original printing of Mage's book but also on the cover of the modern paperback edition, as the logo for the 1989 meeting of the African Literature Association in Dakar, and even on the sides of plastic bags distributed by Editions Karthala, an Africanist publisher in Paris.

Fifteen years after Mage's trip, Commandant Isidore Derrien set off into the interior of West Africa at the head of a well-supplied military expedition of forty-nine men. Sent by the French Ministry of the Navy and the Colonies, the expedition had as its goal to survey part of the route inland from Saint-Louis as far as Kita, 1,250 kilometers from the coast, for the purpose of building a railroad that could connect the Senegal and Niger Rivers. Derrien published a report on the survey in 1882.

The most important product of the expedition for the French was a series of six large maps, on a scale of 1 to 100,000 (1 centimeter equaling 1 kilometer), that cover the area from Medine, on the Senegal River east of Kayes, 250 kilometers eastward to Kita. One of the maps contains what geographer Thomas Bassett described to me as the only reference to African buildings in the entire region covered by the six maps: "Cases de Griot," or griot houses, at a village called Faraba, eleven kilometers southwest of Kita in a wooded plain.

It is not clear why the French cartographer identified griot houses on the map rather than those of chiefs or kings. One answer may lie in the growing awareness of the importance of griots and the realization that Faraba may

4. Sketch of griot playing *kora*. From Mage, 1868.

have constituted something of a center for a profession that played such a key role in relations among political leaders. According to a griot from Kita named Moumouni Diabaté, who heard the story from his father, Massa Diabaté, the "Cases de Griot" at Faraba were once the headquarters of the Kouyaté, the griot clan that served the founder of the Mali empire, Sundiata Keita, and claims the highest rank among all families of griots today. The Kouyatés, along with other clans, protect the sacred objects of their profession in a house in nearby Kita. A color photograph of this house serves as the cover of *L'Assemblée des djinns*, Massa Makan Diabaté's novel about griot conflict in Kita.

Dramane Dembélé, who interviewed Moumoni Diabaté, asks in his research report, "Did the house in Kita replace the one in Faraba? It is quite possible, since Faraba is part of the administrative region of Kita. . . . One can still find members of the clan of the Kouyaté in Faraba" (Dembélé, 1992). Faraba may have lost its griot focus as Kita and the villages closer to it developed, especially with the arrival of the French in the 1880s and the establishment of a fort there. By marking the griots' homes in Faraba, the French explorers were perhaps recognizing the power of the Kouyaté griots and the influence they have had.

Speculation about the significance of Faraba must be balanced by evidence of other griot activity in the region. Just forty kilometers south of Faraba, across the Mali-Guinea border in Niagassola, is a far more significant center of *jeli* activity. It is also a locus of rivalry with the bards of Kita. What is described as the original *balafon* owned by Sumamuru (or Sumanguru), the blacksmith king conquered by Sundiata (Son-Jara) when the Mali empire was created many centuries ago, is kept in a sacred house and maintained by Kouyaté *jeliw*. Members of the Keita clan in Mali attempted, in fact, to take control of it at one point and bring it back to their country.

Whatever the real reason behind the unusual focus on the "Cases de Griot" in a single tiny village, it is clear that the French surveyors were well aware of the multiple roles of the griots who served African leaders, and this understanding was shared by others who marched inland to explore and conquer the region. Joseph Galliéni, a leader in the French conquest of West Africa, described the capture in 1887 of one of the last resisters of French expansion, Mahmadou Lamine, by an African army loyal to France. Galliéni reported (1891) that when the bearers assigned to accompany the body of the dead leader to the French camp began to tire, the griot, as ambassador of Musa Molo, the ruler who captured Lamine, solved the problem of duty versus fatigue by cutting off the head of the resister. In his narrative of these events, Galliéni included an engraving of the griot holding the head as well as two others, one of a griot on horseback, another of a griot being roasted alive for his involvement in an assassination of a local ruler.

Long before the completion of the conquest of most of West Africa, the cities on the coast were growing rapidly. In Saint-Louis, the city that served as both the capital of Senegal and, in a larger sense, the administrative center for the other parts of West Africa that were falling under French control, griots were seen as a social plague. Administrative records for Senegal as early as 1793 reveal orders from a colonial officer to the mayor of Saint-Louis to announce that "all of the griots and the blind people of Grande Terre should leave the island of Saint-Louis and never return" under pain of arrest, prison, and flogging, while a more tolerant warning nine years later from the interim commandant Charbonnier orders the mayor of the city "to forbid all wandering musicians or griots from making their racket any later than nine in the evening so that public tranquillity may be respected" (Alquier, 1922; my translation).

In spite of these threats and warnings, the problem for the French did not disappear. In 1846, one inhabitant of Saint-Louis decided to appeal to Paris for help on the griot menace. A member of the colony's advisory council, Héricé, sent off a report to the Ministry of the Navy and the Colonies in October to point out the need for certain improvements, including measures to get rid of or establish better control over the 1,200 foreigners, that is, Africans from other parts of the region who had settled in Saint-Louis. After introducing his report with a brief, one-page section warning about drought and famine facing the city, Héricé turned to the influx of dangerous foreigners who imported what he described as corruption, fanaticism, superstition, family troubles, poison, and incurable diseases in exchange for rapidly accumulated fortunes at the expense of the African inhabitants of the capital. The worst of the lot, according to Héricé, were the marabouts, anti-Christian Islamic religious leaders who took advantage of people by selling them talismans meant to protect them from punishments. Second on his list of evil foreigners were griots.

> The griots . . . from Cayor, Yolof, and Walo . . . live at the expense of the Senegalese population and extract from them almost by force the ill-merited rewards of their vile profession, which consists of playing the drum to amuse the youth, play-acting, with songs and dances, on street corners where they congregate. . . . It is all so indecent, so outrageous for public morality, that it is really astonishing that the police have not yet taken notice of such horrors. . . . What is really strange is that everyone complains publicly about the

impudence of these people, who will strip you clean, but nobody goes after them! (Héricé, 1847, p. 9; my translation)

Héricé also criticized other classes of people and called for enforcement of existing laws in order to establish better social control. The author's view of griots as an urban plague foreshadows the negative views of many African city dwellers a century later.

EARLY TWENTIETH CENTURY

By the beginning of the twentieth century, the French had consolidated their power in West Africa and installed local administrators. Much information on local culture began to flow back to headquarters in each colony, to the office of the governor general for French West Africa in the new capital of Dakar, and to the Ministry of the Colonies in Paris. This information often came in the form of reports by *commandants de cercle*, the equivalent of the French prefect who administered departments, the basic political and geographical units in France.

H. de Lavallière, the *commandant de cercle* in Siguiri, a town in Upper Guinea, served two stints there from 1905 to 1906 and 1908 to 1910. He wrote in his "Cercle de Siguiri" one of the most detailed studies of griots to emerge from the late colonial era. His unpublished comments, buried in the archives of the Institut de France in Paris, are worth citing in detail.

> Griots. The Diali or griots were musicians and the bards of the country. There were also epic poets, for sometimes their songs were only a history of the wars that had stirred up the country. By their frequent contact with rulers, they have been called to witness before their very own eyes the different events that constitute the history of the country. They have preserved the flavor [of these events], and it is from them that one can still find today information that is more or less correct. Griots are in general much more intelligent than the other Malinkés. (This caste still exists but its influence has diminished considerably.) They are known here for casting spells and for having the evil eye. A free man will never marry his daughter to a griot. They can only marry among themselves or marry captives. Like the blacksmiths, they are stigmatized and remain always as griots. The griots here are like griots everywhere, exploiters par excellence. Griotes assist their husbands in tam-tams (celebrations). (Lavallière, 1911, p. 250)

In a separate school notebook, the author includes a special section, "Chiefs and Griots."

> To speak of gaoulos, djelis, griots, is to recall the epoch of the poets, troubadors, and performers.

At each residence of a black ruler one or two families of this caste are established who, like those of the blacksmiths, are looked down upon, from the point of view of their origin and their profession. They form an agglomeration of parasites who live apart and who marry only "Gnénos," a generic term for artisans: weavers, "sagnobés," blacksmiths, "ouaïlobés," "garanké" leather-workers, "sakhé" sadlers, "mabo" wooden utensil makers, all looked upon by the rest of the population as a body of people of low condition.

The griots, like their brothers the gaoulos, the djelis, have a prodigious memory. For generations they have religiously preserved the war stories, poems, genealogies, and songs that they always repeat with the same words and for good reason. It is the most precious inheritance that they can pass on from father to son and one on which is based their entire existence. They enrich this repertoire with new and lyrical items as time goes by. Thus, without hesitation and all at once they can list eighty names in the genealogy of a person who is known. If that person is near them in the middle of a group, they highlight him by recounting the meritorious acts of his ancestors in order to obtain recompense, which is never or rarely denied them. When they get nothing, they say all kinds of idiocies and create for him an obscure, despised ancestry.

Confused, he crawls away, for a griot is never beaten, and to argue with him is to lower oneself even in the eyes of the members of the caste to which one belongs.

Lavallière observes that in addition to their traditional role as word-smiths, griots in the region have other functions, executing condemned prisoners and managing the current affairs of the chief, becoming so valued that they are not allowed to leave his side, "especially during discussions, trials, and deliberations, in order to support his criticisms and to approve his decisions."

But Lavallière seems to sense what many other observers of the griot world—including some of the most distinguished griots themselves—have observed during the twentieth century: that the good old days will never return.

All their songs, their mimicking gestures, their tales with the savor of fables, poetic reflections—of the burning tropical sun, are beginning to lose their original cachet. . . . They no longer have that limitless freedom to exploit the elite of a generally proud and naive population. Today they evoke without any fire the exploits, the glories (the star of their rulers being eclipsed by the presence of that of the new dominator), the descendants who constituted and who still constitute the only vanities of the race with eyes of orphans, worn down and degenerate.

Lavallière's lengthy observations contain in germ many themes that will reemerge in later chapters. His observation that griots are more intelligent than others stems from the common belief that good memory and keen awareness of human relations are marks of intelligence, a notion that, though difficult to prove, underscores the growing awareness among administrators that griots were key people in the societies the French governed. This awareness is heightened by Lavallière's conclusion that the information held by griots is of some value. As for Lavallière's closing comments about the decline of the profession and the rise of aging griots to the status of royalty, we can certainly find examples today of griots who are treated in such fashion. It is hard to gainsay Lavallière's suggestion that the verbal art of griots was changing. Still, were he alive today, Lavallière would be astonished to see a griot performing on the stage at Carnegie Hall or with a symphony orchestra at the Kennedy Center.

❊ ❊

The origin tales discussed at the beginning of this chapter and the written accounts that contribute to our understanding of the more recent history of griots lead to three conclusions.

First, the profession is indeed quite old, probably more than a millennium. Until the last Arabic manuscript from the region is deciphered — out of the tens of thousands scattered across West Africa and Europe — and the last ancient city is excavated, scholars will only be able to speculate about the origins of griots in the region. In the context of a millennium or two, the past century of the colonial era appears as a very recent event. It is a period, nevertheless, whose impact is still changing the world of griots.

Second, from all of the texts, oral and written, it is increasingly apparent that griots have an extraordinary power over people, elites and masses, because of their verbal talents. It is a power that cannot be explained in simple terms of praise-singing.

Third, although most Europeans achieved only a partial understanding of griots as the result of travel, trade, war, and diplomacy, their accounts provide valuable resources when these narratives are carefully sifted to separate truth from prejudice. But to grasp more fully the nature of *jaliya* or *jeseretarey*, it is time to listen to the verbal art of these poets themselves, the subject of the next chapter.

❋ 3 ❋
The Verbal Art of Griots

Just as the blacksmith works with metal, the griot works with words, an analogy that makes the term *wordsmith* fit as a partial synonym. For *griot*, the comparison, however, goes beyond the notion of working a basic medium—iron or words—because blacksmiths and griots share a common social status among artisans, as seen, for example, in the Mande term for them, *nyamakalaw*.

What distinguishes the verbal art of griots and griottes from those who fulfill some of the same functions in other societies—such as poets in the Western tradition—is that the speech of these African wordsmiths combines both poetic art and, in many cases, a much less clearly defined power. In the Mande world it is known as *nyama*. To understand and appreciate the verbal art of griots, we must "listen" to their polysemic and multifunctional discourse as it is heard in the local context.

The obstacles to understanding for outsiders are many. They include the transfer from spoken word to print, the need to know the original languages in which the griots express themselves, and the fact that some of their speech is simply undecipherable. But a sampling of the many kinds of texts that scholars have recorded, transcribed, and translated—praises, genealogies, songs and poems, proverbs, and epics—can give readers from parts of Africa outside the Sahel and Savanna regions, as well as from other continents, a way to appreciate the artistry of these bards.

For literary scholars, these texts reveal that African literature can no longer be judged solely in terms of novels, plays, and poems written by African authors in Western languages. For researchers in other disciplines, such as history and anthropology, these different genres of verbal art tell much, not only about griots themselves but also about their relationships to others, both in the past and in the present. For the generalist reader, the praises, genealogies, songs, tales, proverbs, and epics of griots and griottes open up a new dimension of world literature.

The semanticist Alfred Korzybski wrote that he "defined man function-ally as a time-binder" because "each generation of humans . . . can start where the former generation left off" (1933, 39). Korzybski's notion of time-binding seems to be retrospective, resonating in some ways with Michel Foucault's idea of the archaeology of knowledge. One need not agree with all of Korzybski's often eccentric ideas about science and philosophy to recognize that griots assume this role of time-binding.

But griots function not only in a retrospective sense, linking past to present, but also, as seen in the hortatory function described in chapter 1, in a prospective sense, because of the impact of their words on the future activities of those listening. In addition, their words take on special value in the present by serving as buffers in human relations, whether between a ruler and his people, between rulers, or between families initiating negotia-tions for a marriage between their children.

The effort to tie past and present to a single event to take place in the near future reflects the griot's view of the two family-oriented concerns touched on earlier and common to many Sahelian and Savanna cultures, *fadenya* and *badenya* (Mande), *baba-ize-tarey* and *nya-ize-tarey* (Songhay), and *mingu babagu* and *bingu yummagu* (also *fandirabe* and *bandiarabe*) (Fulbe), all meaning father-child-ness (rivalry) and mother-child-ness (cooperation). *Fadenya* implies two kinds of competition. The first is between male children of the same father but different mothers; it leads to extreme forms of rivalry in the present, such as what occurred between Askia Moussa and his brothers. The second is a longer-term rivalry between the son and the father's reputation for a place in the family history. In both cases, one's reputation rests not simply on deeds but above all on the way griots and griottes portray these accomplishments for generations to come.

Praises

The most widespread verbal form for griots' portrayals are praises. In the first chapter, I listed praise-singing as one of the many functions of griots, and I made many references to this activity in the descriptions of griots in chapter 2. The evidence in both chapters indicated that praise-singing was the most audible form of a griot's participation in social events but was also misunderstood and criticized by travelers. Here, this function will be framed in the broader context of the other forms of verbal art. From the texts it will be apparent that the praises sung by griots reveal a much deeper and more complex relationship between patron and artist than is evident from the performance itself.

The praise song is usually a description in words of what an individual has done and the qualities that he or she demonstrated in carrying out the deeds. The words of griots in the form of praises—or insults—hold enormous power over people. Griots did not, however, invent praise-singing. The genre appears in many parts of the continent, as evidenced from Judith Gleason's survey, *Leaf and Bone: African Praise Poems* (1980). The Yoruba in southwestern Nigeria have created a highly complex form of praise called *oriki*, sung by people who do not need to be part of an endogamous professional group (Barber, 1990).

In the Sahel and Savanna regions of West Africa there seems to be a tradition of praise-singing by hereditary griots. The cross-cultural nature of this tradition appears in the overlapping nature of some of the terms for it, most of them linked to *jamu*. For the Soninké-speaking peoples claiming roots in the Ghana empire, "praise song" is one of the meanings of *jamu* (Bathily and Meillassoux, 1976, p. 64). In Bamana, *jamu* is a verb meaning "to praise someone, to express recognition" (Bisilliat and Laya, 1972, 8). *Jamu* means "family name" in Bamana and Maninka (Lucy Durán, personal communication, 1996). John William Johnson told me in 1996 that by extension it also means reputation in the same Mande languages. A Fulbe variant is *jammude*. Jeanne Bisilliat and Diouldé Laya suggest that *jamu* is a word of Bamana or Malinké origin, while Jean Pierre Olivier de Sardan argues that it is a Soninké word (1982, pp. 401–402). For Hausa-speaking peoples, *kirari* (praise-epithets) and *take* (shorter vocal or drummed praises) are the most common terms (Furniss, 1996, pp. 73–74). Whatever the case, praise-singing takes many forms and is not limited to griots.

Praises can be sung for people of the past or for those in the present. Sometimes they are somewhat narrative in form, telling what a person did. In *The Epic of Son-Jara*, when the hero uproots a baobab tree, the event is so extraordinary that it generates a series of new praise names. In this scene, narrator Fa-Digi Sisòkò employs several names for the hero, including Biribiriba, Magan Kònatè, and The Wizard, in addition to the new names that emerge from the baobab incident.

1460 Biribiriba came forward.	(Indeed)
He shook the baobab tree.	(Indeed)
A young boy fell out.	
His leg was broken.	

The bards thus sing, "Leg-Crushing-Ruler!"
"Magan Kònatè has risen!"   (Indeed)
He shook the baobab again.   (Indeed)
Another young boy fell out.   (Indeed)
His neck was broken.   (Indeed)
And thus the bards sing, "Neck-Breaking Ruler!"
"Magan Kònatè has risen!"   (Indeed)
The Wizard has uprooted the baobab tree,
And laid it across his shoulder.   (Mmm)
Nare Magan Kònatè rose up.   (Indeed)

(Johnson and Sisòkò, 1992, p. 60)

These praise names all flow from one of the most central episodes of the epic, underscoring the fact that the once-crippled child is now endowed with great physical strength. The uprooting of the tree is significant, but it is the impact of this act on others in the praise poem that serves to announce Son-Jara's future role as a powerful military hero. The praise song and the praise names arising from this incident become permanent verbal monuments that fix both the hero and the griot ancestors of the narrator in a specific moment on the timeline of Mande history.

Power comes from the past, and it also stems from links to other belief systems, such as Islam. The praises of the court poet Hajiya Maizargardi for the Emir of Kano, one of the most powerful men in Nigeria, reflect the close link between ruler and religion in northern Nigeria.

8.   Glory to God, master of Mecca and Medina
9.   Master of the City of Kano, Master of Zaria . . .
10. Sleep Well, Defender of the Faith
11. Emir of Kano Alhaji Ado Bayero, sleep well, son of Abdu.

(Mack, 1981, p. 301)

Praises do not need to be integrated into a longer narrative and do not always need to be focused on events. They may stand alone, and in some cases they can be sung by individuals who are not griots during such everyday events as pounding millet with a mortar and pestle. Among the Songhay and Zarma of Niger, the *zamu* praise poems, or poems about names, are sung to praise or encourage people who are going about their daily tasks. For women, these praises may include references to beauty, abundance, and motherhood. For men, they may refer to physical strength, power, and wealth. The praise poems may also link the individual with historical figures. Bisilliat and Laya (1972) note that "the *zamu* is the actualisation of the past and the actuality of the everyday. Thus, the subject of the praise poem about Amadou is still living today, and one can assume that the zamu praise poem is a process of continual creation, depending on circumstances" (41; my translation). There are other kinds of people who sing praises and who are not linked to the hereditary group generally described as griots—for example, a special class of bards who praise and narrate the feats of hunters.

Praises sung by griots are different from those sung by others in many ways. They are, for instance, the most deeply ingrained form in their multigeneric repertory. Apprentice griots learn the basic praises for great heroes and notable clans at an early age. For this reason, these praises have an almost automatic character about them and become key transitional components between episodes in much longer narratives such as epics. Johnson, in his discussion of the rather complex system of prosody that can be discerned from close study of the Mande epic, explains the praise-proverb mode in the following way:

> Some bards recite praise-proverb mode very rapidly. Functionally, this mode is often employed as a link between themes in the narrative mode. . . . Sometimes the bard seems to use this mode as a mindless way of organizing his forthcoming theme or themes. (In Johnson and Sisòkò, 32)

Here is an example of what listeners hear often in *Son-Jara*:

495 Ah, bards,
   He who would cultivate
   Let him cultivate
   Son-Jara is done!
   He who would deal in commerce,
   Let him deal in commerce!
   The Wizard is done! (Johnson and Sisòkò, 114)

But what may appear on the surface to be an automatic response or a transition between episodes of an epic may on occasion mask a much deeper power rooted in the words of griots. Barbara Hoffman (1995a) argues that many researchers, both African and non-African, have miscon-strued the nature of the power conveyed in the words of Mande *jeliw*. She discerns a basic inconsistency between the public discourse about them and their praises, on the one hand, and the behavior of people toward these artisans of the word, on the other.

Nobles, who seem to look down on *jeliw*, often serve as sources for much research on the profession. From my own experience, one reason appears to be that visiting scholars of every nationality, African and non-African, are sometimes required by protocol, as well as by the research authorization rules in the host country, to meet first with local authorities—village chiefs, canton chiefs, *prefets*—before interacting with informants. The result is that the gaze of these outsiders may be framed by the nobles' perspective, which is frequently negative on the subject of griots.

This tendency to provide a distorted lens through which to study griots contrasts sharply with a social reality in which nobles depend on these verbal artisans to carry out so many functions requiring words. The result is something of a paradox—people appear to outsiders to despise griots, yet on certain occasions the subjects of the griots' praises give these word-smiths, quite literally, the clothing from their own bodies. In the Mande world, Hoffman asserts, the explanation for this confusing situation lies in the relationship between *nyama* and words.

When Hoffman began her research in Mali in the mid-1980s, she witnessed many scenes in which "nobles would empty their coin purses of a month's salary in return for their *fasa* or praise song, an act they perform not just once but over and over again throughout the course of their lives." She asked, "What is it about public praise that has such power for the Mande people?" (1995a, p. 38). In the course of her four-year apprentice-ship as a female griot, or *jelimuso*, she discovered that it was difficult to verbalize the reasons for this power: "Many noblewomen love the griots' songs and sing them to themselves when no one else is around to hear, repeating them quietly, like personal charms. They feel the power of the griots' words, power that moves, that enables—power that, like other power structures in the Mande world, is articulated in obscurity."

By situating the roles of griots in a broader context, that of *nyama*, the mysterious life force or occult power that one must have in order to overcome *nyama* emerging from other sources, human or otherwise, Hoffman learned that griot language—what she terms in the Mande context as *jelikan*—is "the most laden with dangerous force (*nyama*), the most powerful in its impact on the hearer, and the most empowering for its speaker. . . . It occurs extensively in the *fasaw* (praise-songs), which are rated by the Mande as particularly *nyama*-laden" (41). She adds:

> In my attempts to discover what it is about praise genres that is so powerful, I found that most nobles could not decipher the referential content of *jelikan*; even more surprising, a large proportion of any individual griot's repertory of phrases is empty of referential content to him/her as well. These phrases are usually not used in isolation, but in strings which may be many phrases long. When asked the meaning of an individual phrase, *jeliw* say that it is its

membership in the class of phrases that can be sung for a person of a specific clan, for a Traoré or a Keita, or a Diallo. Its meaning is not the sum of its parts. The obscurity of its referential content in the performance context is an important aspect of the *nyama* of *jelikan*.

Hoffman compares the speech of sorcerers, *dibikan*, with that of griots, *jelikan*, by noting both similarities—each is composed largely of noun phrases—and striking differences. Where *dibikan* is spoken at night, in a low voice, and in a closed context, the words of *jeliw* in the form of praises may be shouted during the day among crowds.

> They are uttered very rapidly, at times like verbal gunfire, bombarding the noble with more sound than can be assimilated, causing confusion. . . . The griot has called the weight of extraordinary achievement from the distant past into the living present of the noble "descendant," a juxtaposition which invites comparison, thus encouraging the noble to swell with pride at the thought of being on a par with such heroism, or to sink with shame at the thought that his/her own reputation will not stand up to the scrutiny—in either case, the emotion thus stirred is literally dripping with *nyama*. (42)

Hoffman suggests that it is little wonder that nobles should be "awe-struck by the effects of *jelikan*." She adds that she has seen "many a *horon's* [noble's] hand quake as it thrust forth a bill, sometimes accompanied by a verbal plea, 'ka nyama bo' (Please take away the *nyama*)." What has often been viewed by researchers as anger and resentment toward griots on the part of nobles, she believes, is really a manifestation of fear of the great power of griots. Hoffman argues that we cannot understand the full meaning of these praises uttered by *jeliw* unless we take into account their control of the *nyama* conveyed by the words.

Hoffman's reference to the outstretched hand of the nobles echoes the description of noble-*nyamakala* relations that one finds in another passage of *The Epic of Bamana Segu*. Toward the end of the epic, *jeli* Tayiru Banbera returns to the theme of nobles in a short passage that reveals the functional difference between the two different social groups.

6545   If the tip of the noble's tongue is too sharp, he is either a thief or a liar.
      That is why, our master teacher,
      If a noble is able to control his feet he pleases us, the *nyamakala*.
      A noble able to control his mouth pleases us, the *nyamakala*.
      A noble able to control his stomach pleases us, the *nyamakala*.
6550   But if a noble controls his hand, we are soon separated from him.
      We do not share the same father.
      We do not share the same mother. (Conrad, 1990, p. 284)

In other words, proper nobles do not speak loudly, they do not dance, and, Conrad explains, they maintain a "cool" stomach because that part of the body is the seat of various emotions. Conrad adds that at another level of meaning, the reference to the stomach serves as an amusing "admonition to the *horon* [noble] from the *jeli* to practice restraint in his personal consumption, and leave more for his precious *jeliw*" (personal communication, 1995); it also introduces the next line about generosity. *Jeliw* perform public speaking and dancing—and they are also not constrained by certain other rules of social behavior. Nobles lose, in effect, their status as nobles when they engage in such activities. But the one area where they are forbidden from maintaining self-control is giving—hence the reference to the hand. A hand that does not give represents a miserly noble and, by extension, a person who lacks the qualities of a noble.

Banbera's lesson on noble-*nyamakala* relations needs to be framed in the larger context of Hoffman's discussion of *nyama*. *Jeliw* define behavior in a manner that suits their profession. But their "teaching" is more than a matter of social territory. It is a question of identity, and they are capable of enforcing the rules they enunciate because of the *nyama* contained in their words.

It is not clear that all praises are equally charged with *nyama*, or even that *nyama* or its equivalent is found in other cultures where there are griots. Given the centrality of the Mande world for understanding these wordsmiths, however, is is evident that we need to reexamine the role of praises as a significant verbal genre by drawing on the insights of Hoffman.

Praises do not always have to be about other people. The griot may praise himself in order to persuade listeners of the value of the verbal art that is being presented. H. T. Norris cites a self-praise song by a Mauritanian *tiggiwit*, Yāqūta mint 'Alī Warakān, a wealthy woman in Nouakchott, the capital city. He explains that she is able to support a comfortable, well-furnished house; and like so many of the *iggāwen* themselves, she jealously guards her songs and recitals, in these days when there is extensive tape-recording for nation-wide broadcasting, and rivalry and competition among the *iggāwen* themselves. She has unlimited pride in her own talents, as the following improvised poem of hers reveals:

> From what ruby, O Lord of the throne, is Yākūta?
> From the source of pearl and ruby she is fashioned.
> In the form of a dark-eyed hurī He has shaped her.
> As He wished, and the people love Yākūta.
> Yākūta, her renown is supreme, and any youth

Who says the name Yākūta, then her name is his sustenance.
There is no lady like her in Mauritania,
Nor in Senegal, nor Gambia, nor Fūta.
She is the full moon, but without a blemish in it, and
Her spouse is the sea, but without a great fish in it. (Norris, 1968, p. 53)

Praises do not need to be limited to people, especially in the modern era. Griots also compose praises for countries and political organizations. During the first political campaigns in French West Africa after the Second World War, many griots contributed praise songs to the RDA (Rassemblement Démocratique Africain), the first major political movement to sweep the region. Badié Bagna, one of the best-known griots of Niger in the postwar period, accompanied local political leaders during these campaigns of the late 1940s, according to one of his patrons, Boubou Hama (1980), and one of his widows, Ramatou Niandou (1989). Bala Diabaté in Kéla, Mali, reported (1992) that he had traveled to Kita, Bamako, Ségou, and the Wassoulou region to sing songs in support of the RDA. The long-term outcome of these campaigns was the creation of local political parties and the eventual independence of most French West African countries from France in 1960. Another outcome was a new generation of leaders who found their way to praise songs.

Edris Makward recorded a praise song in 1973 from M'Bana Diop, a Senegalese griotte. Excerpts reflect the national pride in Léopold Sédar Senghor, one of the leading statesmen of West Africa. They also reveal the natural affinity of griots to those who hold political power.

You all know of the year 1960
It is in 1960 that Senghor became our leader.
All nations respect us.
Everybody respects Léopold. . . .
He obtained degrees and diplomas and the *baccalauréat*.
These were not enough.
Agrégé de grammaire.
You made the demands
And the country got its independence.
Through your intelligence the deltas were developed,
In addition to other projects that you had initiated. . . .
When we were behind, and when we were on the brink of disaster,
It was you who took the initiative,
You appealed to the people to have patience and to pray. . . .
You brought back peace and harmony.

Oh! Léopold, oh! Independence is pleasant!
You are not a man of war.
Not a shot fired, not a sword drawn. (Makward,1990, pp. 33–34)

M'Bana Diop saw this as a "development song" to help her country, as well as a political song. Makward reports that "M'Bana insisted on the fact that she sang it first at an annual convention of the UPS (Union Progressiste Sénégalaise), Senghor's party" (34). He adds that the song is not typical of Wolof praise songs because it lacks genealogy, a weakness, he explains, that is due to the distance between the Wolof narrator and the Serer sources of Senghor's family history. To know a clan's genealogy, the griot must spend a lifetime with the family or study hard on his or her own.

In addition to the work of Bisilliat and Laya on Songhay praises, Arnston has studied the genre for the Maninka and Koranko for a recent chapter that includes a track on a compact disc (1998). Other scholars have studied praise names for particular cultures (Seydou for the Fulbe, Zahan and Dieterlen for the Bamana). Given the diverse occurrences of the form as well as the call for a new approach by Hoffman, one can only agree with Stephen Belcher that the time has come for a broader comparative study of the genre (personal communication, 1997).

Genealogies

Praises about deeds or qualities are usually framed or conveyed in genealogical order. In the case of *The Epic of Askia Mohammed*, *jeseré* Nouhou Malio simply runs down a listing of both father and child, varying it occasionally with a reference to the village of descendants.

735   He fathered Nayo Gandaize Harigoni
       He fathered Watta Cisseyze Samsu . . .
       The village of Fabay is Deba
       The village of Samo Nyamo is Waloga. (Hale, 1990a, p. 229)

From the printed texts, there seems to be little "art" in such listings. But in performance the genealogy takes on a particular rhythm when it is called out, one that is quite distinct from other genres. The introduction to the video "Griottes of the Sahel" (Hale, 1990b) includes a brief scene of a griot recounting a genealogy. The audience can see and hear the combination of sound and gesture in the recitation. The narrator begins to gesture, stabbing at the air in front of him with a forefinger to mark each name and repeating in an incantatory fashion the family and given name, preceded or followed by either the word *village* or *fathered*. The repetition creates a hypnotic effect as the "film" of the past is rapidly run past the listeners. The repetition serves also to emphasize, in a hammering way, the name of each person.

Neither narrative nor description of deeds interferes with the roll call of ancestors. One reason for this is perhaps mnemonic—the list was memorized in a certain fashion, and to interrupt would be to risk upsetting the ordering of names. Another reason for such a spare listing is to emphasize the equality of all of these great names from the past. By appearing on the list, they acquire immortality and greatness. The genealogy becomes a sacred thread linking past and present. Its function is to legitimize those in the present, while its art lies in the repetitions, the parallelisms, and the synergy of word and gesture.

The genealogies, as noted in chapter 1, may also include references to the heritage of the narrator. An example from a Fulbe epic reveals more clearly the effect of this self-referential kind of genealogy. Pahel Mamadou Baïla, a Fulbe *gawlo* from Kouniékarie in the Macina region of Mali, comes from a family that originally lived in the Fouta Toro region of northern Senegal. The family migrated eastward during the nineteenth century, following the military campaigns of El Hadj Omar Tall. In the opening lines of *L'Epopée de Samba Guéladiégui*, a Fulbe epic about an eighteenth-century hero that was recorded in 1974 in Dakar by Amadou Ly, this *gawlo* links his own talent with that of a distinguished ancestor.

8   My ancestor was called Farba Sanambilo
9   He was the first *farba* [dean of griots] that the Fouta knew;
10 He was the father of Kiné Sala
11 Who was the father of Déwa Kiné,
12 Who was the father of Oumar Demba,
13 Who was the father of Mamadou Baïla;
14 Mamadou Baïla is my father. (Ly, 1991, p. 19; my translation)

In this description, the genealogy rolls to a sudden stop with the narrator himself. It is carefully framed by the reference at the beginning to a famous ancestor—the dean of griots in the Fouta Toro—and at the end by the current narrator. The names in the middle serve as links between the most distant past and the present, establishing a kind of implicit balance as well as cause and effect: greatness in the past leads to greatness in the present. The 3,176 lines that follow become an extension of that past.

The function of recounting genealogies is not always limited to griots. Elders from all segments of society know something about these lists of ancestors because genealogies are normally viewed by their local audiences as major sources of their history. But historians are often skeptical about the value of these orally conveyed lists. Africanist historians such as David Henige, Jan Vansina, and Joseph C. Miller have focused attention on the question of what can be legitimately gleaned from these genealogies. In *Liptako Speaks*, Paul Irwin was able to draw heavily on oral accounts and genealogies collected in eastern Burkina Faso and western Niger for a history of the region.

These listings remain of considerable value to historians able to interpret them in the context of other data. But more research is needed on the art of genealogy, because these links with the past are no less important from a formal perspective than they are for historians.

Tales

Tales constitute what may be a more widely heard form of oral art than any other in Africa because in many societies they can be told by almost anyone, not just professional wordsmiths. In the Sahel and Savanna regions no one has a monopoly on tale-telling, but griots, because of the wide range of their knowledge, are particularly talented.

The Senegalese veterinarian Birago Diop collected many tales from griots before and during the Second World War, then published them as *Les Contes d'Amadou Koumba* (1947) and *Les Nouveaux Contes d'Amadou Koumba* (1958). In the course of his frequent travels, Diop stopped one day at a shop owned by his uncle Amadou Diawara near the confluence of the Senegal and Falémé Rivers in eastern Senegal. Mohammadou Kane describes Diop's encounter there with a family griot.

> He was introduced to an old griot, Amadou Koumba N'Gom, who, hearing the name of his mother, sang his genealogy. . . . It was as if Birago had met another member of the family. For a week, they met each evening. Amadou Koumba, unstoppable, told, recounted, recited, sang. The shop of Amadou Diawara became for some time the headquarters of Birago Diop's missions in that part of the country; thus, each evening brought him back to the master who was also the repository for the past and of the traditions of the family. (Kane, 1971, p. 37; my translation)

Kane explains that Diop picked up many of his stories not only from Amadou Koumba but also from a variety of other sources—a brother, a grandmother, and another griot, Guewel M'Baye, the *guewel* of his family, who spent six months each year in Dakar at the Diop home when the veterinarian was growing up.

The tales that Diop collected from these griots and from other sources focus to a large extent on animals, a feature that caused several Parisian publishing houses to reject them. But they represent a wide range of types within the genre, from morality tales ("The Inheritance") to comic stories ("The Excuse") and myths ("The Humps"). The tales emerge as both entertainment and instruction. Their collection and publication represent a pioneering effort to convey to new generations of readers—African and non-African—the wisdom of a genre that is without doubt the most accessible in all of African literature.

The difference between tales that can be told by anyone in the evening and those told by griots is that these professional artisans of the word possess a slightly different world view. Their stories may reflect what Annik Thoyer-Rozat, in *Le Riche et le pauvre* (1981) [the rich and the poor], terms "feudal ideology," the perspective of those in power, because griots, more than any other members of society, are keenly sensitive to social differences stemming from birth, deed, or misfortune. *Le Riche et le pauvre*, a fifty-page Bamana tale recorded by Thoyer-Rozat from *jeli* Tayiru Banbera of Ségou in 1971, tells of a rich young man, Faamanjè, and his friend Faantannjè, a poor boy. They become involved in many escapades with women and elders; in the end, as Thoyer-Rozat points out, it is the position of the rich man that is strengthened, thanks to the help of his poor friend, who enables him to marry the daughter of a king.

Tales, then, are among those genres that griots share with other members of society, although the professional wordsmith may bring to the story a somewhat keener awareness of interpersonal relations and, above all, a greater sensitivity to the power structure in which he or she operates. Tales, though basically narrative in form, may also contain other verbal genres, such as songs and poems.

Songs and Poems

The difference between praises and other short poetic forms, such as songs and poems, may not always be clear, because both griots and griottes sing a variety of songs to mark special events that involve people. And the difference between songs and poems may depend on circumstances; a song may be sung on one occasion, while its words may simply be spoken on another occasion.

One of the oldest songs in the Mande tradition is "Janjon," or "The

Brave Warrior's Song," which was sung when young men went off to war. Traditionally, those who danced to this song had participated in battle or risked death in some manner. As John Hutchison and Kassim Kone indicate, in more recent years it was sung "to incite national pride and to keep people going during difficult times through the history of modern Mali" (1994, p. 15). But here are excerpts from a version often sung by the Malian *jeli* Ban Zoumana Cissoko.

> The brave men are no more, the brave men are no more,
> The Bamana who offered slaves to people are no more.
> The drinkers are no more, its drinkers are no more. . . .
> The carriers of bundles of guns are no more. . . .
> Those who carried the axes to flatten villages are no more. . . .
> The carriers of bundles of arrows are no more.
> The carriers of man-killing knives are no more. . . .
> Oh Leading Vulture Mawule
> People are not equal
> Its dancers are no more, the dancers of Janjon are no more. . . .
> The day Batoma died was a terrible day. . . .
> The day Mamadu died was a terrible day,
> The mankilling dog among the people from Npebala,
> Mamadu departed from this life.
> He disappeared with the mankilling swords. . . .
> I have not seen anyone like you.
> Death destroys a person but not his [name] reputation. (Hutchison and Kone, 1994, p. 15)

The focus here is on the past, on how brave men were in those days, and by extension on how far those in the present must go or how much they must accomplish if they are to match the deeds of yesteryear. The *jeli's* identification with the past seems so complete here that it appears as though nothing in the present can ever match the past. The manner in which he presents the past reflects in fact a deep disdain on the part of Ban Zoumana Sissoko for the changes in contemporary Malian society, including the modern profession of *jeliya*. The younger generation of griots is less familiar with the ancient power structure and more sensitive to new lines of authority that have developed since independence. The result has been calls for new songs.

In many cases the line between praise song and song is hardly clear. The issue can become even more ambiguous when the person composing the song is both a griotte and the wife of the hero, a king.

A canton chief married Yaram N'Deer, the aunt of the Wolof griotte Mbana Diop, in accordance with a tradition of some Wolof kings who take one wife of griot origin among the many they may marry. He went off to fight against the Moors at the battle of Baray Kaat. When he returned from his victory, loaded with booty but wearing clothes full of bullets, his wife composed the following song:

Brave Mbabaa!
Brave Mbabaa! Yaram Diop
Fara Penda Aadam Sal [ruled 1827–40]
That Tuesday you crossed the river at Dagana.
5   You spent the day at Ngor Madd.
You distributed the ammunition
Among your men at Barey-Kaat.
You left in the afternoon for Asbuum where you spent the night.
There, you killed Ahmet Faal, you
10   Killed Maallik Kiis and their slave Wulnaa Siri
The Moorish women wept and cried "Weeyli! Weeyli!"
Yamar said, "Who ever says 'Weeylli! Weeyli!' will die."
Fara Kumba, Mataaar Naar.
Ooh Jaajee!
15   Brave Mbabaa.
He is worth singing about.
Sara Koumba, Matar Naar. Woi Jaajee!
Brave Mbabaa!
Brave Mbabaa, Yaram Joop.
20   He [Yamar] fought against Tarxiis at Ngor Madd and burned Saabu Siri.
This is what he got at Xuuma Jankiri.
Mbaye Joop, the country of Samba Wadd.
The Wind of MaaSamba Xosifor [name of warrior's horse]
They all sang: Brave Mbabaa, he is worth singing about.
25   Fara Kumba Mataar Naar,
Ooh Jaajeey. (Makward, 1990, pp. 27–28)

This song accomplishes multiple functions, Makward explains: it tells the story of a campaign against the Moors and includes both a praise song, known in Wolof as the *taag* mode, and a song mode, or *woi*, which means both song and poem.

The difference between a song and a poem may reflect only the mode of transmission—the song is sung, the poem written. But as Beverly Mack points out in her study of Hausa women's oral poetry (1981), the line between the two may be blurred by a common terminology. Whether written or oral, the song or poem is called *waka* (plural, *wakoki*). Written *wakoki* may be given orally, but oral poems are not written down (11). While there are differences between written (*wakar baki*) and oral (*wakar rubutu*) poems by men, for women they are almost the same (13). Mack explains that "all *wakoki*, unlike much Western poetry, are performed primarily with the intention of entertaining an audience rather than as an expression of personal introspection" (15).

> The women who compose written *wakoki* model both the content and form of their works on earlier styles. For them the *waka* is an instructive art form, a means of teaching proper behavior, a vehicle for explanation of new social trends and descriptions of far-reaching news events . . . oral *wakoki* . . . are less didactic than women's written material. (18)

Hausa *wakoki*, which cover a wide range of topics and occasions, can, like the Songhay and Zarma *zamu*, a more focused genre, be composed and performed by both professional and nonprofessional women, though the professional *marok'a* or *zabiya* are much freer to do so in public. What distinguishes Hausa poetry from other forms in related Sahel and Savanna societies appears to be the cohabitation of two linked traditions, the oral and the written. Mack's research on Hausa women poets underscores the fact that in certain areas, the line between professional and nonprofessional performers is often broken.

Songs and poems, along with praises, are the stock-in-trade of griots. They may echo a tradition that goes back many centuries or be created on the spot for a person or event. It is in these short compositions that the verbal art of griots most approximates that of the troubadours of the European Middle Ages, with which they are often compared.

Proverbs

Bernth Lindfors (1968) has entitled an article about proverbs in the novels of Chinua Achebe "The Palm-Oil with Which Achebe's Words Are Eaten." Folklorists would call that a meta-proverb. Much of the cultural weight of Achebe's novels is conveyed by proverbs, and one could say the same about this rhetorical device in the verbal art of griots. By framing a statement in proverbial form, the speaker, griot or otherwise, is calling upon the wisdom of an entire culture. Here, more than anywhere else, the message is carried to a large extent by the medium.

In *The Epic of Askia Mohammed* (Hale, 1990a), *jeseré* Nouhou Malio places a proverb in the mouth of a ruler and then figuratively turns to his audience to ask if they have understood the full meaning. To appreciate this example of proverb, some context is needed.

In the epic, a war breaks out during the seventeenth century between the Songhay of Gao and the attacking Arma, a mixed army of North Africans and Europeans sent by Morocco and based upriver in Timbuktu. The cause of the war appears to be a conflict in Gao that pits one part of a family against another. On one side is the ruler, Soumayla Kassa and his son Amar Zoumbani, whose mother was a captive woman. On the other side are the ruler's wife Sagouma and her brother. When Soumayla Kassa orders the death of his brother-in-law, Sagouma kills her twin sons who were fathered by the ruler, and leaves to search for an Arma warrior who will help her avenge the killing of her brother.

The resulting war finds Soumayla Kassa and Amar Zoumbani on the battlefield one day without water. Amar comes to his father with news that he has found some water in a pot. When his father discovers that the pot and the water were used by farmers to wash millet just before they were forced to flee because of the war, he turns to his son, who has drunk some of the fouled water, and declares, "What misfortune! Even if one buys a house cat for 50,000 CFA francs [$200 at the time of the recording], it will only catch mice. You have returned home, Amar Zoumbani, you have returned home, you have returned home" (lines 1410–12).

Two lines later, narrator Nouhou Malio asks his listeners, "What does it mean, he has returned home? The fact of being a captive, that is the insult that he made to him" (lines 1414–15). What emerges is the uncomfortable reality that Soumayla Kassa never freed the mother of Amar Zoumbani. The result is that Amar will always be viewed—and behave as—a captive, not as a noble. The proverb about the house cat sums up the subtle distinction in his status and behavior in a manner that combines ancient wisdom and modern commerce. It also reveals a fundamental paradox in the social structure: one can become a captive or a noble overnight, depending on the circumstances of war and family relations.

Proverbs are the most ubiquitous example of verbal art, spoken by every mature member of a society. Their use reflects a full grasp of the cultural values of a people and reveals a readiness for adulthood. Mamadou Kouyaté, the *jeli* narrator of the prose version of Sundiata edited by Djibril Tamsir Niane, underscores this point when he places proverbs in the speech of the hero and his half-brother.

> "Mother is calling us," said Sundiata, who was standing at one side. "Come Manding Bory. If I am not mistaken, you are fond of that daughter of Mansa Konkon's."

"Yes brother, but I would have you know that to drive a cow into the stable, it is necessary to take the calf in."

"Of course, the cow will follow the kidnapper. But take care, for if the cow is in a rage so much the worse for the kidnapper."

The two brothers went in swopping proverbs. Men's wisdom is contained in proverbs and when children wield proverbs it is a sign that they have profited from adult company. (Niane, 1965, p. 29)

Given the role of griots as conveyers of this cultural heritage, as well as the frequent need to speak in indirect terms when revealing hard truths, the proverb is a privileged device. Although there is no evidence to confirm that griots use a higher percentage of proverbs in their verbal art than other members of society in everyday speech, a reading of a series of African epics supports the belief that proverbs are indeed important components of these long narratives. David Conrad lists proverbs appearing on 89 of the 285 pages of the *The Epic of Bamana Segu* recounted by Tayiru Banbera (Conrad, 1990, p. 357).

Epics

Proverbs are only one of many different verbal forms that occur in epics. Praises, genealogies, tales, and songs, as well as shorter rhetorical devices such as proverbs, sayings, metaphors, and comparisons all contribute to make up what the Western world calls epic. Little more than a quarter century ago, there was debate over the existence of epic in Africa. It was sparked by Ruth Finnegan's comment in a note in *Oral Literature in Africa* (1970) that the existence of epic on the continent "does not seem to be borne out by the African evidence" (108). It appears that Finnegan's judgment was based on several circumstances: the lack of long poetic narratives from the continent available in European translations, the difficulty of conveying African systems of prosody in Western poetic forms, and a legitimate debate over the distinction between panegyric, similar to praise, and epic, a genre oriented more toward narrative.

Starting in the late 1960s, a small corps of scholars from countries in Africa, Europe, and North America began to record and publish long poetic narratives from African sources, a phenomenon that eventually prompted John William Johnson to publish an essay entitled "Yes, Virginia, There Is an Epic in Africa" (1980). By the late 1980s and early 1990s, a few of these texts could be found in anthologies of world literature read by first-year students in American universities and colleges. The *Harper-Collins World Reader*, published in 1994, included epic texts describing the founding or development of the Ghana, Mali, and Songhay empires as well as other political units in Madagascar and Egypt.

By the mid-1990s, there were enough epics in print or on tape to prompt Johnson, this writer, and Stephen Belcher to assemble excerpts from twenty-five of them for *Oral Epics from Africa: Vibrant Voices from a Vast Continent* (1997), the first anthology of African oral epic texts. Shortly thereafter, Lilyan Kesteloot and Bassirou Dieng published *Les Epopées d'Afrique noire* (1997), a volume that also includes African epics composed in written form. The West African texts are quite diverse in content, ranging from the creation of the Ghana and Mali empires many centuries ago to the resistance of a Senegalese hero against the French in the 1880s. But they share to a large extent the features of epics found in other parts of the world. The narrators tell of heroes who, in many cases, were born under difficult circumstances, grew up to fight battles, conquered territory, resisted invasion, and propagated Islam or an African belief system (see map 7).

The themes and motifs of these epics diffuse across the Sahel from people to people, creating a rich blend of narrative that is known around the world as epic. Why, then, the continuing debate over whether the epic exists in Africa? One cause is the nature of the term *universal*. Until now, when Western scholars defined genres as universal, their frame of reference was largely European, and epic meant Homer's *Iliad*. As Johnson points out in the introduction to *The Epic of Son-Jara* (Johnson and Sisòkò, 1986, 1992), there is persistent concern about the application of *epic*, a Western word, to Africa. He asks whether one should view the long poetic narratives in Africa as "ethno-aesthetic constructs" definable only by local listeners, who give their own particular names to these accounts, or take "a more cross-cultural point of view." Ultimately, he leans toward the adoption of the term *epic*. While recognizing that "no one epic tradition is identical to any other epic tradition," he concludes that "the similarities of various examples of this genre are so striking that I hold the latter view" (1986, p. 6).

Johnson's Criteria

Basing his position on what he finds in *The Epic of Son-Jara* and similar texts from West Africa, Johnson argues for a holistic model of epic that depends on both textual and performance considerations. He lists a variety of features that are specific to the Mande epic as well as, in many cases, other African oral epic traditions.

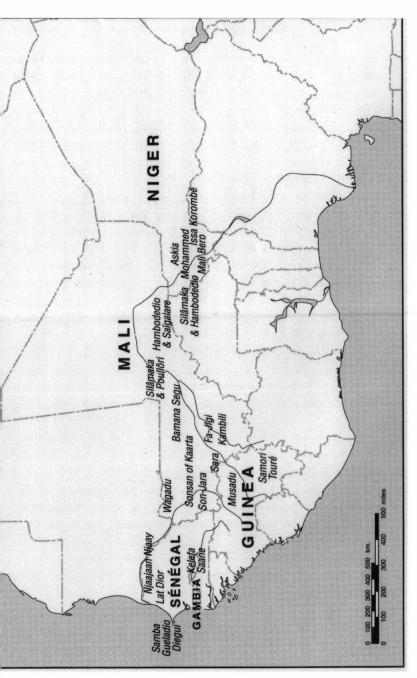

Map 7. Regional sources of selected West African epics.

POETIC LANGUAGE

In the Mande oral epic tradition there are several poetic modes, which can be likened to meters, with different functions for each: the narrative mode recounts the story, while the song mode highlights events in this story. The praise-proverb mode provides a transition between narrative events in the story. Within each mode, the prosody governing the poem is characterized by what Charles Bird has described as language-external constraints. They contrast with the language-internal constraints typical of Western poetry, controlled by grammar.

To understand this system, Johnson explains, one must be aware that Mande languages are tonal: meaning changes with tone. The external constraints may include variations in tone for individual words based on differences between poetic and colloquial speech. The result is that there is much shifting of linguistic accents to conform to the musical accompaniment, a process that might lead to changes in meaning without the maintenance of the context. Johnson writes: "It is this shifting of tones to conform to prosodic stress pattern, which is non-phonemic in normal speech, that proves the text is poetic" (1986, p. 31).

Through a series of diagrams, Johnson shows how aesthetic tension builds or decreases in each of the poetic modes, depending on the degree of variation from the norm in melody or rhythm of the voice and instrument. Bird, in a lecture in 1978, described aesthetic tension by drawing an analogy between two hypothetical performances. The first would be the way a child might play a tune such as "Twinkle, Twinkle, Little Star," picking out notes on a piano in a manner that leaves no doubt about the tune and thus creates no aesthetic tension for the listener. The second would be the way the jazz trumpeter Charlie Parker might rework the same tune into a nearly unrecognizable form, creating enormous aesthetic tension for the listeners, who would continually measure the talent of the trumpet player by the extent of his creative musical reconfiguration. It is this ability to play upon the Mande audience's sense of aesthetics, heightening and diminishing tension in the different modes, Bird explained, that distinguishes the master *jeli* from the apprentice.

NARRATIVE FEATURES

Johnson identifies three levels of structure: the episode based on groups of themes, the three modes of poetry already described, and smaller units such as motifs, genealogies, praise names, and proverbs. Johnson cites two kinds of episodes: core, normally present in all versions, and augmenting episodes, which are not as essential for the main story but may be recounted by the demands of the context. Both of these different kinds of episodes are not always recounted in the same order because of flashbacks or simply forgetfulness on the part of the *jeli*. Although the *jeli* may know many of these episodes in the form of a very long mental text, most often the epic is performed in excerpted form, Johnson explains (1996b).

HEROIC CONTENT

The Mande hero must break with tradition, pursue his own path, and go through a series of transformations as he acquires power. These changes occur on what Johnson describes as the *fadenya* axis, the competitive, single-minded, achievement-oriented mode described earlier as father-child-ness, as opposed to the more domestic, cooperative, and collective mode known as *badenya*, or mother-child-ness.

LEGENDARY TRAITS

Although the Mande peoples view the epic as history, Johnson sees the narrative as composed of a series of legends of varying lengths, beginning with the origins of clans. The narrative as a whole is a legend in which the hero is "molded into an heroic pattern defined by Mande society" (1986, p. 46).

LENGTH

Another feature of Mande epics is their open-endedness. They may be very long or very short. The most appropriate measure of length for an oral epic is either hours required for a performance or number of lines performed per minute. Once the text is transcribed and published, we tend to apply the terminology of writing—lines and pages. One needs to be aware of this almost unconscious shift from one mode of describing the narrative to the other. The text of *Son-Jara* that Johnson published contained 3,083 lines, but many other texts of this epic that he collected or worked with were shorter or longer. The longest epic to appear in print to date is the 7,942-line *Epic of Bamana Segu*, recounted to David Conrad by Tayiru Banbera during six recording sessions from February 28 to March 11, 1976. In a note, Conrad (1990, p. 9) compares the rate of delivery of Tayiru Banbera—7,942 lines in ten hours and five minutes, or 794 lines per hour—with that of Fa-Digi Sisòkò, who recounted the 3,083 lines of *Son-*

Jara in one four-hour session, about 771 lines per hour. Length is largely a function of the griot's knowledge, the composition of the audience, and the occasion.

The difference between a long praise song and an epic, Johnson suggests, lies in both the form (epics contain narratives, praises do not), and the length. Epics can be measured by hours or by thousands of lines, while praise songs are much shorter performances and are limited to a few hundred lines.

MULTIFUNCTIONAL FEATURES

The Mande epic serves a variety of functions. Descriptions of contacts between clans convey a model for relations today, with explanations for joking relations between some clans and conflicts between others. They also provide bases for national unity because of the traditional reroofing ceremony at the sacred house of the Mande that takes place in Kangaba every seven years, an event that attracts participants from all parts of the diaspora. On this occasion, the *jeliw* of nearby Kéla may recite the Sundiata epic inside the mud-walled, thatch-roofed structure for the Keita elders. In a broader sense, the story of conquest and reestablishment of social order serves as a charter for the building of a state that became a great empire by the fourteenth century. The performance of the epic also constitutes an event of great entertainment value for its listeners and serves as a catalog of the customs and values of a people.

CULTURAL AND TRADITIONAL TRANSMISSION

Utensils, weapons, religious paraphernalia, animals, plants, beliefs, foods, and customs such as birth, marriage, and burial all appear in the epic, which, as Johnson suggests, becomes a mirror for society and a force for enculturation.

MULTIGENERIC TRAITS

Just as songs may contain both narrative and praise, the epic usually includes a variety of other verbal forms. Johnson argues that "the multi-generic structure of epic is an important defining feature of this form of oral folklore" (1986, p. 57). The narrator embeds legends within legends, each of which may contain praise names, folk etymologies, proverbs, incantations, curses, and oaths.

Other Epic Traditions

The pattern outlined by Johnson applies to the Mande epic but not necessarily to all other epic traditions in the Sahel. Published Songhay epics, for example, share some but not all of the traits (narrative and praise-proverb, but not song mode), and the Hausa-speaking peoples do not have an epic tradition comparable to that of the Mande or the Songhay. But for many cultures of the Sahel and Savanna regions, the epic is a major component of their oral heritage—the Moors, the Wolof, the Mandinka, the Fulbe, the Soninké, the Bamana, the Maninka, and the Songhay.

A reading of some of these other epics reveals not only recurring features such as those described by Johnson (praise songs, legendary structure, etc.) but also, as one might expect, a full range of the more common poetic characteristics familiar to readers of epic around the world: metaphor, comparison, parallelism, repetition, metonymy, and dialogue. In *La Prise de Dionkolani* (Kabinè, Kesteloot, Dumestre, and Traoré, 1975), one finds a variety of these features. *La Prise de Dionkolani* is an episode in the Bamana oral tradition chanted by Sissoko Kabinè, a *jeli* whose verbal art the volume's editors, Lilyan Kesteloot and Gérard Dumestre, describe in their introduction as very typical of many griots in West Africa.

Kesteloot and Dumestre focus in particular on the repetition of *à kó* (he said) in lines spoken by the same character:

à kó Nyeba
à kó ń nàkun yé sìgili yé
à kó sánfedalan tà í ká ò bila dùgu mà. (lines 546–48, p. 72)

The passage offers a small but telling example of the problem of conveying African systems of poetics in translation. The rendering of these lines in French that appears on the facing page masks the poetic repetition of the original and reads instead as follows:

He said to Nyeba
"I came to sit down for a while,
"Take this mat from up there and place it on the ground." (73; my translation)

Kesteloot and Dumestre cite other poetic elements of the performance that echo some of Johnson's observations—changes in the cadence of the delivery, variations in the rhythm of a word or phrase—that do not survive the transition from tape recording to printed text. But not everything is lost in translation. They give examples of speech patterns that reflect Bamana expressions and are translated directly: the village whitens means daybreak, the price of honey mead means tax, that warms my stomach means that it irritates or surprises, they shortened him means they cut off his head. These examples of symbolic speech contribute in a variety of ways to the poetic style of the narrator.

Comparisons are also common features of Kabinè's verbal style: "as if a swarm of bees attacked them," "as if a beehive attacked them," "he made it [his horse] fly like a top, he made it fly like a calabash in the wind," "it was so clear that one could have picked up a needle on the ground." Even more common than comparisons are the metaphors that recur throughout the text as a refrain: "Dionkoloni is a nest of wasps," "Dionkoloni is a nest of scorpions." Kesteloot and Dumestre cite one metaphor that extends for several lines:

> From here to Kala,
> We say that it is the male side,
> Ségou is the female side of the river.
> Da is on the female side.
> Isn't Da none other than a woman? (26)

These devices constitute the "art" in the verbal message of the epics, but their role is more than simply artistic. Form contributes in a variety of ways to theme in these narratives. In *The Epic of Askia Mohammed*, for example, Nouhou Malio employs metaphor to convey in indirect and symbolic terms the negative character of the son who overthrew his father and tried to kill his brothers. Without ever mentioning this brutal past, he simply cites a metaphor:

644   Moussa, son of Zara, said that he is iron. . . .
648   He said that he, among his rival half-brothers, is the horn of the great
      ram. (Hale, 1990a, p. 223)

Malio also uses repetition, not simply for emphasis but also to indicate the passage of time or movement, often in the form of ideophones, words that convey meaning by sound. To describe the way a horse moves, he says the word *bal* six times to emphasize the notion of speed. Earlier in the epic, he repeats a single phrase three times ("Si continued to have the boy work, Si continued to have the boy work, Si continued to have the boy work," lines 101–3). Metonymy occurs in references to cavalry as simply "horses" in order to stress the sheer number of riders.

Comparisons sometimes appear to link past and present in a striking juxtaposition of traditional and modern images. In a passage where Askia Mohammed seeks help from his mother, he sends a *sohanci*, or sorcerer, flying through the air hundreds of miles to obtain help in the form of magic devices from Kassaye. Malio compares the flight of the *sohanci* to both a traditional referent—a hawk—and to a modern counterpart—an airplane.

> He went away from the crowd, and took off all his clothes.
> Suddenly he took off into the sky.
> The sohanci flies fast.
> They fly faster than airplanes.
> They go faster than a hawk. (Hale and Malio, 1996, p. 29, lines 404–8)

The reference to airplanes may seem to be a jarring intrusion of Western influence on a verbal form that is firmly rooted both in the past and in the artistic heritage of a particular people. But in this case, the airplane comparison in a description of a battle that occurred five centuries ago announces two features of African epic that bring us back to the question of ethno-aesthetics raised by Johnson. To understand the significance of these rhetorical links with the present, we must both draw a distinction between "early" and "recent" epics and take into account the variability of epic texts from one source to another.

Much of the collecting, transcribing, translating and publishing of epic texts during the past two decades has focused on heroes and events from approximately the eighth to the eighteenth century, a millennium that includes the three great medieval empires of the region—Ghana, Mali, and Songhay. These narratives seem to be ethnic-specific accounts of particular heroes who contributed in some way to the creation or maintenance of a society. But as we come closer to the present, in particular the late nineteenth and early twentieth centuries, external influences and references begin to appear; they include greater emphasis on religions, on technologies such as the railroad, and on European colonizers (Dieng, 1993).

At the same time, the hero begins to appeal to a wider range of people as his struggle takes on the sharper lines of *jihad* to spread Islam and mount a defensive war against an enemy armed with modern weaponry. The result is a narrative with a greater sense of immediacy. The griot who recounts *The Epic of Lat Dior* or other texts about the late nineteenth and early twentieth century is speaking about heroes who are still remembered in stories and, in some cases, photographs.

The following excerpt from a short epic text about Diery Dior Ndella Koumba offers a striking but typical example from the oral tradition of the encounter between the French and the Wolof. In this scene, the hero, a Wolof prince, is called into the office of a French officer in the city of Thiès, Senegal, to answer questions about slave-dealing. The narrative is based on an incident that occurred in April 1904.

235   Only Diery went up to the second floor.
    He entered and they offered him a seat.
    The interpreter sat down.
    The wife of the Commandant sat down.
    The Commandant raised his head and spoke volubly in French to Diery, who did not reply.
    The interpreter said to him, "Don't you know that the Toubab is speaking to you?"
    "I don't understand anything of what he is saying, just as he would not understand any that I will say to him."
    "Don't you know that I am an interpreter?"
    "What is an interpreter?"
    "Everything that he will say in French I will translate into Wolof."
    "And everything that you will say in Wolof, I will translate it into French."
    "Therefore you are a funnel?"
    "Exactly."
    "The funnel lets the oil flow.
    "And before the end of this discussion, I will say something that you will not dare translate."
    "You will not dare tell me something that I cannot translate."
    "We shall certainly see," said Diery.
    The Commandant spoke.
    "Are you Diery?" translated the interpreter.
    "Shame to him, with his red ears," Diery said to him, "even among the Lawbé, one would know right away that I am Diery."
    "He says that it is he," translated the interpreter. (Dieng, 1993, p. 457; my translation)

The encounter led to a fight during which the French officer, Lieutenant Chautemps, was mortally wounded and the hero escaped, only to be hunted down and killed a few days later (22). Incidents such as this one between the French and the Wolof remain quite vivid in the imaginations of the people of Senegal today.

Diffusion and Fluidity

The evolution of African epics in the modern period, in particular their diffusion on cassettes and on the radio, helps to nourish a narrative tradition that still competes with written forms such as the novel and the play. Epics and fragments of epics, such as those about El Hadj Omar Tall, who conquered a large part of West Africa during the late nineteenth century, have diffused from Senegal to Niger and are recounted in a variety of languages ranging from Fulbe to Zarma.

The spread of many of these epics outside their original ethnic boundaries stems from several causes: the heroes covered great distances and conquered various peoples; griots travel much more today, thanks to modern transport; and radio carries the stories across many modern political frontiers.

The versions may differ, however, depending on the local perception of the hero. The fluidity of these texts is hardly a new phenomenon, because oral texts are themselves extremely dynamic. There is no "right" version of an epic. Gordon Innes collected and published three versions of the Sundiata epic (1974) and found a variety of differences that seem to depend, as Belcher suggests, on individual rather than regional differences (1999). Each clan of griots has its own version, but differences may emerge within a clan depending on the degree of study and travel by a particular member.

These epic traditions, recorded in a variety of circumstances from the colonial era to the present, by hand and by tape recorder, constitute an extraordinary verbal maze with an incredible number of points of contact. To date, Belcher is the only scholar who has undertaken a thorough and systematic study of these various traditions and their variants, from the Wolof and Soninké narratives through the Mande world to the Songhay. His work will help us grasp for the first time the regional nature of the West African epic tradition.

Although it is widely believed that griots' words are passed down unchanged from father to son—a belief expressed to me in 1980 in no uncertain terms by the Nigérien filmmaker Oumarou Ganda—the reality is that each performance is a re-creation and reinterpretation of the past. As I have indicated, the griot may know the core episodes of the story very well, but inevitably there are too many to recount in one or even several sessions. Which ones to include will depend to a large extent on the circumstances of the performance, especially the audience. Whether or not one includes a lineage, event, or praise may depend on who is listening. Although one encounters formulaic expressions frequently in the epics, the texts are not simply a collection of formulas strung together, as the theories of Albert Lord (1960) might suggest.

While recording a version of the Zarma *Epic of Mali Bero* in the palace of the Zarmakoy, or traditional chief of the Dosso region, in Niger on March 25, 1981, I stopped the tape recording at the request of the ruler, who said a few words to the *jeseré* to the effect that he should shift his narration in a slightly different direction. Then he asked me to turn the machine back on. He wanted to be sure that I had the "right" version from his perspective—a version that included or excluded some episodes about his family or was deemed particularly appropriate for the foreign re-searcher.

A version of the rise of the Mali empire may differ considerably depend-ing on whether it is being told for the Keita clan, the descendants of the hero, or for the Traoré clan, whose ancestor, a general in Son-Jara's army, was sent to serve as governor of the Senegambian region in order to move him away from the center of events.

Esoteric Texts

Hoffman's comparison of the speech of *jeliw* and the language of *dibi*, cited earlier in this chapter, underscores the degree of obscurity in the epic. Just as the subjects of a praise song may not understand many of the words in it, audiences cannot understand all of what they hear in an epic.

In the Mande world, Jan Jansen notes, there is a hierarchy, not only of knowledge but also of expression of knowledge: "Children are not allowed to speak formulaic lines. . . . Only when jeliw become old are they considered to be able to tell epic stories in a meaningful way" (1994, 122). The result, he explains, is that there is a hierarchy in the right to express or narrate certain texts. Young people not only cannot know the meanings of texts; they also cannot pronounce the words without violating social values.

During his research to record *Sundiata* in 1958, Niane reported (5/21/98) that when he approached griots in the town of Baro in Upper Guinea, he was considered to be too young and inexperienced to listen to the master *jeli*. For this reason, Mamadou Kouyaté, a journeyman griot who was about forty years old at the time and who had traveled throughout the Mande region, was assigned to Niane to recount the epic. Kouyaté warned Niane not to seek more information than he had been given by his source.

Some of the words are so old that no one can decipher them. For example, many of the archaic Soninké words that appear in the texts by Songhay *jeserey* are undecipherable, not only by researchers but also by the griots themselves. Deformed over centuries, these words represent fading fragments of a distant heritage that has traveled a thousand miles over nearly a millennium.

That creates a problem for researchers. Should they simply skip those lines, creating a more reader-friendly text, or list them as undecipherable? A half-century ago, the answer would have been to leave out these seemingly nonfunctional and extraneous fragments. Today the focus to a much greater extent is on the accuracy of an original transcription, with all of the ambiguities, mysteries, and untranslatable items included. That is the only way to maintain the authenticity of the text. For *The Epic of Askia Mohammed* (Hale, 1990a), such an approach meant the inclusion of nearly a hundred lines of undecipherable or partially undecipherable words.

Perspective

From the foregoing it is clear that African epics — like epics elsewhere — are highly complex poetic narratives that convey the largest amount of cultural information of any of the verbal forms maintained by griots. Scholars are only beginning to understand the nature of epic in Africa, but it is increasingly clear that one cannot impose a Western framework on African epic.

Isidore Okpewho's *The Epic in Africa* (1979), the first attempt to examine the genre from a continentwide perspective, was to some degree framed in a European context in order to legitimize the notion of epic in Africa. Today, as more texts become available, it is evident that African epic must be viewed first of all from an African perspective. The results of such an approach may eventually lead to a redefinition of the epic in a global context.

⚶ ⚶

Several conclusions emerge from the evidence on verbal art presented in this chapter.

First, if it is evident that griots hold a monopoly on certain narrative forms such as praises and political epics, the monopoly does not cover all genres. Under certain circumstances, genealogies, tales, songs, even some kinds of epics may be recounted by other members of society as well — elders, grandmothers, women in general, hunters. In the Mande world, hunters have their own nonhereditary keepers of the oral tradition. The function of praise-singing may actually have come from hunters.

Second, in spite of the fact that griots share the general role of creating and transmitting verbal art with other members of society, it is clear that no single group bears as much responsibility as they do for such a wide range of functions dependent on words. The spoken word is their raw material. The forms in which their words are shaped—praises, genealogies, tales, songs, proverbs, epics—are so diverse and complex that we may justifiably call griots wordsmiths, not simply bards, for their verbal art serves a wide variety of social functions. Just as one goes to a blacksmith to have anything fabricated or repaired in metal, one normally goes to a griot for almost any affair requiring skill in verbal expression.

Third, what distinguishes hereditary griots in the heartland of the profession, the Mande world, is their membership in the group of people known as *nyamakalaw*. The words of the *jeliw* and to some extent those of their colleagues in other parts of the region carry far more meaning than the simple definitions that we may or may not able to find for them in dictionaries. This meaning is embedded in the ephemeral yet powerful "material" that griots and griottes process in order to guide people through the births, initiations, weddings, installations of chiefs, wars, and funerals that mark a society's cultural history.

Finally, if there is now widespread agreement that the epic exists in Africa, it may be time to take another step toward greater precision in nomenclature by focusing more closely on the particular features of what Johnson calls ethno-aesthetic constructs. When speaking about these narratives in a broad, comparative sense, we should certainly maintain the term *epic* as a valid descriptor. But as with the regional word *griot* and the more ethno-specific Mandinka term *jali*, it may be appropriate at this point to begin to integrate local terms for long poetic narratives into discussions about the nature of the epic genre.

The Wolof say *cosaan* or *woy jallore* for epic, praise song, tale of great exploits, and genealogical song (Kesteloot and Dieng, 1989, p. 13). For the Fulbe, it is *hoddu* (epic story as well as the lute played to accompany it; Seydou, 1972, p. 47). Among the Moors, who have a rich and complex tradition of both oral and written poetry, *thaydina* is a musical and poetic form of some length that contains both praises and accounts of deeds. It used to be reserved for great war chiefs (Guignard, 1975, p. 36). Norris points out, moreover, that unlike many other poetic forms used by the Moors, the *thaydina* is a genre limited to the *iggawen*, griots of sub-Saharan origin (1968, p. 41). In the Mandinka region of The Gambia, *tarikhou* refers to long narratives (Durán, 1995b, p. 201). In Upper Guinea, Conrad reports that the same term, *tariku*, is commonly applied to long narratives (personal communication, 1995). It comes from the Arabic term for history, *tarikh*.

Among the Bamana and Maninka, the most common words for epic are *wasala* and *maana*. *Wasala* suggests completeness, inclusion, and thorough interpretation of all events and people in the narrative. *Maana*, a more typical term for epic, does not imply such great detail (Kassim Kone, personal communication, 1995; John Willliam Johnson, personal communication, 1995; Bailleul, 1981, s.v. *maana*); it can be used for both griot narratives and hunter stories (Lucy Durán, personal communication, 1996). In Songhay, the noun for a long narrative is *deeda*, a story about the past that often involves a blend of genealogy and narrative (Hale, 1990a, p. 66).

One can only hope that a team of researchers collectively fluent in all the languages of the region will someday undertake research on this matter. The outcome might help us to understand more fully the individual cultural identity of these narratives at the same time that we situate them in the vast global family of epics.

The masks and other artwork taken from Africa by colonial-era collectors often seem to have lost their power when exhibited in museums today. In the same way, the printed words of griots seem to have lost the power they had when sung or uttered in performance. Words on the printed page, like masks in a display case, cannot convey the atmosphere of the event at which they were expressed. If it is difficult for us to grasp fully the nuances of African systems of prosody from the printed text, it is even harder to comprehend the power that lies behind the mask of words created by griots and griottes. One reason for that difficulty is that these words are so often spoken or sung in a synergistic blend of voice and another medium, music, the subject of the next chapter.

✵ 4 ✵
Music across the Griot World

It is difficult to separate the musical art of griots and griottes from their vocal art. The two forms work together in a synergistic fashion that produces a powerful effect on audiences and often surprises those who seek to learn about one or the other in isolation.

When Banning Eyre, the American guitarist and writer, went to Mali in 1996 to learn more about instrumental music there, he discovered during a seven-month stay with Jeli Madi Tounkara that the words were far more important than the music. While he learned much about guitar technique from his mentor, the unusual power of the words sung by the *jelimusow* at weddings and naming ceremonies where he served as a backup musician came as a surprise (National Public Radio, October 17).

By contrast, the American linguist Charles Bird learned that his quest for Bamana words could not be carried out effectively until he understood the link with the music that accompanied them. Bird was studying Bamana syntax in 1966 and teaching in a training program for Malian English instructors. He had explored as many kinds of syntax permutations as he could find when he finally decided to seek new variants that might occur in much longer forms of speech than what he had been using for his research. Malian colleagues recommended that he work with a griot. Eventually Bird arranged for a Bamana *jeli* from Ségou, Amadou Diabaté, to come to his office in Bamako. Diabaté arrived with an *ngoni*, a four-stringed lute, and began to sing. Bird recollects: "I was nonplussed by it. I wanted language to analyze syntactically. The music was interfering a lot. . . . I couldn't use the data. I asked him to come back without the instrument. This time he drummed on the table. He needed something to drive his language. That struck me — there was an organizing force in the language" (Bird and Kendall, 1988).

Bird's discovery of the importance of music for the verbal art of the griot does not mean that everything said, chanted, or sung—genealogy, epic, praise—must be accompanied by music. But it underscores the fact that music is a common and highly significant feature of most Mande verbal art. The same may be said of griots elsewhere, from the Wolof in Senegal to the Hausa in Niger and northern Nigeria, though many features of the local and regional nature of their music await further research.

For the European traveler to Senegal in the seventeenth century who visited a ruler surrounded by griots chanting praises or for a modern music lover who goes to a concert in New York that features a vocal performance by a griotte, the new musical experience may produce both fascination and a variety of questions. Do all griots play the *kora* or do those from other parts of West Africa play different instruments? Why is the *kora* played only by men? What kinds of instruments do women play? How large is the repertoire of these musicians?

The answers to these questions underscore the regional nature of the profession and help explain the relationship between the genders of its practitioners as well as the way the music of griots is diffused outside of Africa. But there is far more to the musical world of griots than can be suggested by these questions and presented in a single chapter. For readers who are deeply interested in the music of griots, from notation systems to variations in performance styles, the work of the ethnomusicologists cited in this chapter provides the kind of detail that falls outside the scope of this study.

The purpose here is more modest: first, to answer the basic questions listed above by drawing on the relatively limited body of research available to date, and second, to encourage future researchers to focus on some of the many other areas that call for more study.

Much of what is now known comes from the work of three pioneering ethnomusicologists: Roderic Knight, Lucy Durán, and Eric Charry. Knight, professor of ethnomusicology and the history of music at Oberlin, wrote his 1973 dissertation on Mandinka *jaliya*. In it he defined the basic repertoire, described the instruments (especially the *kora*), identified the major stylisic features of the vocal music, and explained the relationship between the two fundamental components, the instrumental and the vocal. Although Knight's work was limited to the Mandinka, it provided in many ways a benchmark for future research on griots and their music across West Africa. Durán, a musicologist who is now a lecturer at the School of Oriental and African Studies, University of London, began to study Gambian, Senegalese, and Malian music in the late 1970s. During the past 15 years, her research, appearing in a series of articles and chapters, has opened up an entire new dimension for our understanding of the female side of the griot profession. Charry, associate professor of ethnomusicology at Wesleyan University, completed in 1992 a landmark dissertation on music from the entire Mande world that provides for the first time a holistic view of the largest and most influential musical tradition in the griot diaspora.

The information in this chapter is based on the work of Knight, Durán, and Charry, as well as that of others who have contributed to our understanding of griot music and its impact, including Susan Gunn Pevar (1977, 1978), Michael Coolen (1991), Lynne Jessup (1983), and Kate Modic (1996).

Although the influence of music produced by griots extends from West Africa to world music and from past to present, the emphasis here will be on the traditional context. Changes in the past decade or two will be reflected in chapters 7 and 8.

Instruments: Diffusion and Confusion

The terms for instruments, like the terms for griots, reflect local languages, not necessarily local differences in the way the instruments are played. The *ngoni*, or lute, that Amadou Diabaté played for Bird differs only slightly in size and number of strings from its cousins, the Wolof *xalam* and the Songhay *molo*. In "Plucked Lutes in West Africa: An Historical Overview," Charry has provided the best introduction to the regional similarities and differences between these instruments (1996b).

In spite of the widespread occurrence of these plucked lutes, it is the *kora*, or harp-lute, that represents the profession to the outside world. Although recordings of the *xalam* and similar lutes are available, the *jali* or *jeli* with the *kora* remains the most common image of the griot that one finds in an American university auditorium, a coffeehouse in Greenwich Village, on the cover of a CD in a music store in Paris, or a flyer advertising the fact that French is spoken in Africa. The reason for the difference between the "domestic" *ngoni* and the "export" *kora* is bound up in the complex interaction of music, ethnicity, and audience.

Any attempt to explain the riddle of the *ngoni* and its cousins versus the *kora* must begin with a survey of the occurrence of all the major instruments played by griots across the region, a topic that could require an entire book. Charry has come closest to this goal in his dissertation, "Musical Thought, History, and Practice among the Mande of West Africa" (1992), a study that includes a wide range of instruments, not all of which are played by griots. The instruments he describes can be analyzed or categorized with traditional European descriptors, but these terms often fail to provide insight into the way Mande peoples think about them.

Charry points out in his chapter on Mande melody instruments, for example, that the European system of classification of instruments by the mechanisms they use for making sounds does not work in West Africa. Although both griots and hunters play different kinds of harps, there is little overlap between the two musical worlds of these distinct groups in society.

> Even though the playing techniques of the *kora* and the various hunters' harps are similar, they live in two different musical realms. It is much more common to find one person playing both the guitar and *balafon*, or to have a *kora* player whose father played the *koni* (lute) because they are all *jeli* instruments. The fact that the playing techniques may be quite different is not as critical as the fact that *jeli* instruments live in their own world apart from hunters' instruments. (87)

The Lute

Discussion of instruments played by griots must begin with the lute (figure 5) rather than the *kora* because the lute "is probably the oldest melody instrument used by griots, dating back perhaps many centuries before it was first mentioined by Al-'Umāri and Ibn Battuta in the fourteenth century" (Charry, 1996b, p. 9). One reason for the deep roots of the lute is its widespread occurrence. With slight variations in size, shape (some curve in slightly at the waist of the resonator), and number of strings (two to five), it can be found under different names with various spellings across the continent. In West Africa alone one finds the following: Wolof—*xalam, xhalam* or *khalam*; Fulbe—*hoddu*; Soninké—*gambare*; Moor—*tidinit*; Maninka and Bamana—*koni, n'koni* or *ngoni*; Mandinka—*kontingo*; Songhay, Zarma, and Hausa—*molo*. The similarity in many spelling variants (*koni, konting, kontingo, nkoni, ngoni*) underscores the fact of the instrument's diffusion.

Durán describes the *xalam* in the following way:

> A boat-shaped resonator is carved from a single piece of hardwood . . . A piece of cowskin is stretched over and nailed to the back of the resonator, either by nails covered with decorated studs or by small wooden pegs. The cylindrical fretless wooden neck . . . pierces the skin sound table at one end and emerges three-quarters of the way towards the other end, acting as a tail piece for the strings. The five strings, nowadays made from two twisted strings of nylon but formerly of horsehair, are tied at the upper end to tuning rings . . . made from

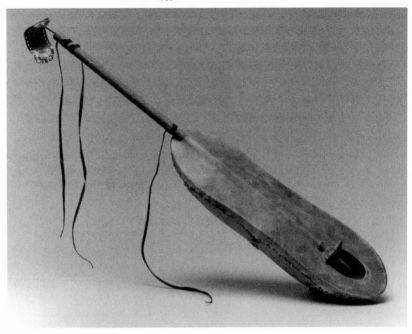

5. Photo of lute by Dwain Harbst.

narrow strips of goat skin wound around the neck. The lower ends of the strings pass over a detachable bridge . . . of calabash fitted on the emerging end of the neck, and are tied to anchor threads which are secured by winding them tightly around the tailpiece. Of the five strings, only two are stopped with the left hand in first position though all five are used to play the melody. (1981, p. 30)

Among each group of peoples, there are many variants. The Wolof, for example, distinguish four kinds of *xalam*: the *diassaré*, the *bappe*, the *n'déré*, and the *molo*. The term *molo*, found as far east as the Hausa-speaking peoples of Nigeria and Niger, underscores the diffusion of nomenclature and the instruments, perhaps the result of migration by the Fulbe (Charry, 1996b, p. 13), while *diassaré*, similar to Soninké and Songhay terms for griot (*gesseré, jarre*, and *jeseré, jasaré*), seems to support his suggestion that the instrument may have come from the Ghana empire.

Charry refers to two bits of evidence that point in Ghana's direction. The first is *Gassire's Lute*, the story that was recorded in 1909 from a Soninké *diari* (*jaare*) in northern Benin by the German anthropologist Leo Frobenius. In Alta Jablow's translation from Frobenius's 1921 German text, there are several references to the lute ordered by the warrior hero as a wooden instrument, thus distinguishing it clearly from the calabash-based *kora*. The other bit of evidence is the fact that no other people in the region have claimed that they invented the lute. Neither clue—one from a single Soninké source who is very far from home and whose text has come down to us without the original transcription, the other an argument from silence—is convincing by itself, but added to the link between the Soninké term for lute (*diassaré*) and the Songhay term for griot (*jeseré*), these clues suggest that further research in the oral traditions of the Soninké and in early Arabic texts from West Africa may offer the most fruitful avenue to follow in the search for the origin of the lute.

One could argue, based on the parallel between Arabic *ud* and Fulbe *hoddu* as well as many similarities with ancient Egyptian instruments, that the lute came from North Africa. But Charry finds the linguistic link alone to be unconvincing, and casts doubt on the tie with early Egyptian instruments. The early Egyptian lute was played by women, not men, and with a plectrum near where the neck meets the body rather than farther down over the middle of the resonator. It had a different bridge and was fitted with three strings that may have been tuned in unison. The neck was threaded through the body in several places, and the neck and body proportions were different from the sub-Saharan version of the lute (Charry, 1996b, pp. 17–18). (See figure 6.)

Charry concludes that there needs to be considerably more research on African lutes before we can arrive at any conclusion, not simply about links between Egypt and West Africa but also about the direction of any influence—east to west or west to east.

There is also continuing scholarly discussion about possible links between the West African lute and the banjo in the United States. Michael Coolen sees many parallels, framed by the history of traffic in slaves, between the Senegambian region and the United States. He explains that the *xalam* is played with two melody strings and two or three drone strings, similar to the banjo, which has one drone string. The playing of the *xalam* also resembles some traditional banjo-playing styles such as "claw-hammer" in which the fingers play the melody and the thumb plays the drone (Coolen, 1991, pp. 13–14).

6. Sketch of woman playing Egyptian lute.
From Manniche, 1991.

Cecilia Conway searched written records to find references to the banjo in this country that date back to 1754 for her study *African Banjo Echoes in Appalachia* (1995). Based on the features of the banjo in this country as well as other evidence, she posits the existence of an African "protobanjo" (190). From the largely African American evidence she presents, it is not entirely clear that the banjo comes from the griot region of West Africa, where the most common instrument of griots, the lute, has a wooden sound chamber rather than the calabash sound chamber typical of early banjos, or if it comes from some other area, such as Ghana. Whether or not the West African lute is the ancestor of the banjo, however, it seems fairly evident now that the banjo has roots in Africa and that there are enough similarities between the diverse stringed instruments played by griots and the banjo to call for further study.

If subsequent research eventually reveals that the West African lute somehow fits into a historical continuum from the ancient Egyptians to African Americans, one reason for the diffusion of the instrument may turn out to be its simplicity of construction and portability. The wooden walls of the resonator, a relatively fragile part of many stringed instruments, are at least a half-inch thick and do not break easily. The lute can be tuned, strummed, carried, and repaired with relative ease. It contrasts with the *kora*, which is sturdy in comparison with a European violin or harp, yet more bulky and less solid than the lute.

The Kora

Unlike the lute with its many names, the *kora* appears to have been invented somewhere in the Senegambian region, apparently by the Mandinka of the Gabu empire, which included parts of The Gambia, the Casamance region of southern Senegal, and Guinea Bissau, farther south (Charry, 1990a, p. 152). It was not until the twentieth century that its use spread eastward to other parts of the Mande diaspora in Mali and northern Guinea (154–55).

There is no Western term for *kora* that can convey an image of the instrument the way the word *lute* describes the guitarlike *ngoni* and its cousins. The most widespread definition of *kora* is "harp-lute." But Knight and Charry believe that "bridge harp" is the best way of describing it.

The *kora* (figure 7) is a rather complex instrument compared with the lute and therefore requires a somewhat more detailed description. Knight (1996) describes it in the following way:

> The body is made from a large half calabash, from 40–50 centimeters in diameter, covered with cowhide from which the hair has been removed. The covering reaches two thirds of the way around the curved sides of the calabash, leaving a shallow dome of the natural surface exposed. The covered portion of the calabash wall is decorated with upholstery tacks in geometric or pictorial designs. A second hole, either round or square, is also cut in this decorated band, near where the right hand holds the instrument.
>
> The player traditionally sits on the floor, holding the instrument with the cowhide facing him and the rounded back of the calabash facing the listeners. The neck, or *falo*—a stout pole of African rosewood—towers above him at 120–130 centimeters. The neck pierces or "spikes" the body vertically and the lower end forms a tailpiece on which the instrument rests.
>
> The player holds the instrument by two wooden handgrips flanking the neck and parallel to it, and plucks the strings with the forefingers and thumbs. The handgrips are long, extending beneath the skin to the lower rim of the body where they reappear. They bear the pressure exerted by the bridge, which rests

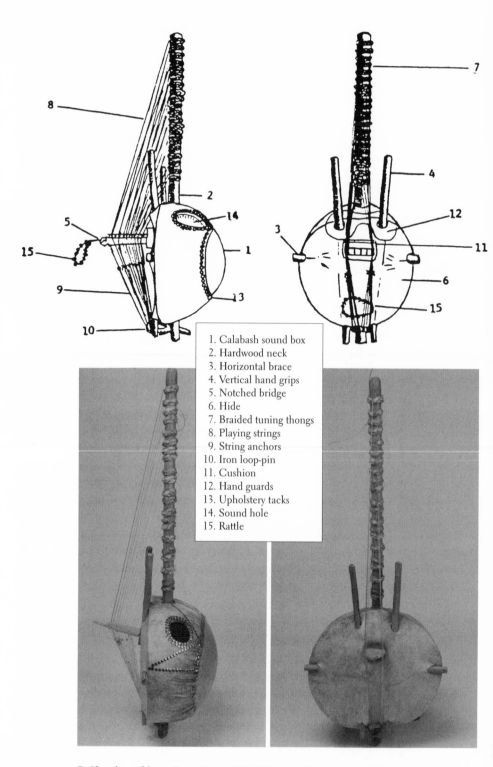

1. Calabash sound box
2. Hardwood neck
3. Horizontal brace
4. Vertical hand grips
5. Notched bridge
6. Hide
7. Braided tuning thongs
8. Playing strings
9. String anchors
10. Iron loop-pin
11. Cushion
12. Hand guards
13. Upholstery tacks
14. Sound hole
15. Rattle

7. Sketches of *kora*. From Pevar, 1977. Photos of *kora* by David Shelley.

between them and just above a crossbar that is also pinned behind the skin. In addition to their practical function, the handgrips can be decorative as well. They are usually cut longer than necessary and carved. In addition, the right handgrip has a musical function: some pieces call for the player to strike it with the forefinger, producing a resonant thump—a technique called *bulukondingo podi*.

The strings (*julo*), made of graded strengths of nylon monofilament line, are attached to the neck via rawhide collars (*konso*) woven in a "Turk's Head" knot. The instrument is tuned by adjusting the collars up or down. Stretching from these collars to an iron ring at the base of the instrument, the strings diverge into two rows and pass over notches cut in the sides of the upright bridge (*bato*). At this point the two rows are essentially parallel to each other, with eleven strings on the left, ten on the right. From the iron ring at the base, forged and then burned into place by a blacksmith, anchor strings reach up to meet the playing strings. Each playing string is tied to its anchor string with a weaver's knot just below the bridge. Before the importation of nylon fishing line in the mid-20th century, kora strings were made from rawhide. The laborious process involved cutting long thin strips, twisting them to form a round cross-section, then stretching each one on a bow to dry.

As suggested by Charry, the origin of the *kora* probably lies in a hunter's instrument, either the Mandinka *simbingo*, a harp with six to ten strings played by hunters' musicians (Knight, 1973, pp. 15–16), or the *donsongoni*, with six strings in two rows.

The strings of the *kora* are held in place above the calabash resonator by a wooden bridge that has shallow grooves cut into each side (figure 8). Ten strings go up the right side of the bridge, as Knight described, while eleven are placed on the left side. The result is two rows of roughly parallel strings. For information on how a *kora* is constructed, see the research of Susan Gunn Pevar (1977, 1978) and Sue Carole DeVale (1989).

The *kora* is a fairly strong instrument, but it is subject to damage in a variety of ways—cracking of the calabash resonator or breaking or displacement of the bridge, which is held in place by the downward tension of the strings. Griots who travel by airplane cannot check a *kora* as luggage without risking considerable damage.

The Ardin

The ten- to thirteen-stringed *ardin*, another harplike instrument (figure 9), differs in many ways from the *kora*. It is played by women *tiggawaten* in Mauritania.

Although the *ardin* is based, like the *kora*, on a calabash resonator

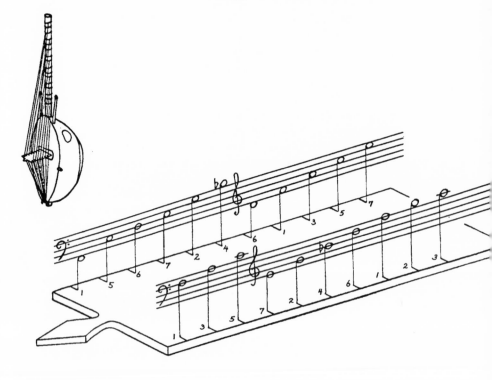

8. Sketch of the bridge of the *kora*. From Knight.

covered by an animal skin and fitted with a long neck and a row of strings placed in vertical, harplike positions, the instrument's calabash is smaller, perhaps twelve to eighteen inches in diameter. The neck is thinner, and instead of fitting across the skin-covered opening, it extends upward at an angle, with the foot of the neck resting on the inside of the calabash so that when the resonator is sitting in the position of a bowl on a flat surface, the neck juts upward from one side. The sheepgut strings are attached to the neck on pegs and to the resonator via a horizontal dowel inserted in the skin covering.

Unlike the *kora*, which is played with the strings facing the male musician, the *ardin* is played like a Western harp with the strings facing away from the *tiggiwit*.

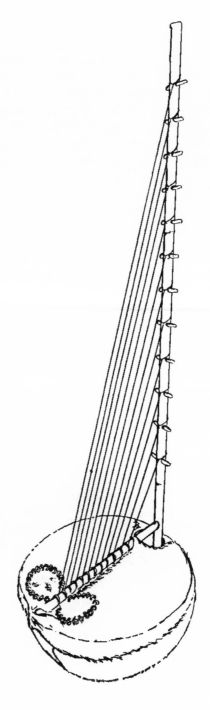

9. Sketch of *ardin*. From La Courbe,
1913, reprinted in Norris, 1968.

The Balafon

The *balafon* is a xylophone made of a series of tuned hardwood bars, or keys, resting on a bamboo frame under which are suspended small calabashes that serve as resonators. The number of keys and the shape of the *balafon* can vary considerably from one musician to the next but normally ranges from seventeen to twenty-two (figure 10).

The musician plays the instrument either sitting on the ground or, with the aid of a cloth strap, standing. The playing sticks are made of hardwood with the striking ends wound with rubber from a rubber tree or from the inner tube of a tire.

Played by men, the *balafon* is one of the oldest instruments in the Mande world. The earliest written reference for West Africa occurs in Ibn Battuta's account of his trip to the kingdom of Mali in 1353, and travelers since then have often mentioned the instrument or drawn pictures of it.

10. Sketch of griot playing the *balafon*. From Dubois.

The most widespread tale of origin for the *balafon* is that found in the various versions of the Sundiata epic. According to this story, the enemy of the Mande, Sumanguru (also Sumamuru), king of Sosso, owned the original *balafon*. When Sundiata's personal *jeli* was sent to Sumanguru on a diplomatic mission, he discovered the ruler's *balafon* and began to play it. Sumanguru decided to keep him there. Only later, when Sundiata's army conquered Sumanguru, did the *jeli* gain his freedom. Then he began to spread the *balafon* to the rest of the Mande world. What is reputed to be the original *balafon*, known as the Sosso-Balla, is kept today in Niagassola, Guinea, by members of the Kouyaté clan of *jeliw*.

In the following passage from *The Epic of Son-Jara*, Fa-Digi Sisòkò links the origin of the *balafon* with the Kouyaté clan (the responses to the right of each line are from the *naamunaamuna* [*naamu*—yes, indeed], the man who responds to each line of the narrative).

1786 At that time, the bards did not have balaphones . . .   (True)
1790 None but Susu Mountain Sumamuru.   (Indeed)

(Johnson and Sisòkò, 1992, p. 68)

While Sumamuru is off fighting, the *jeli*, known as Dòka the Cat, obtains the *balafon* mallets from a hawk, who keeps them in the owner's absence, and learns to play the instrument. When Sumamuru returns, he asks the *jeli* to play and is so impressed by the song and the music from the *balafon* that he decides to keep him.

1859 He said, "Ah! what is your name?"
      "My name is Dòka the Cat."   (Mmm)
      "Will you not remain with me?"
      "Not I! Two kings I cannot praise.
      "I am Son-Jara's bard.
      "From the Manden I have come,
      "And to the Manden I must return."   (True)
      He laid hold of the Kuyatè patriarch,
      And severed both Achilles tendons,
      And by the Susu balaphone set him.   (Indeed)
      "Now what is your name?"   (Indeed)
      "Dòka the Cat is still my name."   (Indeed)
      "Dòka the Cat will no longer do."   (Indeed)
      He drew water and poured it over his head   (Indeed)
      And shaved it clean,   (Indeed)
1874 And gave him the name of Bala Faseke Kuyatè. (70)

The Drums

Charry describes three kinds of drums played in the Mande world—two beaten by *jeliw* and one by non-*jeliw* (1992, pp. 173–80).

The hourglass-shaped *tama*, found not only in the Mande region but also throughout the Sahel and Savanna (it is called *kalangu* among the Hausa) ranges from eight to eighteen inches long and is fitted with heads whose sound can be varied by changing tension on the cords that hold them in place. The drummer holds the instrument under his arm and varies the sound by squeezing the strings against the narrower part of the barrel. He strikes the top head with a curved stick held in one hand and with the fingers of his other hand. Among the Dagbamba of northern Ghana, whose hereditary drummers were influenced by the northern Nigerian tradition, a similar drum is called the *lunsi*.

The larger *dundun* drum, fourteen inches or more in diameter and over two feet long, produces a deeper bass sound. It is played with two sticks as an accompaniment to the *jembe*. Charry notes that among the Xasonke (also spelled Khassonké), it is played only by the *jeli*. In northern Ghana, the Dagbamba drummers play the *gun-gon*, a drum similar to the *dundun*, beaten with only one curved stick.

The *jembe*, an instrument not usually played by griots, is a goblet-shaped drum held between the legs of the musician and played with the hands. It is usually about thirty inches tall, with a narrowed lower part, perhaps six inches in diameter. The top is shaped like a large bowl. Associated with blacksmiths in the Maninka and Susu regions of Mali and Guinea, the *jembe* is one of those instruments that can be played by both hereditary griot musicians as well as non-hereditary performers. Charry (1996a, pp. 67–68) finds that the names of *jembe* players often reflect either blacksmith or noble origin, but not usually *jeli* roots. Although "it is uncommon for jelis to play the jembe, perhaps because they recognize that it is not one of their instruments," one can find examples of griots who have adopted the instrument. The most evident example is Adama Dramé. Charry suggests one explanation for Dramé's adoption of a traditionally non-griot instrument. "While jelis in core Mande areas recognize that the *jembe* is not one of their instruments, in more distant areas this tradition may have been transformed, hence Adama Dramé's assertion that the *jembe* is a *jeli* instrument in Burkina Faso."

In Mauritania, the large *t'bal* drum, similar to a kettle drum, was once played to announce wars but today is used to accompany songs about bravery or combat. Women *tiggawaten* as well as male *iggawen* play the *t'bal* by hand. In other parts of the Sahel, women also play drums. There are cases of women in the Mande who play drums but are not *jelimusow*.

The Karinya

Like the *ardin*, the *karinya* (also *karinyan, karanyango, nege,* or *newo*) is one of the few instruments played primarily by women. It is a type of tubular bell made from a piece of pipe or a rectangle of iron rolled into a tube about six to eight inches long and about an inch in diameter. The instrument is pierced with a hole on one side and a slit running the full length on the other side. A string running through the hole and between the middle and index fingers is wrapped around the middle finger on one hand. The musician holds a metal striker, or awl, called the *loyo*, in the other hand and hits the bell. With the *newo* braced across the left palm and the *loyo* held close in her right hand, she rotates her wrists, striking the bell near one end, then on the other. The volume can be soft or loud and festive.

Nege, one of the words for this bell in The Gambia, is a generic term that means "iron" or any metal instrument. In Mali, *karinya* or *karinyan* is more typical. Durán notes that though the instrument is played mainly by women, hunters and male Khassonké griots, or *jalis*, also play it. The difference, however, is that they scrape the instrument rather than strike it.

Instrumental Icon: The *Kora*

In spite of the widespread diffusion of the different variations on the lute, it is the *kora* that serves as the instrumental icon of griots outside Africa. For example, Durán noted in 1981 that there was not a single recording devoted entirely to the Wolof *xalam* on a European or American label, even though *xalam* music is heard often on the radio and is widely available in the local commercial market (29).

There are at least three reasons why the lute remains relatively unknown. First, for outsiders who do not know the languages of the songs, the attraction of griots lies more in the instrumental music than in the verbal art. In this context, the *kora* appears as a far more complex and fascinating instrument than the *xalam*. Those who encounter a *kora* for the first time are amazed by its construction and the delicate sounds it produces, which, Durán notes, give "a superficial impression of the flamenco guitar" (1978,

p. 754). Second, the *kora* originated on the extreme west coast of Africa, an area that has had contact with Europe for centuries. Musicians there have been traveling to France and the Britain for generations to perform for audiences at colonial expositions and other events featuring the cultures of Africa. During the past few decades, some of the Mandinka *jalolu* from The Gambia who claim that their ancestors invented the *kora* have broken into the Western entertainment world with a success that seems at first to be out of all proportion to the size of their tiny country. Third, the *kora* has grown in popularity during the past century, according to Durán's informants, because of a Mandinka *jali* named Jali Madi Wuleng and his student, Koriying Musa Suso, who served Kelefa Saane, a warrior whose tune became the first song composed for the *kora* as well as the apprentice's first tune to learn (1978, p. 755).

Durán suggests that one other reason why the *kora* has come to overshadow the other instruments, the *kontingo* lute and the *balafon*, "is because of its wider melodic range and flexibility of tuning" (755). It is perhaps this range and the parallels with Spanish music that have prompted the entertainment industry in Europe and the United States to show more interest in producing recordings of *kora* music than other kinds.

The external appreciation of music produced by griots is thus heavily biased toward the *kora*. It is a bias that may diminish over time, depending on changing musical tastes outside Africa, the ability of griots who play lutes to gain wider entry to external audiences, and changes in the mix of griots and griottes who travel to new venues. Paradoxically, because of its complexity, the *kora* serves both to attract new audiences to the art of the griot and to blind these listeners to the larger dimensions of the music produced by lute-players in Africa.

Instrument, Gender, and Venue

Why is the *kora* played only by men, while the *ardin* is plucked by women? What are the deeper gender meanings associated with the music of griots? Why are some events where music is played viewed as "male" while others are "female"?

When asked why only men play the *kora*, griots simply reply that it is a man's instrument and the women have their *karinyan*, or *nege*. The only women who play the *kora* appear to be female researchers who studied the instrument and its music from a scholarly perspective. Knight explains that "a fair number of non-African women are taking up the *kora* and coming to Africa to study it" after first working with griots such as Jali Nyama Suso who have come to the United States for academic residencies (1987, p. 8). Their acceptance as students by male griots may reflect two mitigating conditions: first, the non-African women come to the instrument from an external social context for which the local rules do not automatically apply; second, the interest of these women is not in becoming a *jalimuso* but is more focused on the musical properties of the instrument itself.

What little we know about the gender orientation of the *kora* is based to a large extent on speculation. Durán, drawing on Knight's theory that the *kora* is descended from the hunter's harp, sees this link to a traditionally male group as the source of the instrument's masculine identity. Knight suggests another, simpler explanation that covers a wide range of instruments: in black Africa men play the melody (personal communication, 1996).

As for the lute, it too is most commonly played by men, although it does not seem to suffer from the same absolute masculine identity as the *kora*. One can find occasional exceptions such as Igudu, the Fulbe wife of Al Haji Garba Bagna in Niamey, who accompanied her husband on the *molo* when he performed.

The *balafon* appears to be a clearly defined masculine instrument, perhaps because of its origin in the oral tradition of the Sundiata epic or because it is an instrument that requires a certain amount of strength to carry and play with any vigor, a reflection of men's self-image as the stronger sex.

The only instruments that are reserved almost exclusively for women, the *ardin* and *karinya*, or *nege*, do not seem to offer particular evidence for their gender orientation. In fact, Knight cites exceptions such as hunter's harp music accompanied by a *neo* scraped by men. More research is needed to give a clearer picture of the gender specificity of all instruments.

No matter what the gender attributes of these instruments, however, they are often played together by a group of musicians. Ensembles composed of a *kora*, *xalam*, *balafon*, and *nege*, or *tidinit*, *ardin*, *t'bal*, and tambourine are typical.

The question of venue for these instruments remains a puzzle open to a variety of interpretations. Sory Camara (1976, pp. 116–18) distinguishes between instruments played at ceremonies involving mainly women and those played at events for men. Drums are beaten most often at events organized for or by women while stringed instruments are played for male events, with the *balafon* serving at both. Camara asserts that participation in women's events weakens a griot's image, while participation in men's events strengthens it. That may be true for the Malinké he describes, but it is not evident that this distinction applies in other parts of the region. If this were the case, for example, among the Songhay and Zarma of Niger, where women appear to be the primary and most frequent clients of griots, there would be no *jeserey* of any repute left.

Camara wonders if the distinction between men's and women's events may have something to do with the effect of the music on the emotions and the attention of the audience. He suggests that drums as instruments of rhythm are particularly appropriate for dancing. The sounds "provoke intense visceral reactions" that tend to carry the individual away. He speculates that the sudden release of tension by dancing to drums may be an escape valve for women in a male-centered society where they cannot contest male authority. His observation that women don't make war but do dance suggests a social dichotomy that appears far too simplistic.

Drawing on a psychoanalytic approach, Camara proposes that the "psychophysiological effects" produced by instrumental melodies are interiorized by men and then somehow focused in other directions rather than immediate release. The gender distinction he makes seems to be highly speculative and somewhat too dependent on an approach that may not withstand closer analysis.

Singing Style

Perhaps the most important instrument used by both griots and griottes is the human voice. Singing in general in the Mande world is divided into two kinds. The first kind is *donkilo* or, as Durán (1978, p. 736) describes it, "'song,' that is, a fixed melody and text which recurs at different intervals of a performance." It is sung at a leisurely pace, often in chorus. The second kind is *sataro*, "'narration,' that is, improvised text, without any metrical scheme, either spoken, or recited to a syllabically set musical line" and performed solo. Durán notes that most *kora* pieces include both kinds. Knight adds that any song accompanied on any instrument can have *sataro* (narration) added to the basic *donkilo* (song), and in many cases *sataro* dominates the performance (personal communication, 1996).

Both men and women sing while performing, though the importance of women's singing varies by region. Knight (1971) explains that a *ngaraa*, or highly talented singer in Mande society, is one who can, in the words of *ngaraa* Nyulo Jobarteh, "split the air with singing, stand before crowds without flinching, and compose words that roll off her tongue with fluidity and clarity, so that her audience understands the content of the text and is moved by it." Knight adds that the singing styles of men and women are identical but the technique is different because men sing at the top of their register while women sing at the bottom of theirs (personal communication, 1996). And he writes: "The greatest compliment that can be paid to a male singer (though this is never done directly) is to equate the beauty of his voice with that of a woman's" (1987, p. 3).

Within the Mande world, styles of singing vary from east (Mali and upper Guinea) to west (Gambia and Senegal), Knight explains (1987, p. 3). The eastern style (*Tilibo*) is slow and majestic: "These are the older songs, with much room for improvisation by the singer, and they are the ones at which the women excel." The western-style (*Tiliji*) songs "are faster and show a greater emphasis on instrumental virtuosity. They are generally composed for the *kora* rather than the *balo*, and the player himself usually does the singing." Knight wonders whether there was a shortage of *jali musolu* in the west during the days of expansion of the Mali empire, a situation that might have led to a greater emphasis on *jali keolu*, or men griots, in the performance context. Whatever the result, today men dominate in the west while women have taken over the stage in the east (Hale, 1994). Durán has explored the phenomenon in more detail in her provocatively titled article "Savannah Sex Wars" (1993b).

There are many similarities between Mandinka and Wolof or Serer singing styles, Durán notes (1981, pp. 32–33). Women singers in both cultures are viewed as more talented than men, and they "cultivate a loud, strident tone of voice which falls off at the ends of phrases." But Wolof singing, unlike Mandinka, includes a blend of choral refrain and recitative by a solo singer. Durán adds that Wolof women singers value close synchronization by mouthing the words of the next line to each other during instrumental interludes. They appear to have two separate styles, one for accompaniment by the *xalam* and another for accompaniment by a water drum made of an overturned enamel bowl or a gourd.

Hausa singing styles are quite diverse, depending on gender and context (Mack, 1981). Furniss (1996) offers examples of the group singing tradition of Mamman Shata, one of the most famous performers of northern Nigeria, which shares a common border with Niger that cuts through the Hausa-speaking region. The lead singer in his group, Shata composes the chorus refrains (*amshi*).

He . . . feeds them to the *'yan amshi* "members of the chorus" . . . his initial verbal phrases provide his lead drummer with the cue upon which to build in making the drum phrases that will accompany his songs. Operating with as many as six or seven men in his chorus and another five or six drummers using,

among others, the variable pitch hourglass drum, the *kalangu*, Mamman Shata
will sing his verses of variable length before his '*yan amshi* mark time with,
usually, a two-line refrain. (132)

Furniss also describes a variety of more complicated patterns of lead singer
and chorus, as well as examples of accompaniment on a variety of instruments ranging from the single-stringed lute to the upturned water drum
(135–36).

What emerges from Furniss's descriptions are many similarities between the musical tradition of Nigeria and neighboring Niger, much
diffusion westward through the Songhay-speaking area, and some features
found farther west in Senegal—for example, the lead and chorus.

Repertoire

The instrumental and vocal music produced by griots and griottes takes
form in a wide variety of songs. The examples of songs given in the
preceding chapter on verbal art give a hint of what is conveyed. Here a brief
survey of the musical repertoires—sung and played on instruments—will
give a clearer sense of the range of music performed.

In the Mande region, Charry (1992, p. 234) points out that the music of
jeliw, like that of other groups such as hunters, has its own corpus of pieces
that are linked together as part of a long tradition and also as part of a
heritage tied to a particular instrument. Each piece has a name, usually
that of the hero who is the subject. Charry estimates that the number of
pieces a *jeli* knows may be hundreds, but he adds that the most important
ones number perhaps twenty or thirty. The length of a performance of one
song can vary from a few minutes to an hour or much longer.

Knight has inventoried the Mandinka *jali* repertoire, but as yet no one
has assembled a much broader inventory for the entire region. The closest
listing of this nature is a chart by Charry (1992, p. 245) that represents on
a map abbreviated listings of some of the most important pieces played by
Mande *jeliw*.

The time periods covered by the pieces listed by Charry range from the
founding of the empire almost to the present. But these differences are
rather fluid and dynamic. Songs from the past are constantly reinterpreted
and transformed in the present. Charry explains that

two very common techniques for generating new pieces in the Mande repertory are to lay new words on top of the same instrumental accompaniment and
to alter an already existing instrumental accompaniment. . . . The parent-child

relationship of some pieces is common knowledge and is readily talked about as such among many musicians: *Saxo Dugu* comes from *Duga, Jula Jekere* from *Janjon,* and *Jaka* from *Hamaba Jata.* The relationship between these pieces may be far removed from each other in terms of region, instrument of origin, or tuning system, but once recognized they do give insight into Mande ways of musical transformation. (252)

These pieces are played at a variety of events, but Charry warns against attempts to define them in terms of functions, because the web of history, circumstance of performance, and many other factors contribute in too many other ways to the meaning of a song to limit it to a song label (235). For example, a popular tune in the repertoire of Mandinka griots, "Kelefa Saane," is about the late-nineteenth-century warrior who never conquered great swaths of territory or became king of a large empire. But, as Gordon Innes explains, there is something in the qualities manifested by the hero that inspires listeners to call for this song (1976, p. 9). On the other end of the historical spectrum, songs about Sundiata or Son-Jara Keita, the man who founded the Mali empire, are widespread, occurring in both traditional and modern contexts and as parts of epics. The meaning of Sundiata for the Mande is so complex and deeply rooted that it is difficult to classify or quantify.

To grasp the meaning of the repertoires, one can approach them from many angles. Charry lists several: by patron and ethnic group, as seen in the wide distribution among five different peoples in a study by Knight of fifty pieces played by Mandinka kora players; by subject, as seen in the extensive network of songs rooted in the story of Sundiata; by age, as described by Knight: early (thirteenth to fourteenth centuries); mid (nineteenth and early twentieth centuries); and late (last forty years); and by instrument and region (*kora* in the Senegambian region, *ngoni* in Mali, *balafon* in Guinea) (Charry, 1992, pp. 250–53).

Mode

Another way of looking at the music of griots is through the different modes that govern its presentation, though the term *mode* itself is open to multiple interpretations and may in some cases find a clearer substitute in "style." Johnson describes, for example, Mande narration in different modes—song mode, praise-proverb mode, and narrative mode— to distinguish shifts in both content and form (1986, 30–38). Guignard (1975) uses the term *mode* in quite another way to describe differences between "white" music and "black" music among the Moors of southern Mauritania. The colors, he argues, do not refer to black African and Arabo-Berber cultures but instead convey two rather different styles, emotional systems or paths that can be attributed to a particular mode. The "white" ones are soft and gentle, in contrast with the "black" modes which give the impression of strength, vigor, and roughness. What is "white" is clear and easy to understand, while what is "black" is obscure and hard to grasp.

The verbal and musical modes described by Guignard and Johnson, along with the comments by Norris, reinforce the impression that the music of the griot world is both more complex and more widely diffused within West Africa than previously imagined. But it is also evident that we have much to learn about the nature of this music and the path it has followed over the centuries.

Tuning and Style

One of the most complex aspects of the music produced by griots is the variations in tuning for some instruments and the playing styles. The reader interested in these topics will need to consult Charry's dissertation (1992) or articles by Knight, Durán, and others listed in the bibliography. What follows here is a sampling that will give some sense of the subtlety inherent in much of the music by griots.

 Knight explains (personal communication, 1996) that the tuning of the *kora* is heptatonic, based on seven tones. The *kora* has different tunings for particular kinds of pieces. Evolved over time, four of these tunings are the most common today: the first is *silaba*, or "main road," which is the one most widely used for western Mandinka melodies and one of the oldest; the second is *tomora* or *tomora ba*, a variation on *silaba*; the third is *hardino*, which is close to *silaba* but allows the musician to include pieces from the eastern Mande region. *Silaba* is becoming more widely accepted because of the greater range of pieces that can be played with it. *Sauta*, the fourth, can be tuned for *hardino* by changing one note, but the same scale with a raised fourth can be obtained from other tunings, Knight explains. Thus the "Sauta sound" is actually quite common and important. Charry, as well as Knight, reports that *hardino* is employed mainly to play pieces from Mali that are accompanied by women soloists, a large and important part of the repertoire (Charry, 1992, p. 230).

Jeli Sidiki Diabaté reported to Charry that *tomora* comes from the name for a region in the Khassonké-speaking area of northwestern Mali. *Hardino* and *sauta* come from the *kontingo* or *nkoni* (the lute), according to another of Charry's sources, Amadu Bansang Jobarteh (228). Charry explains the link between the *kora* and lute tuning systems by suggesting that *kora* players in eastern Gambia tuned their instruments to match the *ngoni* players who were migrating from Mali.

Kora players see their style in two forms: *kumbengo*, or a fixed melodic pattern, and *birimintingo*, improvised and ornamented music. Knight explains that the *kora*

> allows stepwise melodic motion to be played very quickly and smoothly by plucking alternately with the right and left fingers. By adding the thumb of the opposite hand, octave doubling is achieved. Fifths are produced by a pinching motion between thumb and forefinger of the same hand, and can be played in sequence when both hands are used. By brushing across more than one string at a time, a triad may be produced, and various other combinations can produce other harmonic sounds. The result is a very rich and varied harmonic texture from which a melody emerges, usually in the upper register, but in the lower as well on occasion. (1971, pp. 27–28)

The tuning systems for the *kora* are linked in some ways to those for the *xalam*. Durán reports that there are two major systems of tuning the *xalam*. The most common is *ardina*, related to the *hardino* tuning of the *kora*, and *ordinaire*, less common. For nearly all of them, the musician usually adjusts only the two highest-pitched of the five strings. Durán points out one particularly significant feature of *xalam* and other lute systems of tuning in West Africa: "The pitch values are not in straight descending order from the top to the bottom string" (1981, p. 35). Instead, the topmost string is actually the third highest in pitch. Blues scholars link this feature with the banjo.

Tuning for the *balafon* varies according to region. In the Mande areas of The Gambia, Guinea-Bissau, and Guinea, it is heptatonic (Jessup, 38), but it differs from the European scale because there are no halftones. In some countries, such as Burkina Faso and Côte d'Ivoire, the *balafon* is pentatonic. Jessup notes that the most common pitch for the lowest note is approximately C sharp, a half step above middle C.

Charry (1992) reports that tuning a *balafon* can be done in two ways: by matching the tuning of another *balafon*, starting at the bass end, or by ear to the instrument itself, a far more difficult process. A slat or key is shaved carefully until it matches the equivalent key on the other instrument, or the tuner simply works at it until it reaches the pitch in his own mind. Knight (personal communication, 1996) adds that to lower the pitch one shaves the keys from the center; shaving the tips raises the pitch.

The styles of *balafon* playing for the Mandinka match the *kora kumbengo*, the basic melody and rhythm that, Jessup explains, is the approximate equivalent of an ostinato pattern in Western music but with wider usage (57), and *birimintingo*, ornamentation and improvisation without any accompanying singing. *Birimintingo* offers "an opportunity for the jali to display his virtuosity by incorporating descending runs, ornamental patterns, faster moving melodic themes, octave displacement, and improvised passages into the music" (58).

The *karinya* is played in accompaniment with the *balafon*. Jessup explains that

> often, it is used casually and quietly, sometimes it fades out completely. At other times, in introductory or bridge passages, it is played in a more forceful manner which supports the virtuosity of the instrumentalist. . . . [the instrument] fits in with the balafon part rather than following the vocal line. It adds emphasis, excitement, and variety to the music. (49)

Regional and instrumental variations influence the style of playing of a particular instrument. Charry notes that the geographical distinctions established by King and Durán match with the influence of the instruments that represent the particular regions. For example, in Guinea, the *kora* is influenced by the *balafon*, while in Mali both the *balafon* and the *ngoni*, or *koni*, have had an impact on *kora* styles. In eastern Gambia it is the *koni* that influences the *kora* most (261).

The tuning techniques I have described can be quite complex. Although the articles published by ethnomusicologists are extremely valuable in helping to understand these techniques, the only way to learn to play one of these instruments is to find a teacher and take lessons. The growing number of griots in the United States, the increase in schools in Africa, and the fascination for novelty in the world of music may produce a new generation of musicians, African and non-African, who play these instruments and the music associated with them.

❈ ❈

The foregoing survey of music in the griot world gives only a hint of the complexity in instruments, styles, and voices. What emerges from this limited collection of data, however, is a series of conclusions that may help orient future research.

First, one encounters a great variety of relations between the instruments—nomenclature, playing styles, and songs—across the Sahel and

Savanna regions. No less than the common social functions identified earlier, the instruments, such as the lutes, and the songs, for example from the Sundiata tradition, underscore the diffusion of these varied musical traditions.

Second, this diffusion does not account for the one-dimensional view of the griot's musical art that has migrated outside of West Africa. In addition to the geographic and cultural reasons cited for the dominance of the *kora*, Knight offers several others of a musical nature: the *kora* is louder, has a wide range, is more versatile, has more potential for modification, and is more suited to virtuoso playing. By its very nature it has a harmonious sound, because the strings are tuned next to each other in thirds, and thus it has an immediate appeal (personal communication, 1996). The dominance of the *kora* may simply constitute the first wave, to be followed by other instruments and styles as African music becomes more influential outside the continent.

Third, the relationship between words and instrumental music is extremely close, but the nature of the link remains elusive. The data presented here underscore Bird's discovery—obtained the hard way—that the two forms of music are inseparable.

Finally, the most striking conclusion to come out of this chapter—at least for this writer, whose background in music is quite limited—is that there has been so little research on the music of griots today. Much of what has appeared is recent and of high quality. But the information now available only points to the great need for more research if we are to understand the incredibly complex and diverse nature of this music as well as how griots manage to acquire the skill to play it. The answer to the last part of that question will be found in the next chapter, where the focus will be on the training of griots, both in music and verbal art.

✵ 5 ✵
The Making of a Griot

Anyone who wants to acquire the enormous range of verbal art and music skills described in the previous chapters must undertake a program of study that might compare with what it takes to earn a doctorate. But there is no university for griots in West Africa, so the training of apprentice griots is mostly informal.

Apprentice Griots

Traditionally, one had to be of griot origin to carry out the functions of the profession. Learning was passed on from father to son in a mode comparable to an apprenticeship. Massa Makan Diabaté describes this process as beginning in childhood with service as a respondent to the lines chanted by the parent, followed by the role of musical accompanist until the age of fourteen, then a period with his or her father's teacher, travel after the age of twenty-one to work as a journeyman griot, and perhaps a period of further training at a center of griot activity such as Kéla (Jacquey, 1984, p. 116). But in fact griots often report a somewhat more diverse and complex learning itinerary that depends on a variety of circumstances over which they may have little control.

Birth

Although there is little information today about distinctive ceremonies marking the birth of griot children, according to Nouhou Malio, a Songhay *jeseré*, there was once a traditional ceremony at birth aimed at inculcating the necessary abilities for the child to succeed in the profession: one would wash the newborn in water taken from seven different houses and then boiled (Hale, 1990a, pp. 179–80). The deep meaning of such a ceremony may not be evident, but the contact with the different water sources suggests both the establishment of a fundamental link with other families in the community and the idea of purity that griots associate with their spoken word.

Childhood

A child born into a griot family is exposed to both the values and the sounds of griot life on a daily basis. Sory Camara explains that for the Malinké, the education of a child of *jeli* origin traditionally included an early differentiation from other children. When boys of the same age engaged in nightly wrestling matches to demonstrate their skills to others and to establish a kind of hierarchy within their group, young male *jeliw* served only as referees.

> The young *jeli* never participates in this kind of physical confrontation which shapes the character of all young Malinké children. Just as his parents teach him that it is out of the question for the child to confront his noble comrades on the same field, in the same way they teach him to recognize that he has a special status. (1976, p. 126)

Camara recounts an incident from his childhood in which two boys, one of *jeli* origin, got into a dispute that prompted the future bard to answer in the manner that he knew best: he insulted the first boy in the crudest possible terms. The victim of this verbal assault then replied in the way he had learned: he slapped the youthful *jeli*. But he forgot the fundamental difference between those of noble origin and those who have the special status of *jeli*.

> When we returned to the village, the little *jeli* told his parents about the event. His mother then took her *karinya* and went to sing a serenade of insults in front of the compound of the parents of the hot-headed little noble. She stopped only when the unfortunate hosts presented her with expensive gifts and apologies. For his impulsive act the first boy received very severe corporal punishment from his parents. (126)

Learning about one's relationship with others is only the beginning of the making of a griot. The question of social status is a highly complex subject that has often been reduced to the term caste, a topic that will be explored in considerable detail in the next chapter. For now, it is important to note that the education of a young griot or griotte may include the early inculcation of awareness about where he or she fits into the social fabric of a community.

Early Training

Awareness of one's position usually includes continued exposure to the verbal and musical arts as they are practiced by family members and friends at home and at ceremonies. In an extended interview with Paulla Ebron, the Gambian *jali* Malamin Jobarteh stated that until he was five he used to sit in the lap of his uncle and was gradually learning to play the *kora*. After his uncle's death, Jobarteh went off to school briefly. At eleven he apprenticed in Brikama with Al Haji Bai Konte, a man who became his adoptive father (Ebron, 1993, pp. 112–13).

The late Gambian bard Jali Nyama Suso described this early stage in more detail: "When we were very young, our fathers used to make a little [*kora*] for us, so we could come to understand how the fingers and thumbs are going. Sometimes with less strings, just to give you an idea of how to do it. When you are very young, you go travelling with your father, and any time he starts to play you join in by tapping out a rhythm on the side of the kora." He explained that "you know the songs very early, because when my mother and my father played someplace we used to join them. That's different from learning the *kora*. . . . Learning the *kora* is like learning a book." He added that the first song students learn is "Kelefaba," about the nineteenth-century hero Kelefa Saane. "When you start to understand that, then you can understand other songs [because] all the notes are in it" (Anderson, p. 1986, 11).

Learning to play one of these complex stringed instruments is not easy. Although I have not encountered child-sized versions of a *kora*, smaller versions of other instruments are not uncommon. I was able to purchase a child-sized, three-stringed *molo* in Niger for my son in 1981, when he was four years old. Referring to the Moor *tidinit*, a four-stringed cousin of the *molo*, and the ten- to thirteen-stringed *ardin*, H. T. Norris explains that "it is not uncommon to find miniature models of both instruments in the houses and tents of *iggawen*. Their sole purpose is to instruct children in the technique of the instruments they are learning to play" (1968, p. 65).

Mandinka *balafon* players interviewed by Lynne Jessup and Demba Sanyang in 1980–81 reported that they began to learn to play as early as four years old, though none sang or recited until they had proved their talents on the instrument (Jessup, 1983, p. 31). The instruments, however, are only part of a more holistic form of education that shapes future griots. Michel Guignard sees the education of Moor griot children as the key to understanding their future personalities. Unlike other children, the griot child is more often allowed to observe adult activities and entertainments.

Guignard writes: "The young griot is pampered, caressed by all, people readily give him presents that he asks for and he is at the center of gatherings where he is invited to show his talents publicly. . . . It is probable that this education leaves traces on his personality" (1975, p. 57; my translation). Charles Bird and Martha Kendall (1988) reported that the same is true in Mali: "Nobles raise children to be very decorous, calm, laid back, [while] griots are looking for children who are going to be outgoing. They put them on the stage when they are infants, and if they want to sing, they do." They described the difficulties that occur from this behavior in other cultures when discussing Djimo Kouyaté, a griot based in Washington, D.C.: "His son encounters problems in school systems in the United States because Djimo wants him to be a griot. Teachers complain that he [the child] is hyperactive, going around giving other students the answers." Kouyaté himself explained (1997) that the lack of opportunity for his children to experience the same environment in Africa that he enjoyed, along with the powerful influence of American society, meant that his children will not acquire the linguistic and cultural knowledge necessary to become griots.

But simple exposure is not enough to learn to play a twenty-one-stringed *kora*, repeat a lengthy genealogy, or chant an epic for five hours. Some children from griot families do not learn these skills and choose instead to exercise another profession. Their children then must find alternative routes into the profession. Nantenegwe Kamissoko, a *jelimuso* in Bamako, reported (1992) that her father was a Muslim religious leader and did not practice *jeliya*. Mariam Kouyaté, another *jelimuso* in Bamako, told me (1992) that her father was a tailor, while Nyuma Mane, a *jalimuso* in Banjul, said (1991) that hers was a healer and sorcerer. Batourou Sekou Kouyaté, a *jeli* from Kita, stated (1992) that his father was a domestic slave dealer during the waning days of that commerce in the late nineteenth and early twentieth centuries.

The traditional path of training from father to son or mother to daughter appears to be marked by many exceptions, depending to a large extent on the situation of the extended family. When the parents of Lamine Kouyaté (1992) died while he was a child, he studied *jeliya* with his uncle Boukary Dramé. Ibrahim Limbo in Timbuktu studied with both his father and his brother, but said in an interview in 1992 that his real teacher was his brother. Aja Nafi Kuyate, a wife of the late Al Haji Bai Konte in Brikama, The Gambia, comes from the most prestigious clan of *jalolu*, but she did not know her father because of his early death or absence and did not learn from her mother. She reported (1991) that most of what she knows today about *jaliya* came from her late husband. Baba Cissoko, the Malian *jeli* who has a weekly radio program, told me (1992) that he learned first from his father, who died before the son could master the profession. He then apprenticed with Senusi Kouyaté and completed his early studies by working with his considerably older brother Magan Sisòkò (Téra, 1974, pp. 5–6). Jali Muso Dramé, from the Casamance region of southern Senegal, reported (1991) that her father died when she was four years old. She went to school for four years, eventually married a *jali*, then divorced him, and finally learned the profession of *jalimuso* from both her ex-husband and her mother-in-law. Pathé Camara, a Fulbe *mabo* who performs with a group in Senegal called the Sory Camara Ballets Acrobatiques, said (1991) that he did not learn from his father, who was a griot, but picked up the violinlike *riti* from his mother, who was not of griot origin. Lamine Diallo, a drummer, was born in Dakar of a Fulbe father from Guinea who was not of griot origin, and a Serer mother from Senegal who sang as an *okawul*, or griotte. He told me (1991) that against his parents' wishes that he continue his schooling, he went off to train as a drummer with Duga Fana Traoré, one of the leading percussionists in the region, then joined the Ballets Nationals du Sénégal in 1966. Hawa Kanuteh, second wife of Jali Madi Kanuteh, explained to me (1991) that she started to learn from her father, the distinguished Gambian *jali* Banna Kanuteh, but then went to school in Banjul for ten years. It was only after she married Jali Madi Kanuteh that she completed her initial training as a *jalimuso* (1991). Michèle N'Diaye, a Lébou griotte from Dakar, explained (1991) that she learned not from her parents but from her grandmother, Bintu N'Diaye.

Beverly Mack (1981) describes the training of Hausa *zabiyoyi* as equally varied. Maizargadi, she explained, "inherited the desire to sing from her musician father," but she

> claims to have been inspired to become a zabiya for the emir when she first saw the front gates of the Kano palace. Deciding to learn proper yabo (praise song) she endeavored to learn the history of Kano's royal line, and returned to sing for the Emir of Kano at a public gathering. He rewarded her, and from then on her career as a royal zabiya grew as she settled in Kano, performing for four different emirs over the past 40 years. (30–31)

Mack also describes other ways of learning—for example, paying a local musician for lessons and then imitating the songs in a manner reminiscent of Qur'anic education. She gives the example of Hajiya Faji, whose parents were not musicians. When she moved to Kano with her husband, she hired somone to teach her to play the *kukuma*, a bowed lute. Mack adds that "the final stages of learning involve 'public' sessions in which a novice can participate among many musicians without spoiling the performance" (33–34). More advanced students learn from others as well as from songs broadcast on radio and television (33).

Formal Training

In addition to family training there are more formal methods, influenced by traditional, Islamic, and Western systems of education. For the Songhay of Niger, *jeseré* Nouhou Malio explained, pupils learn three lines per night around a fire. The *doudal*, or hearth, parallels the Islamic *doudal*, or school, where students learn three lines from the Qur'an at each session. The children contribute their share of sticks and dry millet stalks to the fire as they acquire the new material. When the beginner has absorbed some basic information, he or she may accompany the *jeseré* at ceremonies. According to Nouhou Malio, this introductory stage lasts for three to four years and ends without ceremony when the apprentice goes off to study with another griot. The student pays for his or her education by working in the fields for the master or by providing fodder for his horse (Hale, 1990a, pp. 179–80).

While working with a griot in Liboré, Niger, only a few miles downriver from Nouhou Malio's town of Saga, I watched two stages of this process in reverse order on the same day. El Hadji Garba Bagna, a member of a distinguished family of griots from Liboré, invited me to follow him on a Muslim religious holiday, Tabaski or Id al-Kebir, on October 20, 1980, as he went about his duties as a *jeseré*. At the start of ceremonies in the morning, he and his entourage chanted praises outside of the home of the canton chief as this local ruler was preparing to go to the prayer ground. El Hadji Garba Bagna led these chants, but he was backed up by younger griots, including nieces and nephews, who sang the refrain and served as a chorus.

Later, after he and part of his entourage had made the rounds of many other homes in Liboré, he returned to his own compound where each of his children, down to approximately age five, repeated a few lines into my microphone. The younger they were, the fewer words they were able to sing. The relationship between ability and age was as clear as El Hadji Garba Bagna's pride in their development. They were all being trained to follow in his footsteps if they wanted to.

Griots in Kéla, Mali, reported to Seydou Camara that they employ the same instructional system (1990, p. 73). But Jan Jansen (1997), who lived in that village for a year, feels that the extent of this formality is somewhat exaggerated by both the griots and by Camara (forthcoming in Austen, 1999).

Kéla, along with Kita, also in Mali, Siguiri and Niagassola in Guinea, Liboré and Dibilo in Niger, and Sotuma Sere and Brikama in The Gambia, is one of a small number of towns where there is a high concentration of griots. One finds griots there for a variety of reasons—ancient patterns of settlement, proximity to a local chief, ties to a local holy site, or simply chance. These griots attract others who come for what one might term advanced training or continuing education in some aspect of the profession—learning an epic, perfecting skills in playing an instrument, or seeking some occult wisdom that is not normally divulged. Often there is a central house for the griots presided over by a master griot, as is the case in Kéla and Kita today.

To call these centers schools for griots is hardly stretching our notion of what constitutes a school. But in fact it was just such an issue that provoked a sharp difference between two scholars who have studied griots and their texts: the American linguist and folklorist Charles Bird, and Gordon Innes, former head of the Africa Department at the School of Oriental and African Studies of the University of London. In the introduction to *Sunjata: Three Mandinka Versions* (1974), Innes commented somewhat skeptically on a "curious belief which has gained currency among some scholars, especially American, that there are griot training centers in The Gambia." In a review of Innes's book, Bird noted that such centers were not unusual in other parts of the Mande world. He explained that

> it is clear in Mali that Keyla is such a center where both young and old bards go to add to their repertoires, discuss interpretations and techniques, and often perform for each other. Bards, in singing their vitae at the beginning of their performances, often cite the places they have visited, particularly places like Keyla that have high reputations as sources of knowledge and these visits add to the bard's authenticity. (1977, p. 356)

Each was talking about a different part of the Mande world, and each was interpreting the notion of school in a different manner—Innes taking it somewhat literally, Bird employing it in what one might term a broader, structuralist way. Bird's view is certainly more appropriate, and it is one that, in the past few years, has taken on the more literal sense that Innes rejects, as some griots have in fact set up new centers for the training of griots.

Whether in a round mud-walled, thatched-roof structure of traditional shape in Kéla or in a square concrete, corrugated-iron-roofed block in a suburb of Banjul, these places for learning the art of the griot can only be called schools. For example, the school at Kéla, which serves as the central meeting place for local *jeliw*, receives students not only from all over West Africa but also from around the world. The dean of griots in Kéla, Bala Diabaté, told me (1992) of students from Kayes and Kita who had come to study with him and other *jeliw* there. He also cited non-Africans, in particular a French researcher who had taken a griot name, Sidikou Diabaté, and the Dutch scholar Jan Jansen, who has since published a version of the Sunjata epic. In all cases, Diabaté reported, the visitors learned both songs and how to play instruments.

Jansen, who lived for extended periods in Kéla on several occasions, explained to me in 1996, however, that the training was not formal; nor did there appear to be many students. But he added that learning permeated daily life in ways that might not be apparent to the outsider.

Students at these centers meet with their tutors, often attend ceremonies with them, and add to or confirm knowledge that serves as the basis for future studies as they travel elsewhere. They pay for the instruction, whether by helping out in the fields, as in the example of children who studied with Nouhou Malio, or by paying with cash or in kind.

The prestige of Kéla is based not only on the reputations of the *jeliw* who live there but also on its proximity to Kangaba, the nearby site of the sacred house of the Mande-speaking peoples who claim descent from Sundiata Keita. The Diabaté *jeliw* of Kéla are the hereditary keepers of the house and the traditions surrounding it. They preside over the hosting of a reroofing ceremony every seven years that attracts thousands of people from all corners of the Mande diaspora. To associate with them is widely viewed as the equivalent of aborbing information from the very fount of knowledge about the numerous and diverse Mande-speaking peoples.

Kangaba was a center of power for the Mande world at a particular time many centuries ago. Today, other centers of power—large cities—have emerged to attract the attention of griots. Now one is more likely to find griots in the capitals of West African countries than anywhere else. The concentration of griots around Banjul, Dakar, Bamako, and Niamey, drawn often by the demands of patrons who have migrated to the city as well as by the opportunity for year-round employment, has contributed to the creation of new and more formal establishments for teaching some of the arts of the profession.

Jali Madi Kanuteh, a Gambian *jali*, has set up a school at 19 Tobacco Road in the Bundu section of Serrekunda, a suburb of Banjul, The Gambia. A sign on the front of the building reads "Manding Music and

Dance School." Inside one finds classrooms, instruments, teachers, and paying students. A private, career-training operation directed by a *jali* who has traveled widely, the school hosts visitors from around the world and its instructors also give lessons in people's homes.

Interviews with several of Kanuteh's advanced students revealed that all were from *jali* families, all were attracted to the school because of the success of Kanuteh, and all paid fees in some form or another, usually thirty dalasis ($3.) per hour for lessons, in spite of the fact that many of them were related in one way or another to the director. One student reported that he was able to raise money to attend the school by doing odd jobs and obtaining support from a sponsor. Another said he had fourteen years of education in Western-style schools. All of these advanced students, ranging in age from nineteen to the early thirties, had studied for several years and often accompanied Kanuteh when he performed at hotels and other locations in the Banjul area. Kanuteh's uncle Papa Susso also took pupils and had built a large house in another part of Serrekunda in order to receive foreign students for extended stays. His center was somewhat less formal but constituted nevertheless another locus of instruction in Banjul. He has started to build an even larger study and research center in Sotuma Sere that will attract both students and scholars.

State-Sponsored Training

The focus at the private schools, whether in Kéla or Banjul, is to prepare griots to practice *jaliya* and to offer training to foreigners. State-owned schools also offer training in some of the arts practiced by griots. The emphasis is more on the musical than the verbal side of the profession, and the students do not need to be of griot origin. But the existence of these institutions contributes, often indirectly, to the maintenance of *jaliya*. They support the griots who teach in them and make the profession—or at least activities associated with it—more accessible to people who are not part of it. Two examples, one from Senegal, the other from Mali, illustrate their roles.

Senegal is home to the oldest public school for the arts in West Africa. Founded in Dakar around 1948 as a conservatory for musical and dramatic art, it became the Ecole des Arts, then the Institut National des Arts, before taking on its present title of Conservatoire Nationale de la Musique, de la Danse et de l'Art Dramatique. This conservatory has several hundred students and more than a score of permanent teaching staff. Students go there from all over Africa to study both Western and African instruments and to become teachers or performers. The Senegalese pop star Youssou N'Dour studied there in the 1970s according to the director, Moussa N'Diaye (1991), who was a student there at the time.

Students can learn to play the *kora*, the *balafon*, a variety of drums, and other instruments in the domain of griots. The Senegalese *balafon* player Balla Doumbia serves there as an adjunct professor, and the drummer Sing Sing Faye teaches there occasionally. Graduates who specialize in traditional instruments can join orchestras in Dakar or strike out on their own.

What is missing is the context of the griot profession and the verbal art. In the 1960s, the focus was as much on research as on training, according to Dansy Camara (1967, p. 32). The school sent people out to record songs from oral sources as part of an effort to preserve the cultural heritage of the country. Today the emphasis on music education and performance appears to be aimed at integrating the musical side of the griot profession into the larger panorama of musical art.

In Mali, Senegal's neighbor to the east, the Institut National des Arts started operating in 1956 as a center for artistic creation. But at first it appeared to some critics to be a place of "servitude" for artisans who were brought there to create items for the French market (Fernand Coulibaly, 1992). Today it offers training in music, acting, arts management, sculpture, woodworking, leatherworking, jewelry-making, and weaving. There are ten music instructors for approximately thirty students. The institute offers instruction in both African and Western instruments. But the approach is slightly different from that at the conservatory in Dakar. All students in music must learn to play both a Western and an African instrument. But the teachers are not griots invited in as adjunct instructors. They are fulltime staff members who have learned to play the *kora*, *ngoni*, or *balafon*.

Instructors and recent institute graduates trained on modern Western instruments learned to play traditional instruments from local griots during a series of four summer sessions from 1986 to 1990. The goals were to discover the theory and practice of traditional musical instruments, become familiar with their technical features, and develop a teaching methodology for them. Once the full-time staff had acquired the ability to play these instruments—and some were quite familiar with them from the start—they were ready to teach new students seeking the arts technician diploma awarded there.

As in Dakar, the goal is to master an instrument, not to absorb the many different skills of the griot. Despite the traditional monopoly that griots hold over music, anyone can enroll. In fact, the schools have helped to break down the barrier. The examples of some of the instructors in Bamako illustrate this social change.

Fernand Coulibaly, an instructor of *balafon* as well as Western musical instruments, reported (1992) that when he wanted to study music, he enrolled secretly at the institute without telling his father. After discovering what Fernand was doing, his father declared that he would never have allowed the young man to follow the path of music. Coulibaly calmed his father's fears by explaining that he was out to preserve the cultural heritage of the country. But Coulibaly told me that other parents were less tolerant. They warned their children never to become griots and to stay away from music.

Dramane Coulibaly, another instructor, reported (1992) that he had been intending to study medicine but was more interested in music. He told me that musicians had a hard time to find a wife because families would not allow their daughters to marry anyone who seemed to be associated with griots. "People thought that once you become a singer you are a griot," he said. "Over time, people have come to understand that it is acceptable now to sing. Now people are not condemned . . . people see that it is a profession."

A third instructor, Tapo Bâ, added (1992) that he did not tell his family what he was planning to study when he went off to Cuba in 1963 on a scholarship that lasted eight years. Aware of the social problems he would face upon his return home after studying music, he married a Cuban woman.

Anyone who comes to the Institut National des Arts intending to become a griot would not get far in the profession simply on skill acquired with the *kora*. This and other schools serve in many ways to diffuse some of the arts of the griot, but they do not contribute directly to the expansion of the profession.

That is what Eric Charry discovered on a twenty-two-month trip to conduct research for his doctoral dissertation in African ethnomusicology. His first stop was at the conservatory in Dakar. Charry's goal was not to become a skilled performer who might displace griots in Africa or abroad but to learn more about the musical art of griots by practicing with master teachers. He discovered that the ratio of students to instruments and teachers would not allow him to learn as quickly as he had hoped, and the context was much too divorced from the traditional environment in which griots operate. So he did what other musicians, both non-African and African, have done in the past: he took private lessons with master teachers, including the talented *balafon* player Balla Doumbia.

Charry then moved on to The Gambia, where he studied on an almost daily basis for six months with one of the most respected *kora* players in the country, Amadu Bansang Jobarteh, as well as with Dembo Konte and others. From there he traveled to Bamako, where he studied with relatives of Amadu Bansang Jobarteh, Sidiki Diabaté, his son Toumani Diabaté, and others in their neighborhood, an area of high concentration of *jeliw*.

The itinerary of Charry in Senegal, The Gambia, Mali, and Guinea was in many ways similar to that of a journeyman *jali* who sought to learn from master teachers in different parts of the region. The difference was that Charry's goal was to learn for research purposes. He did on occasion play with some of his instructors at public events—for example with Balla Doumbia in a Dakar restaurant for a visiting Japanese delegation—but such events were exceptional.

A final type of instruction can be found in national ballet or ensembles. These groups have toured both within and outside of their countries in one form or another since the colonial expositions of the late nineteenth century. In some countries, such as Senegal, private groups perform at hotels; they also perform in Europe.

Since independence, the state-sponsored groups have become cultural flagships for their countries, drawing on a pool of artists to assemble a dance panorama backed up by instrumental and vocal music typical of a country. While most of the performers are fully trained when they join, the participants are constantly changing and new members must be integrated into the shows. For this reason, the groups practice almost every day.

Based on my visits to rehearsals of a privately sponsored group in Dakar in 1991 and a state-sponsored group on tour in the Caribbean and the United States in 1993, it appeared that the training going on in these troupes is extremely intense and focused. Most participants are not of griot origin, but among the instrumentalists one finds many players who claim to have griot roots. The existence of these groups, for both cultural and commercial purposes, undoubtedly exerts a powerful influence on younger and less experienced performers who come to them for training and the chance to travel.

Master Griots

Griots learn from many sources—from other griots at ceremonies, by listening to the radio and to cassettes, by watching television, and especially by traveling. John Johnson has observed that such training, often carried out "on the fly," leads to differences in words, phrases, and texts. But by the time griots reach the age of forty or fifty, at least in the Mande world, if they have great talent, people begin to call them *ngara* or *ngaraa* (sometimes pronounced *nara*), or master griot (Johnson, 1986, p. 29). In the Songhay world, the master griot is *jeseré-dunka*, *dunka* being a variant on the Soninké word for chief, *tunka*, that goes back many centuries to the Ghana empire. After the griot's talent is recognized, his or her role turns increasingly to training new generations.

The griots themselves are keen observers of differences in ability. When I was collecting versions of *The Epic of Askia Mohammed* in Niger in 1980–81, the next-to-last level in the long sequence of references given by people who reported that they knew a talented griot was usually a *jeseré* who referred me to a *jeseré dunka*.

Not every child who undergoes training becomes a full-time practicing griot. Guignard cites the examples of several young Moor griots who went to school and eventually obtained civil service jobs, positions that did not prevent them from keeping up their musical activities (1975, p. 65). A brief look at the careers of three griots shows that the decisions on which path to follow are not always easy or comfortable. Their careers also illustrate the dynamic and synthetic nature of the profession today. Although many griots in West Africa follow a path that absorbs little outside influence, these three performers exhibit an openness to new ways that guarantees the survival—and evolution—of the profession.

Career Paths of Three Griots

ADAMA DRAMÉ

Adama Dramé, a *jeli* who grew up in Burkina Faso, started to learn to play the *jembé* drum from his father. Dramé reported: "My father showed me some rhythms, especially the *dansa* and then the *sandia* and then the *bondiala*. I knew how to play them, but I was weak because I was only eight years old" (Dramé and Senn-Borloz, 1992, p. 34). When other *jembé* players arrived in his hometown of Nouna as part of a troupe of traveling Malian magicians, he spent his evenings with them to learn other rhythms. Dramé's growing fascination with music contributed to a decline in his success at school, and at the end of the fifth year, his teacher told him he would have to repeat the year. At that point he had to decide which path to follow.

> I told my teacher that I did not want to go to school anymore. He said "Why?" I said, "I don't know. But I've never repeated a year, so if this year I have to stay back, that means that school is really not for me."

"What are you going to do if you don't go to school?"
"I'll make music, that's what my father did."
"But how can you even think of that. Being a griot is no kind of profession!"
(p. 34; my translation)

When his father realized how serious Dramé was about becoming a *jeli*, he took his son on tours of the villages around Nouna, especially at the end of the harvest season.

After his father moved to Ouagadougou, the capital of the country, and began to perform more often, Dramé's skills began to improve, but his relationship with his father soured. His father was a perfectionist and wanted his son to play only what was in the repertoire of the group. Any divergence prompted the father to beat his son publicly. Whether the conflict between the two was due to the Mande value of *fadenya*, which places the son in competition with the father for a place in history, or the father's desire to make sure that his son had fully mastered the necessary musical skills, the result was that Dramé finally left home to join the Ballet National of Burkina Faso, the next step on his career ladder (37–39).

AL HAJI PAPA BUNKA SUSSO

In the case of Al Haji Papa Bunka Susso of The Gambia, the decision to abandon a Western-style career in favor of the griot profession came after university studies. Papa Susso's extraordinary career, related to me in an interview in 1988, illustrates how the different cultural forces of Africa and the West can influence the choices of someone of *jali* origin.

Born in 1947, he grew up in a large extended family of considerable *jali* talent in Sotuma Sere, near the Senegalese border in eastern Gambia. His father and six uncles, including Bamba Susso, one of The Gambia's greatest bards, all lived in the same compound with their wives and numerous children. From infancy he was surrounded by the sounds of Mandinka *jaliya*. His father sent him to nearby Bakadaji Primary School in 1954 and then in 1960 to Armitage High School in Georgetown in order to give him the option of choosing the career he wanted. When he completed his high school education with honors in 1965, his father invited friends to the house to confirm the young man's talent as a *jali*. He had to answer questions about tuning, *kora* construction, and other matters, as well as perform for the visitors. These *jalolu* then agreed that he had fully qualified for the profession.

The newly confirmed *jali* decided, however, to work as an agricultural assistant in the Ministry of Agriculture and Natural Resources before accepting a scholarship to attend Cuttington University in Liberia, where he earned a bachelor of arts degree in business administration in 1969. He returned to The Gambia to serve as a senior accountant in the Ministry of Works and Communications as well as a financial attaché and liaison officer for the Gambian Embassy in Freetown, Sierra Leone.

Papa Susso soon realized that he could not live on what he considered to be a very low civil servant's salary, so he decided to return to the family tradition. He traveled to Sotuma Sere to tell his father of the decision. After attending a celebration organized by his father in honor of the reconversion of Papa Susso to the profession, the former accountant returned to Banjul to become chief *kora* player for the Gambia National Ballet, a government-sponsored troupe.

In 1974 he resigned to form his own cultural organization, Manding Music and Dance Limited. It was the beginning of a career that took him to concert halls in London, Paris, New York, San Francisco, and Tokyo, where he performed alone and with symphony orchestras, and also to hundreds of schools and universities.

DJIMO KOUYATÉ

Djimo Kouyaté was born in 1947 into a family of *jalolu* in Tambacounda, Senegal, whose ancestors came from The Gambia, Mali, and Guinea. He told me (1997) that he is the 149th generation descended from Balla Fasseké, the *jali* of Sundiata Keita. He learned the profession from his father until he was seven, then from a master *jali*, or *ngara*, named Sata Mady until age eleven.

At that time, his older brother returned from a period of *kora* training with Amadu Bansang Jobarteh in Brikama, The Gambia, and became the *kora* instructor for his other brothers. Kouyaté continued to learn not only the verbal and musical arts from his father and older brother but also what he calls the *savoir*, or morality and rites related to the profession.

When he was thirteen, his father died, and, against his own wishes, he was obliged to accompany his brother to Dakar, where he enrolled at the École des Arts to study piano. His aptitude and success with the Western instrument led to an offer by one of his professors to send him to France for further studies. He declined this opportunity because he did not want to become the first member of his family to leave the profession of *jaliya* completely.

His brother arranged for Kouyaté to try out with the Ballet National du

Sénégal. He was awarded a position as *kora* player, drummer, and dancer, then went on tour. He attempted to keep up with his schoolwork whenever the troupe was in Dakar. Fascinated with the staging of the company's performances, he learned another skill, that of lighting engineer. Twice during his service with the troupe, once in Chicago in the early 1960s and once at the Festival des Arts Nègres in Dakar in 1966, he was offered an opportunity by Duke Ellington to join the African American musician's orchestra. Both times he refused because he did not want to abandon his family.

In 1981, he left the ballet for a series of teaching positions in the United States. Today he serves as an adjunct professor of non-Western music at the University of Maryland and maintains an active schedule of performances in public schools under the aegis of municipal and state arts agencies. Although he holds firmly to the traditional music that he learned from his father and older brother, his exposure to other forms has marked his career indelibly: he performs both jazz and traditional music for diverse audiences.

Pattern, Drive, and Origin

In spite of the diversity in the training of griots, a pattern emerges that appears to be typical. The itinerary of a griot or griotte might be something like the following:

1. The child absorbs the griot world at home, including the values and sounds.

2. Then from age seven to ten he or she follows more focused training, both vocal and instrumental.

3. The child, especially the young adult, follows a master griot to local ceremonies and plays an increasingly visible role as his or her talent develops. If the training remains within the family, the child learns more when the family goes on tour to other villages during the dry season.

4. After more training, the young adult may go off to visit other regions or other countries, learning from other griots.

5. By middle age, the most talented persons are increasingly referred to as master griots or griottes. At this point, if not earlier, they may be heard on the radio or seen on television fairly often. Their impact is multiplied by these modern media, and they may be viewed as national cultural treasures. After they die, the government may memorialize them with a stamp, as Mali did for Ban Zoumana Cissoko (figure 11) and Niger for Boubacar Tinguizi (figure 12).

11. Stamp from Republic of Mali honoring Ban Zoumana Cissoko.

Whatever the path, one cannot underestimate the importance of individual drive to learn and ambition to succeed. When I returned to Niger in 1980 for fieldwork with Songhay griots, one of my working assumptions— a faulty one—was that the only talented griots were old. One day while recording an epic from a rather talented young griot in Kwarey-Haoussa, a small village an hour's drive upriver from Niamey, I turned to another listener to ask why this young man was so good. The reply was "A na

REPUBLIQUE DU NIGER

100F

POSTES 1978

TINGUIZI

CHESNOT   EDILA

12. Stamp from Republic of Niger
honoring Tinguizi.

chow"—he has studied. In other words, it is not enough simply to be born
into the profession.

If that is true, what about those students who are not of griot origin who
come to the hearth, or travel from other continents, to learn from a griot?
Can they also be griots? One hears many different responses to this
question. Charles Bird has argued that anyone can become a griot. But
Gérard Dumestre, the French linguist who has published epic texts from
Mali, told me in 1990 that this idea was ludicrous.

The controversy is rooted in two basic questions. First, how much
cultural and professional literacy can an outsider actually absorb? One

might expect the answer to be as much as anyone else, if one puts in the time, which may be several decades or more. Second, and perhaps more important, will an outsider be given access to the kind of secret knowledge available only to those who are born into the profession? The answer here depends on the teacher.

One can imagine a situation similar to one the American anthropologist Paul Stoller found himself in after two decades of work with the Songhay master sorcerer Adama Jenitongo. Stoller had acquired far more knowledge from healers and sorcerers than almost anyone else in western Niger. Even before the death of his teacher, Stoller was often called upon by people in Niger who knew of his background to put his knowledge to the service of local clients. Although he does not claim to have learned everything there is to know about the profession of sorcery in the Songhay world, Stoller advanced far enough along the path to mastery to be recognized as a well-qualified sorcerer—and also to know when to quit.

It is quite plausible, then, that an assiduous student of nongriot origin could devote sufficient time to acquire considerable knowedge of *jaliya* or *jeseretarey* in at least some parts of West Africa, although that would probably not be the case in major centers such as Kita and Kéla, where there exists a powerful proprietary feeling about information that belongs to a collective of professionals. It is a knowledge that many griots refuse to share completely with audiences and foreigners for a variety of reasons. Djibril Tamsir Niane, the Guinean historian, discovered this when he worked with Mamadou Kouyaté to collect the version of the Sundiata epic that is the most widely read in the world today. The *jeli* warned his interlocutor, "Do not ever go into the dead cities to question the past, for the spirits never forgive. Do not seek to know what is not to be known. . . . I took an oath to teach only what is to be taught and to conceal what is to be kept concealed" (Niane, 1965, p. 84). In an interview in 1998, Niane confirmed not only the significance of that warning, but also the limitations on who was appropriate to learn and who was qualified to teach, constraints governed by the age and status of the student and the teacher.

❊ ❊

The barrier remains between griots and their listeners. Not only should the audience not ask too many questions, but the griot should be cautious in revealing his knowledge. It is a concern that Stoller respected when publishing esoteric texts he learned from his sources, and it is one that I shared when working with a team of Nigérien colleagues on *The Epic of Askia Mohammed*. One result of that concern may be a large number of undecipherable lines. The consequences of overstepping the sometimes unstated limits of access to esoteric knowledge can be fatal—or at least perceived as fatal. The death in 1976 of the famous Malian *jeli* Wâ Kamissoko was widely viewed at home as retribution by his colleagues for his having revealed too much to outsiders. He had participated as the central figure in seminars organized by the SCOA Foundation in Mali in 1975 and 1976 for scholars working on the history of West Africa (Rouch, 1990; Moraes Farias, 1993b, p. 14).

In spite of warnings such as that by Mamadou Kouyaté, one finds numerous examples of people of nongriot origin, particularly nobles, who turned to the profession to make ends meet. Although it is unlikely that they would rank among the most talented, they may well have enjoyed a lifetime of experience as subjects of praises and narratives sung by griots, and for this reason the verbal art of these wordsmiths was quite familiar to them. The full extent of the nobles' knowledge and, above all, their professional standing, remains in doubt. Griots do not accept them. When I asked about them in 1992, Bala Diabaté in Kéla replied, "I will kill the noble with my mouth," meaning that he would destroy the man's reputation with words.

Foreigners and those of nongriot origin can only proceed a certain undefined distance on the path to acquiring the skills and knowledge of a griot. Students of the musical art of the griot who travel to West Africa to study with them and to learn to play their instruments are well aware of this. Their teachers understand it, too, whether they are in West Africa or abroad. Amadu Bansang Jobarteh and Jali Nyama Suso, each of whom spent a year at the University of Washington in Seattle, and Papa Bunka Susso, who has held many artistic residencies in the United States, as well as others who have traveled outside Africa, are happy to teach students the rudiments of the *kora* and even how to sing a basic praise song. But not every item in the griot's baggage is open to the public.

The cumulative nature and proprietary status of the knowledge of griots are the two most important factors in distinguishing their talents from those who seek to imitate them. The griot is both scholar and performer, and, as with anyone in these two professions, there is an almost infinite gradation in quality from apprentice to master. The differences between griots may be difficult for outsiders to discern, but they remain obvious to those who are born into a culture or who have lived there for a long time. And as with other scholars and performers, the griots' learning continues forever.

When I asked Songhay *jeserey* in Niger how long it took to become a master griot, they all gave the same answer: *a siin de mé*, there is no end.

The distinction between those of griot origin and those who are not, evoked at the end of this chapter, underscores the reality of the social structure in many West African societies that support these wordsmiths: to become a griot, it is best to be born a griot, for they are somehow inherently different from everyone else. The reasons for that deeply rooted difference will be examined in the next chapter.

❉ 6 ❉
Would You Want
Your Daughter to Marry One?

No aspect of the griot profession is subject to greater debate than the social status of the wordsmiths. On one hand, griots appear to be the respected keepers of the heritages of families, clans, and societies. On the other hand, if one were to stop a hundred people on the street in Bamako and ask if they would be happy to have a daughter marry a griot, the response would likely be a mixture of laughter and disdain at the idea—except for those of griot origin or those so poor that they might see some economic benefit in such an arrangement. How can one explain such a paradox? To understand the ambiguity surrounding the issue of the status of griots, one must look at the issue from several perspectives, including those of the griots themselves.

Outcasts

As seen in early writings of Europeans, griots in the Senegambian region appeared to be social outcasts, living outside or on the margins of society, behaving in what seemed at times to be an outrageous manner.

Burial

David Conrad notes (in Conrad and Frank, 1995, pp. 4–7) that among the artisans in what is known in the Mande world as *nyamakalaw*, the griots attracted the most attention from Europeans not only because of their highly audible activities but also because of the interment practices reserved for them. They were placed in the hollow trunks of baobab trees (see figure 13), a custom that Europeans assumed meant low social status. These outside observers could not reconcile such a bizarre form of burial with the important roles that griots played. Conrad cites many sources who linked the practice to the devil.

13. Sketch of burial of griots in baobab tree. From Dapper.

The reason for tree burial remains unclear; there is evidence, Conrad suggests, to interpret this practice as a fear of polluting the soil by bodies that possess some sort of occult power. The result, he argues, is to underscore the negative qualities attributed to all people who are commonly identified as members of a caste.

Around 1940 a Catholic priest named Father Bourgoin, assigned to the town of Diofène on the Petite Côte of Senegal, south of Dakar, decided that griots converted to Christianity did not have to be buried in trees. He arranged for a Christian burial of a *guewel* in a cemetery that contained the bodies of free or noble people. He did so in spite of the opposition of the people of Diofène. That year the region was plagued by locusts and crickets. The resulting destruction of the harvest led to so much local dissatisfaction with the priest that the bishop of Dakar was forced to reassign him. From that time on, griots were allowed into Diofène only during festivities (Silla, 1966, p. 748).

In 1955–56, the "griot tree," a large baobab, was cut down in Dakar to make way for urban improvements. Inside were found numerous skeletons, many of them recent and presumably those of griots (Flutre, 1956, p. 223).

Today the burial custom is disappearing in the face of demands by griots for equal treatment and because of social change influenced by other cultures. But change comes slowly.

One fictional portrayal of the demand for change seems to illustrate quite accurately the depth and nature of popular sentiment about griots. In the novel *La Princesse de Tiali* by the Senegalese author Nafissatou Diallo (1987; *Fary, Princess of Tiali*, 1987), one reads the story of a marriage between a beautiful young woman of *guewel* origin and a prince who is a dwarf. The unusual alliance generates a variety of intense and disruptive reactions among the characters. When the princess falls ill toward the end of the novel, her husband reports that "she continues to be delirious and asks me to destroy 'Gouey Guéol,'" the burial trees for griots (101). Warned that such steps would violate both tradition and the wishes of his subjects, the prince seeks advice from his marabout, who played a key role in removing objections against the unusual marriage. After seven days and seven nights of meditation, Tierno the marabout declares:

> Seven white sheep and seven red bulls will be sacrificed and their meat distributed to the village. Bowls of millet paste and soured milk will be shared among the families. Then you will burn the trees. The spirit which tortures the princess and causes her terrible illness is hiding in one of the numerous tree trunks. The fire must be lit from logs coming from the baobabs at the four corners of Mboupbène, east, west, north and south, in the night from Thursday to Friday.
>
> After that you will build a cemetery according to the tradition with graves dug in the earth. You will face serious problems, Prince Bocar Djiwan Malick. Your life will be in danger. Your subjects will be angry with you, some because of the new cemetery, others because of the profanation by fire. But most important to you is your wife's life. (102; I have modified slightly the translation of Ann Woollcombe)

The prince's decision to follow the marabout's advice, made after three days of reflection, leads to attacks against the village of his wife's parents in an outbreak of "fratricidal fighting without precedent in the country's history. Three attempts were made on Bocar's life and failed. Fary's children several times barely escaped kidnapping" (102). The novel concludes with the abolition of the tradition of burying griots in baobab trees. Although this description of events comes from a novel set in the precolonial past, the extraordinary measures taken to change the custom of burial in trees for griots and the powerful reaction of other members of society mirror in fictional form a deeply held and widespread view that griots are fundamentally different from other people and must be treated accordingly.

This resistance to change is evident in Louis Diène Faye's account of the protocol for burying a griot according to the Serer tradition in Senegal. After describing in some detail the process for inserting the body into the baobab tree, he explains that the purpose of tree burial is to avoid polluting the earth. In the conclusion of his discussion of the subject, he points out that "today griots are beginning to bury their dead in the earth. But they are obliged to spread a mat in the floor of the grave. Then one throws sticks and grass onto it before respectfully placing the body of the dead griot in the grave (1983, 41; my translation).

"Caste"

Both the geography and the full meaning of baobab burial remain unclear, but for Conrad there is no doubt that the impact of this custom contributed to the image of *nyamakalaw* conveyed by other members of society, especially nobles and freemen: all of these artisans, griots as well as blacksmiths, potters, and weavers, were quite different from everyone else. In European languages, one word emerged during the colonial era to signify that difference: *caste*.

The notion of caste, more commonly associated with societies in India, served as a convenient way to label all artisans, despite considerable differences between India and Africa. Today, *caste* is employed by scholars, journalists, and the public to explain the difference between the artisans and the other two components of most societies in the Sahel and Savanna: those who are noble or freeborn and those who are of captive origin. But expressing the difference as "caste" suggests that there is some form of hierarchy and raises the basic question of just where do "caste" people fit into the tripartite social structure.

Fatima Mounkaila has suggested that whatever their origin, caste people are widely perceived to be of captive origin, at least in Niger; they appear as social climbers who managed to change their status by acquiring skills that are in demand (Hale, 1990a, p. 41). In other parts of the Sahel and

Savanna, the distinction between artisans and those of captive origin appears to be somewhat clearer.

But whatever their origin, the belief that they are of low status conflicts with the reality of daily life. If they are at the bottom of the social ladder, why would people fear them so much? Why would listeners give them so much in the way of rewards? Why would they be featured in the media, travel with presidents, and appear on postage stamps? The short answer is that griots are not of captive origin and are not of low status.

Diango Cissé argues that the *nyamakalaw* are quite different from the pariahs of India:

> Far from being despised to the point of having to live in an isolated fashion from the rest of the village community, men of the so-called castes are really feared because of a certain "power"—power with the word in general (praises for griots, magical incantations by blacksmiths). (1970, p. 211)

Cissé and other scholars see the social structure more in terms of clans or guilds. Bonnie Wright (1989, p. 2) argues that the notion of hierarchy does not fit well in West Africa. She asserts that "the West African caste system, rather than being composed of hierarchically ranked groups, is really best understood as a set of groups differentiated by innate capacity—or power—sources. The inequalities of the system are less ones of rank than of culturally defined realism of power." John Johnson takes a similar view when he describes the people who carry out different social functions as "socio-economic family monopolies, and not hierarchical pecking orders" (in Johnson and Sisòkò, 1986, p. 22).

Sory Camara (1976, pp. 65–66) explains that in the Malinké world the so-called people of caste, the *nyamakalaw*, are neither noble nor captive; he suggests that the view of their inferiority stems from the lack of social mobility. Because he sees both noble and captive traits in their behavior, he places them in a separate category, outside the basic hierarchy framed by nobles and captives. Camara's study, apparently intended to give a more positive view of griots, nevertheless provoked a hostile response from one family of griots, that of Adama Dramé and his cousin Fatim. Referring to a passage on page 158 of Camara's *Gens de la parole* about griots and society ("Here are men who did not make war, men who sing and play instruments, things which ordinarily are the domain of women"), Fatim responds:

> What is described there, it is defamatory, for me and for my caste. . . . the essence that comes out of it [the book] is that for society the griot is a really superfluous character. People fear griots: they will exploit you, because when

they sing, it is in order to make people give them money. They rob you, knowing well that what is said is false. Thus, they show that the griot is really a plague for society. (Dramé and Senn-Borloz, 1992, p. 19; my translation)

Fatim adopted the word *caste* here no doubt because it is so widely used in West Africa.

Before proceeding, one must ask just what *caste* means and what its significance is for understanding griots. The research of Tal Tamari has thrown the entire subject into a new perspective. In an article in the *Journal of African History* that reflects research for her 1987 thesis "Les Castes au Soudan occidental: Etude anthropologique et historique" (The castes of Western Sudan: An anthropological and historical study), she retained *caste* as an appropriate term to describe an "endogamous ranked specialist group" that forms a small percentage—5 to 20%—of the population among the fifteen peoples in fourteen states of West Africa where they are found" (1991, pp. 221–24). But from her archival sources as well as from fieldwork in Mali she found a considerable overlapping of terms for the different professions (weavers, blacksmiths, carvers, potters, griots), great variation in the number of castes in a given society (from one among the Dan to twelve among the Tukulor and Fulbe), and ambiguity about who was and who was not part of a caste. In general, Tamari's research confirmed several widespread beliefs: first, that free people cannot carry out many of the functions of caste people, but caste people do not always make a career of their caste's specialty; second, that caste people are nearly always considered to be inferior to freeborn but superior to slaves; third, that caste people do not marry or have sexual relations with free people; fourth, that caste people may carry out specialized social functions: for example in many cultures blacksmiths perform circumcisions while griots serve as messengers. But in spite of the differences, Tamari asserted that caste people "were subjected to few forms of social segregation and avoidance behavior other than endogamy itself" (1991, p. 230). The fact that they often lived in separate neighborhoods, she suggested, was less a function of isolation than a reflection of the fact that each lineage tended to have its own part of a village.

"Caste" can sometimes be a trait that depends on the eye of the beholder, especially across ethnic and functional groups. Tamari termed the Somono fisherman of the Niger River in Mali "quasi caste" people because the Bamana consider them to be casted, while others see them as noble or free. What complicates the issue further is that *caste* is associated with clan names, and these names circulate across peoples, changing rank as they travel. Iba Der Thiam, former minister of education in Senegal, notes that family names such as Thiam and Lam are viewed as upperclass in Tukulor society, while Fatou Sow affirms that among the Wolof they are sometimes looked upon as inferior (Coulibaly, March 1, 1990, p. 6).

In the contemporary context the issue of caste is slowly breaking down as the result of a variety of social, economic, and occupational changes. The awareness of these changes appears in a variety of ways, including epics about heroes of the past. For example, in *The Epic of Bamana Segu*, *jeli* Tayiru Banbera contrasts the power of *nyamakalaw* in the late eighteenth and early nineteenth centuries with their influence today.

> In those days, to be a *nyamakala* was like precious gems.
> If one of us destroyed a noble's reputation, the noble lost his place in
>   society.
> If we praise a noble beyond his rank, no one will keep up with him.
> 2230 If a *nyamakala* told his patron to get beans, he would buy butter.
> In those days there was no wealth but nobility.
> Oh, nowadays nobility is dead.
> We live in a day when people have many possessions.
> If a man does not respect his given word but is rich,
> 2235 Even if he is not a Muslim and does not respect his given word,
> People will include him among the nobles anyway.
> In former times material wealth could not rank a man as nobility.
> In those days it was your given word and your behaviour that made
>   you noble.
> It was not because of your wealth that you would get someone's
>   daughter in a marriage.
> 2240 It was your honour and conduct that got you a wife.
> But honour is dead today.
> We now live in a time of money.
> If you have no money, you have no right to speak.
> Even with your own things, others will make the decisions and let
>   you know about it later. (Conrad, 1990, pp. 136–37)

While the *nouveaux riches* acquire the status of nobles, some penniless nobles turn to other means to survive. One can now find nobles in professions formerly occupied solely by so-called caste people. At the same time, new trades based on Western technology attract workers from all social categories. But the sense of difference and of hierarchy rooted in the notion of caste is a feature of social life that escapes no one because it is so deeply rooted in society.

Tamari believes that the concept originated in joking relationships between clans, a feature that is common in the Mande world (1991, p. 239). These relationships, based on an exchange of blood, match the most widely heard origin tale for griots (see in chapter 2). "Contracted in conditions of extreme inequality," Tamari notes, these arrangements tended to tie griots, blacksmiths, and other professionals to certain clans over time.

Tamari's study of the different words for individual caste groups, as well as her examination of the term to represent them, *nyamakala*, found with some variants not only among the Mande-speaking peoples but also among other societies of the region, suggests either that "caste institutions developed independently among each of these three peoples [Manding, Soninke, and Wolof], or, having appeared among one or two, they were adopted by the other(s) at so early a date that no trace of foreign origin has been left in either language of social structure" (247).

In a more recent study, Tamari argues persuasively from linguistic evidence that the notion of caste spread from two terms:

> Only four West African languages have collective designations for caste people. These four languages—Manding, Soninke, Wolof, and Fulfulde (Fulani and Tukulor)—distinguish a total of five terms: Manding nyàmakala, Soninke ñaxamala, Wolof ñeeño, Fulfulde (Fulani and Tukulor) (nyeenyo/nyeenybe), and Fulfulde (Tukulor only) nyaamakala. There are strong reasons for believing that these diverse terms have developed from only two etymons: Manding nyàmakala and Wolof ñeeño. (1995, p. 65)

No matter how deeply rooted the notion of caste, as reflected in the terms mentioned above, the nature of caste in the West African context appears to be dynamic: caste characteristics undergo change. Tamari identifies several different kinds of changes: "increase in importance of secondary occupation, until it became the primary occupation; a complete change of occupation; change in rank and in the nature of relations with the majority occupation" (1991, p. 247). She cites several examples: Yaya Wane's research on the Tukulor, which includes examples of woodworking groups that had a secondary occupation as musicians, and who shifted to music full time; the notion among some Soninké peoples that griots were once blacksmiths (248); and the frequent assimilation of caste people to host cultures.

These examples all underscore the notion that caste activities, and by extension those who participate in them, are subject to change, a trait that conflicts with the idea of caste as a permanent, almost genetic feature. This degree of flexibility inherent in caste also may explain, at least in part, the ability of some contemporary performers who are not of griot origin to enter professions associated with music (see chapter 8).

The issue of caste, then, is rather complex, echoing in different ways throughout Sahelian and Savanna societies. Some researchers contest the use of the term *caste* to describe the position of griots, and I believe it will be best to place the term in quotation marks when it is used to refer to the situation in West African societies of the Sahel and Savanna regions. I agree with David Conrad and Barbara Frank, who argue that local terms rather than *caste* should be adopted. In their 1995 volume *Status and Identity in West Africa: Nyamakalaw of Mande*, Conrad and Frank announce in the preface that they will use the term *nyamakalaya* to represent the world of those who have been for so long called "casted" artisans (ix–x).

This attempt at greater precision underscores the fact that those who come from an artisan background are perceived in many ways as different from others—different almost in an ethnic sense. In other words, griots and other artisans constitute what amounts to a separate people in the minds of the people among whom they live. This difference can be expressed in many ways, but blood, race, and profession recur often in discussions about the distinction between people of artisan origin and other members of society. In other words, where outsiders distinguish clearly between ethnicity and social function, local people see a continuum that blends both.

Marriage

The basic rule against marrying outside of the artisan group remains deeply rooted in the collective memory of societies. Exceptions become part of the mythology of the region. For example, one explanation for the creation of the *guelewar* noble-warrior class among the Serer of Senegal many centuries ago is a migration of some Mande people from east to west that was caused in part by an inappropriate marriage between a princess and a griot. These warriors are supposed to have gone into exile for seven to nine years in the Gabou region of eastern Gambia, where they lived in a grotto without revealing their identity. Henry Gravrand, citing several oral versions among the Serer, implies that this legend led to a widespread belief that *guelewar* women—those who claimed roots in Mali—were libertines. He cites others examples from Serer history of the phenomenon of noble women with griot lovers. In the case of the Mande princess, her husband kept his griot status, but their children became nobles (1983, pp. 250–51).

Today such marriages remain the exception. Adama Dramé (in Dramé and Senn-Borloz, 1992), recounts the extraordinary story of his failed attempt at marriage to the mother of his child. When his prospective in-laws in Bobo-Dioulasso, Burkina Faso, found out that the father of their pregnant daughter was a griot, they were quite upset: "The father says to me no, there is no more marriage between us, because me, I am Jéli, I am only a jembéfola [drummer]. He, he was from a noble family (Horon)" (67). To prevent further contact, the father arranged to have the jeli arrested. Dramé concludes that it was all "because I am only a jembéfola. They wanted to prove to me that they were drivers, that they were Nobles, therefore they could have me locked up" (69).

During the interrogation at the police station, officers noted that his profession, as indicated on his national identity card, was griot. One of them exclaimed, "You are a griot. You don't work. Go on, off to prison!" (69). Dramé escaped from this situation only because one of his co-performers, a jelimuso who was a wife of the police chief, intervened along with 200 women from Bobo-Dioulasso. They refused to accept the arrest of one of their favorite jeliw.

Dramé's cousin Fatim reports that planned marriages had fallen through for her on several occasions because of the view that she was of an inferior "caste" (Dramé and Senn-Borloz, 20).

A Senegalese student named Thiam, interviewed for a newspaper series on the issue of "caste" in contemporary society, complained bitterly that she had lost an opportunity to marry her suitor because of the intervention of the man's parents who did not want their son to marry someone of artisan origin (Coulibaly, March 8, 1990, p. 6). One Senegalese civil servant of similar background reported that after completing studies abroad he had married a European woman "in order to escape the humiliation" that he would face if he attempted to marry outside of his group after he returned home (Coulibaly, March 1, 1990, p. 6).

Employment

Discrimination against griots and other "casted" people also affects those who practice new professions imported from Europe. Kaba Kouyaté, a primary school teacher from the Khassonké region of Mali, near Kayes, expressed great pride in his jeli heritage when I interviewed him in 1992 at the Ecole Normale Supérieure, Mali's leading institution of higher learning in the liberal arts, where he was completing advanced studies to become a high school teacher. His father, he reported, received a medal in Bamako from the visiting president of Côte d'Ivoire, Félix Houphouët-Boigny, for services as a jeli during the electoral campaigns of the Rassemblement Démocratique Africain (RDA) in Mali in the 1940s and 1950s. The RDA was a regional political organization that gave birth to the independence movements and national parties. But Kouyaté explained that in his village, a *jeli* could not become the secretary-general of the political party.

Like Dramé, he too had encountered discrimination. When he first began to teach, he expressed interest in a woman colleague of Fulbe origin. After her father learned of this romantic interest and of the *jeli* origin of the suitor, he warned Kouyaté to stay in his place and to limit himself to singing the daughter's praises. In his professional life, Kouyaté explained, he encountered no difficulty with his students or their parents. People accepted him as a teacher, yet made no connection between the traditional function of the griot as teacher and the modern role of the instructor in a state-sponsored school. But although corporal punishment was permitted in the school, parents of noble or free-born children would complain if he were to strike one of their offspring.

In both Mali and Senegal, however, one can find examples—perhaps they are exceptions—of people of artisan origin who have held high office. Writing in 1966, six years after independence, Ousmane Silla observed that the issue of "caste" did not seem to affect politics to a very great extent in Senegal. He found people of *nyeenyo* origin in the legislature and in the executive branches of government, but in the rural areas there was still some resistance to their being in positions of power. In one region on the Senegal River, local leaders had refused to accept the nomination of a *commandant de cercle* of "caste" origin (732). He explained that

> all nominations for jobs or important posts in the government had been marked, however slightly, by the imprint of "caste." We see some ministries occupied essentially by people of the same family, coming from the same clan, and from the same caste. These aspects of caste in Senegalese political life do not in any way paralyse the action of the state and of the government. But one cannot help but note the persistence of certain forms of traditionalism in the workings of the state. (Silla, 1966, pp. 733–34; my translation)

The first president of Senegal, Léopold Sédar Senghor, reports Villalón (1995, 58), "admitted intentionally challenging caste prejudices in making presidential appointments, once protesting: 'There used to be caste prejudices. . . . I always take them into account, I never speak of them . . . and I think that, now, we have surpassed these prejudices of caste'." Villalón reads Senghor's statement as evidence that caste in government is still a very sensitive issue.

In Mali after independence, people of griot origin held positions in the regional administration of Kita, a center of *jeliya*. As Mali made the transition from colony to country in the late 1950s and early 1960s, two people of *jeli* origin, Moussa Sylla, a Soninké originally from Mopti, and Makan Kouyaté, a descendant of an old Kita *jeli* family, became very influential (Hopkins, 1972, pp. 128–29). Both were in the field of public health, and each took advantage of the fact that under the new rules of society, all members were equal. But there were problems. As Hopkins explains, the government of Mali wanted to eliminate discrimination against *jeliw* and other *nyamakala*, but also to suppress the special privileges these members of society enjoyed, in particular the rewards they received at ceremonies (189). Some members of society, Hopkins notes, felt that "dieli, other nyamakala, and descendants of slaves ought not to have positions in Kita." But he adds that "the success of *dieli* in particular shows the limitation of this attitude" (206).

One of the best known public servants of griot origin was the Malian writer Seydou Badian Kouyaté, who held the post of minister of planning and rural development from 1960 to 1966. He continues to be active in the politics of Mali as a leader in an opposition party. In Senegal, in the broader context of people of artisan origin, one can cite Habib Thiam, prime minister from 1981 to 1983; Iba Der Thiam, minister of education; Keba Mbaye of the International Court of Justice in the Hague; and Amadou Maktar Mbow, former director general of UNESCO. All of them are identified as members of this group, known as *nyeenyo*.

But what about higher rank? A sidebar in one of the news articles on "caste" (Coulibaly, 1990, March 1) provides both the question and the response: "Could a caste person become president of the Republic of Senegal? The question is an open one when one is aware of the extent and the survival of the phenomenon" (my translation). The reporter's conclusion is that such an event is not likely. Although the religious and judicial texts governing life in Senegal exclude any considerations of "caste" in human relations, the sentiment against mixing nobles and "caste" people remains strong. This extends beyond the matter of marriage and includes those who would like to enter a profession traditionally reserved for persons of artisan background.

The most striking exception to the general rule is Salif Keita, the Malian singer. He shares a clan name with Sundiata Keita, founder of the Mali empire. But he is an albino and for this reason he was rejected by his father at birth. He was rejected once again when he began to take up music and is still told by his father that a Keita should not be making music (Seck and Clerfeuille, 1986, p. 98). When his career began to develop, he started to integrate *jeli* songs into his repertoire, a move that angered the country's *jeliw*. Today there is more widespread acceptance at home for this internationally known performer, but no one seems to have forgotten the paradox of his profession and his origin.

Ali Farka Touré, another singer from Mali with a noble clan name, that of Askia Mohammed Touré, the ruler who brought the Songhay empire to its apogee in the late fifteenth and early sixteenth centuries, encountered similar difficulties. But he told me in 1993 that he was able to blaze his own path into the entertainment profession because of another family activity related to music, that of healing and sorcery, which often require music (see also Durán, 1992). Although neither Keita nor Touré claims to be a griot, the fact that both men sing music that is in some ways rooted in the musical tradition of their respective peoples reveals to contemporary griots that these nobles are crossing a professional and social boundary normally closed to them.

Identity and Difference

In Camara Laye's autobiographical account (*L'Enfant noir*, 1953; *The Dark Child*, 1954) of growing up in Guinea as the son of a Malinké blacksmith, the father (in both the French original and the English translation) refers to his profession as a "race." The term that he used originally in his dialogue with his son was undoubtedly *siya*, a word of considerable ambiguity. Barbara Hoffman explains that "'siya' is sometimes best translated as 'race,' sometimes as 'kind' or 'lineage,' 'genotype' or 'seed,' 'origins,' or 'ethnicity'" (1990a, p. 30). The interpretation depends on the context in which it is employed. When referring to griots or blacksmiths, *siya* indicates the distinctive identity of the people who practice those professions.

A teacher from another part of the region echoed this sense of identity during an interview in 1992 in Bamako. When I asked Sidi Ahmed Ag Alhassane, a fourth-year student at the Ecole Normale Supérieure in Bamako, about his ethnic origin, he replied "smith." Knowing that he came from a Tuareg family in Menaka, a town in eastern Mali near the border with Niger, I asked him again, and he replied, "Tuareg smith." Tuareg society, like other societies in West Africa, maintains the basic tripartite social structure, although the noble-captive relationship seems to be more symbiotic than elsewhere but also more clearly defined, with the Tuaregs appearing light-skinned and identifying themselves with a particular clan, those of captive origin dark-skinned and of a different ethnic group.

Illustrating Tamari's observation about overlapping professions, Ag Alhassane confirmed that Tuareg smiths also serve as griots, although it is the women who usually do the singing at events while the men may play a three- or four-stringed instrument. As if to emphasize his initial reference to his social identity as a smith, Ag Alhassane pointed out that smiths were thinner than other members of society, with skin that was darker than that of nobles but lighter than the tint of slaves. For him, smiths constituted a clearly definable people, not to be confused with their Tuareg hosts or the slaves of those people. In this context, it would be unthinkable for a blacksmith to marry either a noble or a slave.

Insiders and Outsiders

One reason for the sense of difference is that griots seem to travel more than other members of society, and in some cultures, the griot comes from the outside. Evidence suggests that among the Fulbe—or at least some groups of Fulbe—griots traditionally came from outside (Dupire, 1970). This is the case among the Zarma of Niger. The Songhay, who share the same language with the Zarma, traditionally provided griots for Zarma ceremonies, according to Boubou Hama, the late dean of researchers on the history of Niger (1980). Today, however, there are many versions of how these bards arrived among the Zarma (Olivier de Sardan, 1982, pp. 224–30).

Although griots are often attached to certain clans and families, they appear as both insiders and outsiders because they also travel widely to perform for expatriates from those groups. This may be especially true in the vast Mande-speaking area composed of many different peoples who speak languages that are more or less related. A Mandinka griot who travels to Bamako, where Maninka and Bamana are spoken, remains within the Mande family but will be perceived as an outsider. He may become part of a diaspora of griots with relatives in many cities. A striking example of this phenomenon is the Diabaté-Jobarteh family, which has roots in both Bamako, Mali, and Brikama, The Gambia.

Power

Griots, as well as other artisans, appear to other members of society as rather different from a variety of angles. But why do the differences inspire fear and, in the extreme, burial in trees? Paulla Ebron argues (1993) that one must understand not simply the difference between these people and others in society, but also the meaning of that difference. Along with Hoffman, she asserts that a major part of that difference lies in the power of the griots over their audiences, a power rooted in a special talent with words. Ebron interprets this talent as that of constructing identity and negotiating meaning.

> They "make culture" through the recitation of genealogies. Jali help construct national identity through their stories of Mande kingdoms. They fashion themselves as cultural authorities, performing for audiences in The Gambia, and internationally, and in these performances identity, culture, and politics are simultaneously enacted and created for and by audiences. (28)

Although Ebron's comments are aimed at the interaction between griots and audiences outside Africa, the notion of cultural authority she describes here explains what lies behind their behavior in the local context. Hoffman suggests that the difference—as well as the social status—of Mande *jeliw* is rooted in their relationship to *nyama*, that special force that is evoked when one carries out certain actions, such as working with iron and speaking words. She sums up a new approach to hierarchy among a recent generation of scholars by reporting that

> the relations between these two groups [nobles and *nyamakalaw*] may be seen as intrinsically connected to each one's capacity to confront and manipulate the energy of *nyama*. Members of *nyamakala* groups . . . are all reputed to be born with greater capacities of control of *nyama* than the nobles. (1990a, pp. 138–39)

Another dimension of the griots' power lies in the control of the collective and individual histories of a people. References to this appear in the descriptions of their role in war. The griot is responsible for linking past, present, and future. Whether a person and his or her ancestors are inserted into, maintained on, or erased from this continuum depends on the griot. It is a cultural pathway shared by many people, some of whom are descendants of warriors or fought not only for the good of the clan or empire but also among themselves. Some griots—for example, Djibo Badié in Niamey, known locally as Djeliba—hold in their memories the power to calm or inflame relations among families today simply by describing conflicts between ancestors that occurred a generation or two ago. It is for this reason, Djeliba told me in 1980, that he is very careful when describing events of the late modern period.

Beyond this broad description of the power of griots, one must cite specific abilities often attributed to them. The most obvious is the ability to destroy a person's reputation with words. Although I have not come across examples of this, the use of verbal power for negative purposes is often cited by nobles as a persuasive reason for generosity to griots. But another less evident reason for fear of griots is the belief that they can use their words in occult ways to achieve their ends. In most West African societies, sorcerers use words as well as other devices to carry out their works. Paul Stoller, a symbolic anthropologist, and Cheryl Olkes give striking examples of the power of words among the Songhay in their study *In Sorcery's Shadow: A Memoir of an Apprenticeship among the Songhay of Niger* (1987). But sorcerers do not hold a monopoly on the use of language for these special purposes. In *L'Assemblée des djinns* (1985), the Malian author of *jeli* origin Massa Makan Diabaté describes several examples of occult power deployed by different factions of *jeliw* in a dispute over the leadership of the profession. In addition, Cheick Keita (1995a, p. 189) has pointed out that "traditionally, the griots have distinguished themselves as social psychologists. As such, not only do they excel in detecting the most secret motives behind human behavior but also they excel in using them in their mediatory role and in their art. . . . The ability to inspire a wide range of feelings gives the griot caste an incredible power over their countrymen."

The Collectivity

If griots are different from other members of society, especially their noble patrons, they nevertheless remain quite closely linked to them, both in daily life and in a psychological sense. Beyond the functional difference of interpreting and preserving culture, the griot seems to constitute the other half, the other side, of a collective personality, one that is allowed to express things and behave in ways that are forbidden to others. Singing, music-making, and other loud behavior are seen as inappropriate for people of noble origin. But without these actitivies, the hard life of inhabitants in the Sahel and Savanna regions would lose much of its cheer.

The notion of the griot as different stems less from the griot than from those around him or her, as Dramé and his cousin Fatim have explained. In other words, identity is defined by context. As Conrad and Frank point out, the identity of this group—and the notion of where it fits into society--stems from how others view griots. If griots, a minority in society, are perceived as dangerous or to be avoided by the majority, then these labels will stick to them.

Ethnicity

The definition of a people by others in society reflects in microcosm the larger ambiguity about the concept of ethnicity in West Africa. One is Bamana or Fulbe not simpy by birth but also by circumstance. The result can be a bewildering list of descriptors for a given people that ultimately make no sense.

Jean Bazin has identified this phenomenon in his essay "A chacun son Bambara" (To Each His Bambara, 1985), arguing that ethnicity—the traits, characteristics, even the name of a people—is often determined by those outside. Ethnicity, he suggests, is a vague and rather approximate notion emerging from human interactions in which people name "others in relation to themselves while naming themselves in relation to others" (94; my translation).

The most common term for Bambara in the language of peoples who are normally designated by this word, Bazin notes, is *Bamana*. But the people known as Bamana have several meanings for this term, none of which is definitive (97). One must, he suggests, take this ambiguity as a given and attempt to read into it the subtle evidence of a complex social history. Thus one can encounter Mande speakers for whom Bamana may mean either people who speak the same language, people who are incomprehensible barbarians, people who are neighbors, people who are foreigners, or simply free people who are not of "caste" origin (110).

Bazin cites the example of a Bamana smith who, like the teacher of Tuareg smith origin or the father of Camara Laye, sees his identity mainly in his professional roots rather than as part of an ethnic group.

> To be a Numu (a member of an endogamous group who are recognized as holding the monopoly on metalworking) or a Jeli . . . is to not be a Bamana. For example, recounting the history of a village, an old Numu will say how his ancestor moved to this area in the company of a Bamana. For it is only by reference to a Bamana lineage fulfilling the function of host (jatigi) that a member of one of these "castes" can join a village community (dugu). (110)

Caste, Tribe, and Dialect

If the notion of ethnicity is so fluid, how useful can the idea of "caste" be in situating and explaining the status of a subgroup in society? One answer may lie in a comparison with two other terms that appear often in reference to people who live outside the Western tradition: *tribe* and *dialect*.

Anthropologists do not always agree on just what constitutes a tribe, but they have attempted to define the term to fit certain conditions, usually involving a common ancestor and a common language. But for the nonspecialist public, including journalists, the term *tribe* is loosely applied to all kinds of non-Western groups, from the diverse Hausa-speaking peoples of northern Nigeria to the vast Swahiliphone world of East and Central Africa. Above all, it is a term that connotes a lack of civilization. But it is not normally used to describe the people at each other's throats in the former Yugoslavia, Northern Ireland, or Cyprus. The same may be said for *dialect*, a word with very clear meaning for linguists. When employed by nonspecialists it often refers to a language spoken by non-Western people. Journalist Maureen Dowd, for instance, described the speech of New York cab drivers as "an exotic range of languages that included the West African dialects of Ga, Efik and Kru" (1986).

Caste appears to follow the same pattern. For the anthropologist, it has a clear definition (people who marry within their own group, which is hierarchically ranked in society), but for the rest of the population, it carries the negative connotations so deeply embedded in descriptions of the lowest stratum of Indian society, the untouchables. By association, *caste* has come to indicate a group of people with whom no one would want to have contact.

High Status

If the differentness of griots, rooted in their verbal power and described in a variety of ways, results in the continued refusal of other members of society to marry one of them, it does not prevent people from listening to their praises, offering them rewards, and glorifying their profession in many other ways. These are all signs of high status, at least for talented griots.

For example, they appear on stamps. Both Ban Zoumana Cissoko of Mali and Boubacar Tinguizi of Niger were commemorated posthumously on stamps (see figures 11 and 12 in the preceding chapter). It is true that the variety of images on the stamps of African countries, as well as on those issued by postal services elsewhere in the world, often gives the impression that almost anything will be used to promote sales. But the appearance of local heroes on stamps (as opposed to airplanes, paintings, and descriptions of animals) is a special event.

The death of a great griot, one who has been heard weekly on the radio, or is invited to the homes of statesmen in many countries, constitutes a major event marked by memorials, obituaries, and other commemorations. When Wâ Kamissoko died in 1976, he was given a state funeral in Mali (Moraes Farias, 1993b, p. 14). The passing of Cissoko in 1989 was marked not only by a stamp but also by articles in Malian publications. In the case of Tinguizi, in addition to the stamp, a regional youth and culture building was named for him. At the funeral of Sira Mory Diabaté, who died October 16, 1989, fifteen cattle were sacrificed. A series of commemorative articles in journals from Mali to the United States later appeared (Bird, 1997; Jansen, 1996a).

Other indicators of the respect shown to griots are the rewards they receive. The most talented griots are richly rewarded for their services in cash, goods, and services. Hardly penniless troubadours, they travel the globe to perform for a variety of audiences and return home with many thousands of dollars. Whether or not one shares the pessimistic views of Massa Makan Diabaté and Ban Zoumana Cissoko that griots have traded the gold of their profession for copper (Keita, 1995b), it is clear that they are well rewarded today. And, as we have seen, the best griots have served at the right hand of their leaders. For example, Samory Touré's griot Morifing Dian traveled with him into exile after the ruler was captured by the French. Dian now is buried near Touré.

Hierarchies

I have referred frequently to "the most talented griots." What has no doubt contributed to the negative view of the profession is the existence of large numbers of not so talented—and in many cases fake—griots, both in the past and today. They constitute an urban plague that has become so serious that governments have attempted to suppress them by establishing new social regulations—for example setting up a professional association.

In 1930 in Saint-Louis, Senegal, colonial government representatives signed an agreement with local chiefs to control the behavior of griots at weddings. The rules included:

Article VII. It is formally forbidden to beat drums at just any occasion (except for public rejoicing, receptions of important people).

Article VIII. Out of respect for a secular tradition, it is agreed that on the occasion of every marriage celebration, the sum of 50 francs will be reserved for distribution among the griots, jewelers, and leatherworkers of the city.

Article IX. The griotte assigned to prepare the coiffure of the bride will receive 40 francs.

Article XI. It is formally forbidden for griots to enter homes in order to flatter young people and thus oblige them to give the praise-singers money. Fathers and mothers of families must prevent such acts if they want to avoid legal action.

All those who violate these articles will be subject to a fine of 500 to 4,000 francs, which will be paid to the government. (Silla, 1966, pp. 764–65; my translation)

The response of griots to these new regulations was to organize groups and assocations to protect their interests. Such organizations were aimed not only at threats from the outside, such as the new regulations, but also from the emergence of numbers of third-rate and fake griots.

It is this split within the profession that explains much of the ambiguity surrounding the status of griots. No one would think of looking down on a famous griot who sits at the side of the president of the country, but the hanger-on at a wedding may inspire charges of being a social parasite, an epithet that often comes to the lips of those who criticize the profession. A closer look at the different kinds of hierarchies within the griot world will help to explain some of the confusion about their status.

The first distinction, at least in the Mande world, which constitutes a very large share of the profession in the Sahel and Savanna regions, occurs between clans of griots. The Kouyatés are often seen as ranking at the top because they are the griots who served the Keita family, which founded the Mali empire. A Keita never gives gifts to griots of lower status in this clan hierarchy. Thus when Kaba Kouyaté, the schoolteacher, held a naming ceremony for one of his children, other *jeliw* attended but did not demand rewards for their praises—until they realized that Kaba's wife was not from the Kouyaté clan and was therefore in a position to satisfy them. The ranking of the other clans is open to debate, with the Jabatés or Diabatés often listed as second, followed by the remaining clans in no particular order—the Sussos, the Kontés, and the Tounkaras.

But this hierarchical difference between clans can take on a much larger meaning in the broader context of the entire Mande world. In Kita, a longtime center for *jeliya*, the leadership of the bards has rotated according to clan, with the Kouyatés remaining in a neutral position. But when the last leader, a Tounkara, died in the early 1980s, his clan attempted to violate tradition by maintaining a hold on the *jelikuntigi*, or leadership position. The conflict was resolved in 1985 only after complex mediation by other griots as well as local political leaders. The event was marked by an enormous three-day celebration that drew thousands of *jeliw* from the Mande diaspora. Hoffman's richly detailed description of the gathering, her analysis of the conflict based on her own attendance there as a Jabaté *jelimuso*, and her subsequent research reveal much about the notion of hierarchy among griots (1990a, 1995b). At the same time, she offers new insights into the relationship of Mande *jeliw* with other members of society.

For another perspective, one can read Massa Makan Diabaté's novel *L'Assemblée des djinns*. Diabaté has recreated the world of rivalry and intrigue surrounding the *jelikuntigi* in Kita from the perspective of an insider in a work that is somewhat critical of his own people. Through the characters in the novel, the reader discovers the pettiness, greediness, and other negative qualities of the groups fighting for power.

A second kind of hierarchy appears across the entire region in the distinction between royal, or court, griots, master griots, journeyman griots, and apprentices (mentioned in chapter 4). The royal griot, who traditionally had the best access to rulers, reigned over all other griots, from the *bajguewel* of the Wolof (Dieng, 1993) to the *jeliba* of the Mande, the *gesereba* of the Bariba (Moraes Farias, 1993b), and the *makadan sarauta* (court singers) of the Hausa (Furniss, 1996, p. 128).

Another category, of nearly equal status depending on the local context, is the master griot, known as *ngara* among the Mande and *jeseré-dunka* among the Songhay. Usually a master griot is forty or fifty years old. He or she may preside over a small community of griots and has acquired great knowledge as the result of decades of study, service, and travel.

In some cases, the difference between royal griot and master griot is difficult to discern. The griot in Zinder described in chapter 1, Mazo dan Alalo, seems to have combined the nobility that is typical of a chief griot with the talent that marks the most skilled *marok'i*. In many cases, it is this kind of talent that leads to the position of royal griot.

Yet another form of hierarchy occurs among musicians. Referring to the Malinké, Sory Camara suggests that those who play stringed instruments are ranked high because these instruments are associated with masculine events. The *balafon* players, who play at all events, are a notch lower, and the drummers come last because their instruments are most commonly played for women (1976, p. 120). The *fina*, Islamic griots who play no instruments at all, would rank at the very top in Camara's scheme because of the importance of the word and their influence, but he notes that Malinké griots rank the *fina* at the bottom. Camara explains this difference by suggesting that the griots are looking at the situation from an internal, griot-centered perspective, while he takes into consideration larger concerns, such as the influence of the bards on society. Ultimately, however, as Camara points out, the *fina* can ask the *jeli* for gifts but not vice versa, evidence if there need be any that the *fina* ranks below the *jeli*.

A final hierarchy, if one may call it that, exists between professional griots and the growing mass of fake griots, including some nobles, who have invaded the profession in search of money. It is a phenomenon probably unheard of a century ago. Today, however, with the economic crisis that has descended upon many countries in West Africa, one finds a growing reversal of roles. In *L'Assemblée des djinns*, the narrator declares, "Griots died when the Whites arrived. . . . Chief of griots! . . . But there are no more griots" (Massa Makan Diabaté, pp. 62–63; my translation). The criticism appears to be aimed as much at the newcomers as at fellow griots who have evolved to meet the changing social conditions.

One of those conditions is the destitution of some noble families who were not able to make the leap from colonialism to the national era. Many of the griots I interviewed affirmed that they had witnessed performances of one kind or another by nobles whom they considered to be "fake" griots.

This role reversal offers a clue to the power of griots. Clemens Zobel has argued that nobles constitute a form of behavior rather than a class or caste. Many griots, he writes, see themselves manifesting forms of conduct that put them on an equal, if not superior, footing with nobles: "The precedence of the *hòròn* [noble] within the realm of action is confronted with the superiority of the *nyamakala-jeli* in the sphere of knowledge" (in Jansen and Zobel, 1996, p. 40). His view is supported by some of the origin tales cited in chapter 2, as well as by the descriptions of some of the oldest and most talented griots, who constitute what amounts to the nobility of the profession.

❊ ❊

The different perspectives reflected by European travelers, nobles, griots, other artisans, and researchers lead to a series of conclusions about the social status of griots today.

First, the term *caste* appears to offer limited value as a descriptor, even though it occurs widely in both popular and scholarly writing. Anthropologists may find *caste* quite useful as the most appropriate term from the vocabulary of their field to describe griots; in fact, Tamari (1987) argues for its use for theoretical and comparative purposes in her thesis. She asserts that the comparison between India and the Sudanic region of West Africa reveals a variety of similarities in the maintenance of systems of castes and clan structures. The data she brings to her analysis are formidable. She believes that objections to the use of the term are based on a misunderstanding of the Indian system. She is careful, however, to point out that there are no relationships between the West African and Indian social structures. For the anthropologist framing a discussion of "caste" in the context of a global comparison between India and Africa, the term may work quite satisfactorily. But *caste* carries a rather high negative charge outside the confines of anthropology as the result of the popular image of the Indian system. It contributes to what many scholars see as an unfortunate simplification and distortion of the complex situation of griots in West African society today. For this and other reasons, Conrad and Frank place the term in quotation marks to distance themselves from it, a step with which I have indicated I agree fully.

Second, it is clear that both the griots and those around them are keenly aware of the significant differences that separate them. These differences are based not simply on social behavior but more importantly on how the behavior impacts on others. It is difficult to identify this behavior in any way other than as a manifestation of social power, following the views of both Ebron and Hoffman.

Third, it is evident that much of what we know about griots and their status in society has come from those who are not griots—primarily free people or nobles who have served as informants or have conducted and published research about griots. Just as the notion of the nature of the Bamana has been shaped by external forces—French colonizers, proponents of Islam, other ethnic groups, anthropologists—so has the idea of the griot, part of the larger world of artisans, come to us from the changing social context in which these wordsmiths operate. But with few exceptions, we have heard little from the griots themselves.

Fourth, we need to reconsider the griot as a distinct but symbiotic component of a complex whole made up of both noble and griot. Fatim, the cousin of Dramé, expresses it in these terms: "If you are Noble, maybe it is necessary for me to be Griot in order for you to be Noble" (Dramé and Senn-Borloz, 1992, p. 20). If, to use Ebron's terms, it is the griot who constructs and interprets culture, then Fatim is certainly on the right path in her comment. Hoffman (1997) argues that the two, noble and griot, are "interdependent and complementary."

Finally, if one balances both the many functions that griots carry out and their own statements of their worth in society against the rather deep-seated distancing of nobles from these bards, at least in a social sense, it appears that the real nature of their social status lies in some ambiguous middle area. They represent an ill-defined "other" that is both essential for the functioning of society and quite uncomfortable for those who seek to establish nontraditional ties with them. It is a role that Sory Camara (1976) and Cheick M. Keita (1995b) have termed as a sort of arbiter. The "otherness" of griots is rooted not simply in their monopoly on certain uses of the spoken word but most importantly on the power of their words to praise, to differentiate, to preserve, and to destroy.

In societies that are permeated with electronic means of communication, people ofter refer to the extraordinary power of the media with a mixed feeling of admiration, awe, and disgust. Many, however, would not decline the opportunity to be the focus of attention of the media. In somewhat the same way, the power of griots inspires fear and awe but also extraordinary pleasure for listeners today in West Africa. Hoffman sums up the importance of this power in the Mande world:

> To speak griot language to someone is to make its *nyama* enter him, to make him bigger with the honor thus bestowed. In the Mande world, control of *nyama* is one of the most important means of exercising power. Unless we, as scholars, take the power of griots into account, we cannot begin to understand, much less to describe, their place in Mande social organization. (1995, p. 43)

What Hoffman describes for the Mande world is true in a more general sense for many other societies that support griots. If griots exercise certain kinds of power over others, then their status must reflect in some ways that capacity. To define that status, as Hoffman implies, we need to understand more clearly the complex dynamics of power relationships that may be quite different from anything we know in other societies with which we are familiar. The evidence presented in this chapter suggests that to the question of whether or not you would want your daughter to marry a griot, the answer may depend to a large extent on where you live, on the identity of your daughter and your family, your relationships with others in society, and the degree to which your values—and those of your daughter—have changed as the result of external influences.

✖ 7 ✖
Griottes:
Unrecognized Female Voices

When Alex Haley searched for links to his heritage in The Gambia, he focused his efforts on male griots. There are no references to female griots in *Roots*, either the video or the written narrative. The lack of any images of griottes stems in large part from a deeply rooted and functionally based gender division in many parts of Africa, as well as from the very limited amount of research on these female wordsmiths.

The lack of scholarly attention on griottes might lead one to assume that they are shadowy figures who stand at the margins of the oral narrative traditions that are recounted by their male counterparts, published in European languages, and read by students around the world. But one measure of the status of a griot is the rewards that the audience provides. The gift of a small airplane to Kandia Kouyaté (Durán, 1989, p. 38), one of Mali's best-known *jelimusow*, suggests that these women performers stand closer to the center than to the periphery of their cultural network. At least that seems to be the case in the heartland of the Mande. Why, then, in the two decades of what we might term the post-*Roots* era, has there been such a silence on griottes in scholarship about the oral traditions of the region?

The answers to this and many other questions are just beginning to emerge in the work of a handful of researchers. The story of how griottes have gone unnoticed for so long is almost as important as why they have now begun to attract greater attention. The purpose here is fourfold: to explain why we know so little about griottes, to report on work now being done by the small group of scholars interested in them, to give examples of the verbal art of these women, and to suggest some avenues of research.

When I asked Haley in 1991 if he had encountered any female griots, he replied candidly, "I never heard of a female griot. . . . Nobody ever mentioned it, nor did I ever think about it. . . . I took it for granted that there were none." Certainly the African American journalist and author did not set out to write an anthropological study of griots and griottes, and he cannot be blamed solely for what seems in retrospect to be an extraordinary oversight.

The omission of griottes from *Roots* was due at least in part to a significant difference between customs on the periphery and those at the center of the Mande world. In the Casamance region of Senegal and The Gambia, on the western edge of the Mande, one finds a great emphasis on the role of men as *kora* players and solo singers, a phenomenon that one can trace to the origin of the *kora* (Durán, 1994). In this region, women tend to play supporting roles in performances. These roles are, however, viewed as essential by male griots. Mandinka *jali* Mawdo Suusoo asserts that "a good instrumentalist does not feel complete unless he has at least one wife who is a good vocalist" (Jatta, 1985, p. 25).

Traditional Gender Bias

If women are important to Mandinka *jalolu*, there is nevertheless a general absence of discussion about griottes in much scholarship on the African oral tradition. Although one can find studies of women as performers in areas outside the Sahel and Savanna regions, as Carole Boyce Davies and Anne Adams Graves point out, some of the available information appears as part of larger studies by sociologists and anthropologists (1986, p. 17). For example, *La Place de la femme dans les rites au Sénégal* (Ndiaye, 1986) includes texts of songs by women, while *Les Zamu ou poèmes sur les noms* offers a collection of chants from the Songhay and Zarma of Niger that can be sung by nonprofessional as well as professional woman singers (Bisilliat and Laya, 1972).

The paucity of scholarship on griottes in particular and women performers in general seems to be symptomatic in a larger sense of the basic gender bias that has marked much social science research by scholars trained in the West, African and non-African. Even the most thorough study to date of griots in a particular people, Sory Camara's *Gens de la parole: Essai sur la condition et le rôle des griots dans la société malinké* (1976), barely mentions the existence of griottes in over 300 pages of highly detailed and complex analyses.

The same is true for one of the most widely read versions of the Sundiata epic. One finds only two brief references to griottes (28–29) in *Sundiata: An Epic of Old Mali* (Niane, 1960, 1965). In my own research for *The Epic of Askia Mohammed* in 1980–81 in Niger, I found no discussion of *jeserey weyborey*, or griottes, by the narrator, Songhay *jeseré* Nouhou Malio, nor did I have the openness of mind to ask about Songhay female griots in the course of many hours of interviews with over a dozen male artisans of the word in western Niger during ten months of fieldwork. My goal was simply to find an epic text that might parallel the *Sundiata* in significance and to learn something about the people who were reported to recount it—male griots.

Female griots are not unknown outside of West Africa. For example, Nantenegwé Kamissoko, a well-known Malian *jelimuso*, visited Penn State in 1978. But she was part of the entourage of *jeli* Batourou Sekou Kouyaté, the featured artist on a tour of many American universities conducted by Charles Bird.

There are numerous reasons for the high profile of male griots, especially outside of Africa. Mamadou Diawara describes distortions that affect the external perception of them.

> The first distortion occurs within the context studied; for this remains—even in matrilineal groups—a men's society, where women, under the sway of the dominant male ideology, do not often proclaim themselves as historians. The second is due to the fact that African studies, regardless of whether research is carried out by men or women, continue to be profoundly marked by the male point of view. (1989, p. 110)

Both Diawara, a male historian from the same cultural heritage as the subjects of his research, men and women from different levels of Soninké society in the ancient Malian kingdom of Jaara, and Barbara Hoffman, an American anthropologist who adopted the identity of a *jelimuso* during four years of research in Mali in the late 1980s, see an even greater and more fundamental distortion in research to date stemming from differences in class. Diawara (1990) has contrasted the many ways noble and slave world views and roles differ in the transmission of oral traditions. Hoffman (1990, pp. 2–3), drawing on both her own work and that of Bonnie Wright (1989) and Martha Kendall (1982), has explored how the noble view of griots as an inferior class literally and figuratively informs the research of both African and non-African scholars. The attention focused on a noble at an event takes on two different meanings, Hoffman explains. For the griot, it is a cause for animation and enlargement of the noble's reputation. For the noble, the griot's activities can be a source of discomfort and embarrassment as well as the occasion for unflattering comparisons between the living and the dead.

When we combine the gender bias of both researchers and noble informants with another bias based on the different world views of griots and nobles, the position of griots moves far down the social ladder and women may seem to disappear from view. The bias generated by this difference in the way two distinct social groups see the world leads to a misunderstanding about the complex nature of the verbal exchange between noble and griot. Hoffman concludes that "while the noble's position of social dominance over the griot is overemphasized in the literature, little is known of the power that griots have over nobles" (6). This holds true whether one is talking about male or female nobles or male or female griots.

Lucy Durán, former curator at the National Sound Archive in London, took a different approach to women griots by first learning about male griots. She studied the *kora* with one of the most respected masters in The Gambia, Amadu Bansang Jobarteh, then became involved in visits of griots to the United Kingdom in the 1980s and interviewed many of them for articles that appeared in a popular British magazine, *Folk Roots*. Through this experience, she became interested in female griots. In 1989, she published a landmark survey article on women singers, "Djely Mousso — Women of Mali," that provides for the first time a variety of insights into their musical art and modern performance contexts in Africa and Europe. More recently, her thorough article on Wasulu music of southern Mali has opened yet another door into the world of West African music, this time by performers who are not of griot origin (1995a).

From Durán's multifaceted work as well as from that of Hoffman and Diawara, it is clear that griottes are more numerous and in some cases even more famous than their male counterparts. Both Durán and Hoffman underscore the fact that in Mali the profession is driven by women. Durán explains:

> It is fundamental to the tradition of the Jalis . . . that the man's job is to play musical instruments whereas the women sing. Of course men sing too but in general women's voices are preferred, especially when it comes to singing the famed praise songs which recount, through improvised lyrics, the origins and history of the various family surnames. Women are also the "animateurs" at every traditional ceremony—whether clapping and singing to encourage the dancers or playing the iron percussion rod (nege), their presence is essential. And so it could be said that the women are the real stars of Mali. (1989a, p. 34)

Hoffman (1990b) echoes Durán's observation by remarking that the world of the griots in Mali, measured by the frequency of events, the number of people involved, the amount of money changing hands, and the variety of new art forms being created, is woman-centered.

Scholars and instructors outside of West Africa who have been reading and teaching *Soundjata* or its English version *Sundiata* for decades may be surprised to discover that women are, at least in Mali, the dominant voices in the modern performance context. There are two reasons for this reaction.

The first reason is that we do not hear the voices of *jelimusow* in the edition of *Soundjata* collected and translated by Niane. Although women play several key roles in the epic, the primary source, *jeli* Mamadou Kouyaté, apparently did not mention *jelimusow* as having any significant speaking parts. But other versions, such as the *Son-Jara* recounted by *jeli* Fa-Digi Sisòkò in Kita in 1968 and translated by John W. Johnson and a team of Malian scholars, give them a voice in the narrative.

In a key passage of the epic, the legal birth order of Son-Jara and his brother Dankaran Tuma is determined by the fact that the *jelimuso* sent to the king to report Son-Jara's birth refused food until she made her announcement. The other *jelimuso* who was to announce the slightly earlier birth of Dankaran Tuma, son of the first wife, Berete, accepts food first, thus delaying the announcement to the king and placing the child in second place. What matters here is that in the linear version of the epic recounted by Sisòkò the *jelimuso* has a voice. In this scene, *jelimuso* Tumu Maniya, referred to here as the Kuyatè matriarch, candidly explains what happened to an enraged Saman Berete, first lady of the Mande but mother of an infant who has now become second in line to the throne.

1106 The Kuyatè matriarch spoke out:
    "Nothing happened at all. (Indeed)
    "I was the first to pronounce myself. (Indeed)
    "Your husband said the first name heard,
    "Said, he would be the elder, (Indeed)
    "And thus yours became the younger." (Indeed)

(Johnson and Sisòkò, 1992, p. 51)

A comparison between the prose version collected by Niane from Mamadou Kouyaté, a text that offers an easily understandable introduction for younger readers, and the version recounted by Fa-Digi Sisòkò, which is more challenging, reveals what is lost not simply in form but also in content—the roles and voices of *jelimusow*.

A second reason for blindness to women is that scholarly interest in texts recorded from oral sources has tended to focus on the longer forms, which are viewed to be the domain of men in West Africa. But women have always shared the stage with men. To understand this paradox, one must begin by looking back at the many early references to griottes by Europeans.

Arab and European travelers encountered griottes at the same time they first took note of griots in the entourages of rulers of West African towns and cities. Amid the confusion and misinterpretation in their portrayals of these male and female wordsmiths, one senses that women were just as important as men in the profession, a view expressed by Raffenel in the citation and sketches contained in chapter 2.

In the late nineteenth century, the first photographic images of griottes began to appear. For example, during the Galliéni expedition from Medina in Senegal to Kita in Mali in 1879–81, a photographer took pictures of local rulers and other dignitaries. One shows the wife of an interpreter from Medina and her "griote" (figure 14). Another is of "Damba Sambala, son of the defender of Medine in 1859, and his griote."

The appearance of griots and griottes in formally posed photographs supports the notion that both were important members of official retinues. Photography at that time was a demanding process. The fact that the expedition leaders saw fit to devote time and equipment to such a subject reminds the viewer that the photographer was not simply taking snapshots of local cultural color to use up a roll of film.

In the twentieth century, as more Europeans began to take interest in the history of West Africa, bringing back both manuscripts from distant cities such as Timbuktu and occasional narratives from oral sources, griottes seemed to fade into the background of the outsiders' focus on the continent. If the more perceptive colonial administrators and researchers in West Africa could see any value in the oral tradition, their interest concentrated on the political epic, a genre usually recited by men in the Sahel and Savanna regions. In 1935, the governor-general of French West Africa, Jules Brévié, sent out a circular letter from his headquarters in Dakar to all administrators, asking them to collect both written and oral documents, including "epic legends," which would help the French to learn about "wars between tribes, migrations, and . . . the social and economic situations in these African countries" (132–33). Today, as scholars, both African and non-African, attempt to piece together the complex cultural history of West Africa, the world of war, diplomacy, and governance, traditionally viewed by men as their domain, continues to attract more attention than songs sung by women at weddings and naming ceremonies.

14. Photo of female griot with wife of Galliéni's interpreter. From Galliéni (Société de Géographie, Paris).

Recent Scholarship

Renewed interest in women in the oral tradition, like the relatively recent focus on women in agriculture by development specialists who seek to understand more clearly the ways particular African societies function, is the product of many contemporary influences. In my own case, as I prepared to undertake research for this book, I realized that men were only part of the story and that I needed to learn more about griottes if I were to arrive at a more holistic understanding of the profession. I returned to

Niger in 1989 with the goal of undertaking a first effort to understand more about the verbal art and social functions of female artisans of the word. Interviews with ten *jeserey weyborey* in both Niamey, the capital, and Yatakala, a small town that is the seat of the local canton chief in the northern corner of western Niger, served as the basis for a short instructional video entitled *Griottes of the Sahel: Female Keepers of the Songhay Oral Tradition in Niger* (Hale, 1990b).

Since then I have interviewed over a score of griottes in The Gambia, Senegal, and Mali, as well as scholars who have worked with griottes. At the same time new data has emerged that gives a much more detailed picture of the role of women in African societies—for example the monumental *Dictionnaire des femmes célèbres du Mali*, a biographical listing of 338 Malian women from the fifth century to 1991 (Ba Konaré, 1993). Most recently, Aïssata Sidikou has conducted research on women singers who are both professional griottes and nonprofessional performers (1997). From this small but growing body of research, answers are emerging to the many questions about griottes: how they train, whether their social functions and verbal art differ from those of the men, and whether they receive the same rewards.

Training and Education of Griottes

In chapter 5, on the training of griots, there appeared to be little difference between the ways griots and griottes learn. They start early and learn from parents, siblings, and other people who can teach them. Although women tend to learn from other women (mothers, aunts, older sisters, and other families), Sidia Jatta argues that fathers also contribute to the education of their daughters, because "male jalis are often more versed in narrating epics and family genealogies than their wives." His observation matches that of Durán, who affirms that *jalimusolu* are exposed to the full range of oral tradition as they grow up. As if to emphasize this point, Jatta's 1985 essay includes a photograph of Fune Kuyaate singing to the accompaniment of her husband, who plays the "*baloo*," or *balafon*. In her lap is a child no more than two years old (p. 26).

If there is any basic difference between the training of men and women, it might seem that men have greater opportunities to travel more widely and to learn from other griots during what might be called the apprentice and journeyman stages. This distinction may be true in the sense that young men, especially in the Hausa world (Mack, 1981, p. 25), are freer to move to the homes of other griots for short visits in order to learn. But information from griottes suggests that they also do a considerable amount of traveling to ceremonies and to other locations. Women travel with their families at an early age. Jatta points out that for the Mandinka in The Gambia, "the most propitious time for training the daughter is when the family is on its seasonal tours. During these tours the family gives more performances for one patron or another. At home, performances are much less frequent" (1985, p. 26).

If the ability to learn from travel varies across the Sahel for those at the beginning of a career, there is no doubt that older and more experienced griottes travel widely, often revealing a history of travel at a formative stage in their careers. Adame Ba Konaré's *Dictionnaire* lists more than thirty female "artistes," the majority of whom are of griotte origin. Most of the entries refer to early trips, often to Bamako, followed by extensive travel throughout West Africa and in many cases Europe.

If travel has always been important for the training of a griot, modern communications technology has played an even greater role in helping to prepare new generations of these wordsmiths. Hoffman noted during her own apprenticeship that some *jelimusow* would record on a cassette player all the songs at a wedding, take them home, and play them over and over again, singing along with them for practice. "It is a very liberating form of training," she told me in 1990, "because the student is not at the whim of anyone." Mack adds that Hausa women singers "are well acquainted with songs broadcast on radio and television, and they often can cite the earlier piece on which the author has modeled the work. It is not unusual to see someone acting out the part of the singer, imitating the voice and, if watching television, repeating the gestures that are an integral part of the performance" (1981, p. 33).

Both griots and griottes can pick up new material by listening to regularly scheduled programs of traditional music in Niger, Mali, and Senegal. But women dominate the field. In Mali in the 1980s women lead singers held an 80 percent share of the music on the radio (Hoffman, 1990b) and in the cassette market (Durán, 1994). There appears to be, then, much more opportunity for women to record and practice songs by women than for men to record and practice songs by men. It is not clear how true this may be for those countries east and west of Mali, but it is evident that the role of radio and television for training griottes should not be underestimated.

Other variations in training occur elsewhere in the Mande diaspora. For example, among the Soninké of the Jarra region, one finds considerable differences due to class and location. The way the oral tradition is learned — formally or informally — depends on whether one is of noble or slave origin, male or female, *geseru* (griot) or non-*geseru*, and from one town or another. Two aspects of the transmission of the past need to be mentioned: first, "information of slave origin remains a female domain *par excellence*" (Diawara, 1989, p. 109), and second, women who recount the past are often the principal historians of their community "because they learn the private testimonies with care; and that ensures them some precedence over the men in this domain" (113).

Professional Recognition

Eventually the most talented griots reach the highest level of achievement with, in the Mande world, the designation of *ngara*, *nara*, or *naara*. Johnson has suggested that among the Mande, at least in the heartland, only men can achieve the status of *nara*, or master singer of narratives. It is a title that is usually obtained between the ages of forty and fifty, he explained (in Johnson and Sisòkò, 1986, p. 25). Durán, however, told me more recently (1993a) that women can also become *nara* or *ngara*. She argued that a *ngara* such as the late Sira Mory Diabaté of Kéla and Kangaba was someone with a gift for words who could sing historical songs as well as praises. Female *ngara* were generally over fifty. What counts, she added, is not gender but ability with words.

Jatta describes a Mandinka *naaraa* as "a female singer who is not only good at singing, but also has tremendous expressive power in narrating family genealogies and epics" (1985, p. 25). The *jelimuso* superstar Ami Koita explained to Durán the procedure for recognizing women who have accumulated the necessary knowledge and developed the ability:

> Ngaaraya is like a diploma. You have to reach a certain level to be considered a ngaara, by the entire [musical] community. It's the elder griots, the elder people who know history well, who can make that judgement. What happens is that an elder will see a singer, at a baptism, for example, and get together with other elders, then all agree to confer this title on the singer. It's not the beauty of the voice, it's the use of the words. (quoted in Durán, 1995b, p. 203)

Epic and Gender

If there is no difference between achievement for men and women, there remains much debate over the issue of epic and gender. Sung or spoken historical narratives are viewed by male griots as the domain of men, whereas long praise songs about historical heroes can be sung by both men and women.

The traditional division of function in the performance of the epic follows the format outlined by Johnson:

Both women and men are involved with praise-poetry and song. . . . The wife will often sing the songs in her husband's epics. Also popular is the musician who accompanies his wife's singing. A full ensemble, such as that of the Kuyatè lineage of the village of Kéla near Kaaba, includes a mastersinger who only narrates, a woman who sings praise-poems and songs, a female chorus, a male naamu-sayer, and several male musicians. (in Johnson and Sisòkò, 1986, p. 25)

What Johnson describes is not limited to the Mande heartland. Mandinka *jali* Papa Susso stated in 1993 that in The Gambia, on the western fringe of the Mande world, the same arrangement holds true: men and women often perform together, the men recounting the narrative part of the epic and the women singing the songs.

Does that mean that women do not or cannot sing epics? The answer depends on how one defines an epic. Jatta (1985, p. 25) lists epic singing among the talents of *naaraa* and there is some evidence to suggest that he is correct in including the epic genre among the verbal forms sung by women griots.

Based on work with the late Sira Mori Diabaté, Jan Jansen (1996a) concludes that in the Mande heartland knowledge of the epic narratives is not gender-limited. He states that "men and women acquire the same information about Sunjata, since they are all allowed to attend the (rare) official rehearsals of the epic," but he adds that in performance women focus more on the praise lines than the narrative. Hoffman observes from her own fieldwork that it is rare for a woman to recount an entire epic (1990b). Durán affirms in a recently published chapter that "despite popular belief to the contrary, it is not uncommon to hear women perform versions of Sunjata and other epics" (1995b, p. 201). Ami Koita supports this view: "Women know the story of Sunjata as well as men, but men can speak the story, women can only sing it. . . . If a man is present a woman will never take the platform from him" (quoted in Durán, 1995b, p. 203).

Durán told me that "the whole issue hangs around the definition of epic, or 'historical' narrative as a genre. Quite clearly, women are excluded from the *tarikou*, but there are several well-known cases of *jelimusow* who sing songs with historical content, in which specific episodes of Mande history are recounted through song." She cited the examples of Nantenegwe Kamissoko, who recorded a long version of Sundiata now played often on the morning "Mande History" program of Radio Mali, and Bako Dagnon and Kandia Kouyaté, both of whom sang Mande epics in public at the International Festival of Culture held in Kita in 1995 (personal communication, 1996).

Although the most visible female performers come from Mali, women griots are also beginning to emerge into the spotlight in other parts of the region. Bakari Sidibe, the dean of Gambian scholars in the oral tradition, reported to me in 1991 that differences between men and women griots were blurring, and that women and female-led groups had begun to appear in The Gambia in the past two decades. He attributed changes to the new social conditions—fewer traditional patrons for men and the need to attract new audiences. Women, he suggested, were playing more visible and audible roles in this shifting environment. And some of them, he added, were very talented and knowledgeable performers.

In summarizing the gender differences between men and women, Durán emphasizes the importance of tradition: "Men specialise in history conveyed through the spoken word (*tarikou*), women specialise in praise through song (*fassa da, donkili da*). Women are denied categorically the right to 'speak' their lyrics" (1995b). Both, however, are part of the epic tradition, and from Durán's perspective, women cannot be excluded from any analysis of that genre.

There appear, then, to be two kinds of barriers—gender and genre. Women traditionally do not narrate the long epic poems recounted or sung by men, yet they know the stories quite well and are expert in singing the songs that form part of the stories. If they sing a song for two hours, does that constitute an epic or simply a form of panegyric, or praise? Until we have some long texts at hand, it is hard to judge, but several other pieces of evidence, one from Mali, the others from Niger, tend to support Durán's view that women cannot be excluded from discussions of epic.

The first is "Sara," a 240-line song about a woman, that was the trademark of Sira Mori Diabaté. Several versions exist. One, recorded by Charles Bird in Kéla, Mali, in 1968, appears in *Oral Epics from Africa*, a collection of excerpts from twenty-five African epics (Johnson, Hale, and Belcher, 1997). Although most of the excerpts from the epics in this volume are in linear form and come from narratives that range from 1,000 to 8,000 lines, the editors have included the full text of "Sara" because, in spite of its length, it bears all of the other hallmarks of epic. Much longer versions may have been recounted at other times and places, depending on the audience.

In the introduction to the song, Bird's observations support fully Durán's argument that women's songs are epics.

The form she [Sira Mori Diabaté] uses is more melodic than the typical Mande male bard's narrative mode. As such it sounds more like praise song (*faasa*), of which Sira Mori was one of the great Mande masters. This is not, however, at all typical of praise song from the point of view of content. Praise songs do not tell stories. This is clearly poetic narrative, and heroic, and therefore by any definition, it qualifies as epic. From the point of view of Maninka speakers, *Sara*, like the Sunjata epic, is called *maana*, the term they use when talking about poetic narratives. (114)

How can one reconcile the culture-specific interpretation by Bird, which places the poem in a local context that makes no distinction according to length, and the Western notion that the only poems called epics are long? Are we stretching the notion of epic beyond what some might term "universal" limits? Perhaps. But whether we call the text a poem or an epic poem may be entirely beside the point from a Maninka perspective.

One other feature of epic performance, however, may explain the comparative brevity of this poem: the issue of episode versus mental text. Johnson warns scholars in oral literature that griots rarely recount the full text of an epic. They tend instead to narrate an episode at a particular event, such as a naming ceremony or a wedding. But they preserve in their minds what Lori Honko has termed "the mental text" and under certain extraordinary conditions—an extended sequence of recording sessions with a researcher or a major ceremony such as the reroofing of the Kamabolon at Kangaba—they may reproduce most if not all of this mental text. It is quite possible that opportunities for women to recount long narratives are so limited by the gender division in epic reproduction and other circumstances that they rarely have occasion to recount a long poetic text. This limitation on women may also fit with the reality that men rank above women in a society such as the Mande marked by patrilineality and gerontocracy (Durán, 1996).

The other evidence that supports Durán's argument comes from research by Aïssata Sidikou in Niger in 1995–96 and 1997. She was seeking songs by women, both professional and nonprofessional, performed in both ritual and nonritual contexts. In the course of interviews with over fifty women in western Niger, she encountered the daughter of one of the most respected *jeserey* in the twentieth century, the late Diado Sékou. Fati Diado, like Sira Mori Diabaté, had grown up listening to her father sing epics. But Fati had followed a different path, which took her to French-style schools run by the government. At the age of twenty-five, with ten years of schooling, she decided to return to the profession she had inherited from her father.

Fati Diado set as her goal to sing epics, both those her father recounted and others that she would create based on her research. In 1995, she sang a version of *The Epic of Sundiata* for a video recording that was based on a written version of the text, probably the original and widely available French prose edition published by Niane in 1960. According to Sidikou (1997), the reborn *jeseré weyboro* also expressed interest in reading more about the heroines of Niger, such as Sarraounia, so that she could compose epics about women.

Her plans, however, have encountered a major obstacle. Male bards, normally the stars of the griot world in her country, are not eager to end up like their Malian counterparts as backup accompanists. At one event, Sidikou reports, when the best-known griot in Niger, Djibo Badié, known as Djeliba, was asked to serve as her accompanist, he refused because he felt it was inappropriate for a woman to sing epics and because he was more accustomed to assuming the lead role in performance (Sidikou, 1997, pp. 136–58).

There is evidence, then, for change in the situation of female griots, perhaps as a result of the diffusion of gender roles from other countries such as Mali and thanks to improved means of travel and new means of sound recording. Bassirou Dieng (1991) has defined these roles as public (for men) and private (for women). In other words, it is the men's task to lead in an official, public way at certain events involving political power, while it is the women's place to take a dominant position at family events, such as naming ceremonies and weddings: "Men are concerned with official and institutional discourse, while women focus on ritual, family, and domestic discourse."

What can one make of a 1,053-line narrative about an ideal wife, Hajara, and her husband, Madugu, that contains a catalog of many different human qualities and family problems ranging from polygamy to divorce and adultery? This is what Sidikou recorded from Safi Hassane, known locally as Chanwo Nya, or Mother of the Mouse, on July 27 and 28, 1995, in Niamey, Niger. The narrative, *The Epic of Good Brides and Young Women*, is not about war and peace or heroes and enemies; it is an episodic portrayal of the relations between the sexes and the wars that can erupt when each side tries to outwit the other.

In the local Songhay-Zarma context, the narrative is a *deeda*, or long story, the same term used to describe *The Epic of Askia Mohammed*. But within this larger category, it is also known as a *saabi*. *Saabi*, explains Sidikou, means "being grateful" in Songhay-Zarma (1997, p. 160). A *saabi*

is recounted at weddings and naming ceremonies, as well as when a woman is about to receive a co-wife into her household. Sidikou describes the poem as a "subversive epic" because it both subverts the male notion of superiority and challenges the traditional view of epic (160).

A *saabi* can be recounted by both *jeseré* and by non-*jeseré* members of society. Safi Hassane is a woman of captive origin, not of *jeseré* heritage. She is called a *nwareyko*, a term used to describe the lowest category of performers, those who hold out their hands to seek rewards for their words. In the eyes of society, however, there is a tendency to lump both the *jeseré* and the *nwareyko* into the same category, hence the belief cited in the preceding chapter that many griots are of low or captive background.

Just as political epics recounted by men serve to illustrate relations between peoples, clans, and other members of society, the *saabi* reveals the nature of relationships between men and women. Sidikou explains that "the *saabi* as a medium of role negotiation and critical discourse in a society is one of the fundamental verbal arts that tell us how these African women think, how they see themselves and other features of their own cultural traditions that they embody, and most of all, how their lives are shaped" (174).

The last episode in the narrative, "the wicked man," illustrates a woman's victory in the ongoing battle with men. The narrator describes a couple who have just married. The wife evidently has second thoughts about the intentions of her husband, who has divorced many women in the past. She goes out to plant millet with him, and, while he walks ahead of her digging holes for the seeds, she secretly dumps them out. As soon as the field is "planted," he divorces her:

964 "Here is your divorce paper
   "You just leave."
   She said, "Oh yeah?"
   He said, "Yes.". . .
   She laughed and said,
   "You did not divorce me first
   "I first divorced you.". . .
   "Any trick a man has out of nastiness,"
   She said "as for a woman, if a man can think of ten tricks,"
   She said "one trick from a woman will trump his."
   She said, "wait for three days,
   "On the fourth day
   "You will know well that it is the time one goes to check one's land

"To see new shoots."
She said, "go to your farm that day"
992 She said "you will know that day that I was the one who divorced you
     first." (Sidikou, 1997, pp. 298–300)

The woman leaves and the man goes to his farm four days later to discover that nothing has emerged from the soil, though his neighbors' fields are covered with shoots. The narrator explains the larger meaning of the events:

1014 It is said by Allah that whatever a man can do
      A woman knows how to trick better
      A deceiving and nasty man,
      And whatever you do out of wickedness
1017 A woman can definitely outdo you. . . .
1021 So you see, he thought the farm was completed, he divorced her.
      He did not know they were only empty holes. (301)

This story, one of many illustrating the relations between the sexes in this Songhay-Zarma *saabi*, suggests that we may need to rethink our definition of epic—at least in the African context. If the notion of epic is limited to the Western ideal of the conquering male hero, half the world's population and much of its literature may be excluded.

If there may be discussion about fitting the *saabi* into whatever definition of epic emerges in the future, it is quite possible that a longer narrative recorded by Sidikou from Fati Djado Sékou in December 1997 will turn out to be the first published African epic by a woman. The 1,462-line narrative tells the story of Fatimata bi Daani, a woman who seeks revenge against a local ruler by calling for help from some of the great heroes of the 19th century, Ham Bodedio, Dondi Gorba Dicko, Amaala Seyni Ga Koï, Bakari Dia, and Boube Ardo Gallo. The text is now being transcribed, translated, and edited by Sidikou.

Given the widespread belief on the part of researchers, both African and non-African, that only men narrate epics, there is obviously a great need for more study of the intersection between gender, genre, and ethnicity before we can understand more fully the roles of men and women in this particular form of narrative in West Africa.

Praise Songs

Both men and women sing praises and songs of great variety about heroes of the past and patrons of the present, some of which have appeared in earlier chapters. Although there may be a tendency for women to sing certain kinds of songs while men sing others, there is no gender barrier, at least in Mali. A woman, for example, can sing a hunter's song about a man, as did Tumu Maniya, the *jelimuso* who played a key role in *The Epic of Son-Jara*:

1671   The Kuyatè matriarch took up the iron rasp.
       She sang a hunter's song for Nare Magan Kònatè:
           Took up the bow!   (Indeed)
           Simbon, Master-of-the-Bush!
           Took up the bow!
           Took up the bow! . . .   (Indeed)
           The Kòndè woman's child,
1683   Answerer-of-Needs,   (Indeed)

                              (Johnson and Sisòkò, 1992, p. 65)

Belcher (1999) points out that this example of a woman singing the "Song of the Bow" in the epic is sometimes changed in other versions to male *jeliw* and to the incident where the hero rises for the first time from his crippled condition. Belcher sees such changes as evidence not only for ideological shifts within the epic, but also for external constraints operating on the performance conditions.

Whether *jelimusow* are composing or performing songs as characters in epics or for friends and important people in contemporary society, their praise-singing, called *fasa dali* among the Bamana, Maninka, and Dioula, is more than simply a matter of voicing kind words about another person in exchange for rewards. As seen earlier, it reflects a complex dialogue that speaks to the power relations between different groups in society. Women, as much as men, are part of that dialogue.

Advice and Solidarity

In the weekly round of weddings and naming ceremonies, griottes play a vocal role as advisers and social arbiters. Evidence presented in chapter 1 showed both women griots and men providing advice in the form of songs. In some cases, women's advice can extend to forms of female solidarity representing much social power. Moor women, for example, sometimes hire groups of griots—presumably women, but perhaps also men—to participate in demonstrations of support and sympathy for women who suffer from unfaithful husbands.

Such manifestations of sympathy are powerful instruments against the men. Indeed, the women spare no money or fortune (usually their husbands') for the party they organize in a show of force. If the unfaithful husband is prominent, they will seize any opportunity to turn the occasion into a popular demonstration for the wife and against the husband, in an attempt to harm him socially or politically. (Gerteiny, 1967, p. 71)

The songs of advice and solidarity may be part of a larger pool of verbal art shared by women of both griot and nongriot origin. Sidikou has recorded songs by women in ritual contexts that are highly critical of men. One form of these songs, sung by both women and by *jeserey weyborey*, is the *marchandé*. Women come together in a circle, led by a *jeseré weyboro*, just prior to a wedding, especially when a man takes a second wife. Such performances constitute a kind of cultural back talk that in some cases frightens men who happen to hear them. Often the songs are sung in ritual contexts that exclude men. One song recorded and translated by Sidikou is rather direct in criticism of a man taking a second wife:

> Marriage is not a problem.
> Chatting is not fighting.
> Here comes your rival.
> Your luck brought her here.
> It is your good fate that brought her here.
> Hold his penis.
> And insert it yourself. . . .
> Spray pepper in his eyes
> By Allah we will spray it back. . . .
> We will rub it on his testicles.
> So he puts it into the eyes of his new wife
> So he puts it into his new wife's eyes.
> So he puts it into his new wife's vagina. (Sidikou, 1997, p. 238)

Sidikou's research on the Songhay-Zarma women's oral tradition is largely specific to western Niger, although she has made some promising comparisons with material from Mali and Senegal. When viewed in the larger context of women's common concerns about domestic abuse, improvident husbands, rivalry between co-wives, and other issues, however, another common regional thread emerges: a generally positive working relationship between professional and nonprofessional singers. Many of the songs she collected can be sung by both *jeseré* and non-*jeseré* women.

In Mali, Kate Modic has found a similarly close relationship. She studied the musical tradition of the Bèn Ka Di (Agreement is Sweet), an association of women of noble or free origin in Banankabougou, a suburb of Bamako. At family ceremonies of members (naming ceremonies, circumcisions, engagements, weddings), they sing, dance, and play a variety of instruments: the *ji dunun* (water drum), the *ntamanin* (small hourglass drum), the *yakoro* (gourd rattle), and the *karinyan* (the metal rod or rasp and striker). These are the same events that *jeliw* and *jelimusow* attend, although women performers are far more numerous than men in the Bèn Ka Di ceremonies.

There are many parallels between the nonprofessional Bèn Ka Di women and *jelimusow*. But a variety of differences emerge that help to define more clearly the frontier between *jelimusow* and other members of society. Although the Bèn Ka Di group is composed of women, its focus is on community support for families rather than increased female solidarity, (Modic, 1996, p. 87). The women recognize that as singers and musicians they are stepping into the domain of hereditary *jelimusow*. For this reason, they have their own *jelimuso* who accompanies them when they perform, and grants them permission to sing (94). The women do not expect payment for their performances. But their lead singer, Mariam Coulibaly, who served as the key source for Modic and whose life story occupies the center of the study, has shifted into an ambiguous zone between that of the noble or freeborn performers she represents and the more clearly demarcated territory of the *jelimusow*.

Modic offers several kinds of evidence that reveal this social encroachment. First, Mariam is the only member of the Bèn Ka Di who demands money for her services. At one point she left the group for one year over a dispute about money (97). Some members of the group resent the fact that she is paid for her performances. Those in the group must ask her permission to sing. The leader is supposed to ask the presiding *jelimuso* for permission to sing, but Mariam does not do so, arguing that Allah gives her the permission to sing (94). Thus, by failing to recognize the authority of *jelimusow* and by demanding rewards for her singing, Mariam is functioning in many ways outside the rules of her noble or freeborn status in society. She does so because she knows she has an excellent voice, superior to that of any other woman in the association; because she badly needs the money; and because more and more women who are not of *jeli* origin are entering the world of musical performance in Mali.

In neighborhood events, where the *jelimusow* and the Bèn Ka Di women know each other, the professional and nonprofessional women mark out their own performance spaces during ceremonies. The *jelimusow* alternate with the Bèn Ka Di women during ceremonies. Modic describes in some detail an engagement party on July 11, 1991, in Banankabougou. The ceremony was overseen by Sali Kouyaté, the *jelimuso* of the Bèn Ka Di group. She gave a speech about the impending marriage, identifying members of the community and emphasizing the importance of the event. After two songs by the Bèn Ka Di women honoring a childless woman, the *jelimuso* continued her speech, identifying other women and praising the family. Modic explains that Sali Kouyaté's speech was necessary for the event to be complete.

In the local context, then, the women place themselves under the official guidance of a *jelimuso*, which, in a sense, enables them to carry out *jeli* activities such as singing. But when they travel to events outside their own world, competition and rivalry can emerge, not simply with other women singers but also with *jelimusow*. According to Mariam Coulibaly, other women could attempt to silence a singer's voice with sorcery or engage in competition for the microphone. Modic cites one example of how the Bèn Ka Di women, invited to an event in Bamako, were nudged aside by a *jelimuso* after only four songs (99).

Modic points out that the women singers are not doing imitations of *jeli* music (242). Although there can be much overlap of the kinds of songs each group sings, in general the Bèn Ka Di women find that *jeli* songs are hard to understand. Their own are far less hermetic and are linked to places, people, and events familiar to members of the community. By contrast, the praises of the *jelimusow* may refer to distant heroes, trace lineages, and contain such highly symbolic speech that they represent a kind of occult discourse. Modic emphasizes the immediacy of the Bèn Ka Di women's songs when she adds that they sing "in recognition of each other's lives. Theirs were personal history praise songs in which a singer would praise another woman for the good deeds she had done for the singer, for other members of the community" (160).

There are also some differences in the way instruments are played. For example, the metal pipe described in chapter 4, known here as the *ngèrenyè*, is struck by *jelimusow* in an alternating pattern on each end, while the women musicians of the Bèn Ka Di scrape the pipe with the striker (105).

In some ways, the Bèn Ka Di members echo the music of another famous singer from the Wassoulou area of their ancestors, a woman who, like them, is not of griotte origin. Oumou Sangaré sings songs of advice that the Bèn Ka Di women also sing (Sangaré, 1993).

Durán describes the tradition in considerable detail in her article "Birds of Wasulu: Freedom of Expression and Expressions of Freedom in the Popular Music of Southern Mali." The performers, she explains, call themselves *konow*, or birds, to distinguish themselves from griots and griottes. "The *konow* are musicians by choice and natural ability, with a 'bird's-eye' view of society, allowing them to comment on social issues in freer musical and textual ways than those of the *jeliw*" (1995a, 102). The performers are generally young and often unmarried women. Their music operates on what Durán describes as a "different 'cultural axis'" than the music of the *jeliw*, who, as hereditary musicians, "have monopolised public performance" (103) in a style that is specifically Malian and associated with the world of hunters. They are musicians by choice, not by heredity. They may sing praises, but they do not sing genealogies or praise names. Their mode is song, not *tarikou*, or spoken narrative (111).

The *konow* of Wassoulou may be male or female. But in the world of men, there does not appear to be an equivalent to the kind of performance by the Bèn Ka Di women where one finds a mix of griot and nongriot performers. There are, however, some men of noble or free birth who, like Mariam Coulibaly, have gone far down the path toward the domain of griots. Coulibaly claimed a "licence" to sing because her grandmother, a great singer in her day, was taken away by a spirit for three months when she was an infant. This heritage, along with her claim of a gift from Allah, serves as her reason for carrying out an activity normally forbidden to women of her origin.

The mixed professional-nonprofessional world of the Bèn Ka Di association might appear to be an exception to the performance rules that only those of griotte origin sing, but in fact there is evidence to support DjeDje's belief that "most women in Sudanic Africa are nonprofessional musicians—that is, their primary source of livelihood is not performing music" (1985, p. 81). She cites Ames's comments on Hausa women ("Among nonprofessionals, women of all ages more often perform music than men" [1973, 133]).

Mack's research on women's poetry, oral and written, in northern Nigeria, supports the view that many women are musicians. One of Mack's informants declared, "Every woman is a singer" (1981, 43). Mack's study of both professional and nonprofessional women reveals that much of the variety of Hausa women's verbal art depends on the context: whether it is inside the home (*cikin gida*), in the streets, or for the Emir or Sultan at his palace. Those who are nonprofessional, especially those who write poems, do not want to be compared with professional singers, whom they view as low status (21–22).

"Although these women do in fact enjoy performances by *zabiyoyi*, they feel unable to admit to such interest. Among certain female artists the social stigma attached to *marok'a* and *zabiyoyi* makes them unwilling to be included in these categories" (22). Yet the highest ranking of these professionals, the *zabiyoyi* who perform for the Emir, enjoy an unusual degree of prestige and freedom to travel.

Patrons

The articulation of a woman's right to escape from domestic abuse, seen in the song by Weybi Karma cited in chapter 1, or to complain about a second wife, mentioned earlier in this chapter, reflects in microcosm the larger role of both griots and griottes as people who articulate the models for appropriate social behavior, whether expressed in a song for a bride or an epic for a chief. Such behavior includes acts of great generosity by patrons of griots. But there are differences both in rewards and in praises for those who appreciate the words of griots and griottes.

From Durán's work, it appears that those *jelimusow* who have become famous and have performed abroad tend to be exceptionally generous in praises for their patrons, perhaps more so than *jeli ke*, or male griots. Durán gives the example of Kandia Kouyaté, whose entire repertoire on one recording is composed of praises for a patron, Babani Sissoko (spelled elsewhere as Cissoko). "Virtually all of her songs, from 1987 onwards, are in praise of Sissoko," Durán adds (1989a, 38).

Tata Bambo Kouyaté begins her 1985 CD *Jatigui* (Wealthy Patron) with an homage song to the same man who had an international reputation for generosity to his favorite *jelimusow*. On the liner of the CD (Globestyle Records CDORB042), Durán explains that it was during Kouyaté's travels in the 1980s to expatriate Malian communities in other parts of Africa that the talented *jelimuso* first met this wealthy patron, a successful and well-connected businessman of griot origin. Durán's description of the encounter reveals how traditional music can be instantly reinterpreted to serve contemporary ends: "Tata's turn came in 1984. Sissoko, then living in Libreville [Gabon], had heard a tape of Tata's music and become so entranced that he returned to Mali to find her." Learning that she was in Paris with a group of musicians, "he followed her . . . and made a grand entrance at one of her concerts. Tata recognised him instantly, and began improvising praise lyrics to him, reciting his genealogies, listing his many acts of generosity. 'Toutou Diarra,' the tune she was singing, was a traditional melody dedicated to a great fighter from Segou, but she renamed it 'homage to Baba Sissoko'—now her most famous composition" ("Jatigui," Durán, 1989b).

Not all women have wealthy patrons or the desire and talent to step onto the global stage. For those whose context is more local, sometimes performance is with a group of women. In some cases, the woman performs with a man who serves as the accompanist on the *kora*; occasionally the man takes the lead. Weybi Karma's nine-member troupe in Niamey, Niger, is made up of female singers backed up by male musicians, mostly drummers, but she is clearly the lead singer and director of the group.

Whatever the gender mix, the matter of rewards for women in the local context raises many questions. In general, women receive less than men, though the Malian superstars are an exception to this rule. Interviews with two dozen male griots in both The Gambia, Mali, and Senegal, as well as data from Michel Guignard, who has conducted research in Mauritania, confirm what seems to be the general tendency of men, especially in The Gambia and Senegal, to treat women as second-class participants. I asked many men how they shared rewards with their female counterparts. The answer was often that the women received far less than the men, perhaps 10 percent to 30 percent.

That was the case not only in The Gambia but also among the Gambian community in New York City. Nakoyo Suso reported to me in 1994 that when she and her cousin Papa Susso attend family events in the 900-member Gambian community in the Bronx, the share for the woman is likely to be 30 percent to 40 percent. One exception was reported to me in 1991 by Mohammed Manjako Suso in Serrekunda, The Gambia, whose female partner, Sayengdeh Suso, also his wife, was so talented and so well known that she insisted on taking a half share of all income. The Gambian *jali* explained that it is the woman who opens the performance for the man and therefore has a very important role to play.

The situation is different in Mali, where women performers of all kinds, not simply the stars, have begun to organize to promote their own interests. Since the overthrow of the Traoré régime and the installation of the democratically elected government of Alpha Konaré, both men and women musicians have taken advantage of greater social freedom to establish new professional associations. Women singers created their own association, and in November 1993 they gave a concert at the Stade des

Omnisports in Bamako to raise money to restore the burned-out Marché aux Roses (Durán, 1994). They were not the first, however, to organize in the region. Associations of people representing different professions have existed for a long time. Ousmane Silla cites examples of jewelers in Saint-Louis and women griots in Senegal. The women's goal is "to revive the Senegalese past and maintain the traditions inherited from their ancestors" (1966, p. 763).

The amounts, the context in which rewards are given, the mix of cash and material gifts, variations between what is given to men and to women as well as according to audience, ethnic group, location (at home, in another part of Africa, in Europe) are topics of considerable complexity that can reveal much about the differences between men and women griots as well as help us to understand their relationship with their patrons. But the data now available only hint at what can be learned from closer study.

Gender and Instruments

Women griots normally play the metal pipe and striker (*nege, karinya, karinyan*) in the Mande world and the *ardin* in Mauritania. They also play gourd rattles and other sound-makers known by ethnomusicologists as idiophones. In general, women—griot or nonprofessional—tend to play idiophones more commonly than any other instrument, and it is unusual for women to play drums and wind instruments associated with power (Djedje, 1985, p. 79). But there are exceptions to these rules, as Modic noted (1996) from research on the Bèn Ka Di women. One can still encounter women who play instruments normally reserved for men. As noted earlier, Igudu, the wife of Al Haji Garba Bagna, accompanied her husband on the *molo* in Niger when I recorded him in 1980, and one of Beverly Mack's principal informants, Hajiya Faji, played the *kukuma*, a violinlike one-stringed bowed lute. In the Hausa world, women appear to play the widest range of instruments—rattles, calabash drums, hand-clappers, tubular, open-ended gourds, and wooden mortars (DjeDje, 1985, p. 78).

✖ ✖

From the evidence presented here, several themes emerge.

First, women griots share the knowledge base of their male counterparts but tend to convey that knowledge in a different form, the song, a component of the epic tradition. It is not clear yet that women griots in general know as much about the many episodes of the past, but there is enough preliminary evidence to suggest that at least some of these women may be as knowledgeable as men in recounting history. As scholars begin to focus more attention on the verbal art of women, we may come to understand better their roles and the nature of their talent. One outcome of that research may be a redefinition of our notion of African epic, a genre widely viewed as dealing solely with male heroes and conveyed by men.

Second, it appears that women griots work closely with nonprofessional women singers to maintain a sense of community. The evidence from the research of Mack, Modic, and Sidikou suggests that while the distinction between professional and nonprofessional women performers survives, cooperation at events and crossing of the boundary that separates the worlds are increasingly common. But much more evidence is needed on these and other issues to enable one to appreciate these multifaceted performers from a more fully informed perspective.

Third, the world of women griots is changing because of several conditions: democratization, new means of communication, more opportunities to travel. Although these factors influence both men and women, the impact on women seems to be greater because they may have enjoyed less freedom than men in the past.

Finally, the comparative lack of research on women griots and the rapid social change occurring in many Sahelian and Savanna countries suggest that our picture of griots and griottes will remain incomplete until further research is carried out. There are many conundrums that may attract the interest of scholars, but I will mention only a few that come to mind as the result of the evidence in this chapter.

The world of griottes needs to be viewed in the broadest possible geographic and human context. For example, the influence of Mande *jelimusow* from Mali on women singers in other parts of the region must be explored in more detail if we are to understand the diversity and unity that mark female contributions to the many different forms of verbal art in West Africa. The research of Modic on one group and, in particular, on the lead singer in that group, opens a door to an area that remains little understood. By the same token, we need to learn more about the impact of non-*jelimuso* music on the world of the *jelimusow*. Are the songs of Oumou Sangaré and other performers from the culturally diverse Wassoulou region, echoed by the Bèn Ka Di women, all that different from the songs of Ami Koita? In a lengthy review of Oumou Sangaré's CD *Ko Sira* in the *New York Times*, Milo Miles (1994), an occasional commentator on world music for National Public Radio, leaves the reader confused about just how her musical heritage relates to that of the *jeli* tradition. But one cannot criticize Miles, because we are only beginning to understand the difference between *jelimuso* and non-*jelimuso* music.

The griottes' own view of the origin of the profession, long obscured by the focus on men, also needs more investigation. There are many etiological tales about the first griot. The most widely reported version, cited in chapter 2, is based on the story of the hunter who sacrifices flesh from his thigh to feed his starving brother. But what about griottes? Are their origin tales related to those of men? The preliminary responses I have collected from women griots are limited and inconclusive. But as Johnson suggests (1996b), if there is a lack of etiological legends about them now, there will be no shortage in the future as these women come to occupy center stage.

Variations in the impact of modern communications technology on men and women also need to be examined more closely. They range from the Mauritanian *tiggiwit*, reported in 1936 to have sung songs over the telephone to students in isolated parts of the country who had paid her by money order (Puigadeau, 1936, p. 193), to contemporary apprentice *jalimusow* who have become overnight stars because of a few appearances on Malian television (Hoffman, 1994) and the veteran performers whose cassettes are sold on every street corner. If, as Durán suggests (1994), for most *jalimusow* "one is only as good as one's most recent cassette recording," what are the consequences for the art and economics of those whose livelihood depends in part on the sale of recordings?

In addition, one must ask what the impact is of the shift from a local to national and global audiences on griottes as well as griots. Durán told me (personal communication, 1996) that in Senegal Kine Lam claimed to be the first griotte to record a "modern" cassette in 1989 and has since developed an enormous following. Is that the result of her music or the technology? Yandé Codou Sène, a Serer griotte who was once Léopold Senghor's favorite praise singer, now has a CD available on World Network. Has her shift to a CD produced by an international company changed her style? Durán reports (1993b) that Oumou Dioubaté and Djanka Diabaté, both from Guinea, "have moved completely away from the tradition, into full blown hi-tech pop—unashamed music for the dance floor," a change that produces "a wall of disapproval from elder members of the West African community towards women who become fully fledged public perfomers." Are they exceptions or part of a growing trend?

Whatever the answers to these questions, it is evident that griottes— *jalimusolu, jelimusow, jeserey weyborey, marok'iya* or *zabiya*, and *tiggawaten*—have always been important as artists. Social and technological changes affecting many West African societies are enabling them to break into new areas of music-making. But more research and more exchange of information among scholars in the many different disciplines concerned with the activities of griots and griottes are needed if we are to arrive at a more balanced view. One focus of that research will be on the way new audiences are influencing the demand for both griottes and griots, the subject of the next chapter.

ℵ 8 ℵ
From the Courtyards of the Nobility
to a Global Audience

When Charles Bird took *jeli* Batourou Sékou Kouyaté, his wife Dionton Tounkara, and another *jelimuso*, Nantenegwe Kamissoko, on a tour of American universities and colleges in 1978, he made an announcement at the beginning of each concert to warn listeners that the words being spoken and sung that evening had tremendous power and might move the audience to respond in unaccustomed ways.

At Penn State and many other stops on the griots' itinerary, few people understood the Bamana songs they heard. But those seated at the University Park campus's Paul Robeson Cultural Center reacted exactly as Bird had predicted. After Kouyaté had played the *kora* for a while, Nantenegwe Kamissoko, backed up by Dionton Tounkara, began to sing and eventually sprinkled her songs with the names of some of those in the audience. They included a professor of African history who was the founder of African Studies at Penn State, an assistant vice president whose office had provided financial support for the event, and the author, who had invited the group to come to perform.

Although Bird had given the names to the performers in advance, hearing them in the context of an otherwise incomprehensible African song created a sense of surprise and shock. Those whose names were called made their way to the stage either to offer a small reward or, more often, and much to the astonishment of the performers, to give a hug, accompanied by audience applause. The person whose name was called for praise received a long red scarf to hold until another person's name was called, at which point the garment was passed on.

The change in atmosphere during this part of the performance was startling. A politely attentive audience of 200 that had come to hear "folkloric" music from Africa was suddenly transformed into a snake-dancing throng, caught up in the music and behaving in a way no one had expected. The event illustrated in dramatic fashion that West African griots could hurdle the barriers of space, language, and cultural context to touch an audience that had limited understanding of the distant continent. The new audiences for griots included not only university students but also researchers, educators, museum directors, librarians, musicians, fans of world music, and a vast diaspora of people in the Western hemisphere who wanted to know more about their cultural heritage in Africa.

The shift from the courtyards of the nobility in West Africa to a global audience was the result of a variety of influences, including the growing interest in griots on the part of researchers such as Bird and the introduction of many new forms of technology. But by far the most important factor in the creation of the global audience for griots was the *Roots* phenomenon produced by Alex Haley. *Roots* generated not only a wave of interest in Africa but also enormous controversy after it appeared in 1976.

To understand how griots made such a dramatic leap from the local context to the international stage, it is essential to reexamine the encounter between these artisans of the word and those such as Haley, Bird, and other researchers who brought them to the attention of new audiences. At the same time, it is important to keep in mind that griots were active participants in this process. Many of them were swift to take advantage of new technologies to expand the performance context. But given the importance of Haley in creating a more receptive audience for griots worldwide, it is essential to begin by reexamining the debate over *Roots*.

Alex Haley and Griots

Haley began to speak about griots many years before the publication of *Roots*. For example, he was one of the participants at the first Manding conference, held in 1972 at the School of Oriental and African Studies of the University of London. A landmark event in African Studies, the conference attracted over 200 participants, including the president of Senegal, Léopold Sédar Senghor, who presented the opening paper, the first of over 100 on a variety of topics related to the history, culture, and languages of the Manding (or Mande) peoples.

It was a full-scale scholarly conference with all the formality one associates with the presentation of papers. But what tied the four-day event firmly to an African cultural context was the presence of over two dozen griots and griottes from The Gambia, Senegal, and Mali. Sent by their own countries, these griots were more than simply folkloric performers at a

World's Fair venue, as were those I saw in New York in 1964. According to the conference report of David Dalby, one of the organizers, they partici- pated in discussions during some of the sessions and also "provided musical illustrations for some of the public lectures" (1972, p. 11).

The Gambian delegation included Lalokeba Drammeh, Balobo Jeng, Rohia Jeng, Fabala Kanute, Nano Sakiliba, and Nyama Suso. Suso had recently spent a year at the University of Washington. From Mali came Fanta Demba, Sidiki Diabaté, D. Diabaté, Nantenegwe Kamissoko, Dion- ton Tounkara (listed as Mme. Kouyaté), Batourou Sékou Kouyaté, N. Sacko, and Djelimadi Sissoko. Senegal sent the largest group: Bakary Cissoko, Banna Cissoko, Djiguiba Cissoko, Soundioulou Cissoko, Fodé Dramé, Banna Kanouté (a Gambian brother of Fabala Kanute who hap- pened to be living in Senegal at the time), Dinding Kouyaté, Ma Hawa Kouyaté, Madati M'Baye, Fanta Sakho, Fatou Sakho, and Noumou Sakho. They participated in events both within the context of the conference—a workshop on Mande music organized by Bird—and outside. They gave a series of public performances at the Africa Centre in London, the Com- monwealth Institute, the University Collegiate Theatre, and the Town Hall of Oxford, as well as on radio and television. During a dinner offered by Prime Minister Edward Heath for President Senghor at 10 Downing Street on June 29, some of them performed a *kora* recital. They made several recordings of their music (Dalby, 11).

The response from both the participants at the meeting and the press in Britain was extremely positive. These griots were not the first to visit Europe, but they had, in a sense, opened the door far wider to include not only researchers but a public that had, in most cases, never heard of them.

Haley attended the conference to learn about what other scholars were doing and to speak, on July 1, about his own research for his family and cultural roots. Geoffrey Haydon, a British filmmaker who had met with Haley the night before, described the reaction to the African American's presentation.

> Next day's lecture to the Manding conference at London University was an emotional affair: a triumph of rhetoric in the face of some discreet academic head-shaking. When he reached the climax of his impassioned tale, Professor Haley brought forward musicians from The Gambia who repeated in song his story of capture by slavers of his great-great-grandfather, Kunta Kinteh. (1985, p. 9)

The French Africanist Raymond Mauny was among those head-shakers. He evidently was not pleased with Haley's speech because he assumed that it was impossible to trace back the heritage of a slave so many generations (Moraes Farias, 1993a). The reaction of some scholars reported by Haydon and Paulo de Moraes Farias was one of the first and most public manifestations of skepticism about the possibility of gleaning anything of documentable value from Haley's oral sources.

If it is not possible to verify the Gambian genealogy in Haley's narrative, one nevertheless can document the impact of *Roots*. It is a safe conclusion that Haley probably did more than any other individual to create an interest in griots throughout the world. He introduced images of them into the homes of readers and television viewers via the different forms of *Roots*. To date, the book has sold 1,645,000 hardcover volumes and 4,288,000 paperback copies in English, as well as millions more copies in various translations (Applebaum, 1997). Approximately 130,000,000 viewers saw at least one episode of *Roots* (Anon., "Why *Roots* Hit Home," 1977, p. 69).

Haley was not the first writer, however, to compose a narrative that featured a griot as a character. For *Bug-Jargal* (1818 and 1826), a novel about the Haitian revolution, the French author Victor Hugo drew on secondhand information from Abbé Grégoire's sympathetic *De la littérature des nègres* (1808) to sketch a five-page portrait of griots that includes a scene with "griotes" whose dancing frightens the narrator. Terms such as "wild demon," "barbaric songs," "grotesque parody," "burlesque grimaces" and "sinister character" pepper the description and reinforce the atmosphere of breathless exoticism in what is viewed by Hugo scholars as one of the author's lesser novels. In 1858, a French officer assigned to Senegal, Victor Verneuil, published a rather light-hearted narrative entitled *Mes aventures au Sénégal: Souvenirs d'un voyage*. It contains descriptions of life in the cities of Senegal that match those of other writers of the era, as well as what appear to be two rather unrealistic tales by a griot who took the author on a journey of discovery far inland. These tales, one about the nature of the devil, the other about a ruler and his kingdom, seem to be based on the author's partial knowledge of the region and a desire to present griots as intelligent and exceptional members of society.

For these two French writers, the griot served to convey the exotic cultural landscape of Africa and its diaspora to European readers fascinated by unknown lands. A century later when Haley began to trace his family's heritage back to The Gambia, the goal was to lift the veil of exoticism and, in Moore's words (1994), to claim "an entire continent for an unmoored people." In his role as researcher for his own heritage and, in a larger sense, for the narrative that would be called *Roots*, Haley became infinitely better

known than all of the other scholars who attended the Manding conference. But he also recognized his need to work with those who had devoted
their careers to the study of West Africa.

By the early 1970s, Haley had written a first draft of the book and was
consulting with scholars on the African chapters. In The Gambia he had
met with Bakari Sidibe, the leading researcher on the oral tradition there.
Later, when Sidibe was in the United States as a scholar in residence at
Indiana University, Haley showed these early chapters to him and to
Charles Bird. According to Bird, he, Haley, and Sidibe went through the
chapters carefully, and both Sidibe and Bird offered suggestions for
changes. Sidibe in particular, Bird told me (1992), wanted to strengthen
the ethnographic details. What Haley was seeking, Bird added, was someone to say that the African chapters where we find portraits of griots were
not completely at odds with reality, and "I think that is what he got from
both of us."

Haley had consulted with other Africanist scholars in the United States,
notably the distinguished oral historian Jan Vansina at the University of
Wisconsin. But none of these researchers was involved in the more
fundamental debate about the qualifications of Haley's source in The
Gambia. For students of griots today, one of the nagging questions to come
out of Roots was just how "authentic" was the information conveyed to
Haley that contributed so much to the story of Roots.

It would take far more than a book to sort out the complex story of
Haley's research. But for an 8,000-word exposé in the Village Voice in 1993,
"Alex Haley's Hoax," Philip Nobile, aided by a team of four researchers,
attempted to do just that by examining some of the late author's papers and
talking with many people who worked with him on Roots. The result was
a devastating attack on the authenticity of Roots presented in an intensely
muckraking style.

Nobile's research, as well as my own and that of other scholars, suggests
answers to these three key questions about Roots and griots: What was the
nature of the contacts Haley had with griots? Where does his encounter
with griots fit into the larger picture of the impact of his narrative? What is
the significance of Roots for the expansion of the griots' performance
context in the 1980s and 1990s?

Haley's contacts with griots are of interest for two reasons. First, Roots
contains portrayals of griots that introduced the profession to a mass
audience. Second, Haley claimed to have met a griot who identified his
ancestor, Kunta Kinte, and referred to his capture in the eighteenth
century.

In the first reference in Roots to bards (Haley, 1976, p. 117), the narrator describes an old griot telling about the African past to young men in the process of completing their initiation into society. The scene reflects the educational process that is part of initiation ceremonies, but the real goal appears to be to inform the reader about the empires of Ghana, Mali, Songhay, and Benin. Later, on the trip home from the lengthy initiation ceremonies, Kunta Kinte tells his age-mate Lamin that a griot is buried in an old baobab tree. Haley's fictional reconstruction of the griot telling stories to the boys about the past is quite plausible, and the brief scene at the baobab tree reflects a custom that can be documented from the seventeenth century at least until the 1950s, although the reason given by Kunta for why griots are buried in trees—"since both the trees and the histories in the heads of griots were timeless"—does not match the more common view that burial of these performers in the ground would pollute the earth.

Those two scenes are embedded in the clearly fictional parts of *Roots* that Haley composed based on what his sources indicated life might have been like in The Gambia in the late eighteenth century. The final three chapters, which bring the reader up to the present, and especially the last, which reveals how Haley went about his research, are supposed to be based on fact. It is here that Haley describes how he met a griot in Juffure and heard him mention his ancestor Kunta Kinte at about the two-hour mark in the narration of Kinte clan history.

Did Haley really obtain his family history from a Mandinka *jali*? If so, did the *jali* know in advance that Haley was coming? There is much evidence to suggest a negative answer to the first question and a positive answer to the second. The evidence also indicates that *Roots* is a far more fictional work than anyone has realized until now. But to limit any critique of *Roots* to these questions is to blind oneself to the larger significance of the impact of the narrative since 1976. To put both issues, accuracy and impact, into a broader framework, I shall examine in some detail the question of Alex Haley's meeting with the griot in Juffure, an event that occurred, according to Nobile, on May 17, 1967.

In an interview in the *New York Times* in 1976, Haley traced his research on *Roots* back to 1964, when he encountered references to his ancestors at the National Archives in Washington that matched what he had heard from his relatives during childhood. From the outset, Haley emphasized that "although it's advertised as nonfiction, perhaps we should call it 'faction.' Every statement in *Roots* is accurate in terms of authenticity—the descriptions of the culture and terrain are based on valid material. The beginning is a re-creation, using novelistic techniques, but as it moves forward more is known and it is more factually based" (Watkins, 1976, p. 2).

After the book appeared, the matter of the accuracy of the key element in his research, the identification of Kinta Kunte by a Gambian griot, came under sharp attack by a British journalist. In 1977, Mark Ottaway traveled to Juffure on a one-week trip to write tourism articles. While there, he interviewed people Haley had met. Then he assembled a list of inconsistencies based on what he learned in The Gambia and on later research in London. He then presented the list to Haley during an interview. One of the inconsistencies, as Ottaway reported in the *Sunday Times*, was that the man who had told Haley the story of Kunta Kinte was "of notorious unreliability . . . [he] knew in advance what Haley wanted to hear and . . . subsequently gave a totally different version of the tale" (1977, p. 17). Haley's response was that "I felt I could only write what I was told. Neither you nor I know exactly what happened. But I stand by *Roots* as a symbol of the fate of my people" (2). Was the journalist simply engaged in "Sticking Pins into a Best-seller" (P.H.S., 1977), the subtitle of a followup item in the same paper two days later, or was there some significance in his discoveries? To understand the controversy, it is useful to begin by tracing Haley's roundabout path to Juffure.

Nobile, in his *Village Voice* article, questioned the existence of the Mandinka words Haley claimed to have received from his ancestors, as well as the timing of his encounters with both Africanists in this country and a Gambian student who helped arrange meetings in Banjul. Haley and the student did in fact travel to Banjul, the capital of The Gambia, where, with the help of the student's father and others, the name Kinte was traced to a particular region on the opposite side of the Gambia River and about twenty miles up the right shore.

As explained in the last chapter of *Roots*, it was in Banjul that Haley first reported hearing about the existence of griots from the group of local advisers organized by the father of the Gambian student. After describing what he was seeking, Haley returned to the United States. He went back to The Gambia sometime later at the invitation of the local advisers to meet Kebbi Kanji Fofana, a man presented to Haley as a Mandinka *jali* who was familiar with the Kinte history. Haley describes in that same chapter his encounter at Juffure with Fofana and the way the man recounted the history of the Kinte clan, including the story of Kunta Kinte who had been taken away "by the King's soldiers." From that point, Haley reports he went on to trace military, shipping, and genealogical records that matched what the griot had told him.

Ottaway, however, returned to London from Juffure with the startling news that Fofana, who had died in 1976, was not a griot at all. A son of the imam, or religious leader, of the village, Fofana had been denied the vacant hereditary post by his people after the death of his father because of his lack of Qur'anic training and his reputation as playboy, Ottaway reported. This information came from local sources, including the scholar Bakari Sidibe and Fofana's son, who said that his father merely spent much time with village elders. Ottaway also interviewed Binta Kinte, the widow of Fofana, who said that the people of Juffure had been expecting Haley when he came on his first trip to the village.

Fourteen years later, when I questioned Binta Kinte about her husband during an interview in Juffure (1991), she told me that Kebba Kanji Fofana had come from a family of griot origin, but had not practiced the profession, though he knew much about the past of the Kintes.

Whatever Fofana's origins, what seems clear here is that he assumed an ambiguous role, somewhere between griot and elder, in order to respond to Haley's request. His ambiguous role does not necessarily invalidate his information.

Another charge by Ottaway was that Sidibe had found other, more qualified sources for Haley but that the American writer had decided to ignore Sidibe. In particular, Sidibe had warned Haley that Fofana was not of griot origin. Haley's response to Ottaway's report, in particular the discounting of Sidibe's warning letter about Fofana, was simply that he had encountered conflicting views from many sources in The Gambia, and had chosen to believe Fofana.

Donald Wright, an oral historian who did considerable research in the Lower Gambia region and interviewed Fofana several times, presented parts of one of the interview, as well as an excerpt from an interview with Bakari Sidibe, in "Uprooting Kunta Kinte: On the Perils of Relying on Encyclopedic Informants" (1981). He found that Fofana knew something about the past but was by no means an expert: "I would guess Fofana recited for Haley what Kinte history and genealogy he knew (accurate or otherwise)—and he likely knew as much as most, since he resided with and was related to the Kinte—and then added to it his own embellishment of the information gleaned from Haley's own tradition of 'Kin-tay' from the United States" (1981, 211). Fofana, added Wright, seemed to have become by middle age "a local entertainer and teller of stories. Thus, he became something of an amateur griot, one who passed on stories heard around the evening fires rather than one who, by traditional lots in life, memorized and embellished long genealogies and family histories handed down for generations" (208). Citing the importance of fitting narratives to the audience, he concluded that "Fofana probably did for Haley just what any good griot might have done for an African ruler several centuries before his time" (214).

Although Wright seems to take an accommodating view of Haley's source, placing Fofana in the broader context of elders who know about the past and who, on occasion, can provide more accurate information than griots, the historian cites Haley as a prime example of how not to carry out fieldwork in Africa on the oral tradition: Haley advertised in advance what he was seeking, apparently failed to tape-record the narrative by Fofana, should not have relied on a single informant, but have made better use of other Kinte material that he had requested Sidibe to collect, and depended too much on one phrase, "the king's soldiers," to date the capture of Kunta Kinte.

Wright did not have access to Haley's papers when he wrote. Philip Nobile, however, was able to examine a variety of documents and recordings before they were placed in the Special Collections Library of the University of Tennessee at Knoxville. He obtained enough additional resources to conduct a wide-ranging series of interviews in person and by telephone with people who had known or worked with the late author in this country and abroad.

One of the greatest surprises to emerge from Nobile's research was a tape recording and accompanying transcript of the meeting between Haley and Fofana in Juffure. It serves as the starting point for the journalist's indictment.

1. The Griot Tape: The encounter with Kebba Kanji Fofana in the Gambian village of Juffure on May 17, 1967, was the defining moment of his career. Upon this single scene he built the church of *Roots*. But listening to the tape recording of the exchange strongly suggests that the events of that pivotal day were fabricated. Fofana recited no lineage of the Kinte clan as worshipfully portrayed in *Roots*. Instead, Haley fed him a few pre-arranged questions, and the griot replied with answers massaged by Haley's Gambian associates. As long as he lived, Haley apparently never let anyone hear the tape.

After brief greetings, Haley got down to business with the translator, A. B. C. Salla, the minister of Gambia's public works. "What I wanted to do," Haley told Salla, "is get a way here to get a specific date . . . and put it to an event like I know the thing was that say [*sic*] in 1760." (Haley's transcript, also on deposit in the archives, omits this stated agenda.)

Next the translator explained Haley's mission to Fofana in untranslated Mandinka, happening to mention the words *prime minister*. With that prompting, the translator quoted the griot as saying: "During the slave trade, it appears that Kunta Kinte disappeared, and Kunta Kinte is the son of Omoro Kinte and Binta, Binta Kebba . . . Now Kunta disappeared and they couldn't find him any more. They thought he was caught by slave dealers. . . ."

"Does he have any idea of the time this happened?" Haley asked.

The translator continued: "He says with the arrival of the British soldiers, and the Portuguese soldiers. They are sent back home to Portuguese."

In *Roots*, Haley did not mention the Portuguese, for whatever reason, and instead has the griot say, "About the time the King's soldiers came . . ." This alteration comported with his decision to have Kunta/Toby arrive in Annapolis in 1767 on a British slave ship. (Nobile, 1993, p. 34)

Nobile explains that the Gambian committee had seen Fofana in advance, prepared him, and reported to Haley their results four days prior to the meeting in Juffure. According to the transcript of the meeting, Nobile reports, "Cham-Joof then read Haley a three-page 'Confidential Report,' dated April 1967, which was subtitled 'Story told by Kebba Fofana Kangi.' The hand-written document, itself partially copied from J. M. Gray's A *History of the Gambia* (1966), contains a preview of what Fofana would say in Juffure about Kunta's capture and the 201-year backdating" (34–35).

Nobile's argument is that Haley embroidered on this set-up meeting to create the emotional description marking the high point of the last chapter of *Roots*. This incident was emblematic of the entire process of the creation of *Roots*, Nobile implies, quoting from a long list of genealogists, editors, relatives, scholars, and friends of Haley to support his case.

The evidence presented by Nobile is convincing, but my own interview with Haley, as well as extensive research with griots, has led me to a slightly different conclusion. Nobile's exposé appeared a year after Haley's death (he died on February 10, 1992, in Seattle, Washington). Three months before he died, I interviewed Haley after he made a speech at The Pennsylvania State University. The context of this interview needs some explanation. We had met briefly twelve years earlier at a reception after a speech he gave at Penn State. I had discussed with him my plans to return to Niger to collect an African epic, and he had encouraged me to undertake the project. When I met him again on the morning of November 7, 1991, I handed him a copy of the book that had resulted from my research as well as a photograph taken of Binta Kinte, widow of Fofana, at her home in Juffure. I explained that I wanted to interview him, and he agreed to meet with me that evening after his presentation.

Like Nobile, I had come to doubt the claims of Haley in *Roots*. But my perspective on the narrative, based on research in four countries in West Africa and interviews with over 100 griots, was different from that of the *Village Voice* journalist. From the research for *Scribe, Griot, and Novelist*, it seemed highly unlikely that a Songhay griot could have recalled specific incidents associated with the name of an ordinary citizen two centuries earlier unless that person was of royal origin and had accomplished something significant in life. The chronology of Songhay rulers from 1463 to 1591 that I recorded was missing many of the names one could find in the detailed Arabic chronicles from Timbuktu—especially those of rulers who had done little or reigned for only a short period. But comparisons between the written and oral traditions had also revealed that both media were marked by a variety of biases—the reason for the subtitle of the book: *Narrative Interpreters of the Songhay Empire*. If *The Epic of Askia Mohammed*, a 1,602-line narrative included as part of the study, lacked references to nondescript rulers, it did reveal far more about Songhay values than the lengthy and detailed Timbuktu chronicles with which I compared it. In other words, the deeper meaning of the text was far more significant than the details. I wondered what the worth of the factual details was for Alex Haley in comparison with the values his narrative conveyed and the impact it had.

What emerged from our discussion late that evening was my sense both of the limitations of Haley's knowledge about griots—for example, as indicated in the preceding chapter, he had not heard of women griots— and of the fact that he had told a story that was quite plausible to his audience. In other words, based on partial knowledge, partial data, and a desire to construct a narrative that would have meaning for his readers, he had created *Roots* in a way that echoed the griot tradition. But what about truth? It simply had to be interpreted at a symbolic level, much as the Songhay griot Nouhou Malio had done for me in 1980 when he recounted the story of Askia Mohammed.

Toward the end of our meeting, I offered my own reading of *Roots* to Haley. He had gone off to The Gambia in search of a story that might be linked to his own heritage. His Gambian hosts had understood quite clearly what he wanted, and they gave it to him. He, in turn, had interpreted their story in a manner that stirred the hearts of millions of people around the world and gave a new sense of pride to people of African descent.

Haley readily agreed to my description of what he had done, adding that he was under no illusion about the nature of the process that he had set in motion when he first traveled to The Gambia. He had stated essentially the same thing in his responses to critics in New York and London by emphasizing the fictional nature of the enterprise. But in the process of marketing his narrative, he and his publishers and advertisers had shifted the fuzzy line between fact and fiction. Haley himself did not go out of his way to restore the balance between the two on the timeline of the narrative. He felt no need to do so because he was operating as a modern-day griot, telling a story of great social and cultural significance to audiences that until then had had little opportunity to learn anything positive about their African past.

In discussions since then with Africanist scholars who have worked with both the written and the oral history of Africa, I find that many of them share my view, including some who were consulted by Haley. Bakari Sidibe agreed (1991) with the interpretation of *Roots* that I gave to Haley. Bird added (1992) that *Roots* was "a marvelous contribution to making people aware. . . . When you take a population of African Americans . . . and all of a sudden show them there is beauty and nobility and majesty in [their past] then you get them to go on. And if they find out that Haley did not have all of the facts right, that's academic nitpicking at a certain point. I would have liked to have seen it better, but, in terms of its overall impact, it was a tour de force, a great contribution. Haley deserved everything he got." The historian John Hunwick, who has devoted a career to studying Arabic-language texts from West Africa, shares Bird's view: "The controversy over *Roots* is unimportant compared to the impact the book had—not so much on perceptions of Africa, but on (for Whites) a real feeling for what slavery was like, and (for Blacks) a sense of triumph over adversity and (and this goes for everyone), the power of the human spirit to survive and retain its humanity" (personal communication, 1996).

Other researchers and journalists might term such a view revisionist at best and downright naive at worst, especially because of Haley's distortions about life in Juffure in the eighteenth century (D. R. Wright, 1997, p. 235). But it is a perspective that stands on the reality of two basic facts about narratives by griots. First, they contain a degree of symbolism that may mask a much more complex social reality which cannot always be stated or detailed. Second, the story of *Roots*, rather than the history of its composition as exposed in the charges, countercharges, denials, and discoveries listed by journalists, has had an extraordinarily profound impact on how people around the world view the continent as well as on the people of Juffure, which now attracts as many as 10,000 tourists each year.

Beyond viewership and publication numbers, *Roots* has generated a multitude of positive responses, ranging from local efforts to collect oral history to the use of the term *griot* to symbolize awareness of and attachment to Africa. David Chioni Moore, an American scholar of African literature, argues that *Roots* must be accepted as symbolic truth (1994, p. 10) and read as a world foundational text that focuses not simply on the re-created origins of a single family but on the reality of a multiracial collection of many thousands of people related to Haley on several continents today. Moore's most recent research on Haley's archives in Knoxville,

Tennessee ("Revisiting a Silenced Giant," 1996) reflects that scholar's view that Haley deserves to be read and studied from a more sympathetic perspective today. His perspective stands in stark contrast to that of the journalist Nobile, who has launched a campaign to have Haley's Pulitzer Prize revoked (Reid, 1997).

If the griot qualifications of Haley's source in Juffure are marginal, one of the great ironies is that in *Roots II: The Next Generation*, the televised version of how Haley went about his research in The Gambia, the person selected to play the role of Fofana was in fact one of the most talented *jalolu* of The Gambia, Al Haji Bai Konte. In a sense, thanks to the narrative *Roots*, large audiences saw for the first time an actual griot recounting a genealogy. Although the late Al Haji Bai Konte is the subject of an eleven-minute film by the same name that is shown by many instructors in African literature courses every semester at universities and colleges around the United States, it is unlikely that the sum of these audiences will ever match the total that saw the Gambian *jali* in *Roots II* in February 1979.

Griots and Researchers

One major impact of *Roots* was on researchers. The performance at Penn State described at the beginning of this chapter was a by-product of a semester-long residency by these three *jeliw* at Indiana University, and it illustrates in the most positive way how academic research can be combined with outreach for the benefit of diverse audiences.

Bird was not the first, however, to invite griots to this country. A few had come years earlier at the invitation of scholars to perform and teach. Jali Nyama Suso at the University of Washington in 1971–72 was the first *kora* player to hold an extended residency in the United States. Griots had visited Europe individually and in groups for several generations, mainly in the context of colonial exhibitions, such as the ones organized by the French in Paris in 1889 and 1931. The Exposition Universelle in 1889 featured a reconstructed African village that included a blacksmith, a weaver, a jeweler, and several griots from a variety of ethnic groups (Anon., May 1, 1889).

A few researchers had worked with griots after the Second World War. The best-known researchers were Birago Diop, the Senegalese veterinarian who began to collect stories in the 1940s in Senegal and Mali; the Guinean historian Djibril Tamsir Niane, who set out to collect an epic in Upper Guinea in 1958; and his compatriot Camara Laye, who followed in the same tradition.

These pioneers were joined by many other scholars during the 1960s and 1970s. Gordon Innes and Anthony King from Great Britain, Roderic Knight from the United States, and Bakari Sidibe from The Gambia conducted research in that tiny but griot-rich country. Christian Seydou and Gérard Dumestre from France, along with Lilyan Kesteloot from Belgium, Charles Bird, John Johnson, and David Conrad from the United States, and Youssouf Tata Cissé from Mali worked in Mali. Laye managed to record epic texts in his home country, Guinea, before going into exile in Senegal.

These researchers came from a variety of disciplines—folklore, literature, music, anthropology, history, and linguistics. They constituted a peculiar kind of "audience" for several reasons. To a large extent they approached the world of the griots from the angle of workers in the medium of print, not voice. Moreover, their interest in what the griots had to say or perform was quite varied—some wanted texts, others wanted music, while still others sought data on the past.

Inevitably the griots responded to this disparate new audience with hesitation. The suspicion and unwillingness to reveal all to the researcher is evident in the way Mamadou Kouyaté narrates *The Epic of Sundiata* to Niane, pausing from time to time to warn him about the absurdity of books and the danger of asking too many questions.

Although both foreign and local researchers faced distrust on the part of griots when working with them, there were fundamental differences in the way they were treated by griots. For African researchers, access to griots was generally easier. They could usually speak the language of their informants more fluently than outsiders. The other side of the coin was that the relationship established between the African researcher and the griot could never be strictly professional. The act of requesting information and of rewarding the informant set up a lifetime link that could not be easily broken. Thus the griot could come to the local researcher at any time to request rewards, secure in the knowledge that he had a claim that could not be rejected.

Bassirou Dieng told me in 1991 that all of the griots he worked with during ten years in the Kayor region of Senegal still came occasionally to his house in Dakar and expected some kind of reward. Mamadou Diawara, who recorded the oral traditions of his own people in what was once the kingdom of Jaara near the Mali-Mauritania border, described several kinds of constraints on his ability to obtain information. He told me in 1992 that he began his research while a student at the Ecole Normale Supérieure in Bamako. Although he had extremely limited resources, he was under three different and overlapping kinds of obligations to the people he interviewed. First, as a researcher, he was requesting a service and therefore was expected to provide a reward for information offered to him, just as any other person might proffer something of value, even symbolic, when assisted. Second, he was viewed as someone who had gone away for a long time and should return with something to give to the people of the village, much as young men who migrated to the coast to find work always returned to share some of the material fruits of their trip. Finally, he was also viewed as a member of a local extended family and therefore was reinserting himself into a complex and longstanding network of subtle relationships and obligations when he returned to meet people. The result was that he did not always find what he wanted. He clearly recalls refusals to talk on the part of some griots for a variety of reasons, not all of which were monetary. For Diawara, the dual role of insider and outsider sometimes worked to his advantage, but on occasion it turned out to be an obstacle. Aïssata Sidikou, a citizen of Niger, faced some of the same obstacles while conducting research in her home country on three occasions from 1994 to 1997.

Neither the local nor the foreign researcher could simply walk into a griot's home and request an interview or a recording of a performance. One had to present oneself with care, and an intermediary was often necessary, someone who knew the griot and could intervene on one's behalf—much in the way griots serve as intermediaries for people who seek services. Laye reports in the introduction to Le Maître de la parole: Kouma Lafôlô Kouma (1978, p. 31) that he had some difficulties in 1958 when dealing with jeliw simply because he violated local etiquette and was not dressed appropriately. When he went to visit Babou Condé on March 15, 1963, in Fadama, Guinea, fifty kilometers east of the researcher's hometown of Kouroussa, he asked an elder how he should approach the belen tigui, or master jeli. He was advised to wear a caftan so that he would not be mistaken for an administrator. He was accepted and stayed for a month to record a version of the Sundiata epic, which he eventually reconstructed and reinterpreted in his own prose style in Le Maître de la parole.

Both local and foreign researchers often resorted to what has been described as the "induced natural context" (Goldstein, 1964, pp. 87–90) in which one attempts to record the performance in a context that is as close to natural as possible. By creating a situation similar to a ceremony, it was presumably less likely that the griot would modify or deviate from what might be expected for a traditional performance. Senegalese scholar Bassirou Dieng explained to me in 1991 how he carried out this approach in Senegal.

When I arrive in a town, I try to create the conditions—a celebration, like the royal celebrations. I kill a certain number of sheep, the entire village is invited to have lunch. I bring in musicians, all the chiefs of the families. The musicians begin to play . . . the griot speaks naturally to his natural audience.

When I videotaped a performance in Karma, Niger, I asked the canton chief, a hereditary ruler, if the griots could perform for him. He acceded to my request, and the event took place in late morning in the entrance hall to his compound. The audience included a score of local listeners and retainers, many of whom had come for a meeting earlier in the morning. The occasion had all the earmarks of what one might term an induced natural context. Even for many of the performances I recorded in Niger in 1980–81 on audiotape, a narration I had requested became, in effect, an "authentic" performance because of the crowd that assembled to hear it. During a recording of a version of *The Epic of Askia Mohammed* in Garbey Kourou, the small group surrounding the *jeseré* that Saturday evening quickly grew to over a hundred, including many people who brought their own tape recorders. Rewards were offered during the performance as newcomers arrived and were recognized in the narrative by the narrator (figure 15).

On other occasions, both the *jeseré* and the researcher sought an environment free of noise and interruption. During a taping I did in Niamey with Boubacar Tinguizi, who had narrated the version of *Silâmaka and Poullôri* recorded many years earlier and published by Christiane Seydou, we had to ask people in the neighboring compound to turn down their television set. During another taping with Djibo Badié, known as Djeliba, he drove me from his home to an empty lot on the edge of town where he was building a new house; experienced with recording in studios, he was concerned with the noise in his own compound. There, sitting on a concrete building block, he recounted *The Epic of Mali Bero* in what amounted to a studio environment under the stars (figure 16).

My colleague at the University of Niamey, Fatima Mounkaila, took the process one step further. She recorded Djeliba in a quiet studio at the Institut de Recherches en Sciences Humaines in Niamey in December 1980. There she could take advantage of first-class recording equipment and a sound specialist. Charles Bird did the same in Mali for some of his recording sessions. When I recorded *The Epic of Askia Mohammed* from Nouhou Malio, he chose the living room of a relative's house because it had electricity, more space, and comfortable chairs (figure 17).

There is a clear sense from many of these sessions that the griots were

15. Photo of Ayouba Tessa narrating epic for audience in Garbey Kourou,
Niger. By the author.

well aware of the importance of recording under the right conditions,
wherever they were. They seemed to be fully familiar with the needs of the
tape recorder, and they wanted to provide the best performance possible.

With the exception of the induced natural contexts, most of the recording sessions as well as the interviews that often preceded or followed them
were basically one-on-one interactions with a small local audience of
neighbors or friends who wanted to listen and watch. The researcher
constituted a privileged audience in many senses of the term, and the griot
supplied what was requested.

As interest in griots by researchers, African and non-African, began to
grow by the 1970s, the audiences began to change. For the researchers,
group meetings produced extended dialogues but also some problems in

16. Photo of Djibo Badié, known as Djeliba, recording *The Epic of Mali Bero* in a vacant lot in Niamey, Niger. By the author.

the encounters between two ways of seeing the past. In 1974, Georges Nesterenko, director-general of the Société Commerciale de l'Ouest Africaine (SCOA), a large trading house that had operated for decades in West Africa, agreed to work with French ethnographer Jean Rouch, his classmate from the School of Civil Engineering in France prior to the Second World War, to establish a foundation that would assist scholars studying West African cultures. Most of the foundation's efforts focused on

17. Photo of Nouhou Malio narrating *The Epic of Askia Mohammed* in a friend's house, Saga, Niger. By the author.

the study of the oral history of the great empires of the Sahel and Savanna: Ghana, Mali, and Songhay. Griots were central to the projects funded by SCOA.

The best known of these projects was a series of colloquia held in Bamako, Mali, and Niamey, Niger, that were limited to a small group of about fifty scholars from Africa and other parts of the world. SCOA brought them together not simply to talk to each other but also to interact with griots, who were invited as special guests. The key to the invitations of the griots, and in a larger sense to the colloquia project itself, was the Malian scholar Youssouf Tata Cissé, who had been working with *jeli* Wâ Kamissoko since 1959.

The emphasis at these colloquia was on discussion and exchange of information, not on performance. Some previously recorded texts, however, were distributed to the participants and served as the basis for broader discussions. The bards answered questions and offered their own views about the past. Kamissoko played a central role in many of these colloquia, and among the outcomes of his participation were new versions of epic texts edited by Cissé. One volume of the 1975 colloquium, held from January 27 to February 1, contains the first draft of a version of *The Epic of Sundiata* recounted by Kamissoko and distributed to the participants. During the colloquium the Malian *jeli* participated in discussions and, with Cissé, took the researchers on tours of the Mande region. A significant feature of these meetings was that the tapes of the week-long colloquia were transcribed and published.

The following year, Kamissoko and Diarra Sylla, who had a deep knowledge of the oral traditions associated with the Ghana empire, participated in the second SCOA colloquium, also in Bamako. This meeting resulted in the publication of the second half of *The Sundiata Epic* as well as a long narrative about the origin of the Fulbe peoples in the Mande world. The third colloquium, held at Niamey in 1977, included several griots from Mali (Sidiki Diabaté, Madani Gawlo N'Diaye, Diarra Sylla), as well as one from Niger, Djeliba Djibo Badié. It also generated texts—a mimeographed narrative recorded from Wâ Kamissoko about Mansa Moussa as well as two shorter fragments about Ghana by Diarra Sylla and Jiri Silla. During the fourth meeting in 1981 in Niamey, which I attended, both Sylla and Badié participated in the discussions and additional texts were printed in various formats.

The SCOA meetings were a collective continuation of a long-standing French tradition of support for research in Francophone Africa. By-invitation affairs designed to focus discussion for a week on a series of topics, they included scholars from Mali, Senegal, Niger, France, Britain, and the United States. What is significant about the role of griots in these meetings is that they were able to participate fully through translators, and scholars were able to ask questions, hear responses, follow up, and respond again. For the first time, groups of Western-trained researchers were able to meet on a collective basis over an extended period to explore a wide range of topics with extremely talented griots. The researchers created, in effect, a new way of eliciting information from these human archives, and the griots themselves realized more clearly than ever before that there was a growing international audience for their words.

From the transcripts, as well as from my own experience during the

Société Conerciale Le Ouest Africaine

1981 meeting, it appears that the griots had relatively little difficulty in dealing with this new audience. But at the 1976 Bamako colloquium, the difference between two ways of knowing and communicating information, that of the scholars and that of the griots, led to a sharp verbal exchange between one of the most distinguished French Africanists, Vincent Monteil, and Wâ Kamissoko.

The *jeli* gave a precise year—1258—for the death of Sundiata. Monteil replied with astonishment by saying that it was impossible for anyone operating in the oral mode to produce such a date, and his follow-up questions, even in print, were conveyed in what seemed to be a disrespectful tone.

Kamissoko replied directly with an equally sharp question: "Am I to understand that it is because we don't know how to read and write that you see that what we know on this subject is not true?" He then proceeded to explain in detail the system of accounting for the passage of time in his village, Krina. Monteil retreated somewhat from his original position of disbelief as the result of this explanation. But Cissé reported later the following rather critical comment by Kamissoko about the incident:

> Most of our "brothers"—the participants in the colloquia—don't understand very much or don't know how to listen to what they are told. Moreover, they work very hard at refuting the information about the history of the blacks that we give to beginners at Krina. In addition, they are very distant, sometimes even distrustful, of our beliefs, of our traditions and customs, and, in any case, of our languages which they don't take the trouble to learn. Finally, I did not always understand the attacks against tradition and the criticisms of me personally. (Cissé and Kamissoko, 1988, p. 16; my translation)

Most of the scholars went to the SCOA meetings as students to listen to the griots and to go on tours with them, and the griots expected their "guests" to manifest the kind of respect that any of their own students would show to someone endowed with great knowledge. In most cases, the participants recognized the extraordinary nature of these sessions not only for themselves but also for subsequent generations of scholars who can read the transcripts today.

The SCOA colloquia contrasted in size, format, and venue with the Manding Conference organized by the School of Oriental and African Studies of the University of London in 1972; the latter was far more formal in tone. But together the Manding conference and the SCOA colloquia marked a new development in the expansion of the global audience for griots. But before *Roots*, griots still remained little known outside the network of Africanist scholars.

The Post-*Roots* Era

By introducing griots to millions of readers and viewers, Haley opened the doors wider for a new audience of scholars in music, anthropology, literature, history, and other disciplines. When they applied for support to do their research, the task of explaining just what a griot was and the significance of these artisans of the word for African Americans became somewhat easier simply by referring to *Roots*.

This new and diverse audience of scholars sought particular information from griots—the text of an epic, the meaning of a praise song, the social functions of griots, a genealogy to match with other historical sources. Griots quickly became accustomed to the visits of these researchers, whose interest in their work heightened the bards' local prestige.

To understand this phenomenon, one needs to keep in mind that the griot was in many ways so ubiquitous a member of the local cultural landscape that audiences tended to take even the best for granted. Although the most talented griots enjoyed respect, which was shown in command performances for heads of state and other dignitaries and occasional visits to other countries, the everyday context of their lives was local. The day that an African or foreign researcher arrived, armed with a tape recorder, camera, and a list of questions, that context suddenly took on wider, sometimes intercontinental dimensions. The griot or griotte now had a contact with someone who might—and in a few cases did—invite him or her to meet new audiences in other countries.

That was the case, for example, when Laura Harris (now Arnston) conducted research on praise singing among the Maninka and Kuranko of Sierra Leone in 1986–88. She discovered that she had become in many ways a patron for the griot who served as one of her major informants, and she had to assume responsibilities that she did not expect. It even affected, for example, her relationship with other griots and governed the way she went about her research (1992a, 1992b).

The audience for griots expanded to include students in many countries outside Africa. The visit of Jali Nyama Suso in 1971–72 to the University of Washington was followed in 1987–88 by a year-long residency by Amadu Bansang Jobarteh, one of the most respected *jalolu* in The Gambia. Roderic Knight, who had trained at UCLA and taught at the University of Washington, invited many Mandinka *jalolu* to perform for his students and teach at Oberlin College.

Other scholars all over the United States became part of the griot network, inviting these performers to come for a few days, a week, or longer. Susan Gunn Pevar, who had done research in The Gambia on the musical tradition of Mandinka *jalolu*, and her husband, Marc, designed an instructional package for Al Haji Bai Konte that included a booklet on the *kora*, a recording, and a video; they also arranged tours and concerts for him. Charles Bird, years after his 1978 tour with Batourou Sékou Kouyaté, performed with Djimo Kouyaté, translating songs and the history of griots and providing introductions.

Griots came to be seen not simply as one-night performers but as artists who could serve residencies of interest to many students. Papa Bunka Susso visited Penn State for a week on two occasions, in January 1989 and October 1994. Each time, I organized approximately thirty events for him in the course of the five working days of his residency. The audiences ranged from a roomful of toddlers at a nursery school to a classroom of teenagers at a junior high school, a gymnasium full of even more curious high school students, many classes at the university (music, folklore, literature, history, even a graduate seminar on the griot), a workshop for those who wanted to learn to play the *kora*, a dance rehearsal for an African American group, a luncheon talk and performance for literary scholars, one-on-one meetings with administrators (vice presidents, provosts, deans, department heads), public performances open to the entire community, a reception at an African American–owned shop downtown, and numerous encounters with people on the street during a performance-stroll along the sidewalk dividing the University Park campus and the Borough of State College.

Visits by griots served many needs. They not only helped students understand Africa, but also helped build ties between the university and the community. At a time when there was growing debate over the introduction of non-Western material into the traditionally Eurocentric general education curriculum, visits by griots and other African performers helped many instructors to educate their colleagues about the significance of African cultures.

Griots and the Public

If there was a tendency for griots to focus their attention on academic audiences, it was in part because scholars knew more about griots, would work hard to obtain the funds and the visas, and could help introduce them to audiences. It did not take griots long, however, to discover that there were much wider audiences outside academia. In London, Lucy Durán helped to arrange visits, concerts, and recording sessions for griots at a variety of venues, ranging from arts centers to the National Sound Archives. The African Service of the British Broadcasting Corporation adopted music by Amadu Bansang Jobarteh for its sign-on music and often broadcast performances by griots.

Those bards who traveled to the United States after *Roots*, whether they came because of contacts with researchers or other groups, found a waiting audience in African American churches, clubs, secondary schools, museums, and concert halls. Some griots, such as Papa Susso, linked up with African American promoters who helped to introduce them to the vast African diaspora in this country.

These and other promoters often played key roles in helping to insert griots into the world music phenomenon that developed during the 1980s. In Great Britain, WOMAD—the World of Music, Arts, and Dance Festival—began to include griots in its annual festival and tours, while magazines such as *Folk Roots* started to feature them in articles researched in West Africa. In New York, the World Music Institute became the most effective sponsor of performances because the director there, Robert Browning, was one of the few persons in this country with both a deep interest in ethnic music and the experience to obtain visas.

Browning started the World Music Institute in 1985 after organizing evening musical programs in an alternative art gallery in Manhattan. By 1990, he was producing seventy concerts a year of ethnic music in a church in Washington Square, Merkin Hall, and Symphony Space. For many griots today, his operation represents something of a beacon because he and his staff have been so generous in helping them through the visa maze and the process of finding performance dates.

The shift from purely academic venues to concert halls that traditionally had invited only performers of high Western culture was a product of social change in this country and a growing sense of social responsibility on the part of sources of funding for these events. John Pareles, one of a team of music critics at the *New York Times* who included ethnic music in their reviews, explained in a 1990 article that for many of these institutions, the "declining classical audience, changes in urban demographics, new goals set by governments and private financing sources and broader ideas of musical quality" led to greater receptivity of world folk music. Ethel Fraim, co-director of the Ethnic Folk Arts Center, another venue for griots, told Pareles: "There is some pressure from foundations for presenting institutions to respond to the community that lives around them." The result, Robert Browning told Pareles, was that "every institution in New York—

Lincoln Center, Carnegie Hall, Town Hall—bought our mailing list" (Pareles, 1990, p. 32).

That same year, when Senegal was featured during the Smithsonian Institution's annual Festival of American Folklife, visitors to Washington could hear a variety of griots among the fifty-six artists performing during a ten-day period of cultural events (N'Diaye, 1991, p. 3).

Although African dance groups that included griots as musicians had visited the United States as early as 1959, when Keita Fodeba's Ballets Africains performed for two weeks in New York (N'Diaye, 1959, pp. 18–20), it was not until the 1970s and early 1980s that griots became so well known as to appear in newspaper reviews. Pareles, Peter Watrous, and Robert Palmer of the *New York Times* wrote occasional reviews of their performances beginning in the early 1980s, but as increasing numbers of griots arrived in the United States, the number of reviews grew considerably in the 1990s.

The reviewers demonstrated great interest in the music, but did not hesitate to offer suggestions when the gulf between artists and audience appeared to be too great. In a review of the performance of *Africa Oye!*, a variety show made up of performers from all over Africa, including griots from some West African countries, Pareles (1989) marveled at what he heard ("It is a pleasure, and something of an education, to see these performers on an American stage") but warned of the tendency to turn traditional rituals into "variety show turns, which may be unavoidable before an alien audience" (May 13, pp. 12–13). Watrous (1989) interviewed Mel Howard, who brought the group to the United States, and learned of the difficulties of assembling a show from such disparate sources. Howard explained that "the basic concept wasn't to do an ethnomusicological program . . . it was to do a musical program. I want to give an evening of music, where the pieces lead from one to another" (May 12).

Performers were eager not only to perform but also to market recordings of their music. The shift to a world music audience with CDs containing songs in Mandinka, Bamana, and other African languages represented a major expansion of the audience for griots. These CDs, however, often remained over the heads of their new audiences.

In some cases, the producers included extensive liner notes that helped purchasers to understand what they were hearing. One of the best examples is *Tabara*, a compact disk of music by Amadu Bansang Jobarteh recorded in 1987 during the *jali*'s residency at the University of Washington and produced by Music of the World (CDT–129) in 1993. The notes contain background on the Mandinka, their bards, and each piece. The list of credits includes the names of Lucy Durán, Roderic Knight, and Eric Charry, three of the most knowledgeable scholars in the world on Mandinka music. For many other recordings aimed at a much wider audience, however, listeners can only guess at what the songs are about and the peculiarities of the music.

In live performances, griots do not normally translate the songs they sing in Mandinka or Bamana. During Papa Susso's 1994 residency at Penn State, I asked him to explain in advance what he was going to sing, and on occasion he did, but the description of the song—the translation of key words—remained rather general and elusive. It was almost as if to translate and dissect would be to destroy.

A significant exception to this rule that also illustrates the range of the griots' impact occurred during a series of performances by Susso with symphony orchestras in the United States as part of an opera titled *African Portraits* by the American composer and musician Hannibal Peterson. It opened at Carnegie Hall on November 11, 1990. The opera traces life from a village in West Africa through the slave trade and up to the musical forms that grew out of the African presence in this country. The libretto includes an English translation of the praise song Papa Susso sings in Mandinka while playing the *kora*.

Peterson took the opera on tour and Susso eventually performed with the Baltimore, San Antonio, Saint Louis, Chicago, Detroit, Philadelphia, and Kalamazoo orchestras as well as the National Symphony in Washington. His role in the opera no doubt represented the first time a *kora* player had ever performed with many of these orchestras, and it was probably the first time that any of the European-style musicians had ever participated in a concert featuring music from sub-Saharan Africa.

For Peterson, inclusion of scenes and music from Africa served as a way of opening one of the most elite forms of music in this country to an audience that had felt largely excluded. He also saw it as an effective educational tool. In the program notes, he explained to prospective sponsors:

> During a recent open rehearsal workshop in Westchester, New York, over eleven hundred children ranging in age from nine to seventeen were enthralled with the sounds of the symphony orchestra in combination with sounds of chains, gun shots, wails, moans, screams, and a man from Africa singing in an African language . . . an operatic production of *African Portraits* would have an overwhelming effect on any school system that would include it as part of their scholastic schedule.

The performances of the opera led to several weeks of outreach by Papa Susso and other performers in school districts in the metropolitan area of each city. The Kennedy Center, which operates a large national outreach program, booked Susso for a two-week residency in April 1997, prior to his engagement with the National Symphony. He was also included as a performer in a children's play about Sundiata based on the version published by David Wisniewski, *Sundiata: Lion King of Mali*.

The example of Susso and the opera raises the more complex question of just how people of different backgrounds respond. One could argue that audiences of European origin and those of African origin, both of whom are products of Western-style systems of education, lack knowledge of Africa. But if both are interested and fascinated in what they see and hear, whether it is an opera depicting events in the history of African Americans or a performance of music by a solo griot, the African origin of the music resonates in a different way for those of the diaspora. Susso reports that his African American audiences tend to respond more warmly and spontaneously to his music. This apparent difference in audience response raises a larger question of control over intineraries of griots outside Africa.

In Britain, the issue appeared in print with the publication of a booklet entitled *The Silenced Voice: Hidden Music of the Kora*, by Galina Chester and her son Tunde Jegede (1987). They complained that African musicians who went to Britain were exploited by their hosts while their music was monopolized by what Chester and Jegede viewed as patronizing and elitist groups and institutions, such as the Commonwealth Institute and WOMAD (World of Music, Arts, and Dance). When I asked Gambian *jali* Dembo Konté about these concerns in 1991, he told me that griots had been misused by people of all races but that he and others had found nothing but support from their British sponsors in scheduling concerts throughout the country, including minority areas such as Brixton. The broader issue of support for the arts of Africa and the African diaspora in Great Britain, raised by Chester, is an ongoing concern that Kwesi Owusu addressed in his passionately argued study *The Struggle for Black Arts in Britain* (1986).

Change in the Audiences

In 1959, the popular African magazine *Bingo* published an article entitled "Les Griots: Sont-ils condamnés à disparaître?" (Are griots condemned to disappear?) by the Senegalese playwright Abdou Anta Ka. The answer from Maurice Sonar Senghor, then assigned to the Ministry of

Education and Health of pre-independent Mali, was that they might serve the Africa of tomorrow as teachers of music, historians, and technical advisers for filmmakers. But he added that the essential thing was for people to "hear them sing not of dead values but of those that are needed for our current life: work, courage, honesty, etc." (Ka, 1959, p. 32). It is unlikely that either Ka or Senghor could have foreseen the way the performance context for griots would expand.

The consequences of the rapid growth in audiences for griots are diverse. Opportunities are more frequent for griots to perform in Africa outside of the Sahel and Savanna, not simply because of migration by some of their traditional audiences to jobs in coastal countries but also because they are now recognized as part of the continentwide cultural heritage. At pan-African festivals, such as FESTAC in 1977 in Lagos, Nigeria, griots from different countries appear on the same stage. Moreover, some griots have set up permanent residency outside Africa, or spend at least half their time away from home. Papa Susso now calls New York his home away from home for six months of the year, although it is merely a base for his constant travels around the United States and to countries such as France and Japan. Others have settled in other U.S. cities: Foday Musa Suso in Chicago, Djimo Kouyaté in Washington, D.C.

The shift from an African to a global performance context raises the large question of whether there has been change in the art of griots. The answers to that question are many, and it would take a whole book to deal with them in sufficient detail. But from the examples of a few griots, one can draw several conclusions.

For Amadu Bansang Jobarteh, the year that he spent at the University of Washington in 1987–88 led to little change in his art. And Dembo Konte, son of Al Haji Bai Konte, told me in 1991 that he composes new songs and explores new styles but does not change his art fundamentally: "Myself, I never change my traditions. When I go to Europe, I am with the traditional ways, I am a typical African, that is my identity, my ancestors did it this way, I don't want to become a 'yey yey' boy." This stance did not prevent Konte and his partner Kausu Kuyateh from producing *Jali Roll* (Rogue, FMSC3020) in 1990, a cassette that alluded to the famous African American musician Jelly Roll Morton and was subsequently reissued as a CD (CD1992 Omnium 2004D). His familiarity with African American music dates back to the 1970s, when he and his father performed with Taj Mahal, the African American guitarist, at a series of concerts in the United States.

For Foday Musa Suso the changes are far more evident. He does not always wear a boubou, as he did for the photo appearing on the jacket of his first recording, but may appear in a dashiki, sporting a golden earring. His music, responding as it does to the variety of forms current in American music today, echoes his change in world view. He plays traditional styles but he also infuses his musical art with jazz. He feels that he must be open to the musical currents flowing through his world if he is to develop as a musician.

The changes emerging from contact with these new, external audiences developing outside Africa match in some ways the changes at home. In a paper presented in 1986, Durán reports that *jalolu* and *jeliw* from the Mande world see their role as having evolved as a result of the shift in patronage—or what we might term audience. When one's patron dies, notes Durán, it is understood that the griot will move on. She quotes an oft-heard line from their griot songs to illustrate this normal change: "yiriba boit, kunolu janjanta (the big tree . . . has fallen, and the birds . . . have scattered)." This saying is almost as common as another one she cites: "Mansolu man bang bari i doyata (The kings have not gone completely, but there are very few left)" (Durán, 1987, p. 235). One result of this changing situation is an increase in the number of politically powerful patrons. Durán observes that

> the area in which patronage continues most strongly is in politics. Many politicians in The Gambia, Senegal, Guinea, and Mali are known to have close associations with particular musicians, often those who are best represented in the record and cassette industry. The entry of jaliya [the activity of jalolu] into the political arena is viewed with some concern by the older jalis [or jalolu] who feel that their music should not be associated with any one political party. Too many songs nowadays, they say, are merely a catalogue of the names of politicians in power. (235–36)

Griots have been drawn to political power since the beginning of the profession, so the shifts today are hardly surprising. Old and new politicians constitute an audience with the same basic values. But one might be tempted to view with alarm the tendency of modern griots to adapt their music to the needs of something as foreign as the Western music industry. Durán, however, sees this trend in a positive light when it occurs in the local context.

> Perhaps one of the most encouraging trends of Jaliya in the last decade is its use in local "pop" music. Many of the well-known bands of the Manding countries, bands like the "Rail Band of Bamako," Mory Kante, Salif Keita and even some non-Manding bands like those of Youssou N'Dour and Baaba Maal, incorporate many traditional Jaliya songs in their repertoire. Some of the personnel of

these bands, especially the guitarists and percussionists, are members of the Jali caste. But recently there has been a tendency for singers to be non-Jalis. Singers like Salif Keita are as conversant with the style of Jaliya as with other styles, and indeed the song for which he is most famous, "Mandjou," is a straightforward example of a praise song for Sekou Touré. . . . The future of Jaliya no doubt lies in the concert hall and recording studio, though without individual patronage, it is bound to alter radically in style. (236)

Charry cites ways male and female performers adapt to these new audiences by pointing to a basic gender difference: men are "the recognized experts in speech and history and women reign in the world of singing," thus creating a distinction in audience. The women, who focus on "the aesthetic of praise," touch an audience outside Africa that consists mainly of African expatriates. "On the other hand, male singers, whose singing is not so deeply entrenched in praising, have been more successful in reaching a non-African audience" (1993b, p. 4).

Instrumental music is an important key to this distinction. Charry explains that

> since non-griots do not have the right to play the traditional griot instruments, they usually become singers or guitarists. When they want to use traditional instruments for their recordings, they hire griots. On the recordings of non-hereditary singers such as Salif Keita and Baaba Maal, for example, the family names of musicians who play the traditional lutes and balafons read like a who's who of griot families from West Africa: Kouyate, Diabate, and Sissokho. (1993b, p. 4)

Thus men have what amounts to an inside track on the path to reaching new audiences. Charry explains that in the 1920s, 1930s, and 1940s, griots began to integrate the acoustic guitar into their tradition. The electric guitar was added to their ensembles with the assumption of power by President Sekou Touré of Guinea in 1958. He ordered that a national orchestra be established and provided the funds for instruments, including electric guitars (1994b, pp. 30–31). Mali eventually followed Guinea in integrating the electric guitar into urban ensembles, though at a slower pace, Charry suggests, because the country did not go through such a rapid modernization process as Guinea in the early days after independence and was less subject to Western influence. Charry points out that although anyone may play the guitar, those with the family names of Kouyaté, Diabaté, and Sissoko are the most talented (1993b, pp. 4–5). He adds that most of these griots are Maninka. The Wolof, Fula, and Soninké griots have not done as well.

In the course of his 1993 presentation entitled "When a Griot Modernizes: A View from the Recording Studio," Charry illustrated his points with
several examples. Nowhere was the difference between the older and the
younger generations clearer than in the excerpts from the Gambian *jali*
Amadu Bansang Jobarteh, played at the beginning of the talk, and his
extraordinarily talented grand-nephew, the Malian Toumani Diabaté,
played at the end (a version of "Kaira" from a cassette entitled *Shake the
World*). For the recording, Charry explained, a Japanese arranger took
Toumani Diabaté's notes and arranged them for violins and synthesizers, a
blending that a *jeli* neighbor described as "trop sophistiqué."

Charry also observed in his 1993 paper that women were more audience
sensitive than men. That may be true in the context of instrumental and
vocal music, but in a larger sense one can conclude that griots in general
are highly audience sensitive. Just as the griot whose king has fallen in
battle is not harmed but must, in many cases, switch loyalties to the
winning side, in a much more general way the griots of today are switching
loyalties to the new audiences they have created around the world. If there
are far fewer patrons at home than in years past, new patrons in search of
what griots have to offer can be found. This mobility may seem at first to be
opportunistic, and in the worst cases it certainly can be regarded as such.
But griots are caught in a fundamental social shift brought on by the
communications revolution of the second half of this century and the
political changes occasioned by the transition from the colonial to the
national era in Africa. They have married their own fundamental flexibility
and audience sensitivity to the new audiences generated by this revolution.
Those of us, African and non-African, who would like to see tradition
preserved cannot stop the forces of change.

During the discussion of papers on griots presented at the 1995 meeting
of the African Studies Association, one member of the audience argued
that scholars should do more to encourage griots to return to the path of
tradition. My response was that it would be presumptuous for scholars,
especially those from outside Africa, to tell griots what to do in any
circumstance. I might have added that in addition to the impropriety of
giving such advice, many factors over which we scholars have no control
are propelling these performers toward new audiences.

Electric Griots

After that same panel, whose topic was griots and technology, one
member of the audience reported to me that she had reduced the title of

the session to "electric griots" in order to convey the excitement of the event to those who had not been there. The papers had included such a wide variety of references to electronic media that the simple term *electric* conveyed more effectively both the content and the atmosphere generated by the discussion.

If the power of the verbal art of griots stems in large part from its medium, the human voice, then technology, electric as well as other kinds, has indeed provided the key to expanding the range of that voice to larger and more diverse audiences in the last half century. Paved roads, air transportation, telephone, radio, television, audio and video recordings, satellite communication, printing, and the Internet all help bring the words of griots to these new audiences. The juxtaposition of the two words *griot* and *technology* does not, however, seem at first to be appropriate.

The term *griot* has come to mean roots, traditions, and a kind of connectedness with the past that contrasts sharply with the constant change that is the hallmark of Western societies today. But one reason why some griots are surviving and even prospering is their ability to adapt to new situations and new ways. That is the case not only in the social sense — adaptation to new audiences and new patrons — but also in the technological sense. Many griots and griottes have taken to technology with an eagerness that contrasts sharply with our image of the village bard, repository of a seemingly static oral tradition.

How can we explain this paradox of tradition and modernity contained in a human vessel called the griot? One answer might be that griots will do anything to reach a larger audience and make more money. But a more complex explanation emerges when we place modern communications media in a broader context and reinterpret the notion of technology to include change that may seem either too subtle or too obvious to non-Africans.

Technology suggests machines, electronic parts, wires, and devices of various kinds. These instruments are, in fact, important for the new performance context that griots have created. But one definition of technology is "the sum of the ways in which social groups provide themselves with the material objects of their civilization" (*Webster's College Dictionary*, 1991, p. 1371). Framed in this broader perspective, technology includes everything made by man. Changes in these ways — even changes in long-standing methods — may be termed technological. My experiences with an African musical instrument will illustrate the point. In 1981, I ordered a three-stringed *molo* from the shop at the Musée National in Niamey because I wanted to learn more about the standard instrument played by the *jeserey* I was recording that year in western Niger. I went to the Musée National to obtain one of these instruments because, in addition to the imaginative displays and the animals one can see there, it supports a large number of artisans who craft jewelry, leatherwork, sculpture, blankets, basketry, and other items in the traditional styles of Niger.

After purchasing the *molo* for approximately twenty dollars, I contacted Zakary Hamani, a young *jeseré* I had met in Ouallam, a provincial capital. He had just moved to Niamey, and I wanted to ask him to give me some *molo* lessons. When he came to my house, he looked at the *molo* and said it needed to be modified. He took it away with the promise that he would return the instrument in a week.

When he brought the instrument back, it looked the same, but there was one change. He had replaced the neck. The original neck was made of a branch from what I think was an acacia tree. Stripped of its bark, it was white and smooth, a trait that made it difficult for the player to maintain the proper tuning of the three strings, which were attached to the neck with leather thongs wrapped around it at different points. Zakary had had the neck replaced with a piece of hardwood with a fine-grained, slightly abrasive surface just right for maintaining the tuning. He had updated my *molo* with a kind of wood that came from the forest region south of Niger.

The change to the instrument was hardly noticeable, but it represented an evolution, a modernization—what we might call an equipment upgrade. Though I thanked Zakary for his work, I was not delighted by the change because I viewed it as technologically incorrect. I didn't realize that in Zakary's eyes the instrument was not a museum piece, but a working *molo*. He had, in fact, high hopes that I would pay him for lessons and learn how to play it—hence the need for the latest version.

The change to the *molo* reflected in microcosm what has happened to other instruments in West Africa. Whenever the Gambian *jali* Papa Susso visited Penn State, he took delight in explaining to his audiences how the twenty-one-stringed *kora* is constructed from a large calabash, a cowhide, and a long wooden neck. But he also revealed how this fascinating and complex bridge-harp, the embodiment of an ancient tradition in design and construction, had also undergone change. *Kora* builders no longer secure the calfskin to the calabash with thongs that make up a neatly tied network on the round side. Instead they attach the hide with many long, shiny carpet tacks that also give a decorative effect. They have made one other change of a more functional nature: the cords are no longer made of strips of antelope hide. *Kora* builders have switched to nylon fishing line, which lasts longer and is easier to obtain.

In both cases, the *molo* and the *kora*, the changes seem rather small. Yet they represent a feature of many African societies that outsiders find rather difficult to grasp: these cultures are not static; they are dynamic. In the case of the *molo* and the *kora*, artisans have changed construction techniques as new materials have become available and as they learn about new ways of designing their instruments. In the 1960s, for example, some griots in Senegal, along with monks at the Ker Moussa Monastery, offered their own changes to the *kora* with the introduction of keys similar to what one finds on other stringed instruments.

But there is change at one's own pace and change at the forced rate of overpowering outside influences. The growth in population in West Africa and the decline in numbers of some animal species may have led to a shortage of antelope skin that might explain the shift to synthetic strings. But this small change also reflects a basic openness to available technology as a means to improve or expand performances. In other words, griots may be vehicles for conveying the past to the present, but they are no more locked into traditional technology than any other member of society in any other profession—the blacksmith who discovers welding, the weaver who adopts color-fast thread, or the carver who finds that Western tools enable him to work more quickly. Where it suits their needs, many griots have embraced modern Western technology without hesitation.

Technology, however, is far more than the substitution or modification of parts of the tools of one's profession. If we take a longer historical perspective, without doubt one of the most significant changes for the griot was the improved transportation that came with the arrival of the coloniz- ers. This change may seem ordinary to those unfamiliar with the chal- lenges of traveling long distances in Africa, but it was quite important in expanding the performance context of griots. Although people used to cover great distances by river transport, by foot, and by animal, the building of roads and bridges and, eventually, the introduction of the railroad and the automobile increased the griot's ability to travel rapidly to more distant events.

Jan Jansen (1996a) underscores this point in his study of Sira Mori Diabaté, the *jelimuso* from Kéla and Kangaba whose performance context expanded somewhat when she was able to travel more easily to Bamako, the capital of Mali, several hours away. This improvement in roads had an impact not only in the local context—a wider range of weddings, installa- tions of chiefs, and naming ceremonies—but also in the region. Where it might have taken weeks in the past to travel from the inland Sahel to the coast, now one could make the trip in a few days to perform for an expatriate audience—one made up of people who came from the interior but had settled on the coast because of work, marriage, or other reasons. It was not unusual for parents to send a train ticket to a griot or griotte in Bamako, Ouagadougou, or Niamey to attend a ceremony in Dakar, Abidjan, or Cotonou.

After the Second World War, griots could travel more easily to the major cities. But it was the introduction of air travel in the 1950s and especially the 1960s that enabled them to expand their performance context to more distant audiences. Although griots had traveled individually and with troupes to Europe in the 1950s, it was not until the 1970s that large numbers of them traveled by air to perform in Paris and London. In real terms the price of air travel continued—and still continues—to drop year by year, shrinking the globe for griots. They now perform in the capitals of the former colonizers as well as in other cities quite distant from West Africa—Moscow, New York, Tokyo, and in hundreds of smaller places. The revolution in air travel, something that Westerners take for granted, has contributed enormously to the shift from a local to a global performance context for griots and griottes.

Even before griots began to travel by air to other countries, however, they were reaching national and regional audiences back home thanks to radio. Around 1957, Radio Soudan began broadcasting from Bamako with a format that included regular performances by *jeliw* (see Newton, 1995, p. 4). These broadcasts were heard at first only in the vicinity of Bamako but later, with the installation of more advanced equipment, reached the entire country.

The audiences for these broadcasts did not need electricity to hear the performers on battery-powered radios, the most ubiquitous form of modern technology in Africa. It is sometimes difficult for those who have never visited Africa to imagine the extent to which radios so quickly covered the continent. The transistor revolution of the 1950s led to the proliferation of radios in nearly every village. By the 1960s, radio broadcasts had become the primary means of mass communication in many countries. In Niger, for example, it often appears as though the entire population tunes in to the radio at one o'clock every afternoon to hear the news and, more importantly, announcements of personnel transfers in civil service positions and convocations of people to attend meetings.

One result of this dependence on radio is the local production and extensive distribution of batteries. The recent invention of a windup radio that does not depend on batteries promises to fill any remaining gaps in the near-total coverage of radio reception in Africa today.

The synergistic combination of radio and tape recorder in the 1970s and 1980s led to an even greater expansion of the performance context for griots. Producers could record griots in natural situations and broadcast their performances; then listeners could record them, make copies, and distribute them locally and to expatriate communities. Today, in any large Sahelian or Savanna city, one can find in the electronics section of outdoor markets stacks of cassettes on which the salespeople have written by hand the name of the performer. These merchants willingly allow the potential purchaser to listen to the cassette before buying. Other traveling sales-people or simply travelers buy them in quantity and take them on trips of a thousand kilometers or more to the coast to sell to expatriate customers.

The cassettes come from a variety of sources. Robert Newton, during his research on the music marketplace in Mali in 1992–94, encountered five kinds of cassettes available to listeners: those copied from recordings by the radio station from the late 1950s to the present (state-owned from 1957 to 1991, privatized since then); those recorded by individuals at local per-formances and then sold to entrepreneurs for dubbing and marketing; those recorded in privately owned studios in Bamako, Abidjan, Conakry, Paris, London, or New York, many of which are pirated either by the original producers or other studios; and copies of local performances distributed among friends (Newton, 1995, pp. 12–13).

This incredibly diverse production has blanketed the market with audio cassettes. It is hard to walk down a street in a city or small town in West Africa without being accosted by someone selling cassettes from a tray or table. Not all of them, of course, carry music by griots, but typically one finds a sampling of tapes by griots and griottes in each display. These cassettes have replaced the few vinyl recordings that were once available at high cost and in limited numbers and are holding their own against the growing flow of more expensive CDs.

The music available from radio and recordings, both those copied from other sources and those recorded at events such as weddings, serves as an important cultural resource not just for listeners but also for griots and griottes—those in training and those who are simply interested in what other performers are doing. In chapter 4 I cited, as one example of the use of technology for training, Barbara Hoffman's description of how *jelimusow* in Mali record songs at weddings and then listen to them at home as part of their training. Durán reported more recently that when she visited the senior *jeli* in Kéla, the late Kéla Bala Diabaté, in May 1995, she discovered that he listened every morning to a cassette recording of the Guinean *jelimuso* Djene Doumbia performing in 1983. This cassette, entitled

Djene Doumbia—la pure tradition mandingue au Hilton, helped to make her a star in the mid-1980s and to obtain her position as the main chorus singer for the Malian singer Salif Keita. Durán explained that the music on the cassette was an "interesting example of the art of a young *jelimuso*" who combined standard songs from the Mande repertoire with her own compositions. She added: "I was surprised to find the elderly and notoriously purist Kéla Bala listening to someone who had since moved into 'Mandé rock,' but he claimed it was because his wife liked the cassette. 'Oh no' said his wife, 'it's Kéla Bala who asks to hear it every morning'" (1995c, p. 5). One can only speculate on what the aging and infirm Kéla Bala found in this cassette from the previous decade—perhaps the pleasure of listening to something a bit different, inspiration for a new form that he might create, or insights on how to create his own hit in his waning years.

No matter how far griots and griottes travel via modern communications and transport technology, the local context remains a privileged space. But it is no longer limited by the acoustic *kora* or *molo.* The amplifier has invaded this space and the results are mixed.

Portable amplifiers arrived on the scene by the late 1970s. In 1980, one of Niamey's best known *jeserey,* Djeliba Djibo Badié, asked me to send him one of these amplifiers from the United States. When I learned from salespeople at music stores in my town that a small portable amplifier would create enormous distortion, I decided not to follow through on the *jeseré's* request. Many years later, while recording griots and griottes in Niger, I discovered just how much distortion could occur. In 1980, I had taped Zakary Hamani on a five-inch reel-to-reel Uher 4000 recorder in Ouallam on Nov. 29. The sound of his acoustic playing was rich and mellow on that tape. Nine years later, I encountered Zakary playing one evening at a wedding celebration in Saga Gorou, a village about 15 kilometers east of Niamey. Both he and I had switched technologies by then—I had shifted from audio to video, and he had found a way to extend the sound range of his music. Only when I approached within 20 feet of the musicians could I make out by the light of a kerosene lantern that it was Zakary. He had attached a microphone to the *molo* and set up another one on a stand in front of him as he sat on a mat with his accompanists. I was shocked at what a small portable amplifier had done to his music. The sound emanating from his amplifier/speaker unit had changed from the rich resonance I had recorded earlier to a harsh, high-pitched twang that was hard to listen to for any length of time. The amplifier had expanded his local performance space dramatically, but at a high cost in sound quality.

The encounter with amplification at a rural wedding was something of a surprise for me. But for those who have heard Mande *jeliw* perform in the United States, amplification on stage is quite normal. *Kora* players perform in front of microphones or drop a microphone into the hole in the upper part of the calabash sound chamber. There may be an occasional clunk or rumble when the microphone shifts inside the *kora* as the griot moves, but the overall distortion is not very noticeable.

During the past few years, some griots have sought to facilitate amplification by having jacks installed on their *koras*. For example, in 1990, the Mandinka *jali*, Jali Madi Kanuteh, was told by an engineer at a performance in New York that he should purchase a jack to simplify the setting up of sound systems. Kanuteh told me later (1991) that he went to a shop on Fourteeenth Street, bought one, and had it installed. He said he does not like the sound it produces, however, and does not always use it. But his brother Brahim thinks that the jack-linked amplification works well with large audiences. Other griots have followed suit. During a residency at Penn State in October 1994, *jali* Papa Susso proudly showed me the jack he had installed on his *kora*. The only thing that prevented him from using it during performances at Penn State was the lack of the right plug for the jack—a lack for which I was grateful. Whether or not we think it is appropriate, however, amplification has arrived and constitutes an important tool for enabling the griot to reach a larger live audience. The impact on the music reflects the quality of the equipment the performers are able to purchase.

Radio and audio cassette remain the most important technological devices that have helped griots and griottes to reach larger audiences. Television is still making its way into West Africa. Although the first television broadcasting in West Africa dates to 1959 in Nigeria, it was not adopted by many other countries until the 1960s (Bourgault, 1995, 104). It is often limited to a small region—usually the capital—and to those with electricity or access to a good supply of batteries, but it draws large audiences. One may find twenty or thirty people watching in a compound at any one time. The effect of television is difficult to summarize because of its complex nature.

Griots have embraced this new technology, though not always with the results they hoped to achieve. In a paper presented at the African Studies Association meeting in 1995, "Technology and Tradition: Television and Jeliya," Hoffman gives striking examples of how Mande *jeliw* and *jelimusow* have used—and been used by—this new medium.

She cites Zumana Yoro Traoré's weekly broadcast, *Rencontre avec nos vedettes* (Encounter with our stars), a forum that attracted a wide range of *jeliw* to its Western-style interview format. Hoffman explains that the program enabled these performers to be seen by "audiences in the hundreds of thousands, topping even the capacity of Bamako, Abidjan, and Dakar's largest concert halls and stadiums." She adds that another consequence of the program was that the Mande term *ngara*, which refers to older *jeliw* recognized as masters who have achieved the highest level of competence in *jeliya*, the art of the *jeli*, came to mean *vedette*, the French word for "star" (1995b, p. 4).

But not all *ngara* benefited equally from television. One of the most famous of Mali's *jeliw*, Baba Sissoko, who was known throughout the country for his weekly radio broadcast, added a televison show to his schedule after the medium was introduced in 1983. But Hoffman says that audiences who had listened intently to his radio programs for years found it difficult to watch his static performance on television.

> During his second season, Jeli Baba began to stand and walk around while he told his stories and played his *ngoni*. Some of the stories were even shot on location. For some, moving backgrounds were built that scrolled horizontally behind the bard as he performed. Eventually, however, under the weight of widespread criticism and even ridicule, these techniques were given up and Jeli Baba left television altogether, returning his performance of *jeliya* to its former, purely oral, medium. (5)

Hoffman adds that the first *jelimusow* to appear on television had the same problem—lack of movement, stiffness, nervousness—but explains that some of them, such as Ami Koita and Tata Bambo Kouyaté, "were successful largely because their performance style was well suited to the visual medium. They not only sounded wonderful, they looked spectacular." The video *Amy Koita: Grande Chanteuse Malienne*, distributed in Paris and Washington by Kalim International, offers a one-hour collection of clips from concerts that show the *jelimuso* in a variety of elaborate outfits.

One problem for griots in adapting to television is that at many ceremonies the focus of attention is on dancers and drummers, not on the singing griot, Hoffman notes. But "by 1990, many *jelimusow* had been successful in adapting their performance styles to suit the demands of audiences whose attention now focuses entirely on the images of them which fill those 19 and 27 inch screens" (6).

What appears on those screens, of course, depends on the editing, and Hoffman provided examples of just how powerful the editing can be. She showed both raw and edited footage of a large crowd of thousands of *jeliw* and *jelimusow* who had descended upon the town of Kita to help resolve the long-simmering dispute over who should become the next chief of the bards there. To maintain some order as the procession marched through Kita, the television crew gave instructions to the different delegations, asking them to raise their hands at certain points. Most fascinating, however, was the way that the tape editors dealt with the status of one *jelimuso* and rivalry between two *jeliw*. Hoffman believes that the inclusion of much footage in the edited version of a young Kandia Kouyaté was "directly attributable to her friendship with the people making decisions about who to show and who to leave out" rather than to her nonexistent role in the resolution of the dispute at Kita (11). But when it came to coverage of the two leading *jeliw* at the event, Kéla Bala Diabaté and Sidiki Diabaté, the editors had to take great care to maintain balance. They did so by reducing the superlatives for one of these bards that dominated the voiceover in the raw footage (12). Hoffman's study of television in Mali serves as a reminder that "what is commonly referred to as 'traditional' behavior is often plastic and dynamic, shaping and adapting itself to new conditions of performance, such as new technologies" (14).

One device that is expanding the range not only of television but of the griot's own network is the communications satellite. Although not all African countries have television available throughout the entire nation, satellites are helping to spread the medium to large areas. Many countries such as Niger and Mali, each the size of Alaska, cannot communicate to distant corners without the aid of a satellite. This revolutionary device contributes to the expansion of the performance context, not only in Africa but in other parts of the world as well, especially because of the current revolution in distance education.

In the case of *jali* Papa Susso's performance at Penn State in 1989, it was thanks to television transmitted via satellite that students at other campuses around the state could see him perform. Interactivity was limited to voice responses to his appearance on a screen, but it did enable the students to call in questions via a phone link. At one point in the broadcast, students at one remote site asked him to turn the instrument different ways in front of the camera to improve their view of his playing technique.

Satellites help not simply with performance but also by facilitating the task of inserting the griot into a global communications network. A Mandinka *jali* in The Gambia, for example, may have a telephone and access to a fax machine, essential devices for dealing with the mediators between him and his global audiences—promoters, tour operators, even researchers. Both the telephone and the fax machine may rely on satellite transmission for communication with the world outside that tiny country. Visitors to the home of Toumani Diabaté in Bamako are often invited to read—and help decipher—the many faxes he receives from agents in Europe who want to book him for a concert tour or a recording session.

The way that griots and griottes have accepted various kinds of modern communications technology and absorbed new styles of performance may give a confusing image of the profession. In 1987, I saw Djimo Kouyaté perform at a meeting in Madison. He played a *kora* whose strings were tuned by keys, and rolled on the floor as part of his act, strumming the instrument while lying down. My instinctive reaction was negative—this could not be an "authentic" griot. From what I have learned about him since then from people who know his work better, as well as from an interview with him, it appears that he may simply have been experimenting both with the instrument and with the performance style. His experimentation does not detract from his talent.

Many of us interested in the preservation of West African culture need to accept the fact that griots and griottes—no less than performers in Europe and elsewhere—are free to experiment and change over time. We may prefer to focus on traditionalists such as Amadu Bansang Jobarteh from The Gambia rather than the next generation who have come to this country—for example, Foday Musa Suso in Chicago. But we cannot adopt a "technologically correct" attitude toward the younger generation by asking them to return to the past so that our image of traditional Africa remains unspoiled by outside influence. Griots who adopt technology, whether old or new, are simply doing what many have done for centuries—adapting in order to deal with the enormous changes wrought by colonialism, nationalism, and postcolonialism and to reach new audiences.

Griots in Print

One form of technology that the griots do not use themselves but which nevertheless contributes significantly to spreading their words is the printed text. Converting the spoken word to the printed medium creates a variety of problems as well as opportunities. The product of writing down an epic or any other words by a griot is quite different from what is spoken.

Nowhere is this difference more evident than in the two versions of the Sundiata epic now most widely available. In the preceding chapter, I pointed out the differences between the reconstructed prose of the Niane edition of *Sundiata*, recorded primarily from Mamadou Kouyaté, and the linear version recorded from Fa-Digi Sisòkò and edited by Johnson. The first is a reader-friendly text that serves as an excellent introduction to the epic tradition, especially for those who might have difficulty with the story—for example, my students in an advanced French course on African literature written in French. But it does not communicate fully the oral nature of the original performance. The second requires more patience on the part of the reader and a willingness to give more than passing attention to the introduction and notes.

The intended audience for the performance is people who are part of the culture. The intended audience for the text is a different group. But beyond the vast cultural gap represented by the sometimes obscure references in the text, the linear form, with its *naamunaamuna*, or man who says "indeed" at the end of each line, echoes similar kinds of discourse, especially call and response, found among the descendants of Africans shipped to the New World. The linear version conveys more accurately than any other printed form the poetic nature of the text and the atmosphere of the original performance.

At an even greater extreme, the print edition of *The Epic of Askia Mohammed*, as I indicated in chapter 3, contains numerous lines in archaic Soninké that are not always understandable even by those of *jeseré* background. For both local and foreign readers with no knowledge of Songhay culture, the epic can be an esoteric and frequently mystifying story.

The textualization of the epic raises the question of whether we are doing any good by fixing a text in print. The traditional view of social progress is that societies evolve in the direction of literacy, with a certain percentage of literacy required for industrial development. One could argue that Western civilization is better off because people can read the *Iliad, Beowulf,* and *The Song of Roland* in books and that we would not be where we are today—for better or worse—if we could not read. Brian Street (1984) rejects this view by asserting that the medium is not what counts. It is, instead, the language that is of greatest importance, a point I illustrated in *Scribe, Griot, and Novelist* when describing the cohabitation of several languages in Niger, some written, some oral (Hale, 1990a, pp. 163–66). The function of the language rather than the medium, written or oral, is significant because language carries culture with it. In West Africa today, Arabic prayers and greetings rub shoulders with French-language newspapers and everyday speech in African languages. The changing mix of these languages, Street argues, is more significant than the medium in which they are conveyed (2–5). Thus, whether an epic is sung in person, played ten years later on the radio, or published in a schoolbook, it offers a rich and diverse catalog of cultural information to its listeners and readers. The technology of printing simply conveys the narrative to a much larger and often quite different audience.

The griots' role in the spread of their texts to the printed medium is not the result of a conscious decision on their part; instead it is the product of contacts with researchers, African and non-African, who want to preserve these texts. Although the griots rarely see the results of these meetings, they appear to be fully aware that the encounter is more than a meeting of two worlds, theirs with that of the West. It is an event that preserves their words, at least on tape and perhaps on paper. Many griots that I and other scholars interviewed seemed to recognize the importance of this preservation, especially the older ones who did not always see much hope in the younger generation.

If some griots and most scholars share the view that audio and textual preservation is important, Johnson (1996c) points to what he terms "a major failing of current published epics . . . the omission of the musical accompaniment." He proposes that epics be published "in a format resembling a musical score or songbook. . . . At the very least, we could include cassette tapes or CDs of the performance with our books, a practice which our French colleagues have managed to convince their publishers to do." He also suggests that scholars could produce videos of epic performances. But the ideal for him would be a hypercard format combining "printed text with translation, notes, and annotations in the text color-highlighted instead of footnote numbered, with a separate section on the CD-ROM featuring an animated performance by the bard with a subtitled translation."

At Tufts University, Dr. Lynda Shaffer and Parker James, a graduate student in history, have embarked on a project that promises to meet some of Johnson's expectations. They videotaped scenes from the *Sundiata* epic performed by students in Guinea and are planning to include them as part of a CD-ROM version of the well-known text recorded by Niane from Mamadou Kouyaté in 1958. The goal is to bring the epic to life for students in junior high school and high school classes. The potential impact of their project was evident at a session at Northeastern University on May 21, 1998, when a scene from the epic was shown to an auditorium of public school students attending a presentation by Niane and a *kora*-player based in Boston, *jeli* Balla Tounkara. The students listened attentively to the brief talk by Niane and to the performance by Tounkara, but came alive with laughter and exclamations when Shaffer and James showed some footage of the iron bar scene from the epic.

The willingness of griots not simply to interact with researchers who bring technology to the field but also to adopt and adapt the technology to reach their own performance goals reinforces the paradoxical image of these artisans as preservers of tradition who are often eager to change their ways. The explanation of the paradox lies in a fundamental ability to survive in the face of change—social, political, and technological. Just as griots adapt to new political situations—the defeat of a patron and the need to serve a new sponsor—they are attempting, in many different fashions, to adapt to the new performance world in which they find themselves. From those who will accept only a microphone to others who insist on a jack built into a *kora* or adjustable pegs instead of leather wrappings for tuning strings, from those who perform occasionally on the radio to those who tour the world and promote their recordings, each is developing his or her own solution.

From the foregoing, it appears that many factors have contributed to the shift of griots from performances for local listeners to encounters with audiences around the world. Alex Haley played a catalytic role in this shift, operating at times in a synergistic fashion with other researchers to bring griots to the attention of the world. Many griots themselves have now seized the opportunity opening up to them and are taking advantage of different forms of technology to continue the process of attracting new audiences. Although it is difficult to measure the extent to which the verbal and musical art of griots is changing to meet the demands of these new audiences, there is no doubt that the rewards for those who travel the globe to perform are stimulating new interest in the profession. In the next chapter, the focus will be on just how that reward system has changed over the centuries and what it means for the profession today.

❊ 9 ❊
The Value of Words

Words, written and oral, can have great monetary value in many cultures. Two examples from the African world underscore this reality. When Alex Haley spoke at Penn State in 1991, he announced to his audience that he would be staying up all night after his lecture to write a book prospectus that he could fax to his agent in New York by the next morning. He even went so far as to thank publicly his student hosts who had found him a typewriter, more powerful light bulbs for his hotel room, and the location of a nearby copy and fax shop that was open all night. Presumably the prospectus from the best-selling author would win a large advance from a major trade publisher. In this case, the value of Haley's words was based on what he had earned over a decade earlier with *Roots* and the expectation that a new narrative by him might attract another enormous audience.

Three months after Haley's death in February 1992, in another part of the world, the director of acquisitions at the Ahmed Baba Center for Research and Documentation in Timbuktu, Mali, purchased a collection of 700 manuscripts in Arabic for $10,000 from an owner who lived in the region. This mass of millions of words on thousands of sheets of yellowed paper and parchment filled a large trunk and required two people to haul it into the manuscript room at the Center. As I watched the container being carried in, the purchase seemed to set off a 450-year-old echo of the remark by Leo Africanus about trade in the ancient city that he visited early in the sixteenth century: "Hither are brought divers manuscripts or written books out of Barbary, which are sold for more money than any other merchandize" (Africanus, 1550).

In each case, money played an important role in motivating the writing or sale of the texts in question. The law of supply and demand governs because there was a scarce product: a potentially lucrative manuscript from

Haley and a finite number of ancient manuscripts from West Africa. But what kind of value can we place on spoken or sung words, which normally leave no printed trace? Can rewards play a role in influencing the flow or form of words that are not written? We know that griots are rewarded for their service, but it is not clear just how the rewards have changed in the modern era, or what the consequences are for the verbal art of the griots who speak them. Answers to these questions will emerge in the description of how the reward system for griots has changed during the past 700 years and what role those rewards play in the survival of the profession today.

In the past griots received a wide variety of goods from their patrons — precious metals, clothing, animals, wives, and in some cases slaves. In the shift from traditional to modern sponsors, the profession has undergone changes. Many traditional forms of reward — clothing, animals, and jewelry — are still given to griots today. But other kinds, such as airplane tickets, vehicles, homes, and, in a case cited earlier, a small airplane, have taken the place of traditional gifts. Although patrons of griots — chiefs, kings, and nobles — still offer rewards for praise songs and narratives that highlight their lineage, other sponsors have come forth with new forms of rewards for the verbal and musical art of the griot.

Early Accounts of Rewards

Ibn Battuta has given us the earliest description of rewards for a West African griot — the sum of 200 mithkals of gold to Dugha at the court of Mansa Sulayman in mid–fourteenth century Mali. There are 4.7 grams in a mithkal. The reward of 200 mithkals, or 940 grams divided by 28, equals 33.33 ounces of gold. At the current rate of a little over \$300 per ounce, we can calculate that Dugha received approximately \$10,000 in today's currency. Of course, the approximate value of this amount of gold in the fourteenth century can only be guessed at because it is difficult to determine how scarce the metal was in Mali. We do know, however, that the sum of 200 mithkals was the equivalent of five camel loads of salt that had been transported 700 kilometers from the Sahara. The common saying about salt at that time was that it was worth its weight in gold because of the distance that it traveled and its importance for people who live in an extremely hot climate. Although the comparison was an exaggeration, the two minerals were linked in the minds of traders because the purest kind of salt was rare and costly. In West Africa it came from the western Sahara (Lovejoy, 1986, 4).

Gold, clothing, animals, housing, and wives were common gifts for griots at the top of the profession. There is evidence to suggest that the most talented or best connected griots lived quite well, both from the rewards they received and from other activities. In the mid-1860s, five centuries after Ibn Battuta's travels to the court of Mali, Eugène Mage, the French officer sent by Governor Faidherbe to seek a link between the upper Senegal and Niger River, described several wealthy griots in Ségou, the capital of the Toucouleur empire of El Hadj Omar. When he arrived in the city of Nioro, 750 kilometers east of Saint-Louis near the border of what is today Mali and Mauritania, Mage was quite appreciative of the opportunity to stay in "a very spacious house, the home of a very rich griot named Samba Gouloumba, father or uncle of a griot I had known at Ségou" (1868, p. 294; my translation). The two-story building had a terrace and airy windows, probably similar to the comfortable stone homes one still finds in Timbuktu.

The rewards offered griots included slaves until the First World War. As indicated earlier, the father of Batourou Sékou Kouyaté, a man who did not practice the profession of jeliya, was a slave dealer at the turn of the century. Kouyaté's father participated in the capture of enemy soldiers in battles both with the French, whose armies were staffed by Africans, and with other rulers. These captives then became slaves who might serve a variety of masters. One of Kouyaté's father's assignments was to distribute the captives, and the son told me in 1992 that his father was instructed to give some of them to jeliw. Kouyaté added that Samory Touré was reported to have given ten villages, with all the people in them, as a gift to a jeli.

Djimo Kouyaté told me in 1997 that one of his ancestors who had served as a general in the army of Foday Kaba in The Gambia received twenty-seven slaves, all of whom the ancestor liberated. Aja Mariama Susso, who was about seventy years old when I interviewed her in 1991, said that her father had been a follower of the late-nineteenth- and early-twentieth-century warrior Musa Molo, who died in 1931. He had given her father a slave named Toumani, who had been captured during a battle at the end of the nineteenth century. Toumani helped provide food for the horses, haul firewood, and do other chores. Bofi Suso, eighty-one years old, whom I interviewed the same day, added that when she was traveling with her husband early in her career, a king gave them a horse and a slave. Mariam Kouyaté, third wife of Sidiki Diabaté (together they were one of the jeli couples most in demand in Mali), told me (1992) that a woman who helped train her, Dienaba Daraba, visited the ruler of Ségou, Babountchi, when she was a child, prior to the First World War. After Dienaba and her mother sang praises for the king, he gave them two slaves. Sidiki Diabaté added that his father told him that he had received a slave and ten head of cattle from a ruler in Guinea-Bissau named Mounjourou, also at some time before the First World War.

Rewards Today

Gifts such as slaves are illegal today, and the social structure that allowed them is in decline. One might assume also that the griot profession is in decline because of the advance of literacy and Western influence. In a study of Kita, a major center of *jeliya*, Diango Cissé, for example, argues that "there was a time when griots could live well from their chants and praises" but that today the profession is no longer profitable (1970, p. 195; my translation). But we get a different view from from Christiane Seydou. In her introduction to several Fulbe texts by Boubacar Tinguizi, she notes that "the function of the griot in Africa is, by far, the most lucrative" (1972, p. 13).

Although in the West we tend to take a somewhat secretive approach to income, in West Africa the rewards given to griots constitute public events. To understand the significance of these rewards in shaping and maintaining the profession, it is essential to examine in some detail a variety of data. The purpose is not to offer an exposé of the economics of the griot profession but to reveal in broader terms why these artisans of the word must be viewed today as professionals rather than human artifacts of a dying folklore. In many cases, the data will be rather precise: names, dates, and amounts of money or other forms of rewards. From time to time, however, I will omit names, organizations, and documentation in order to avoid the possibility of legal complications for those involved.

The evidence for the wealth of griots often appears in indirect forms. For example, Agnès-Fatoumata Diarra, in her study of Zarma women in Niger, *Femmes africaines en devenir* (1971), reports the expenses for a marriage, one of the most common family celebrations where one will find griots. Griots are listed to receive as much as $20 each, a week's wages for a skilled worker at the time. Griots' income from weddings is highly variable, depending on the circumstances, time of year, and number of griots at the event. Assa Kouyaté, a *jelimuso* in Bamako, told me in 1992 that she receives from $10 to $60 at a typical wedding but sometimes is given much more. In a society where the per-capita annual income may be measured in hundreds rather than thousands of dollars, these figures represent substantial sums.

Installations of chiefs, which can last several days, are rarer than weddings, but offer greater opportunities for rewards. In a detailed study of gift-giving during the installation of canton chiefs in three Hausa localities of Niger, Guy Nicolas (1968) reported a wide range of rewards. In one group of five griots, the average of rewards for praise-singing was $115. When Nicolas conducted this study in the early 1960s, $115 was the equivalent of three months' salary for a skilled worker in the cities.

My own research on rewards at installations of chiefs in 1980 yielded comparable figures. Garba Bagna, a *jeseré* in Niamey, told me he earned $200 from a three-day installation of a chief, while his wife Igudu received $48. Income such as this helped him to maintain two homes and make a pilgrimage to Mecca—though it is likely that even the air ticket for that trip was a gift. These figures match those reported earlier (chapter 7) for the rural *jeserey weyborey* from Yatakala, Niger ($200 to $400). Batourou Sékou Kouyaté pointed out that a few weeks prior to our interview in 1992, a *jelimuso* who had accompanied him to Ségou to attend the wedding of the son of Fanta Damba, a well-known *jelimuso*, had received diamonds as a reward.

Griots and griottes who live in the country can do almost as well as those in the cities, in part because they are willing to travel. Ayouba Tessa reported to me in 1981 that after he and his son Oumarou Ayouba, both Songhay *jeserey* who lived in Garbey Kourou, a small village sixty kilometers north of Niamey, traveled nearly 1,500 kilometers to Abidjan during the dry season to perform for several months for the expatriate Songhay community there, they returned home with $600 and a large supply of handwoven blankets and other gifts. Thus a short seasonal trip to perform in Côte d'Ivoire might be worth $1,000—a year's wages for a skilled worker in Niamey in 1981 and several times what a farmer might have expected to earn in a year.

At the western end of the Sahel, data are similar. Judith Irvine includes in her 1973 dissertation, "Caste and Communication in a Wolof Village," a chapter on the financial aspect of relations among professional groups. She lists both income and expenses for several griot families from 1960 to 1970. By subtracting income from outgo, she was able to identify the undocumented income from the *guewel* heads of households. The amounts ranged from $400 to $1500 per year and represented the largest share of household revenue. As a group, the griots, in comparison with other households in the sample, including those of noble families, appeared to be the wealthiest (415–16).

More enterprising griots, especially those who have broadened their networks, do much better. The career of Jeli Madi Kanuteh, who works primarily at home in The Gambia, illustrates one career path. He joined a jazz band for $10 per month, then traveled to Senegal, Guinea Bissau, Liberia, Sierra Leone, Ghana, Côte d'Ivoire, Burkina Faso, Mali, Togo, Niger, Benin, Sudan, Nigeria, Chad, Libya, Congo, and Zaire before settling down at home, playing each night in a hotel for $100. He organized a group that was paid $600 per evening, then toured Europe and the United States several times. In 1991, he told me that his estimated average annual income was $5,000, far more than the average skilled worker earned in his country.

Teaching and Live Performances

In addition to weddings, griots have several other sources of rewards for live performances. These days they also earn income for recorded performances, which I cover in the next major section of this chapter.

Sources of Rewards

Among the sources of rewards for "live" griots are tuition from giving lessons to students and income from performances for the tourist industry, tours and visits in Africa, state-sponsored troupes, ceremonies and events, the media, and foreign tours.

TUITION

One source of income that is often more regular than the pattern of revenue from ceremonies, especially for griots who spend most of their time at home, is instruction. Jali Madi Kanuteh's school in the Serrekunda suburb of Banjul attracts students from all over the world. He charges from $3 to $5 per hour for lessons. Toumani Diabaté, who was both a student and a teacher at the Institut National des Arts in Mali in the late 1970s and early 1980s, told me in 1992 that he was paid $3 per hour then but often went for several months without receiving his salary.

Seyengdeh Suso reported (1991) that in Banjul she charges young girls $100 per month for lessons that last for nine months. The intensive training takes up the entire morning and part of the evening. The *jeliw* in Kéla described in chapter 5 were proud to declare that they charged much higher rates. A student from Kayes mentioned by Bala Diabaté paid $7,200 for two years of training, while another pupil who came from Kita, a *jeliya* center of great repute that is little more than 150 kilometers north of Kéla, paid $1,200 and five head of cattle for three years of study. When I asked how much he would charge an American, Diabaté replied only half-jokingly that he would want $8,000 and a tractor. Diabaté may have inflated these figures considerably. Jansen, who was in Kéla a day after my visit, told me in 1996 that Diabaté had expressed to others some embarrassment about making such claims. There is little doubt, however, that students from outside the Kéla area, African or non-African, would be expected to contribute more than local residents for instruction.

For an American graduate student on a tight research budget, such sums are out of the question. When Eric Charry undertook a series of apprenticeships with griots in West Africa, he was able to pay only a token amount. The unstated but clearly implied message of his relationship with his tutors was that the symbolic payment represented a commitment to provide assistance then and later in a variety of other ways. He helped out in emergencies while studying with griots, obtained instruments for his instructors, arranged tours of the United States, and provided other services (Charry 1994a, personal communication, 1996c). Charry's relationship with his teachers depended on a mutual sense of respect rooted in a common interest in the music they played. Jansen had the same experience in Kéla, where he was obliged to carry out his initial research on a limited budget but was able to compensate his hosts in a variety of other ways that were of value to them (1996b).

Fifteen years earlier in Mali, John William Johnson encountered *jeliw* who already had considerable experience in dealing with foreigners and therefore a keen sense of the exchange value of their verbal art. Johnson's goal was to record texts for his doctoral thesis. A typical performance fee at that time was $20 to $40, but Johnson discovered that some of the most famous griots had set prices and conditions that put them out of his range as a graduate student. Kele Monson Diabaté, the best known *jeli* in Kita at the time, had developed a verbal package of performances (30, 60, 90, and 120 minutes), each with its own rate. Johnson told me in 1988 that he had paid $100 for a thirty-minute recording session. Others, such as Wâ Kamissoko, were simply beyond his means. Charles Bird added during the same interview that he had worked with Kamissoko several times but could not afford the $200 price for a single epic.

THE HOSPITALITY INDUSTRY

Hotels offer another form of regular employment. Toumani Diabaté reported to me in 1992 that he received $200 per month for performing for two hours a day at the Hotel de l'Amitié in Bamako, the largest and most modern hotel in the country at the time. Mohammed Manjako Suso explained in 1991 that the group he often performed with at the beachside hotels outside Banjul was composed of over forty musicians and singers and was paid $300 for an hour. But that kind of work is seasonal, occurring mainly in the winter.

TOURS AND VISITS

After the harvest in the early fall, Mandinka *jalolu* from The Gambia go to countries such as Senegal, Mali, and Guinea Bissau where they are paid in cows and sheep.

Describing these seasonal tours, Sidia Jatta (1985) emphasized that griots did not depend on a single patron in each village. Drawing on the experience of Amadu Bansang Jobarteh's parents, Jatta outlined a typical tour for Mandinka *jalolu* in the past. Two families would get together, with the leadership reserved for the senior *jali*, whose job was to manage the group and take care of any problems that might arise. When they visited a village where both he and the other family head in the group had primary patrons, each would be hosted by the primary patron while the other members of the group would be lodged with secondary patrons. They would perform first for the primary patrons, then for the secondary patrons, although the performances were open to the public. Every resident was invited to listen—and to offer rewards (22–23). After the tour was over, the leader would give each member "whatever he deemed fit from the amount of money, clothing, and other gifts received." Jatta emphasized that what the griots received were gifts, not payment for services: "That is why in Mandinka we say: *Ka jaloo so* (to give to a *jali*), not *Ka jaloo joo* (to pay a *jali*)" (21). Jatta added that rewards were not automatically offered for each performance.

Jatta noted that though such traditional tours are still made occasionally by griots and their families, new arrangements are replacing them. He described how three or four *jalolu* sometimes rent a taxi together to go on tour: "When their arrival in a village coincides with nightfall, they will stay with a patron overnight. Otherwise, the longest they will stay is between thirty minutes and one hour. The reason for this is simple: since the car they use is hired on a daily basis, the more patrons they visit within a day, the more money they are likely to make" (21–22). What Jatta described appears to reflect a basic shift in the definition of rewards from gifts to payments.

STATE-SPONSORED TROUPES

Some griots are employed in government-sponsored troupes that tour the world. In the Ballets Africains of Guinea, there may be numerous performers of griot origin, but there are only one or two *kora* players. When I spoke with Fodé Kalissi in Fort-de-France, Martinique in June 1993 and again when the troupe visited Penn State to perform that October, he reported that he had traveled the world for five years with the company. But he added that because all performers were employees of the state, the salary was minimal, a statement confirmed by the European managers of the group during conversations in Fort-de-France and echoed by Amadu Bansang Jobarteh, a former performer for a state-sponsored group, who is quoted by Jatta:

> The best analogy to a musical troupe is a troop of soldiers under the control of a commander. Troupes such as the Gambian National Troupe are managed and controlled by Western-educated persons and the *jalis* are given no say. Whenever they give a concert, the money received belongs to the government. The *jalis* get nothing other than their monthly salaries. This is quite contrary to everything we *jalis* know from inheritance. I was a member of the national troupe for a very short period. [After one performance] I gave them back their uniform and withdrew from the troupe. I told them that the whole thing was alien to me and that I was not a soldier to be regimented in that fashion. (1985, pp. 22–23)

It was the low salaries paid to government-employed artists that prompted another Mandinka *jali*, Papa Susso, to leave the Gambian National Ballet and launch an independent career. But not all troupe members are unhappy. A *balafon* player, Mawdo Suusoo, observed that "when I toured in my own district, in traditional fashion, for a period of a month, visiting my patrons, I made more than I earn in a month with the troupe; in fact, what I now earn in a month might well have been given to me by a patron in one day." Although Suusoo complained about some problems with the troupe, he added that "the troupe assures me of a certain fixed income at the end of every month, however small that income. One cannot go to beg one's patrons every month!" (Jatta, 23).

CEREMONIES AND SPECIAL EVENTS

Rewards to individual griots at ceremonies and special events can be quite variable, but the total amount of gifts distributed often adds up to an enormous amount of money and goods. Bofi Suso, the grandmother of Jeli Madi Kanuteh, reported to me in 1981 that when she was much younger, she had attended the inauguration of Diaru Coulibaly as ruler in Basse, The Gambia. There were 2,000 people at the three-day ceremony, including sixty griots. Over forty cows were given to them, much cloth, and 6,000 British pounds. Haja Nuse Kanuteh, one of the wives of Fabala Kanuteh, a *jali* who traveled often with the former head of state of The Gambia, reported (1991) that she once received over $1,000 from President Dauda Jawara during a celebration for visiting African presidents. She had received that amount of money in other countries, but never before in The Gambia. Foday Musa Suso, another Gambian *jali* who lives in Serrekunda (not to be confused with the *jali* of the same name who has been based for many years in Chicago), reported (1991) that he received nearly $1,000 at a party to celebrate Senegalese independence day in 1990. This amount would cover all of his expenses for six months.

More typical are the amounts reported by Aji Nafa Kuyate, wife of the late Al Haji Bai Konte and mother of Dembo Konte, who told me in 1991 that at a wedding ceremony that year she had received $150 from the bride, another $100 from guests, and cloth worth about $35. Mariam Kouyaté in Bamako reported (1992) that the day before I interviewed her, she had received $400 and four *boubous*, expensive outfits, at a wedding at the home of the wife of the late Modibo Keita, first president of Mali. Batourou Sékou Kouyaté pointed out in 1992 that he had received a ton of rice and $400 at the wedding in Ségou where his partner had received diamonds, mentioned earlier. *Jalimuso* Nyuma Mane reported in 1991 that in her group of ten women, each performer had made about $1,000 the previous year.

THE MEDIA

Griots perform on radio and television, either occasionally or on regular programs.

Ismaila Mane, an assistant information officer at Radio Gambia, told me in 1991 that griots were paid a contractual rate of $50 for thirty minutes, once a week for one or two months. But income from state-owned radio and television can vary considerably depending on the economic condition of the country and the novelty of the performer.

When I asked Toumani Diabaté in 1992 how much he had received from radio and television appearances, he replied that he had been paid little or nothing since 1987. Payments were controlled by a Malian national agency that set royalty rates, collected them, and then transferred the money to an account held for the performer, he said, and when he inquired in 1991 to see how much money was in his account, he was told that for the preceding three years it amounted to $40. He added that he eventually received $15. Mariam Kouyaté, who is married to Toumani Diabaté's father, explained (1992) that in the early days of independence, griots and griottes were well paid by radio and television producers but that today no money was available. For this reason, she and her husband no longer would agree to perform or to be interviewed on the state-owned media.

FOREIGN TOURS

The figures I have cited vary considerably. Nevertheless, measured against prevailing levels of revenue in local economies they emphasize the comparative prosperity enjoyed by griots. But these amounts pale in comparison with what the most talented or enterprising griots can earn outside their country.

Many griots know they are wanted to perform when a plane ticket arrives. Mariam Kouyaté told me in 1992 that several weeks earlier she and her husband had gone to Burkina Faso when they learned that plane tickets had arrived for them to go to Burundi. Some of these trips are to attend expatriate weddings, and there is no way of knowing how much money will be offered at the event by the guests.

Concerts are different. On average, a griot who travels to France, England, the United States, or Japan can expect between $500 and $1,000 per performance. A tour may include ten or twenty performances. Toumani Diabaté reported (1991) that he earned $8,000, $10,000, and $13,000 respectively for his first three tours of the United States, in 1989, 1990, and 1991.

A one-week residency at a university can net several thousand dollars, while a year as a visiting professor can pay anywhere from $30,000 to $50,000. One Gambian *jali* reported that he received $30,000 in four months in New York in 1990. Income for a single six-month season in 1988–89 for another well-known Gambian *jali* was $50,000. For 1994–95 and 1995–96, he earned close to $80,000 before taxes.

Most of the income comes in the form of performance fees paid on a contractual basis, but, as at home, a chance encounter with an appreciative listener can generate a generous gift. Papa Susso reported (1988) that when he was playing at a Sheraton Hotel in New York, a wealthy American industrialist heard him, sent a limousine to pick him up the next day, welcomed him into his home, and asked him to compose a praise song. Susso complied and added a translation; he was paid $1,000.

Men versus Women

So far I have not distinguished between men and women in the matter of rewards. But as I indicated in chapter 7, female griots generally receive less than a half share when performing with men, although there are many exceptions to this rule.

In Niger, Mamata Sunna, a member of a troupe run by a woman, Weybi Karma, explained that in general

> in this profession, the female, the *jeseré weyboro*, does not receive as much rewards as men, because whatever the circumstances, the man is always ahead and the woman comes after him. That is why when women share something with men, men take a bigger share and women a smaller share because they are superior to women. (Hale, 1990b)

It is most likely that with this interpretation of the reward differential she was articulating in her professonal role the traditional values of the Songhay-Zarma peoples rather than offering an opinion on whether men are intrinsically superior to women.

If women and men perform as a team, men accept the rewards and may distribute from nothing to one-half to the women. Aja Nafi Kuyate explained (1991) that the matter of division of rewards "was not part of our tradition, because the man is taking care of me, providing food, clothing, housing, and resolving all problems, therefore it is not necessary to share the money." Bofi Suso calculated in 1991 that if the man received $100 he would give $10 or $20 to his wife for the purchase of cloth, and added that the wife would be quite happy because it was the man who was in charge of family finances. Foday Musa Suso agreed with this view when he explained (1991) that "I have the entire responsibility for my wife and expenses, so if I received $100 I give her $30." Aja Mariama Suso put the percentage at 40 (1991), a figure echoed by Haja Nuse Kanuteh (1991), wife of *jali* Fabala Kanuteh, and Jalimuso Dramé, wife of Manjako Suso, who emphasized the importance of the husband's role in taking care of all family needs.

That traditional view was repeated by many griots and griottes, but Sayengdeh Suso (1991) hinted that the days of women's tacit acceptance of this gender differentiation were numbered:

> The experience people now have is not the same as in the old days. The women are thinking now that if they get money they'll build a house, get cloth, and buy goods. In the old days, they just bought meat to cook for their husbands.

Nyuma Mane stated (1991) that she might receive $100 at a wedding and it would be shared equally among all the members of her group. Two of Jali Madi Kanuteh's wives, Hawa Kanuteh and Joma Kuyate, said they each received a share equal to that of their husband when they performed with him (1991).

The inequality one finds among most couples contrasts with the widespread belief among *jalolu* in The Gambia that it is the woman's performance as the opening act that brings in the rewards. Roderic Knight reported, for example, that Gambian *jali* Al Haji Suntu Suso expressed the hope of marrying a woman who could sing well and make him wealthy. Knight added that "every *jali ke* [male griot] hopes to have a true . . . *jali muso* for a wife" (1987). Since he made that observation, Knight wrote in a subsequent article (1991, p. 62) that Al Haji Suntu Suso in fact had found a wife, "Kankaba, a fine singer," and had prospered from performances for the expatriate community in Paris.

These examples from Niger and The Gambia contrast to some extent with the situation in Mali, where many *jelimusow*, as seen in chapter 7, have assumed a dominant position. In "Savannah Sex Wars," Lucy Durán describes how

> the instrumentalists (all men; few women play instruments) complain that the women singers take the lion's share of the money for themselves. The virtuoso Malian guitarist Bouba Sacko, president of the newly formed Association Amicale des Artistes and regular accompanist to Mali's top vocalists, claims that "one of the main motivations behind the forming of this organization was to protect the interests of the instrumentalists." (1993, p. 43)

Batourou Sékou Kouyaté reported that when he performed with Dieneba Traoré, she would get 75 percent and he would receive 25 percent. He explained to me in 1992 that

> it is the *jalimuso* who gets the most because she is the one who sings, she is not obliged to share equally with the male accompanists. She has the microphone, she receives the money. She does most of the work, she gets the people to give, she names the ancestors . . . it is not easy to sing in public, she [must] go into the crowd. The *jalimuso* is more important than the *jali ke*.

This reality is visually evident in a video of Ami Koita, in which the performer works the crowd, inspiring men to step onto the stage with handfuls of money that the *jelimuso* simply throws up in the air.

The most striking example of the kind of rewards received for Malian stars is the small airplane mentioned earlier. It was reported to have been given to Kandia Kouyaté by Babani Cissoko, one of her wealthy admirers and a businessman of griot origin who wanted her to be able to fly directly to his airstrip (Durán, 1989).

There is a difference, however, between "star" *jalimusow* and the less famous women who attend local events with men. Lamine Kouyaté in Bamako explained (1992) that if cloth was given as a present, it went to the women; if cash, it went to the men, though each man would give 40 percent of it to his female partner. This view was echoed by Bala Diabaté in Kéla (1992). Cash management as a male role was confirmed by Nantenegwe Kamissoko in Bamako, who said that if a husband received $400, a wife probably would see very little of it.

Some griots in Mali reported that cash should be shared equally with their wives, although Sidi Ali Oumar in Timbuktu told me in 1992 that if the woman was not his wife, she would receive less. Another griot from Timbuktu, Ibrahim Limbo, said that he would give 25 percent of rewards to any woman who might accompany him, without distinguishing between his wife and other women (1992). Beya Kouyaté from Basse, The Gambia, reported the same division of rewards, 25 percent for his wife.

The differences probably reflect both regional variations—Bamana versus Songhay and Fulbe—as well as variations in reputation. A woman who has achieved the local equivalent of stardom, with cassettes and videos in circulation, is treated differently from the neighborhood *jelimuso*. But the larger regional difference—that between Mali, where women play an increasingly dominant role, and the Senegambian region, where men still control the stage—can cause clashes when performers from each region meet in a different country.

That occurred several years ago when one of Mali's female stars was to perform in New York. She and her accompanist for the occasion, a Gambian living at the time in New York, disagreed over the distribution of rewards for the performance because of their different origins within the Mande world. In The Gambia men tend to play the lead role, while in Mali the woman performers dominate; in this case, the woman expected to decide how to divide up the performance fee. The difference was quickly resolved when it became clear that the man had the appropriate visa to perform but the woman did not: he therefore controlled the distribution.

Expatriate versus Foreign Audiences

Changing audiences and larger rewards, especially outside Africa, are helping to maintain and in some ways increase the corps of people who sing praises, epics, and other forms of verbal and musical art. There is also a difference, however, between the tour organized for a non-African audience in Britain, where there is a sizable minority of African origin but relatively few from the countries of the Sahel and Savanna that produce most griots, and performances for an expatriate community such as the one in Paris, where one finds many residents from Mali, Senegal, Guinea, and Niger. They tend to congregate in neighborhoods on the periphery of the city and maintain an active cultural life that includes naming ceremonies and weddings.

Sékou Kouyaté, a Malian *jeli*, estimated in 1991 that there were 200 to 300 griots working in Paris either part-time or full-time to serve the needs of the expatriate community. The editors of *L'Afrique à Paris* reported that the chief griot in the city, Brulaye Diabaté, was the head driver at the Embassy of Mali, and they provided a list of performers (Dyan and Mandel, 1984, pp. 129–31). Diabaté served as a kind of coordinator and dispatcher when griots were needed. In fact, it was through a Nigérien woman friend who knew a Malian neighbor who contacted this chief griot that I was able to arrange to interview Sékou Kouyaté and another *jeli*.

Even where the expatriate community is small, as in the case of the Gambians in London and Washington, "home" can generate a powerful pull. Jali Madi Kanuteh told me in 1991 that when he was in New York in 1990, some Gambians in Washington had sent a car for him so that he could be driven to the capital to perform for them. They gave him and his group, composed of Papa Susso and two other musicians, $2,900 for their performance.

Rewards at Home versus Rewards on the Road

There is a difference between rewards at home and cash on the road. The traditional patron who gives the griot anything—a blanket, $10, a goat—seals an unwritten life contract with the bard. The griot may now ask the donor for anything at any time, and the patron is normally under the obligation to do his or her best to accede to the request. The African community in Paris, whose income may be higher than what can be earned at home, will have slightly less frequent contact with griots but can afford to be more generous—and usually is. The concert promoter, on the other hand, gives the griot a check for $750 and may not see the performer again for several years, if at all. The relationship is not personal; it is commercial. The patron back home knows and understands the griot's verbal art; the promoter, in many cases, only appreciates the number of people who can be attracted to pay for the performance.

Recorded Performances

The words-for-rewards exchange I have described so far refers to live performances. When performances are recorded, an entirely new set of problems emerges. The griots sometimes receive royalties from these sound recordings, though it is also quite common for them to be given a one-time payment.

As for royalties on printed texts, it is rare to find formal arrangements for several reasons. There is no way that a researcher can know in advance, at the time of the recording, whether the griot's words will be transformed into print.

In 1980–81, I collected over a score of versions of Songhay and Zarma epics from *jeserey* in western Niger. In each case, I explained the purpose of my request—to help Americans learn more about the oral art of griots. Most often, griots did not ask before the performance how much I would give them. They simply said that I should offer whatever I wanted. Implicit in their response was that I should appreciate their verbal art in the same way as any other local listener. After the event, when I gave them $40, I explained that I was well aware that the griot could earn many hundreds of dollars at a wedding or other ceremony, but that this was more than I could provide. I concluded by emphasizing the symbolic nature of the payment. The funds came from a grant of $1,200 from the University of Niamey, where I was teaching, and covered only part of the cost of recording narratives from the many griots I worked with that year. Costs included not only informant fees but also travel expenses as well as the transcription of the tapes. It was not until I was well along in the collection and text-processing parts of the project that I began to focus on one of the epics. It took ten years and the help of a team of researchers from Niger to transform the recording of that epic into a printed text that appeared in a book.

For the foreign researcher, a major difficulty lies in differentiating himself or herself from the concert promoter back home. In one case, a Senegalese griot refused to see me unless I paid $600, his fee for performing in New York, which was half of my research budget for that trip. Another well-known griot in Dakar, the late Soundioulou Cissoko, reluctantly agreed to an interview for $80 but began to tap on his watch at precisely one hour, indicating that my time was up. His fee matched that of others of his stature. Isabelle Leymarie reported (1978) that the president of the griot association in Dakar charged $100 per hour.

The validity of paying anyone for an interview or a performance is open to question. We look askance at reporters who pay subjects for interviews.

But in the context of the unusual researcher-griot relationship, unless there is a pre-existing and long-term tie, the lack of any form of reward amounts to an insult.

If the researcher and assistants manage to transcribe, translate, and annotate an epic, and then write an introduction to it, another problem occurs in finding a publisher. In today's tight academic publishing climate, it is often difficult to find publishers for such seemingly exotic material. Sometimes the researcher has to subsidize the publication, or accept publication in a series that pays no royalties.

One of the longest and most detailed epics to appear in print, the nearly 8,000-line Bamana epic by Tayiru Banbera (Conrad, 1990), appears in an extremely expensive ($85) volume that is part of a little-known series, Fontes Historiae Africanae, published by Oxford University Press for the British Academy. Although the collector, translator, and editor of this monumental work, David Conrad, managed to get the text into print fourteen years after it was recorded, he never saw any royalties from the publication and thus had none to share with the Banbera family. Jan Jansen, who published a version of the Sundiata epic from Kéla, had a similar experience; as he told me in 1996, his subsidized publication generates no royalties for either the researcher or the informants.

Another problem is that even if the name of the griot could be put on the eventual contract with the publisher, there would be no simple way of remitting the funds to someone in a remote area who, like the vast majority of Africans, functions outside the global banking system. There are, nevertheless, ways of overcoming these obstacles. The French ethnographer Jean Rouch, as well as other researchers, have proposed that performers receive a share of royalties from texts that are recorded and published, perhaps 20 or 30 percent. If the royalties cannot be built into a contract, the researcher can nevertheless distribute part of his or her own share to the informant.

In my own case, I have been sending a one-third share of the modest royalties from *Scribe, Griot, and Novelist* to the family of the late griot Nouhou Malio in Saga, Niger, because his version of *The Epic of Askia Mohammed*, which appears in the appendix, is one of three narratives that are the focus of the book. I send the money, on which I have paid U.S. taxes, with people who travel to Niger and who can be counted on to deliver it in person in the local currency. With the publication of the English version of the epic in paperback (Hale and Malio, 1996), I now send a 50 percent share of its royalties to the family.

Djibril Tamsir Niane reports that he shares the royalties from *Sundiata* with members of the family of the late Mamadou Kouyaté, who never fail to stop at his bookshop when they travel to Conakry, Guinea. His system is less formal than mine because of the nature of his long-term relationship with the Kouyaté family, but he achieves the same goal.

The situation with sound recordings is far more complex. There is, for instance, an enormous amount of piracy of recordings, both from the radio and from cassettes. The extent of it is difficult to measure, but some estimates place pirated distribution of commercial recordings as high as 90 percent of the total number of cassettes in circulation.

An even knottier problem involves negotiations between the performer and the recording company. In the past, griots benefited from a patron who took care of many of these details. Today, griots and other African musicians may have an agent, a manager, a promoter, and a record company producer, all of whom may want a share of the proceeds. None of them matches fully the traditional description of a patron such as Sidi Mohammed Sacko of Abidjan, principal sponsor of *jelimuso* Fanta Damba.

One example illustrates the nature of the problem. A well-known Malian *jeli* reported to me in 1992 that he had been invited to tour the United States for three weeks. He would do fifteen concerts in twenty days. The tour would generate $13,500 in fees, but after expenses he would be left with only $5,000. When he showed me the faxes, contracts, and other papers, I had difficulty understanding what they were all about, but it appeared that the costs of production and distribution of his cassettes as well as expenses from earlier trips were being charged against the income of the tour, a practice that seemed to be in accordance with the terms of the contract and industry tradition. To the *jeli*, however, the numbers did not add up, and he decided to cancel the tour.

To me, it appeared as though both parties, the promoter and the performer, were sincere in their negotiating stance, but each was speaking from a set of values that the other could not understand. The performer told me that he was learning how the tours function, with payments for the hotel, the airfare, and the commissions all coming out of fees and royalties, but he added that this system was totally contrary to African values which call for the host to take care of everything and the griot simply to perform. The cultural difference was so great that he could not tell his family at home that he had to pay for his hotel, even though that was the way the system worked. When I explained to a British promoter the circumstances of this difference, he replied that the American promoters appeared to have been following the rules of the profession, but had been too direct and too honest in describing the details of the arrangements.

There seems to be considerable differences in how these tours are set up, depending on the role of the individual performer. Toumani Diabaté told me in 1992 that in France in 1984 the promoters had paid for the air tickets while in Britain that was not always the case. One company had invited him to tour for three months in Canada, Japan, Britain, Finland, Italy, and France at the rate of $200 per day and a bonus of $14,000 at the end of the tour. The World of Music, Arts, and Dance (WOMAD) had invited him to tour for nine weeks at a little over $1,000 per week for concerts in Denmark, Spain, France, Britain, Finland, Canada, and Japan, but he turned the offer down because he felt he was included simply as a *kora* player. He added that his relationship with WOMAD went through a variety of twists and turns as he attempted to negotiate for more royalties for recordings and access to the local promoters who handled the organization's tour in each country.

What emerged from my discussion with him was evidence not only of tensions between two different ways of looking at the performer, African and Western, but also of differences between the artist's self-image as a star and the promoter's view of him as a supporting member of the group—a problem that occurs in many negotiations in the entertainment industry worldwide. Perhaps that is why Diabaté affirms that his best experience was in Japan in 1989; there he was paid $4,000 per concert for four appearances.

The wariness of griots is justified by experiences in Europe and elsewhere. During a concert in Germany in June 1993, a promoter is reported to have absconded with the receipts, an incident that prompted another African performer to switch plans just as he was about to board a plane from London for Germany (Gold, 1993). In the United States, another Gambian griot, who had entrusted his taxes to a promoter, discovered too late that the Internal Revenue Service had never received the money; he was forced to negotiate a settlement with the agency.

Problems with sponsors are not limited to promoters. Fanta Sacko, one of Mali's best known *jelimusow* in the late 1960s and 1970s, revealed to Lucy Durán that when she performed in Kita for a delegation of the government of Mali, the event had been recorded and her songs had been distributed in Germany, but she had received nothing for her role in the event, even though she went to the president of Mali to complain (Durán, 1993a). A similar problem occurred for Amadu Bansang Jobarteh with the British Broadcasting Corporation. For many years, the African section of the BBC broadcast, without payment, a recording from the Gambian *jali* as sign-on music for programs. It was only after receiving complaints about

the practice that BBC representatives finally paid some money to the *jali* —
then stopped using his sign-on music (Ledger, 1993; Durán, 1993a).

When Sidiki Diabaté, father of Toumani Diabaté and nephew of
Amadu Bansang Jobarteh, was a member of the Ensemble Instrumental du
Mali, he earned no royalties from the many copies of the Sundiata disk and
cassette that were recorded and sold in France, although he was eventually
given a plot of land. Toumani Diabaté told me (1992) that his father
received $60 in retirement pay once every three months. He added that
when his father toured the United States and performed seventy-seven
concerts in three weeks with the Ballets National du Mali, he received only
a salary, no per diem.

Griots breaking into the Western market are of course well aware that
they must share their rewards with agents and promoters. As Nicholas
Gold, director of World Circuit in London, points out, "by the time they
have made two or three tours, they have a clear sense of how the system
operates" (1993). But the relationship can be difficult. At a meeting of a
state arts council in 1989, a Gambian griot was scheduled to make a
presentation to support an application for a grant that would enable him to
perform in public schools. When his promoter arrived late and the *jali*
complained about the lack of punctuality, the promoter took umbrage,
punched his client, and left. The *jali* was awarded the grant but the
incident marked the end of his relationship with an exploitive promoter.

Even when griots and other musicians establish satisfactory relationships with recording companies, there are sometimes difficulties in remitting royalties. In 1992, the royalty on compact disks in Britain was about
$1.50 each. The average CD cost about $5,000 to make and, in the case of
griots, sold from 2,000 to 15,000 copies, according to Gold (1993). When
the time comes to remit funds, if the performer does not have a bank
account in his home country, he or she must find someone with an account
who will agree to serve as the conduit. The practice of opening bank
accounts in Francophone Africa is far more limited than in other parts of
the world because the fee structures are so high. Most griots and griottes
deal only in cash. The other solution is to hold the funds until the
performer's next visit to Europe.

If the recording company wants to communicate with the griot, then a
path must be established. For those in the capitals in Senegal, The
Gambia, and Mali, a telephone call or fax suffices. But in the case of Ali
Farka Touré, a well-known singer who is not of griot origin but who reveals
much griot influence in his music, the director of World Circuit in London must send a fax to Bamako, which is then conveyed via a twice-a-week

aid agency helicopter to Niafounké, a small town 500 kilometers northeast on the often impassable road to Timbuktu. It is a town without a telephone system or municipal electricity.

The rewards for griots who perform overseas or in other countries are far greater than at home, not only because expatriate audiences are so delighted to hear music from home and the standard of living is much higher but also because the audience may represent a diverse expatriate population made up of both working-class and professional people.

Roderic Knight has described the world of Gambian and Senegalese *jalolu* in Paris who perform in restaurants and for expatriate families in their homes. At the entry level, employment may be found in African and Caribbean restaurants, playing soft background music for small rewards amounting to $20 at most; those who have standing arrangements at more upscale establishments earn several times more. They and other, older *jalolu* visit Gambian and Senegalese families for naming ceremonies and Muslim holidays and may receive hundreds of dollars (Knight, 1991).

In the United States, there may be fewer opportunities in restaurants because the expatriate communities are smaller. But in a city such as Washington, home of many African embassies and international institutions that employ professionals from Africa as well as cabdrivers and students from all over the continent, there is a strong interest in griots. The high point of Batourou Sékou Kouyaté's twenty-eight-concert tour of the United States with his wife and Nantenegwe Kamissoko was their two-night stand at the Baird Auditorium of the capital's National Museum of Natural History. The house was full both nights according to Charles Bird, with hundreds of dollars piling up on the stage as people came forward with gifts. The audience included a large contingent of diplomats and other members of the African international community assigned to Washington. After expenses, Kouyaté returned to Mali with $15,000 for three months of performances and teaching (Bird and Kendall, 1988).

The matter of rewards for griots raises questions about the intent of the person giving the gifts and the talent of those who receive them. The assumption is that there is a correlation between the talent of the griot and the rewards he or she is given. The most talented appear to benefit the most from the largesse of their patrons. But Djimo Kouyaté (1997) takes a different view. He argues that the gift does not recognize the griot but instead focuses the spotlight on the donor. "People express their own values when they give. . . . People who can do what their ancestors did, do it for themselves, not because of us. They participate in the values of their family." In other words, giving a great gift to a griot is a means of immortalizing oneself in the family history, in the same way that achievement on the battlefield was recognized in past generations. Kouyaté's interpretation of gift-giving fits with the Mande notion of *fadenya*. In life, one is the rival of one's ancestors as well as one's siblings.

One might interpret the extraordinary gift of $300,000 to a high school band in Florida by Babani Cissoko in the light of Kouyaté's comment. Cissoko is the Malian businessman of griot origin who gave an airplane to Kandia Kouyaté. In the case of the airplane, the gift marked the donor as a man of extraordinary means and generosity, someone never to be forgotten in the oral tradition of late-twentieth-century West African griots. In the case of the unidentified high school band seeking funds for a trip to perform in the 1997 Macy's Thanksgiving Day parade in New York, however, the motivation of the *jeli* donor may have been less to impress the people back home with his wealth and power than to extricate himself from a difficult legal situation.

After the gift to the high school band was reported in U.S. newspapers, Cissoko's name turned up in investigations of 1996 electoral campaign financing. Cissoko, identified as a millionaire philanthropist, had been targeted by the Democratic National Committee as a prospective donor and invited to have dinner with President Clinton in December 1996, according to a report in the *New York Times* (Van Natta, 1997). But a week prior to the scheduled event, it was alleged, Cissoko had been arrested in Europe on charges of attempting to smuggle helicopters out of Miami to Africa and to bribe a U.S. Customs agent. Although the charges were eventually reduced, Cissoko was sentenced to serve four months at a federal prison and four months of house arrest in Miami.

Cissoko understood intimately both sides of the patron-griot relationship because he was both a patron and a griot. Although the contexts were quite different—Africa and the United States—the result of his gift in both cases was the same: he attracted enormous attention to himself and, in a sense, proved Kouyaté's theory about the relationship between donor and recipient.

Another question arising from the discussion of rewards is that of talent. Not all griots benefit from the rewards of increased demand. Bakari Sidibe argues, in fact, that some of the most talented griots are not reaping the fruits of overseas travel because they do not have the right connections, or because promoters do not recognize their talent. That may be true to some extent, because the differences between an average *kora* player and a virtuoso are not likely to be apparent to a foreign audience hearing the instrument played for the first time. As audiences become more familiar with these performers, however, one may expect that the best will attract more attention no matter where they live. The profession is gradually evolving from "folkloric" status to the kind of recognition accorded the most talented performers on an international level.

That shift, along with the growing rewards that accompany it, seems to be having an impact on the supply of griots. This phenomenon is difficult to document, but each time a griot returns home with the fruits of his trip — a new car, an addition to a house, electronic equipment — younger performers are inspired to learn more about the profession in order to follow the same path. As references to griots increase in the media and the griot as a figure becomes more fully integrated into the network of world artists, demand will increase.

If there are no more rulers handing out sacks of gold to griots like Dugha at the court of Mali, it is evident that many griots are surviving today and that the profession will continue in large part because of the rewards generated by increased demand. The time is not far off when a griot or a griotte will become a multimillionaire international star and join the pantheon of popular musicians from Africa who are now sweeping across the world music scene. But it is hard to believe that such performers will be able to maintain the traditional verbal art and social functions outlined in chapters 3 and 4. In the conclusion to this study, I will attempt to look more deeply into the future to speculate on just what may happen to these artisans of the word in the next millennium.

❈ 10 ❈
New Millennium Griots

It is difficult to predict just what the future holds for griots and their influence on world culture. The evidence presented in the preceding chapters leads to a series of conclusions about the profession and a variety of speculations and questions about its future, especially when one sees how the younger generation is adapting to external cultural influences. Nowhere is this more evident than in the family of Tiémoko Cissoko, better known as Soundioulou, one of the best-known griots in Senegal.

During my interview with Soundioulou in 1991, the seventy-year-old Mandinka griot reported that he had been the first *jali* to be heard on the radio in Francophone West Africa, an event that occurred in 1943 or 1944, apparently after the Free French turned the tide in their favor in West Africa. He implied that he had been a pioneer in the broadcast of a traditional musical form via a technology that was still quite novel in the region. His son intervened to confirm what his father was saying, and to report that he himself was taking this family tradition to new dimensions of performance that were about as revolutionary to the griot world as flying was to the West in 1900.

The father, Soundioulou, came from Ziginchor, capital of the Casamance region in southern Senegal, below The Gambia. He reported that he had been crowned "king of the *kora*" in 1966 by Sékou Touré, the president of Guinea, at the inauguration of the Palais des Sports in Conakry. Later the government of Senegal had awarded him the rank of chevalier and then the title of officer in the Ordre du Mérite, the equivalent of the French Legion of Honor, for his long service as a griot—service that one could trace back to the struggle for independence in postwar Francophone West Africa. Soundioulou's claim to be the leading *kora* player in Senegal was not an idle boast. Lucy Durán (1988) once described him as "Senegal's most famous *kora* player" (p. 37). (See figure 18.)

18. Photo of Tiémoko Cissoko, known as Soundioulou, playing the *kora* at his home in Dakar, Senegal. By the author.

Soundioulou Cissoko embodied what one might call the pure tradition of Mandinka griots. The son who was present during the interview, Papa Abdoulaye Cissoko, had learned from his father and was in many ways the inheritor of a talent and profession that went back for generations. But as Prince—the professional name Papa Cissoko had adopted—began to tell me more about his own development, a new path for the future of griots began to emerge in a startling manner. He was, it seemed, literally and figuratively flying into the future with his innovative projects (see figure 19).

Prince explained that earlier in the day he had met with a technical adviser in the office of the president of Senegal to discuss the process of patenting his latest invention: a computerized *kora*. This involved not simply the kind of electric amplification discussed earlier but the coupling of a *kora* with a personal computer and a synthesizer to create combinations of all kinds—the *kora* with a violin, the *kora* with a piano, and so on. Other griots, such as Toumani Diabaté, had performed with bands that had a synthesizer. But the direct linking of the *kora* with a synthesizer via a personal computer constituted a leap into the latest in high-tech music-making. For those who would like to preserve tradition in a glass case, the obvious question might be "Where did he go wrong?"

In fact, Prince had studied at the conservatory in Dakar, learned the Western system of notation and performance, gone off to Brussels for advanced study, including aviation lessons, and then returned to Senegal in 1988 to launch *Black Opera*, a stage show that contained music from Louis Armstrong and Beethoven's Fifth Symphony—all done in Mandinka. In the process he had changed the tuning of the *kora* to F major to facilitate the synthesis of two rather different musical traditions. After describing this extraordinary itinerary during my interview with his father, Prince then sang for me "When the Saints Go Marching In," accompanied by the *kora* in a manner I had never heard before. Soundioulou smiled as I listened in a state of astonishment to this theme song for New Orleans jazz played on a *kora*.

The potential loss of traditional values and styles in such a shift seemed enormous. But Prince explained that in order to engage audiences in Mandinka music, he first had to catch their attention with Western sounds. Then he would shift to traditional tunes. His goal, in a sense, was to penetrate the Western musical tradition with the *kora* in order to draw new audiences to an interest in Africa. His approach, however, was not purely musical. He had studied the careers of performers in the West and come to several rather perceptive and perhaps cynical conclusions about the reali-

19. Photo of Papa Abdoulaye Cissoko, known as Prince, playing the *kora* at his home in Dakar, Senegal. By the author.

ties of the music industry. He asserted that "show business has three things: no faith, no law, and no religion." The American contribution to show business, via Michael Jackson, he added, was "a look, a character, and a style."

When I asked what he did today, he replied that he did not go to naming ceremonies or other events of that kind because participation would not match his "look, character, and style." Instead he conducted workshops on music and dance. With what he earned he continued his aviation lessons. He added that in the past he had worked extensively in tourism. He was not the only member of his family to be exploring new audiences; he noted that his brother Malang Cissoko, based in Helsinki, was currently performing in Denver.

Prince emphasized throughout our conversation that he owed a great debt to his father, and believed he was continuing a tradition that was many centuries old. But he wanted to make his mark in his own way. His father supported his experimentation, pointing out that each generation must follow its own path—another example of the Mande value of *fadenya*. It would have been difficult for Prince to outdo his father's reputation as the most famous *kora* player in Senegal. But the son might find his place in the family genealogy—and in music history—with the innovations he planned to bring to the instrument.

Prince's clear focus on the future might seem to be cut off almost entirely from the past. But in fact he traces the musical art inherited from his father all the way back to Egypt. His historical consciousness seems to be longer than that of any other griot I encountered. He pointed out the link (cited independently by Eric Charry and discussed in chapter 4) between the *ardin*, the Moor harp similar to early Egyptian instruments, and *hardino*, one of the systems of tuning for the *kora* today. For Prince, this link symbolized the deepest roots of West African music and a point of intersection between Africa and the West. In other words, just as Egypt has influenced the West, it has also had an impact on the rest of Africa. For him, the performance of Beethoven's Fifth Symphony on a *kora* represented a modern synthesis of two very different musical traditions that can be traced back 5,000 years.

It is not at all clear where Prince will land in his flight into the future or what his impact will be on the griot profession. However, the interview with him and his father, as well as the variety of evidence presented in previous chapters, leads to a series of conclusions, speculations, and questions that force us to rethink our notion of where griots have been and where they are going.

An Ancient Profession

The profession appears to be as old as the civilizations of the West African Sahel and Savanna regions—and perhaps older. If Ibn Battuta found royal griots flourishing in mid-fourteenth century, then it is plausible to assume that these wordsmiths had been participating in the major events of society centuries before then.

Evidence that holds the potential to push the origins back into the first millennium may come from the thousands of Arabic manuscripts scattered across West Africa, from Mauritania to Lake Chad. Many have not been collected, and those that are now housed in African libraries and archives, such as the Ahmed Baba Center in Timbuktu, Mali, and the Institute for Research in Social Sciences in Niamey, Niger, or in European locations, such as the Escorial in Spain, are still awaiting analysis by scholars.

The problem is that very few scholars are working in this field and few resources exist to hire additional help. For example, before the Tuareg rebellion in northern Mali in the early 1990s, only a handful of researchers traveled to the isolated city of Timbuktu each year to consult the Ahmed Baba collection. Efforts by scholars such as Charles Stewart at the University of Illinois to obtain funds to systematize the Ahmed Baba collection by using modern computer equipment have not been successful. In Niamey the lack of a permanent Arabic specialist and microfilming equipment has slowed the processing of texts from the Boubou Hama collection housed in the Institute for Research in Social Sciences, a unit of the University of Niamey. The earliest of the texts in these two collections dates to the thirteenth century, but judging from Arabic inscriptions on tombstones in Gao, it is likely that older texts will emerge from future research.

Writing in Arabic did not arrive in West Africa until late in the last millennium and early in this millennium. Archaeological evidence, however, goes back thousands of years and may push the origin of griots back to well before the time of Christ. Evidence of the past two decades (cited in my discussions of the origin of the term *griot* in the introduction as well as in Appendix G) has shifted the roots of Sahelian and Savanna cities from the Middle Ages to the Roman era. It is reasonable to suggest that the profession of griot is not simply six centuries old, dating to the time of Ibn Battuta, but at least a millennium and perhaps two millennia old. Evidence for this dating will come from future archaeological work on the thousands of tumuli scattered across the region.

Although it is not clear what kind of material culture will support the dating of the profession to an earlier time, some of the instruments they played had metal parts that may have survived. Other circumstantial evidence, such as the placement of burial sites, may yield clues to the existence of griots thousands of years ago.

The number of researchers conducting archaeological research in the Sahel and Savanna is small and the resources are limited. But at least in the case of Mali there is considerable interest at the top level of the government: President Alpha Konaré is a historian and archaeologist with a keen personal interest in promoting further research.

Measuring the Power of Griots

From the different windows on the world of griots in this study—researchers, patrons, and the griots themselves—it is apparent that these wordsmiths are not simply a caste of parasitic buffoons or minstrels clinging to ancient ways. They are instead a dynamic and distinct element of many West African societies.

Griots possess a kind of verbal power that links them inextricably to those who hold other forms of power in society—or who would like to appear as holding such power. Cornelia Panzaachi points out that for anyone who wants to pass for a noble, "failure to give to the griot would result in being unmasked" (1994, p. 195).

In fact, griots appear to operate at the center of a complex human network that depends on their participation for many kinds of social functions. The work of Barbara Hoffman suggests that we need to reframe the perspective on griots by including them in the discussion and by examining more closely the nature and extent of the power they wield over other members of society.

Adapting to Social Change

The traditional nature of the profession masks an inherent adaptability that has enabled griots to survive for so many centuries through the rise and fall of empires, the imposition of colonialism, the pressure of nationalism, the resurgence of neocolonialism, and, above all, the onslaught of many waves of Islamic and Western cultural influences that continue to sweep across the Sahel and Savanna regions. In the face of these social changes, griots have responded to new audiences, technologies, and systems of reward in ways that guarantee their survival for a long time to come.

Whereas griots competed centuries ago with religious leaders for the attention of rulers and those of the upper classes, today they have developed a much more symbiotic relationship with these other men of the word. This trend began to emerge generations ago (Hale, 1985), but it is taking on new dimensions in some countries. Fiona McLaughlin points out (1997) that in Senegal, marabouts often speak to a crowd in public through the intermediary of a *guewel*. In fact, the *muezzins*, who call people to prayer, are often of *guewel* origin. Today there is a new form of Islamic popular music marked by praise for marabouts. McLaughlin argues that when popular singers of *guewel* origin sing such songs, they undertake a shift from the griot-noble relationship to the *taalibe* (Islamic pupil)–marabout relationship. Although the relationship changes, Mc-Laughlin notes that the form of the praise song does not change. It becomes, instead, a praise to god, via the marabout. McLaughlin concludes that by attaching the form of the *guewel*'s praise song to the Sufi tradition, popular singers have created a new genre that enables them to straddle creatively the boundary between the roles of the *guewel* and *taalibe*.

What McLaughlin describes for Senegal is occurring on a broader scale as some movements within Islam in West Africa begin to demand greater adherence to the rules of the religion. One by-product of this demand is greater availability on cassettes of music and stories about heroes from the recent past, from El Hadj Omar to Samory Touré, who fought in the name of Islam to create kingdoms that resisted the French (Dieng and Hale, 1994). Whatever differences might have appeared between griots and religious leaders in the past have faded somewhat as a more traditional form of Islam takes stronger hold in Sahelian and Savanna societies. To understand this synthesis, there is a need for more research on the interface between Islam and the griot tradition.

Multifunctional Character

From the listing of their diverse activities, it is clear that we can no longer translate the term *griot* as simply praise-singer or story-teller. *Griot* reflects in microcosm the complexity and dynamism cited on nearly every page of this study. Born of the interaction between many cultures, African and Western, the term *griot* has entered the vocabulary of so many languages it can no longer be suppressed entirely in favor of local terms. The meaning of *griot* to audiences outside Africa is still evolving as the result of different sources of information about them, ranging from *Roots* to world music. With griots entering into the print, visual, and electronic media in so many ways, the term will become more widespread, and people will begin to understand the nuances that it represents.

Equal Billing for Women

The focus on male griots can no longer hide the roles of women. If *griot* and its local terms serve as pathways to help people understand both the regional nature of the profession and the cultural specificity of *jali, jeli, jeseré*, etc., part of that understanding must include a recognition that women, as well as men, have always played a role. The focus on male griots in the past, rooted in so many causes, can no longer veil the presence of women on the various stages that make up the griots' performance context.

Women's emergence into the gaze of the outside world is a recent phenomenon. But it is likely to grow not only because of technology, but also because of internal social change, the increased interest in women on the part of researchers, and women's own efforts.

Griots on Their Own

As griots adapt to new audiences and new technologies, we—researchers and audiences in Africa and outside—cannot intervene to channel or change what they do. At best, those interested in preserving material from the past can contribute to international efforts to record, transcribe, translate, and publish narratives and other verbal forms from griots. But just as the texts have undergone change over the years, they will continue to change in the future—perhaps at a faster rate. Though griots may still participate in naming ceremonies, weddings, and other events, we cannot step in between current and future audiences to freeze griots and griottes in a particular social context.

In New York, as the population from the Sahel and Savanna grows, demand will increase for griots' services at events. Whether or not those events will include circumcisions may depend on changes in U.S. law on some aspects of these ceremonies, especially genital cutting of females, a subject of intense interest as the result of the success of a recent suit on behalf of a woman from Benin who fled her country for the United States because she feared the practice.

At the same time, griots may become in greater demand at rituals of other peoples. Papa Susso reported that he has been asked to perform nine times at circumcisions in Jewish families in the New York area. He also was asked to play at political events for leaders such as the former mayor of New York, David Dinkins. One wonders, however, whether the ceremonial interest in griots, like the voracious appetite for musical novelty in the world today, will somehow absorb and then cast aside the customary activities of griots from Mali, Senegal, and other countries.

Diversity in the Griot World

As details of the griot world begin to emerge owing to wider dissemination of information such as that provided in this book and in videos, performances, and interviews, both the griots themselves and their multiple audiences—researchers, music lovers, and others—need to be reminded of a reality that is not likely to change: there is much diversity within the griot world.

Although I have identified a variety of common features about the profession in the preceding pages, there are many variations from one society to another. Generalizations can lead to misinterpretations, especially if one depends on the views of theorists who have had little or no interest in Africa.

This caveat operates on the microlevel of a phenomenon such as the griot tradition within a particular region. For example, one specialist in African oral literature, drawing on the literary theories of Mikhail Bakhtin, could not understand why there was no audience response listed in the text of *The Epic of Askia Mohammed* (see Okpewho, 1996). In the neighboring Mande world, one finds the *naamunaamuna*, the man who responds at the end of each line to encourage and confirm the words of the griot with "naamu," loosely translated as "indeed." But for the Songhay, this audience tradition is far less common. The attempt to generalize from part of one region to another area based on Bakhtin's theory of laughter and some familiarity with the Mande epic tradition led to a series of fundamental misinterpretations of the epic text, the cultural context, and the performance situation.

In spite of the diffusion of the griot tradition across the Sahel and Savanna, one cannot ignore the specificity of local conditions. The African epic tradition, no less than the West African griot tradition, reveals an extraordinary variety from one area to another.

Preservation of the Past

Although the profession is still in a state of flux, two factors are contributing to the preservation of the verbal and musical traditions of griots: migration and technology, both at home and abroad. Although changes in immigration rules in countries such as France and the United States may slow the flow of immigrants from Africa, expatriate communities have taken on a life of their own and are growing at a steady rate. Thanks to the full range of technology, from telephone to airplane, the people of these communities are as much in touch with their cultural roots as were other immigrant communities of the past. The latest communications technologies make it much easier for expatriate communities to maintain ties, not only among themselves but around the world.

Paul Stoller has studied a small community of Songhay and Zarma traders in New York. These people, from the center of West Africa, are far less numerous than their Senegalese, Gambian, and Malian counterparts who trade on the streets of Harlem. But the fact that the Songhay and Zarma have established a foothold and that it is growing suggests that the time is not far off when Djeliba Badié will fly in from Niamey to sing *The Epic of Mali Bero*. He would join a stream of other griots who have made New York a frequent destination in the search for both new and old audiences. The numbers will depend on the success of these new communities and their ability to build the demand for griots in ways that have yet to be calculated.

At the same time, governmental and nongovernmental organizations at home will, I believe, step up efforts to nourish as best they can those activities that preserve a sense of social cohesion. In many countries the impact of outside forces is multiplied by an economic crisis that offers no quick solution. In these difficult times, though people have less money to spend, they may hold on to their traditions as a symbol of a more prosperous and happy past. Central to these traditions is the griot.

Current forms of technology, as well as others to be developed, will contribute in another way to the preservation of the griot heritage. As the world shrinks rapidly to communities of people on the Internet, the barriers of space and time are disappearing. It will become less and less necessary for listeners around the world to enjoy the sounds of griots only on recordings. Interactive video and electronic communication will come to play an increasing role.

Although only a small number of countries in Africa are on the Internet, the rate of change in this medium is so rapid that one is likely by the early part of next century to find people in tiny African villages communicating electronically with the rest of the world. The recent adaptation to laptop computers of the generator that powers windup radios is a promising step in this direction.

Of the griots working in the United States who are listed in Appendix A, Djimo Kouyaté now has an e-mail address, and another, Balla Tounkara, can be reached via an African promoter living in the Boston area who also has an e-mail address. Just as some griots have taken to sound technology and, as seen with Prince, to computers and synthesizers to reach new audiences, it is likely that more of them in the future, in the United States, other countries, and in Africa, will take advantage of the Internet as a way of communicating and advertising.

If, with a few exceptions, members of the current generation of griots operating internationally have not had the opportunity to attend a university, many of their children will. In June 1996, for example, Papa Susso enrolled one of his sons at Columbia College in Missouri, an institution where he once performed.

Everyone Is a Griot

In spite of debates about the merits of the word *griot*, the term is now being applied by a variety of people on both sides of the Atlantic, from writers to scholars, usually in a positive manner, but on occasion as an insult. The diversity of this phenomenon leads on occasion to the reinforcement of stereotypes.

Many writers see themselve as griots because of the way they tell about the past. Responding to a question about a poem he had written on the death of a union organizer, Martinican writer Aimé Césaire declared that his role as a poet was "to be . . . one of those 'griots' who link the people to its history" (1960, p. 23; my translation). Senegalese novelist and filmmaker Ousmane Sembène sees the African filmmaker as the griot of modern times (Pfaff, 1984, p. 40). Maryse Condé, the Guadeloupean writer, also views the modern writer as a "contemporary griot." But in an analysis of her best-selling novel, *Ségou*, the critic Chinosole sees her as a somewhat subversive one both because of her clear-eyed view of the fall of an African empire and because of the critical voice she gives to one of these wordsmiths in another novel, *A Season in Rihata*. He also implies, however, that the irreverent tone of her novels is heightened by the fact that she is a woman and most griots are men, a view that echoes the widespread lack of knowledge about women griots (Chinosole, 1995, pp. 93–95).

The term *griot* can be applied also in a negative sense. In a short but highly critical study of the relations beween France and Africa, Sékou Traoré termed the former president of Senegal, Léopold Sédar Senghor, the "griot" of Francophonie, the amorphous international community of French speakers and organizations linked by the French language (1989, p. 22). For Traoré, the term *griot* implied that Senghor had sold out to the French.

In the examples just cited, the references to *griot* remain within the context of the African diaspora. But today, the notion of the griot is being picked up by others whose connections to Africa vary considerably. For example, the titles of two books on Jean Rouch compared the French ethnographer to a griot. Since then, an author of one of these books, Paul Stoller, who is sometimes viewed as the scholarly son of Rouch because both conducted extensive research on the belief system of the Songhay in Niger, described himself as a griot in an essay title, "The Griot's Tongue" (in Stoller, 1997). Explaining how he came to write *In Sorcery's Shadow* and *Fusion of the Worlds*, first-person narratives of his training in Songhay sorcery and healing, Stoller argues that to weave together the diverse and often conflicting threads of anthropological research, one must face up to the realities that the researcher is part of the world in which he or she works and must convey that world in all its complexity rather than filter it through a predetermined theoretical grid: "The scholar's burden, the griot's burden, was to create the past" (24–43).

The insertion of the term *griot* into the non-African world carries with it both positive and negative connotations. The conservative Republican former speaker of the U.S. House of Representatives, Newt Gingrich, who came to power in 1994 amid considerable publicity about effecting major changes in government, was compared to a griot by one critic. Under the headline "The Many Persona of Speaker Gingrich," Gannett News Service writer DeWayne Wickham remarked: "given that he's such a good talker, the speaker-to-be no doubt will use the oral tradition of the griot—aided by his talk-show boosters—to hawk his slanted version of events, thus enhancing his role as minister of propaganda" (1994).

Today, anyone who links past and present can be described as a griot. The American writer Studs Terkel, who recreates the past through interviews with people who have experienced the events of the period, describes the seventy people featured in his book *Coming of Age* (1995a) as "our griots." These "griots" range in age from seventy to ninety-five, and include economist John Kenneth Galbraith, the first woman mayor of Pittsburgh, Sophie Masloff, and Victor Reuther, co-founder of the United Auto Workers union. For Terkel, they were like griots because they could recount into his microphone the stories of their lives and of the events of the twentieth century (1995b, 1995c).

The American historian of religion and columnist Martin Marty has described his first encounter with the term—in a Moravian prayer from a book given to him by friends of that faith. After picking up the habit of reading from it each morning, he reported: "On February 2 we read the prayer, 'Help us to be faithful storytellers, griots, narrators and teachers, Lord, Amen.' Amen! If the Moravians say we should want to be something, we will. But what do we want if we want to be griots?" Marty then went on a search for the meaning of the term, eventually finding it in the *American Heritage Dictionary*. Marty concluded:

> I can't tell you how happy I am to add the word to my vocabulary as a teacher, editor, writer, lecturer, "village-and-family" member, devotionalist, and believer. Yes, a "griot" is what I'd like to be when I grow up. Proof of this pudding about the value of storytelling? You'd have forgotten the word as quickly as you heard it had I not put it in a sort of story. (1995)

The identification with griots of writers, filmmakers, anthropologists, politicians, and people in other walks of life is likely to continue as the term spreads via the media. This diffusion will contribute both to greater awareness of the existence of the griot tradition in West Africa and to more confusion about the nature of the profession as the term becomes generalized.

The most extreme example of this phenomenon appeared at the 1987 Panafrican Festival of Cinema in Ouagadougou, Burkina Faso, during a colloquium entitled "The Oral Tradition and New Media." An Ivorian scholar, poet, actor, and director, Niangoranh Porquet, described himself as a griotist and griologue in a startling presentation he called "La Griologie." He sees "griologie" as a new multimedia way of conveying information to the world. From the text alone it is difficult to determine whether he actually believed in what he was saying or was attacking in ironic manner the fascination of others with griots. He provided a list of terms to help readers understand the concepts he presented: *griologie*—the study of griots; *griotude*—the values of griots; *griotisation*—the means to stage African performances; *griotique*—the style of acting; *griographie*—the world of griotique; *griotiseur*—the practitioner of griotisation; *griotiste*—the philosopher of griotique; *grioticien*—the practitioner of griotique; *grioturgie*—the playwright of griotique; *grioture*—the writing, speaking, and drumming of griotique; *griotegie*—griotique tragedy; *grioterie*—griotique comedy; *griotscenie*—the staging of griotique; *griothèque*—the collection of books, tapes, videos, and films about griots; *griotoire*—the repertoire of griot activities. Whatever his intention, the term *griot* here became lost in verbiage that further confuses the unsuspecting reader (in Bachy, 1989, pp. 55–67).

Questions in Search of Researchers

Although I have brought together a variety of information in this study, much of the data simply opens doors to new questions that will be answered by another generation of scholars. Here are a few of the many questions that are emerging from the diverse mass of data about griots.

What is the impact of griot music on world music? The career of Senegalese singer Youssou N'Dour offers clues. The mother of Youssou N'Dour was a *gawlo* of Tukulor or Fulbe origin who married a noble and had to give up her profession. Without the kind of support evident in families of griots such as the Cissokos, Youssou N'Dour nevertheless sensed a deep urge to sing. He started as a youth, singing at circumcision ceremonies in Dakar, then moved on to a theater troupe and a band. Eventually, he ran away from home when his father told him he could not go off to The Gambia with another group. After negotiations with his parents, he attended the Ecole des Arts, the predecessor to the conservatory attended by Prince Cissoko, and was allowed to join a band in Dakar. He formed his own band in 1979 and made his first trips abroad to Paris in 1982 and London in 1984 (Durán, 1988). Today, amid the extraordinary variety of styles and songs he sings, one can hear praise songs and other echoes of his *gawlo* roots. But the echoes are often drowned out in the synthesis of new sounds and what Prince Cissoko would call new "looks."

In the July 12, 1992, *Boston Globe* appears a picture of Youssou N'Dour wearing a baseball hat, blazer, tie, and jeans. The caption reads: "Senegalese singer Youssou N'Dour is a modern-day griot, a traditional African storyteller" (Gonzalez, p. B25). It is a claim that must have come not from the interviewer but directly from the musician, who affirmed in another interview, "I am a modern griot" when describing the message of his song "Toxiques" about the crime of international dumping of toxic materials in Africa (Coxon, p.15). Coxon described the musician in terms of his strong tenor voice, the *mbalax* rhythm that drives his music, and, above all, the "extraordinary synthesis of languages, musical styles, traditional elements, and technology" with echoes of rhythm and blues, jazz-rock, and "traditional styles."

An earlier critic took the term *griot* quite literally when criticizing N'Dour. In an unsigned editorial for *The Gambia News-Letter*, a publication aimed at the Gambian community in Sweden, the author accused N'Dour of selling out to "the neo-colonial elite of the Gambia and Senegal." He pointed out that while N'Dour sings of the poor, he performs only for the rich. The critic, evidently a member of the opposition to the government in The Gambia, which had just survived an attempted coup only by the grace of intervention from Senegal, viewed N'Dour as someone who "stripped himself of any moral responsibility and covers himself behind the griot tradition of singing songs of praise to the rich and powerful. But even those griots that sang at the courts of ancient kings took [a] stand on the moral and social questions of their times even if they had to express them somewhat carefully" (Anon. 6/84). For that critic, Youssou N'Dour, inheritor of the griot tradition, had taken the wrong path.

For Europeans and Americans, however, N'Dour seemed, at least in his earlier years, authentically African, if not 100 percent griot in his style. In a review of a 1986 concert in Philadelphia, the critic noted that N'Dour was seen by most Americans as an "exotic, elemental force" which "at climactic moments . . . straddles the border between exaltation and keening." Peter Gabriel, a pop star who has toured with N'Dour, warned, however, of the need to maintain a certain identity: "Part of what is good about Youssou's music is that it *is* different from the mainstream" (Lambert, 1986, p. 28).

As N'Dour attempted to open up the U.S. market to his style of music, however, he appeared to one critic to lose his way. In 1989, Peter Watrous of the *New York Times* described a performance at the Ritz in New York. A bored audience suddenly woke up when Senegalese members of the audience began to step on stage to give N'Dour money and to dance. Whatever the content of the music, the audience response echoed in some ways the reaction of people listening to a famous griot. But the show as a whole, Watrous commented, seemed to be missing something: "In his attempt to change his music to fit a non-African pop sensibility, he's often made rhythm secondary to melody. . . . Without a resourceful band, or clear arrangements, the music has a tendency to seem watery and insubstantial, the result less of evolution than of a badly planned attempt to find a marketplace" (1989b).

By 1992, the time of the *Globe* news item cited earlier, N'Dour had linked up with Spike Lee to release a new album in an attempt to break through the anonymity that marked his visits to New York (Anon., *Time*, 5/4/92). The process of adapting to the new market seemed to one critic to have shaken but not destroyed N'Dour's African roots. The links to the griot tradition, however, seemed to be fading. Jon Pareles, the *New York Times* reporter with the greatest interest and perceptivity when it comes to West African music, attended N'Dour's concert at the Apollo Theatre in Harlem and reported that the context was high tech and highly polished: "He sings in a fervent tenor voice, with the turns and swoops of Arabic music; where he used to soar in syncopated lines, recalling West Africa's jali (griot) music, some of his melodies now land on the downbeat like Western pop." For Pareles, nevertheless, if "the language is adjustable, the roots are intact" (1992).

One reason for N'Dour's difficulties in breaking through in the United States was a failed attempt to cross over to English-language singing. In an article-interview, one critic explained that "The Lion" has been a failure, but with "Eyes Open" N'Dour had finally achieved success in this country (Rule, 1992).

In a detailed biographical article on N'Dour, Lucy Durán observed that the Senegalese singer's work with Peter Gabriel had "an immeasurable impact" on his performances, especially in the stage presentation. The singer and his musicians now dance, she noted, "their movements subtly choreographed, with considerable wit, to reflect the subject of the song" (1988, p. 37).

To answer the question of griot influence on modern rock stars in West Africa and by extension on world music, one will need to study not simply the songs but also the music and the movement over the entire career of a singer such as Youssou N'Dour. One starting point will be the recent film by French filmmaker Béatrice Soulé, *Velvet Jungle*, which traces fifteen years of the musician's career. But to understand the griot influence more fully, researchers will need to learn the languages he uses—Wolof, Dioula, Fulbe, and French.

Other musicians also claim griot roots and are attempting to negotiate the twisting path from their past to the global audiences without getting lost in the process. The passing comments of the reviewers I have cited give a hint—and only that—of the evolution of musicians of griot origin such as N'Dour. A wider range of critics from a more diverse group of publications is needed. The long-term judgment on the impact of both the roots on the musician and the audience on the roots will come not from reviewers but from an extended and highly focused study of the career of a single musician such as N'Dour, framed in the broader context of what other performers have done and are doing.

One place to start will be the lengthening shelf of books on music from Africa that I list in Appendix E. To varying degrees, these studies will help the reader who wants to learn how the evolving music of griots contributes to or is part of the larger world of African music.

Is world music becoming "Mandified"?

To understand more clearly the impact of particular strains, one ultimately must focus on the most significant force in griot music, that of the Mande world, whose influence is growing not only in West Africa but also in world music. One might make an analogy between English, the language of the Internet, and Mande, the musical force of the Sahel and Savanna. No one knows just what will be the result of the worldwide use of

English on the Internet. Will it lead to the more rapid marginalization of languages such as French? Or will it give new life to lesser-known languages? It is hard to tell just how the phenomenon of world music will change in the next few years as more performers from the Mande diaspora disseminate their music via the various forms of media available to them.

Will the wave of "Mandification" drown out or marginalize the other musics of West Africa, especially those of traditional performers? Will Paris become a Mande province, as the cover of one magazine declared in 1987 (see Knight, 1991, p. 52)? Or will the increased benefits of rapid electronic communication enable a world audience to distinguish more clearly between all of these cultural forces simply by shifting to a different Web site?

Eric Charry's dissertation on Mande music (1992) is the essential starting point for any understanding of the future of Mande music as a force in regional and world music. Recent conference presentations and articles by him and by Robert Newton offer tantalizing hints about the future of Mande music.

One reason for the influence, of course, is the large number of griots from the Mande world, compared to the performers from the periphery. Wolof, Moor, Songhay, and Hausa griots may attract more attention in the future, but for now they are overshadowed on the world stage by their Bamana, Maninka, and Mandinka colleagues.

The number of CDs and other media forms now appearing from that part of Africa is considerable. One of the most recent and most elaborately packaged is *Jali Kunda: Griots of West Africa and Beyond* produced by a team that included Foday Musa Suso, the Gambian *jali* based in Chicago. In a cardboard box with a picture of Suso teaching his son Saiku to play the *kora* on the cover, one finds a ninety-six page booklet filled with glossy photos of *jalolu* and scenes of life in The Gambia. The booklet contains short essays about the profession and its music by Suso, Robert Palmer, and others, as well as track notes for the accompanying CD. The package provides a fascinating introduction to the world of griots, although it leaves the reader with the impression that the center of this world is the Mandinka people of The Gambia. The mix of music on the CD includes several tracks with accompaniment by Philip Glass on piano and Pharaoh Sanders on saxophone, further evidence of the growing synthesis of different instrumental traditions.

Another reason for the phenomenon of Mandification may be the technical influence of some of the instruments. In addition to the appearance of the *kora* and the *ngoni* in contexts that include Western instruments, there is one piece of evidence to indicate that the style of the *kora* as an instrument has had an impact in the United States. In 1986, Robert Grawi invented the Gravikord, an instrument based on the *kora*. With twenty-nine strings, it is a stainless steel, electronically amplified harp-lute with an open lyre-shaped bridge that arranges the strings ergonomically to be more comfortable than the *kora*. The instrument was displayed among eighty objects chosen to illustrate the African contribution to American music in winter 1997 at the Metropolitan Museum of Art in New York. Grawi teamed up with a flutist, Pip Klein, for a concert there on January 31, 1996, in which he mixed African and American popular styles.

What is the impact of griot music on African American musical forms such as blues and rap?

Paul Oliver has pursued the matter of linkages between the African traditions and the blues on a broad scale in *Savannah Syncopaters: African Retentions in the Blues* (1970). He discovered a variety of apparent convergences, ranging from the use of high voices to systems of tuning and picking styles. Sam Charters took a more personal approach by going off to West Africa in 1974 in search of the roots of the blues. He met with a variety of griots in The Gambia and other countries. There he, too, discovered similarities between the blues and the music of griots—singing styles, rhythmic figures, texturing of voice, and accompanying rhythm. But he also found extensive differences—Arabic and Spanish influences, such as flamenco music (1981, p. 125).

In part because of the research of Oliver and Charters, blues scholars now routinely refer to griot music in discussions of the origins of this form. William Barlow claims that early blues performers were "African-American variations on the famous West African 'griot' tradition." He sees them as "descendants of the griots, carrying forward the historical and cultural legacy of their people even while they are setting a new agenda for social discourse and action" (1989, pp. 7–8). The impressionistic travelogue of Charters and the studies of more recent scholars have begun to open the door to further comparisons between blues and griot music, but much more research needs to be done.

The same is true for rap music. In *Rap Attack 2: African Rap to Global Hip Hop* (1991), David Toop suggests that contemporary rappers may have roots in the griot tradition, but he offers little evidence. Many musicians, however, see an obvious link in the narrative elements in the art of griots and the same features in rap.

Was Br'er Rabbit a Griot?

In a study of a collection of Wolof stories from The Gambia, Emil Magel discovered that in restricted storytelling contexts, the hare character was often portrayed as a griot because of his quickness, perception, and, above all, verbal skills. By "restricted context" he means evening sessions in the homes of griots—occasions that would not normally be marked by the presence of nobles. "In such restricted contexts," Magel writes, "the hare is consistently identified as a member of the *gewel* caste" (1981, p. 189). Magel cites a variety of sources linking the hare and the *gewel*. He then offers a series of examples of the animal in roles that support the symbolic link with a human counterpart. Magel concludes that the hare in these particular contexts is a "manifestaton in narrative form of the ideals and values to which *gewel* aspire. In these contexts, it cannot represent the Wolof Everyman but only the Wolof *gewel*, exclusive of all other caste members" (199).

Is this an isolated case that is overshadowed by the usual association of Br'er Rabbit with West African trickster tales? Or can we simply conclude that Br'er Rabbit of the African American story tradition descended from a variety of West African rabbit stories, including those that identify the animal character with griots?

Paul Cimbala offers one clue in his discussion of Black "musicianers" in the 19th century. "Slaves paid special tribute to their musicianers by making their favorite trickster, Br'er Rabbit, a fiddler and by recounting stories concerning their musicians in the same style as the animal trickster tales," he reports (1995, p. 19). For example, in a narrative recorded from an ex-slave in Texas during the 1930s, Br'er Rabbit, portrayed as a trickster, plays the fiddle in an encounter with Br'er Fox (20).

Other scholars suggest that the influence of griots on the African American tradition is more generalized and evident not simply in tales but also in other forms of discourse such as preaching. The editors of *Call and Response: The Riverside Anthology of the African American Tradition* argue in the introduction to their massive, 2,000-page collection that

> a few northern people were able to draw on the African tradition of the poet-historian, called the *griot*, along with the discipleship of preaching—which was the only acceptable form of public utterance allowed to slaves—to emerge as literate spokespersons for their people.... Thus, like their African predecessors, early African American ministers such as Allen, Liele, and Jones, and, to varying degrees, other black writers and spokespersons of that era became political leaders of a society that functioned within a society. Using the inherited verbal artistry and eloquence of the griots, they crafted sermons,

prayers, narratives, hymns, poems, essays, and songs to educate, uplift and stir the African American spirit toward social action. (Liggins *et al.*, 1997, 3–4, 26)

The volume's editors offer as evidence parallels between West African epics and slave spirituals such as "Go Down Moses" (42–44) as well as between sermons and prayers in epic narratives and counterparts in the African American tradition.

In *Exchanging Our Country Marks: The Transformation of African Identities in the Colonial and Antebellum South*, Michael A. Gomez argues that same point but from a different angle. He suggests that the usual identification of African American ministers with West African priest kings is misplaced, and proposes instead that it may be more beneficial for scholars to re-examine the role of the West African *griot* as re-creator of the past. "The *griots* and their progeny would have . . . taken advantage of the opportunities presented by Christianity, and especially the Baptists, to learn new words and master their delivery. Black preachers, as was true of the *griot*, established reputations based upon their ability to tell and retell 'the story.' . . . The black preacher, particularly in the Baptist tradition, developed a unique style of delivery, a kind of 'sing-song' sermon that was part speech, part exhortation, part ballad, all performance" (1998, pp. 280–81). Gomez points out that while the preacher he describes "may be the spiritual descendant" of the griot, "he had to transcend that role" under the particular conditions of the slave environment.

The evidence proposed here, ranging from Br'er Rabbit to the African American preacher tradition, remains limited but fascinating. More research will be needed, however, on both sides of the Atlantic. In particular, we need to learn more about the roles of animals in different ethnic groups and pay careful attention to the origins and destinations of slaves. Large numbers of slaves arriving in the New World did not come from the Sahel and Savanna region, but originated among coastal peoples such as the Yoruba and the Ibo, whose verbal heritage was as rich as those of peoples from the interior of West Africa but did not include griots. Searches of records of names of slaves in the 17th and 18th centuries for clear indicators such as Kuyate, Kwateh, and Katey, along with examination of narratives by owners of plantations and their families that offer detailed descriptions of particularly talented or unusual slaves, may nevertheless provide the clues needed to identify the earliest griots to arrive in this country.

What is the impact of griots on contemporary African American society? Aside from the numerous examples of usage by African Americans described in the introduction to this study, the image of the griot is beginning to appear in areas that might seem to be totally unrelated to West Africa. The Kwanzaa ceremonies, based on a set of principles enunciated in Swahili vocabulary and rooted in East African cultures, were created by Maulana Karenga in 1966 as an African American holiday. Some participants in these ceremonies assume the role and title of griot to tell stories about the past. In *The Complete Kwanzaa*, Dorothy Winbush Riley (1995, pp. 256–58) includes an excerpt from *Sundiata*, while in *A Kwanzaa Keepsake*, Jessica B. Harris (1995, p. 23) provides an explanation of what a griot is and encourages a family member to play this role by writing down family information. The inclusion of references to griots and texts by them in these ceremonies suggests that there may be far more to the griot influence in contemporary African American culture than is immediately evident.

Is the griot profession becoming feminized?

There is a small but growing discussion among scholars about the gender of the profession. It is fueled by several observations. In many countries, it is the ceremonies organized by women that attract griots. Christopher Miller, drawing on Sory Camara (1976), notes that griots are in some ways neutral in sexual identity because they can "participate as women while remaining men" (Miller, 1990, p. 263). Oumarou Watta, referring to the Songhay world in a chapter entitled "Griots and Women," argues that "griots and women have a great deal in common. The former are the latter, and vice versa" (1993, p. 167). He adds that "women and griots are catalysts of poetic thought. . . . Women cannot live without *gesere*. *Gesere* are not without women" (168, 187). The validity of these observations awaits further research that will have to depend less on Western psychoanalytic theories and broad generalizations and more on conversations with griottes and griots themselves in a variety of societies.

In addition to the matter of gender as it relates to men, there is also a question about the changing roles of women in the profession. Mamadou Diawara sees the electronic media and the expanded performance context as playing major roles in the shift in Mali from men to women as the dominant performers. As women's voices have taken over the recording market, men are literally fading into the background. Evidence of what he describes as "a clear feminization of the artist's profession among griots" comes from a report from a griot in Mali, Bréhima Camara, about another *jeli* who must stay at home for months to take care of the children while his wife, "one of the griot-entrepreneurs," leaves for Paris to perform (1997, p. 42).

Can Griots Represent All of Africa?

For the reader who has never studied any aspect of African cultures, the diverse evidence about griots presented in this book may give the impression that these wordsmiths speak for Africa when in fact they represent in cultural terms only one section of the continent—West Africa—and then only part of that section, some of the cultures of the Sahel and Savanna regions. Interest in the United States in griots, as we have seen, boomed after the *Roots* phenomenon in 1976 because of the link with the African American minority in this country and a long-suppressed thirst to understand a distant past. Griots represent a part—and only a part—of Africa that contributed significantly to the slave trade. If it is, then, quite appropriate that African Americans rediscover their origins through the interpretation of West African cultural history conveyed by griots, there is a danger that a single perspective will be too limiting.

Paulla Ebron addresses this issue in her 1993 dissertation on Mandinka *jalolu* when she describes the ways griots negotiate identity, not only within their own cultures but also between Africa and other cultures. At the level of an individual performance in the United States, for example, it is easy for a griot to generalize by saying that "in Africa we do it this way. . . ." The griot suddenly becomes the articulate spokesperson for all of a very vast and diverse continent. But in fact, the problem of interpreting Africa is multi-layered, beginning with the regional bias presented by griots and extending to more specific issues of just which griots and which cultures will be represented.

The matter of who represents a culture in a pluralistic world is bound up in politics, economics, and the complex interactions of agents, governments, organizations, and the griots themselves. In the mediated exchange between two cultural worlds—Africa and the West—each side may deal from the outset with a large number of unknowns and misperceptions.

It is likely that such negotiations during the first few decades of the post-*Roots* era are only the first step in a much longer process that will lead to more knowledgable partners on both sides. More of the most talented griots from West Africa will go abroad as audiences come to appreciate and better understand the nature of the musical art being conveyed. But it is unlikely that the verbal art of griots will ever be understood in performance abroad as fully as it is at home because of the language barrier. It is more likely that griots, like some singers, will attempt to cross the language barrier by giving performances in English.

In spite of these problems, it appears that griots will become a constant source for increasing world understanding of Africa. Given both the extraordinary distortion of African cultures in the outside world and the focusing of attention almost exclusively on the crises of the continent, from bloody coups to devastating droughts, the task of giving a more balanced view of Africa's peoples will continue to be a difficult one. Each appearance of a West African wordsmith in a classroom or concert hall helps to erase the cultural graffiti represented by widespread stereotypes (see figure 20).

❊ ❊

What, then, can one conclude about griots and their role in the global village? Griots have survived from before the time of Ibn Battuta to beyond the time of Alex Haley. They probably existed for a millennium before the Berber traveler crossed the Sahara to Mali, and it is likely that thanks in part to *Roots* they will be flourishing for centuries to come through the next millennium. They represent an enduring synthesis of word, music, and

20. Photo of Papa Bunka Susso lecturing in a classroom at The Pennsylvania State University. By the author.

human dynamics. If, from the questions I have posed, it is evident that researchers have much more to learn about griots, it is certain also that griots have much to teach their new audiences around the world, especially about the rich cultural heritage of their diverse African societies.

Epilogue

A striking example of that educational process occurred on June 3, 1998, at the Community College of Philadelphia, an urban institution that enrolls 40,000 students. Faculty members there, under the leadership of Professors Fay Beauchamp and David Prejsnar, obtained a two-year grant from the U.S. Department of Education to prepare instructors in a variety of disciplines (literature, foreign languages, anthropology, history, political science, philosophy, religion, art) to create new courses about Asia and Africa as well as to infuse other courses with a broader global and comparative perspective on the peoples from these areas. Visiting professors from many disciplines came to the seminar for brief residencies of one to three days in order to make presentations in their own specialities.

One of the faculty development seminars, however, included a day-long presentation by two Gambian griots, Sarjo Kuyate and Nakoyo Suso. In the morning, the pair performed and answered questions from an audience of students and faculty. In the afternoon, they met with the instructors participating in the training project in order to engage in longer discussions and respond to more queries. By their presence in the seminar, they were engaging in a form of instruction that would have a multiplier effect. Two griots were teaching 25 instructors who would, in turn, teach thousands of students about Africa in the years to come.

Appendices

※ A ※
Griots Working in the United States

The following is a partial list of West African griots who live in the United States. For more complete and up-to-date information, consult the griot Web page at http://www.la.psu.edu/~thale/ or send me a message at tah@psu.edu. The African Performance Clearinghouse coordinated by Robert Newton at the University of Wisconsin's African Studies Program also supplies information about African performers, including griots such as Toumani Diabaté. The Web address is: http://polyglot.lss.wisc.edu/afrst/clear/html. Newton can be reached by e-mail at afrclear@macc.wisc.edu or by phone at 608-265-9151.

Cheick Hamala Diabaté, c/o Kader Tounkara, 1905 East West Highway, Apt. 104, Silver Spring, MD 20910. Tel. 301-589-2743.

Mamadou Diabaté, 222 West 116th St., Apt. 3W, New York, NY 10026. Tel. 212-749-6421, 212-662-1293.

Djimo Kouyaté, 319 16th St. SE, Washington, DC 20003, and P.O. Box 50042, Washington, DC 20091. Tel. 202-546-0610. He may also be contacted c/o Akua Kouyaté, the administrator for his organization, Memory for Africa, Inc., at 202-726-1400, or at dkouyate@wam.umd.edu.

Keba Kouyaté, c/o Rufus Cappadocia, 201 E. 15th St., New York, NY 10003. Tel. 212-995-8379.

Sarjo Kuyate, 265 E. 176th St., Apt. 3C, New York, NY 10457. Tel. 718-294-2074.

Foday Musa Suso, 2120 South Harper Ave., Chicago, IL 60615. Tel. 773-324-4132.

Al Haji Papa Bunka Susso, Apt. 3G, 333 E. 181st St., New York, NY 10457. Tel. 718-563-3936.

Balla Tounkara, 4 University Rd., Apt. 201, Cambridge, MA 02138. Tel. 617-661-3961. He may also be contacted c/o El Hadj Msam (uncle of Djibril Tamsir Niane) at 16 Kennedy Rd., Cambridge, MA 02138. Tel. 617-876-3153, and at elhadjmsam@aol.com.

❈ B ❈
Films and Videos Featuring Griots

Documentary and Instructional Films and Videos

For the first three items below, the distributor is Roderic Knight, 89 Pyle Rd., Oberlin, Ohio 44074. More information on them is available on his Web site: http://www.oberlin.edu/~rknight.

Music of the Mande: Part I, Music for the Warriors, Hunters, and Ordinary People; Part II, Professional Music: Mandinka Jaliyaa with the Kora. Filmed in The Gambia originally on Super 8 film in 1970 and 1982 by Roderic Knight and converted more recently to video. Part II, 47 minutes, contains rare footage of scenes three decades ago that include performances by *jalolu* who are no longer alive (Al Haji Bai Konte, Jali Nyama Suso, Fabala Kanuteh, and Jali Mori Suso) as well as Amadu Bansang Jobarteh and Al Haji Suntu Suso. Footage of griots greeting the presidents of The Gambia and Sierra Leone at the airport, a child-naming ceremony, and how to build a *kora* provide context.

Jali Nyama Suso: Kora Player of The Gambia. A rare recording of Jali Nyama Suso performing four classic tunes, Ala l'a ke (Allah's deed), Jula Faso (Merchants' tune), Yundumunko (Man from Yundum), and Masane Sise (Masanneh Sisay), while serving as an artist in residence at the University of Washington in 1971–72.

Mande III: Gambian Tantango Drumming. Contains five scenes filmed in 1970 in silent Super 8, with separately recorded sound added later: Lenjengo/Seruba (recreational drumming), Nyaka Julo (playing in the field at rice-planting time), Kanyelango or Dimbo Tulongo (Young Mothers' Play), Nyoboringo (wrestling match), and Kankurango (masked dance). OMV-009, 1992. 35 minutes, 24 pp., notes.

Al Haji Bai Konte. 12 minutes. Describes the life of the late Mandinka griot Al Haji Bai Konte from Brikama, The Gambia. Includes local performance scenes with his son Dembo. In Mandinka with English narration by Taj Mahal. Produced by Marc Pevar and Oliver Franklin. From Marc Pevar, 606 Ridge Avenue, Kennett Square, PA 19348. Tel. 610-444-1157, e-mail mpevar@ravenet.com.

Griottes of the Sahel: Female Keepers of the Songhay Oral Tradition in Niger. 11-minute video about griottes, or *jeserey weyborey,* in both the urban context of Niamey, Niger, and the isolated town of Yatakala. In Songhay and Zarma with English voice-over. Item 24633, Audio Visual Services, Pennsylvania State University, University Park, PA 16802. Tel. 1-800-770-2111, e-mail avsmedia@psulias.psu.edu

Amy Koita, Grande Chanteuse Malienne: Concert à Bamako. 60-minute video of Amy Koita, one of Mali's most popular woman singers of *jeli* origin, performing on stage in various venues in Mali. Her dress, the backup musicians, the audience, and those who come on stage to offer rewards reveal how the superstar *jelimusolu* of Mali have adapted to the late-twentieth-century context. Kalim International Video item 549. 99, rue du Faubourg St.-Denis, 75010 Paris, France. Tel. 45-23-47-41. My copy was purchased in a small shop in the Adams-Morgan section of Washington.

Great Great Great Grandparents' Music. Documentary portrait of a family of *jeliw* filmed in Burkina Faso. In Jula (Dioula), Bwamu, and Moor, with subtitles in English. African Family Film Foundation. 90 minutes. Contact Taale Laafi Rosellini, African Family Film Foundation, Box 630, Santa Cruz, CA 95061-0630.

Born Musicians: Traditional Music from The Gambia. Documentary on Mandinka vocal and instrumental music. In Mandinka and English. Produced by Geoffrey Haydon and Dennis Marks. Third Eye Productions. 60 minutes. No information available on distributor at this time.

Feature Films and Videos

Djeli, Conte d'Aujourd'hui. 1981. Directed by Lancina Fadika-Kramo. An attack on the notion of caste by presenting a narrative that begins with an origin tale of griots as hunters and then moves forward to a love story involving a griot and a woman from another social group. Filmed in Dioula. 90 minutes. Films du Sabre. Distributed by AUDECAM (Association Universitaire Pour le Developpement, l'Education, et la Communication en Afrique et dans le Monde. Tel. 45-51-28-24, fax 45-56-10-72. 100, rue de l'Université, 75007 Paris, France.

Jom ou l'histoire d'un peuple. 80 minutes. In Wolof. Directed by Ababacar Samb-Makharam, co-produced with Zweites Deutschen Fernsehen television in Germany. This is a frame tale in which a griot from the present seeks to unify two groups of strikers who cannot agree on how to proceed. He succeeds in unifying them by taking them into the past to a conflict in which a man kills a French administrator, then commits suicide. This event is presented through the narrative of an earlier griot. Baobab Films (Senegal) and ZDF Mainz (Germany). Distribution in France: Sumafa Production.

Keita: L'Héritage du Griot. Directed by Dani Kouyaté. In Dioula and French with English subtitles. Feature film about a *jeli* who visits an urban family to teach the child about the past. Includes scenes of the Sundiata epic. 94 minutes. California Newsreel, 149 Ninth Street / 420, San Francisco, CA 94103. Tel. 415-621-6196, e-mail newsreel@ix.netcom.com.

✹ C ✹
Selected English Translations
of Epics by Griots

All texts are in linear format and translated from the original language unless otherwise indicated. Not all are in print at this time, but all may normally be obtained via interlibrary loan.

Conrad, David C. *A State of Intrigue: The Epic of Bamana Segu according to Tayiru Banbera*. Oxford: Oxford University Press, 1990. The longest linear epic now in print.

Diop, Samba. *The Oral History and Literature of the Wolof People of Waalo, Northern Senegal: The Master of the Word (Griot) in the Wolof Tradition*. Lewiston, Maine: Mellen Press, 1995. Contains a version of the Wolof epic of Njaajaan Njaaye.

Hale, Thomas A. *Scribe, Griot and Novelist: Narrative Interpreters of the Songhay Empire. Followed by The Epic of Askia Mohammed Recounted by Nouhou Malio*. Gainesville: University of Florida Press and African Studies Center, 1990.

——, and Nouhou Malio. *The Epic of Askia Mohammed*. Bloomington: Indiana University Press, 1996. This is a slightly revised paperback edition of the epic text included in the preceding volume.

Innes, Gordon. *Sunjata: Three Mandinka Versions*. London: School of Oriental and African Studies, 1974.

——. *Kaabu and Fuladu: Historical Narratives of the Gambian Mandinka*. London: School of Oriental and African Studies, 1976.

——. *Kelefa Saane: His Career Recounted by Two Mandinka Bards*. London: School of Oriental and African Studies, 1978.

Jablow, Alta. *Gassire's Lute*. New York: Dutton, 1917. Prospect Heights: Waveland, 1991. Based on a version collected by Leo Frobenius in 1909 that tells the story of the Ghana empire. Suitable for junior high school and high school students.

Johnson, John William, and Fa-Digi Sisòkò. *The Epic of Son-Jara, a West African Tradition.* Bloomington: Indiana University Press, 1986. Second edition, in paperback, with a new introduction, 1992.

Johnson, John William, and Magan Sisòkò. *The Epic of Sun-Jata according to Magan Sisòkò.* Bloomington: Folklore Publications Group, 1979.

Johnson, John William, Thomas A. Hale, and Stephen Belcher. *Oral Epics from Africa: Vibrant Voices from a Vast Continent.* Bloomington: Indiana University Press, 1997. Excerpts from 25 epics, 19 of which are by griots.

Laye, Camara. *The Guardian of the Word.* New York: Fontana, 1980. Translation by James Kirkup of *Le Maître de la parole: kouma lafôlô kouma.* Paris: Plon, 1978. A reconstructed prose version of Sundiata.

Niane, Djibril Tamsir. *Sundiata: An Epic of Old Mali.* London: Longman, 1965. Translation by G. D. Pickett of *Soundjata, ou l'épopée mandingue.* Paris: Présence Africaine, 1960. A reconstructed prose version most suitable for secondary school students.

Watta, Oumarou. *Rosary, Mat and Molo: A Study in the Spiritual Epic of Omar Seku Tal.* New York: Lang, 1993.

Wisniewski, David. *Sundiata: Lion King of Mali.* New York: Clarion Books, 1992. An extraordinarily well illustrated children's version.

✵ D ✵
Audio Recordings by Griots

Diabaté, Toumani (*kora*). *Kaira*. Hannibal Records HNCD 1338, 1987. Five tracks: Alla L'Aake, Jarabi, Kaira, Kankaba, and Tubaka. Brief but excellent liner notes by Durán.

——, Ketama, and José Soto. *Songhay 1*. Hannibal Records HNCD 1323, 1994. Ten tracks containing a variety of Spanish and Mande songs.

——. *Songhai 2*. Hannibal Records HNCD 1383, 1994. Ten tracks containing a variety of Spanish and Mande songs, presented in blend of European and West African instruments. Ten pages of liner notes on performers and songs.

——. *Djelika*. Hannibal Records HNCD 1380, 1995. Eight tracks: Djelika, Mankoman Djan, Cheick Oumar Bah, Marielle, Kandjoura, Aminata Santoro, Tony Vander, Sankoun Djabi. In addition to *kora* by Diabaté, group includes an *ngoni*, a *balafon*, and two basses. Excellent liner notes.

Diawara, Djeli Moussa. *Cimadan*. Celluloid 66910–2, 1992. Nine tracks: Cimadan, Boubafati, Fotemogoban, Chéri-coco, Vérité, Ayo, Haîdara, Dembaya, Imakoun. Mix of mostly contemporary and some traditional tunes by group that includes Diawara on *kora* with keyboard, *balafon*, bass guitar, *ngoni*, electric guitar, trumpet, trombone, and saxophone. Brief liner notes.

Jansen, Jan. *An Bè Kelen/We Are One: Griot Music from Mali*. PAN 2015CD, 1994. Ten classic songs, many from the Sundiata epic tradition, by *jeliw* and *jelimusow* in Kéla, including the late Bala Diabaté: Sunjata Fasa, Tiramagan Fasa, Fakoli Janjo, Sumaoro Fasa, Simbon, Jeliya, Tara, Datuluma, A Yelema, Kouyata. Excellent notes and photos in liner notes by Jansen.

——. *Bonya/Respect: Griot Music from Mali #2*. PAN 2059CD, 1997. Eight songs about love, friendship, and praise of great men and women by *jeliw* and *jelimusow* in Kéla. Mamadi Bitiki, Kaninba, Lamine Cisse, Kunnadi Lolo, Bala Fasa, Sara #1, Sara #2 (by Siramori Diabaté), Bangali Fode. Excellent liner notes include biographies of performers, summaries of songs, a translation of Sara, and a bibliography.

Jobarteh, Amadu Bansang (*kora*). *Tabara: Gambian Kora Music*. Music of the World CDT 129, 1993. Eight classic tunes from the Mande repertoire: Tabara, Jula Faso, Lamban, Kelefaba, Fode Kaba, Hama Ba Jata, Jule Jegere, Alfa Yaya. Recorded in 1987. Four pages of well-written liner notes.

Koite, Sourakata (*balafon*) and Diombo Kouyaté (*kora*). *Les Griots*. Koch International 322412, 1990. Ten tracks: Diaraby, Tamala, Facoli, Mory Karambolo, Wouli, Tounkara, Edhioula Diekere, Fary Boulo, Cocola Pinceaux, Tambacoumba. Brief liner notes on musicians and songs.

Konte, Dembo (*kora*), Kausa Kuyateh (*kora*), and Mawdo Suso (*balafon*). *Jaliology*. Xenophile 4036, 1995. Nine tracks: Serifu Sidi Haidara, Yussufa Nyabali, Alhaji Sidia Diabi Tesilimang, Dudu Touray, Tunko Darbo, Alisewa, Adam Ning Nahawa, Ke Koto Mani, Lambango. Excellent liner notes by Durán.

Konte, Lamine. *La Kora du Sénégal*. vol. 1. Arion ARN 64036, 1982. Fourteen tracks, including poems by Senghor and Damas set to music: Africa, Yarabi, Mama Tamba, Dioula, Yobaléma, Domba, Yasso, Casa di Mansa, Négritude, Femme Noire, Etait-ce une nuite maghrébine, La légende Baoulé, Hoquet, à New York. Brief liner notes about the performer and music in general, but little on the songs.

———, *La Kora du Sénégal*, vol. 2. Arion 64070, 1989. Eighteen tracks: Lale Kouma, Fodeba, Nagnol, Malon, Gna Terra, Kotoba, Coumpo, Kairaba, Dunya, Koulandian, Koumbu Sora, N'Teri, Abaraka, Mba, Telephonista, Afrikavalse, Fode Kaba, Moussol. Very good liner notes by the musician.

Kouyaté, Sékou (*ngoni*). *Mali Stars*. Mélodie 38106–2, n.d. Eight tracks: Diagnaba, Hommage à Jean-Marie, Kone, Sinigne Sigui, Alassane, Keleya Kele, Sada, Fanion Diarra, Yayi. Group includes *balafon* and other instruments. No details in liner notes.

Kouyaté, Sory Kandia (*ngoni*). *L'Epopée du Mandingue*, vol. 1. Syliphone/ Bolibana/Mélodie 42037–2. Recorded in 1970. Four classic Mande songs, including Djanjon and Siiba, as well as a praise song for Keme-Bourema, younger brother of Samory Touré, and a love song. Brief liner notes.

———, (*ngoni*). *L'épopée du Mandingue*, vol. 2. Syliphone/Bolibana/Mélodie 42038–2. Recorded in 1970. Four classic Mande songs, including Lamban; the praise for a Bambara ruler, Toutou Diarra; the song for great warriors, Douga; and the song for a warrior of Gabou in southern Senegal, Kedo. Brief liner notes.

Kouyaté, Tata Bambo. *Jatigui*. CDORB 042, 1989. Six tracks, beginning with the patron for this CD: Hommage à Baba Cissoko, Ainana Bah, Mama Batchily,

Aorou Bocoum, Goundo Tandja, Amadou Traoré. Brief but excellent liner notes by Durán.

Suso, Foday Musa. *The Dreamtime.* CMP CD 3001, 1990. Eleven tracks containing a mixture of traditional and contemporary music accompanied by *kora* and other African instruments: Futula Mussoli, Morning Light, Mba Ndin Seedy, Under the Tree, Kana Boori, Early Walk, Finger Work, Moving Shadow, Dunia, Bunfa Silence, Fuladu. Brief liner notes.

——. *Jali Kunda: Griots of West Africa and Beyond.* Ellipsis Arts, 1996 (part of package that includes a glossy illustrated book). Box 304, Roslyn, NY 11576; tel. 516-621-2727, e-mail elliarts@aol.com. Fifteen tracks recorded in The Gambia, Senegal, and Guinea Bissau from a wide range of musicians and including some accompaniment by piano (Spring Waterfall), saxophone (Samma), and electric *kora* (Lanmbasy Dub): Alla l'aake (Senegal), Sunjata (Guinea-Bissau), Sinyaro, Mariama, Spring Waterfall, Jula Faso, Sunjata (Senegal), Lanmbasy Dub, Jula Jekereh, Lambango (Gabu, Guinea-Bissau), Samma, Sorrie, Yata Kaya, Lambango (Tabato, Guinea-Bissau), Allah l'aake (The Gambia). Brief liner notes.

Suso, Jali Nyama. *Gambie—l'art de la kora: Jali Nyama Suso.* OCORA Radio France C 580027. 1996. Distributed by Harmonia Mundi. Eight tracks: Jimbasengo, Kuruntu Kelefa and Kelefabaa, Kura (with singer Jali Kani Sumano and *kontingo* player Abdulai Samba), Alifa Yaya, Fanta (with guitarist Ansumana Diabate), Yundum Nko, Cheddo, Tabara.

Suso, Salieu (*kora*). *Griot.* Lyrichord, LRYCD 7418, n.d. Five tracks: Kuruntu Kaliafa, Jimbo Sen, Simbun Ba, Siddy Yellah. Good liner notes by Sherrard and Chen.

Susso, Al Haji Papa Bunka (*kora*). *A Gathering of Elders.* Water Lily Acoustics WLA-AS-25-CD, 1993. Traditional Mande tunes (Ala-Lake, Tabara, Kunkuba, Kaira, and Mamya), some accompanied by vocals of contralto Pat Patrick and soprano Michelle Lawyer, who also sing Steal Away and Amazing Grace.

——, in *African Portraits.* TELDEC 4509-98802-2. Opening solo "Dafengba" accompanied by *kora* in operatic history of Black people written by Hannibal Peterson and recorded in live performance with the Chicago Symphony Orchestra. Extensive liner notes describing the opera.

Wentz, Brooke, and Randall Grass. *Divas of Mali.* Shanachie 64078, 1996. Eleven previously issued songs by the best known women singers of Mali, both griotte and non-griotte: Sanougue Kouyaté, Tata Bambo Kouyaté, Nahawa Doumbia, Hadja Soumano, Ami Koïta, Coumba Sidibé, Fanta Damba, Yahi Kanouté, Kandia Kouyaté, Djeneda Diakité, and Sali Sidibé. Brief descriptive notes for each performer.

✼ E ✼
African Music Books
That Include Sections on Griots

This brief bibliographic survey will give the reader a sense of where the music of griots fits into the much larger and quite diverse world of African music today.

John Gray's *African Music: A Bibliographical Guide to the Traditional, Popular, Art, and Liturgical Musics of Sub-Saharan Africa* (1991) does not cover North Africa but does provide considerable detail on a country-by-country basis, and includes for the remainder of the continent extensive discographies and a variety of indexes. It is the essential starting point for research on African music.

Two earlier works, Francis Bebey's *African Music: A People's Art* (1969) and John Chernoff's *African Rhythm and African Sensibility: Aesthetics and Social Action in African Musical Idioms* (1979), offer overviews that take a holistic approach and include a few references to griots and more than a few pictures of them, though no chapter is devoted to their music. Two other books that focus more closely on the African American connection are Paul Oliver's *Savannah Syncopaters* and Sam Charters's personal narrative, *The Roots of the Blues*.

Books appearing in the past decade give the reader a clearer sense of where the music of griots fits into the larger context. E. Nago Seck, a Senegalese disk jockey and music promoter of griot origin, and Sylvie Clerfeuille, his French collaborator, assembled *Musiciens africains des années 80: Guide* (1986), a modest volume that opens with a brief but useful two-page chapter on griots before going on to a series of six entries about musical styles (*mbalax* for example) and forty-six about individual musicians and groups.

Ronnie Graham compiled *The Da Capo Guide to Contemporary African Music* (1988), which offers brief country-by-country descriptions of music and a short discography. Although it is now out of date, the introduction has an excellent survey of the music industry in Africa, and the sections on the lesser-known countries such as Guinea-Bissau are particularly valuable. In 1992, he published a second edition under the title *The World of African Music*. Although I have not seen it, Charry describes the book as an important complement to the first volume.

In *Rockers d'Afrique* (1988) Hélène Lee describes the ascent of modern African musicians, some of whom are of griot origin—for example Mory Kanté, subject of an entire chapter. She frames griot musicians in the larger context of modern rock music from Africa in a popular, breathless, journalistic style that gives the reader a superficial "you-are-there" feel for this new music.

Wolfgang Bender's more scholarly *Sweet Mother: Modern African Music* (1991) offers an analytical narrative that begins with a lengthy survey chapter, "The Griot Style," on the Sahel and Savanna regions. It is particularly useful from a historical perspective.

Chris Stapleton and Chris May's *African Rock: The Pop Music of a Continent* (1990) includes brief sections on the best-known stars from the Sahel and Savanna, including Youssou N'Dour.

John Collins's lengthy *West African Pop Roots* (1992) includes a comparatively short survey chapter by Flemming Harrev, "Francophone West Africa and the Jali Experience," in a volume that focuses primarily on sub-Saharan Anglophone Africa.

Graeme Ewens's *Africa O-Ye! A Celebration of African Music* (1991) is notable for its large format, many color illustrations, and inclusion of information from parts of North Africa in a chapter entitled "Islamic Inflexions."

World Music: The Rough Guide (1994), edited by Simon Broughton, Mark Ellingham, David Muddyman, and Richard Trillo, includes an excellent article on griots of Mali and Guinea by Lucy Durán framed in a chapter on West African music that gives an overview of the contemporary music scene from the recording industry to the Senegambian stars.

Africa: The Garland Encyclopedia of World Music (1998), edited by Ruth Stone, is a massive 851-page volume that is probably the most extensive work of its kind to appear to date. The West African section, nearly 100 pages long, includes in-depth articles on Mande and Hausa praise-singing. Some of this music can be heard on a CD that accompanies the volume.

❊ F ❊
Ethno-Specific Terms for Griots

In each West African language—Wolof, Moor, Bamana, Songhay, Bariba, Fulbe, and others—there is not just one term but often several for *griot*. And in some cases there is considerable ambiguity about the local terms because of overlaps between the profession, the name of the ethnic group, and the descriptor for the subgroup of artisans.

Wolof

The word for griot is *guewel*, sometimes spelled *gewel*, although there was once a complex nomenclature to designate subcategories according to the kind of music performers sang, the instruments they played, and their behavior in public. They were the *tamakat* (drummers), *xalamkat* (players of the stringed *xalam*), and the *gawlo* (singers) (Diop, 1981). They were all part of a group of artisans known by the general term *nyeenyo*. In the Waalo kingdom in the northwestern part of Senegal, on the border with Mauritania, the *sab-lekk* were musicians, and they included the *tamakat* (drummer) and the *xalambaan*, who played a violinlike instrument, and the *baw-lekk*, or griots who acted as clowns. This social structure from the past is disappearing under the weight of external cultural forces (Barry, 1985).

Mande

As might be expected, the nomenclature for griot among the many Mande-speaking peoples—the Bamana, Malinké or Maninka, Dioula, Mandingo, Mandinka, Khassonké, etc.—varies from southern Mauritania to Senegal, The Gambia, Guinea-Bissau, Guinea, Mali, Côte d'Ivoire, and parts of several other countries. Throughout the region, griots fall into the general category of *nyamakala*, what Conrad and Frank define as a "major professional class of artists and other occupationally-defined specialists" (1995, p. 1) that includes blacksmiths, potters, weavers, woodcarvers, and leatherworkers.

For the Mandinka of the western Mande in the Senegambian region, the term is *jali*, with *jalimuso* for women and *jali ke* for men. The plural of *jali* is *jalolu*. *Jaliya* is the profession or activity of griots.

In the central Mande area where the Bamana and Maninka variants are spoken, primarily in Mali, the term for griot is *jeli*, with *jeliw* as plural. For woman the equivalent is *jelimuso* and *jelimusow*. The master singer, male or female, is known as *nara* or *ngara*.

Within these broad differences, one finds a variety of subgroups. For example, among the Khassonké, a Mande people on the western frontier of Mali, there were two broad categories of griots, the *laada-jalolu*, who were attached to a particular family and therefore benefited from certain privileges not available to other griots, and the *naa*, the newcomers, or itinerant griots. A chief griot was a *jali-kuntigo* (Sékéné-Mody Cissoko, 1986, pp. 160–61) or *jalikuntio* (Durán, 1996). The term *laada* and variants of it mean "privilege," and recur in related areas such as among the Soninké.

Throughout the region, there are griots associated with particular groups, though there is an important distinction between many of them and the hereditary wordsmiths who are the focus of this study. The *funé*, also spelled *fina*, handles oral arts associated with Islam (Conrad and Frank, 86), and the *donso-jeli* or *sora* serves as the griot for hunters by celebrating their exploits in the field (Cissé, 1994, pp. 64–65). These bards, however, are different from other griots, notably because they may come from any segment of society (Johnson and Sisòkò, 1986, pp. 28–29).

Soninké is related to the Mande family of languages but remains somewhat more distant than the others. For this reason the terms for griot are more distinct. One Soninké word for griot is *geseré* (pl. *geserun*), sometimes spelled *gessere*. The Soninké are split into several large subgroups, which accounts for the diversity of terms. In the case of the Kusa, their griot is called *kusatage* ("smith of the Kusa," Meillassoux, Doucouré, and Simagha, 1967). Fatoumata Siré Diakité explains that *geseré* means "griot of the Wage fraction," or subgroup. Master griot, she adds, is *fade geseré*, *fade* being a term "given to anyone who has acquired a certain notoriety in what concerns his personal activities" (1977, 11). Pollet and Winter distinguish between the *geseré*, who may know some history, and the *dyare* or, in other spellings, *jaare*, whose job it is to praise nobles to the accompaniment of music (1971, p. 217).

These differences reported by scholars who have studied the cultures of the Soninké-speaking peoples are dwarfed by the complex terminology collected by Mamadou Diawara, a Malian historian who researched the Jaara kingdom that dominated an area on the western Mali–southern Mauritania border in the fifteenth and sixteenth centuries. Diawara, who comes from this region, drew on archival sources and an extensive range of oral informants to create a highly detailed portrait of the social structure of the kingdom. Today Jaara is no more than what he describes as a modest village thirty kilometers east northeast of Nioro in Mali. From the tapestry of different kinds of wordsmiths who served the rulers of

Jaara, one can understand the importance of hierarchy and ethnic or clan origin in defining differences between griots. It is also clear from Diawara's research why he believes that the general term *griot* should be proscribed (1990, pp. 40–46).

The *laxaranto* (sing. *laxarante*), people skilled with words, include the *geseru*, the singers and musicians traditionally attached to the aristocracy of the Ghana empire and more generally serving the Soninké people, and the *jaaru* (sing. *jaare*), who carry out the same functions for people who are of Mande origin but live in the Soninké milieu. Diawara notes other differences based on whether or not the griots are linked to the nobility in an official way. The *laadan nyaxamalo*, for example, serve the court of the ruler. Within this group one finds the *laadan jaaru*, or court griots, who are linked to people of Mande origin; the *laadan geseru*, the court griots whose patrons are the Soninké; and the *mancahinlenmu*, who provide instrumental music. Diawara lists many other terms for specialized griots who appeared in society as the result of circumstances occurring four centuries ago.

The Soninké-speaking world is composed of peoples who claim descent from the Ghana empire of the eighth through the eleventh century. Given the age of the empire and the dispersion of many Soninké peoples throughout West Africa, it is not surprising that they should have so many terms for griot. As will be seen with the Songhay terms, their influence spread quite a distance from southern Mauritania over the centuries.

Songhay

On the right bank of the Niger River in western Niger, heartland of the Songhay who fled south from Gao after the fall of the empire in 1591, the term for griot is *jeseré* (pl. *jeserey*), with *jeseré-dunka* for master griot and *timmé* for descendants of master griots. *Jeseré-dunka* becomes in many cases the name of the person who exercises the profession (Olivier de Sardan, 1982, pp. 225–30). The reason for the similarity between Songhay and Soninké terms (*geseré*, *jeseré*) is that the ruler of the Songhay empire in the late fifteenth and early sixteenth centuries, Askia Mohammed Touré, was probably of Soninké origin; Touré is a Soninké clan name. When he came to power in 1493, it is likely that Soninké griots migrated to his court. This would explain why Songhay epics were maintained for centuries in Soninké, a tradition that survives in the archaic Soninké terms sprinkled throughout *The Epic of Askia Mohammed* (Hale, 1990a, 1996) that I recorded in 1980–81. The Zarma people of this region, who live primarily on the left bank of the Niger River in western Niger, speak a dialect of Songhay, but they use *nyamakaale*, the Mande term for people who are artisans (Olivier de Sardan, 1982, p. 310), perhaps because, according to their oral traditions, they migrated from Mali several centuries ago. They also use *jasaray* (Bernard and Kaba, 1994, p. 164). A third term listed by Bernard and Kaba, *nwaarayko*, points to a category of griots whose hands are always outstretched, a form of behavior that associates them with beggars (244). The word *gawle*, which appears in other societies, indicates for the Songhay the lower-class griot who seeks only to make money from his songs (Olivier de Sardan, p. 157). *Jeserétarey* is the profession of griots.

Bariba

To the south of the Songhay empire, in the northern Benin region of Borgou, an area once controlled by the Songhay and heavily influenced by their culture, Jacques Lombard (1965, pp. 203–14) categorized griots of the Bariba-speaking peoples in terms of social status, with those at the bottom called *gasira*, flute players who may praise anyone. At the same level he lists the *yereku*, popular singers. A step above them on his scale are the *kororu*, hunters' griots who sing unaccompanied by instruments. The *barabaru*, another notch higher, play the drum. Next is the *bara sunon*, a high-ranking griot who associates with chiefs, and the *gnakpe*, the personal griot of the chief. At the very top of the hierarachy of griots is the *gesere*, attached not simply to the chief but to the throne. The leader of all griots is the *Ba-Gesere*. The term reported to Moraes Farias during a decade of research in northern Benin is *geserebà* (1992, 1993a).

Fulbe

Songhay terminology, influenced by Soninké and in turn influencing peoples such as those who speak Bariba in northern Benin, bridges a considerable distance in time and space: the Ghana empire of the Soninké dates from the eighth to the eleventh centuries. Songhay, nearly 1,000 kilometers east of Ghana, did not emerge as a power until the fifteenth century, after the decline of the Mali empire. By contrast, the Fulbe, known also as the Fulani and the Peul, created a variety of kingdoms scattered across West Africa. Some lasted until the late ninteenth century. The Fulbe employ a network of terms for griot that further complicates the nomenclature. One finds words that change from one region to another, from one subgroup to another, even from one kind of activity to another.

For those of the Fouta Toro, a region inland on the left bank of the Senegal River in northern Senegal, the generic term is *gawlo* or, less often, *mabo*, but *farba* designates master griot, while the *awlube* knows the genealogy and praises for a particular family (Seydou, 1972, pp. 15–24). The *bambaado* (pl. *wambaabe*) play the *hoddar*, a lute, or the *nyaa nyooru*, a kind of violin.

Farther east, these terms take on different meanings, with the *mabo* speaking to nobles and the *gawlo* interacting with other elements of society. But Seydou, citing Gaden, suggests that *mabo* is actually a word of Mande origin (19–20).

One reason for the diversity in terms for Fulbe griots is the great spread of these people across West Africa from Senegal to northern Cameroon. In the introduction to *Status and Identity in West Africa: Nyamakalaw of Mande*, Conrad and Frank (1995) offer a fascinating discussion of the ambiguity generated by the terminology for Fulbe griots. A summary of their diverse sources will illustrate the problem.

They cite (8) one Senegalese scholar, Yaya Wane, whose 1969 study of social stratification among the Tukulor of Senegal lists *galabés* as griots who sometimes worked in leather, while another source, the French ethnographer Jean Cremer, saw them in 1923 as simply a category of people from a particular region, the Fouta Djallon. For him, the *jawambe* (sing. *jawando*) were Fulbe griots higher up the social scale but beneath the *mabow*, who are similar to the Mande *jeliw*. Conrad and Frank also cite another French anthropologist, Louis Tauxier, who classified Fulbe griots in 1927 as *bambabe* or *niémmbé*. The *tyapurtaw*, another Fulbe group, were listed by a third French scholar, Dominique Zahan, "as the lowest class of Bamana griot, and bards of the Fulbe."

The most confusing aspect of the Fulbe terms *mabow/mabubé* and *jawambe/ diawando* was the blurring of the boundary between professions, classes, and ethnicity. Citing a variety of sources from the past century, Conrad and Frank found a number of different identities attributed to *jawando*: courtiers and weavers (Delafosse), griots (Arcin and Cremer), lower-class nobles (Gaden), businessmen and go-betweens (Moreau), and traders, cattle raisers, and teachers (Tauxier). One source (Pageard) indicated that the *diawambe* were prohibited from acting as griots; another (Urvoy) described them as "a branch of a Tukulor lineage who speak Fulfulde and are fanatical Muslims" (9).

The nineteenth-century German traveler Heinrich Barth, Conrad and Frank note, listed the *jawambe* as a distinct ethnic group known as the Zoghorân who were separate at least until the sixteenth century, when they became assimilated into Fulbe society. A contemporary source, the Senegalese historian Ibrahim Bathily, sees them as an ethnic group with particular professions. He divides the *Diawando* into several groups: the *Diawandos*, the *Lahtimbés* (slaves of the *Diawando*), and the *Kida Mabos*, source of the *Mabo* griots. By matching Bathily's view with other sources, Conrad and Frank explain that much of the confusion over the professional activities of the *mabow* stems from the fact that as they were being assimilated into the vast Fulbe society, they took on a variety of social functions ranging from trade to education. Zahan, they add, found evidence for the *mabow* as bards among the Bamana, tanners and weavers among the Fulbe, and blacksmiths and bards among the Tuareg.

The terminology for Fulbe griots, then, is highly complex and fluid, shifting over time and space depending on the gaze of the classifier and the migration patterns of a people who have probably covered more territory than almost any other in West Africa. *Mabo* and *jawando* seem to be the most generally recognized terms, but it is evident from the foregoing that local context is more important than any system of classification one might attempt to invent.

Moor

In some areas, the nomenclature appears to be relatively straightforward. As Norris has explained, the Moor term is *iggiw*, sometimes spelled *iggio* (pl. *igga-wen*) (1968, p. 35). The female is the *tiggiwit* (pl. *tiggawaten*).

Mossi

According to Skinner (1989, p. 35), the Mossi of Burkina Faso employ the word *bendere* for griot, with the chief griot called *bendere naba*.

Dogon

Geneviève Calame-Griaule describes the Dogon griot as *genene* (1987, p. 487). But the relative simplicity of terminology available here may be due simply to the lack of research on this particular aspect of this society by specialists in music.

Hausa

Farther east, the Hausa-speaking peoples of northern Nigeria and western Niger designate griots by *marok'a*, with *marok'i* (masc. sing.) and *marok'iya* (fem. sing.). But these terms cover a vast and diverse collection of musicians, some of whom consider themselves to be a *marok'i*, or hereditary griot, while others do not (Besmer, 1983, pp. 40–41). In the 1960s, Ames and King studied Hausa musicians in Zaria and Katsina, two northern Nigerian emirates with very long histories and a highly stratified ruling class. They produced (1971, pp. 62–96) a list of musicians categorized by a variety of collective terms, such as *mabusa* (wind-instrument players), *magu'da* (women specializing in celebratory ululating), *maka'da* (drummers taken in the broadest sense of the term), *maka'dan Sarki* (musicians for the Emir), *marok'an baki* (professional acclamators), *marok'an hakimi* (griots in the service of a high official), *marok'an sarakuna* (those who may be in the service of any high office-holder including the Emir), and *zabiyoyi* (professional women singers).

These terms, however, serve only to designate an even longer and more diverse listing of musicians divided into more specialized categories. One can appreciate this incredible list only by placing it in the context of a broader metaphor for the subject. If *griot* represents the top and therefore most visible linguistic feature of the pyramid and the local terms such as *jeli* and *marok'i* constitute the supporting ethnic blocks that are not always evident to those unfamiliar with these wordsmiths, then the list of performers prepared by Ames and King might be viewed as an example of the deepest and most complex substratum of these performers' diverse world. Not all of those listed are still identifiable today. Ames and King attempted to distinguish between what we might call hereditary griot and nongriot musicians. But it is difficult to separate the two amid the extraordinary variety of these artisans of word and music. Ames and King classify them by five broad categories: drummers, lutenists, blowers, acclamators, and talkers.

In *Poetry, Prose, and Popular Culture in Hausa*, Graham Furniss (1996) looks at these performers from a different perspective, distinguishing between free-lance singers and those who are "tied" to certain patrons. Although he does not use the term *griot* anywhere in his study, nor focus much on the hereditary nature of the griot's art, the descriptions he offers of the many different performers and the citations from texts and interviews establish a variety of parallels with their hereditary counterparts to the west. Some of the activities of griots in the Hausa-speaking world do not match completely those in the more unified Wolof-Mande-Songhay region. But in contrast with those peoples who do not maintain griots as a distinct group, one of which will be discussed briefly below, it is clear from the research of Ames (1975) as well as that of Furniss and other scholars that the Hausa are very much part of a long tradition of hereditary musical and verbal art that extends from Senegal almost to Lake Chad.

Dagbamba

In northern Ghana, one finds an echo of the Hausa griot tradition in the Dagbamba drummers. These hereditary performers, known as *lunsi*, are professionals who perform what David Locke describes as praise drumming for chiefs as well as others in society. Their groups include instrumentalists, singers, and reciters of "epic chronicles" (1990, p. 14). They migrated around 1100 from northern Nigeria, which may explain the reason for the similarity between some of their activities and those of their counterparts in that region.

Tuareg

On the opposite side of the griot world, the Tuareg, who live in the Sahara and on the northern fringe of the Sahel, especially in northern Mali and Niger as well as southern Algeria, offer an even more distant reflection of the griot world. They do not have a separate griot tradition. But their artisans who work in metal, wood, and leather, known as *enad* (sing. *inadan*), carry out so many of the functions of griots, such as singing songs at weddings and serving as go-betweens (Rasmussen, 1997, pp. 60, 93) that they must be mentioned as somehow related to though not directly a part of the griot world. Most widely known as blacksmiths, these artisans have so many technical and social functions that this term seems somewhat limiting.

G
Theories for the Origin of the Word *Griot*

French

The most common explanation for the origin of *griot* is that it comes from French and therefore represents a colonial influence. This view is based on the fact that Saint-Lô's *guiriot* is the earliest appearance (1637) of the ancestor of the term *griot*. But French travelers suggested other origins in their own language. In 1778, Le Brasseur, a colonial administrator in West Africa, asserted in a note in a report to a French admiral that

> a *grillot* is a species of negro actor whose theatrical costume resembles that of Harlequin. He has two or three hundred rattles (*grelots*) attached to his legs and belt, and makes them move when he is on stage with a variety and a cadence that would not shock the most delicate ear. The sound of these rattles is backed up by the sound of a box that the negroes make with a piece of hollow tree and that they cover with a piece of goat skin stretched very tightly and held on the edges by pegs made of wood. The people dance to the sound of this monotonous instrument. . . . The grillots are liked and despised by people just like actors in Europe. They are not even looked upon as members of society, and they can only marry among themselves. (27)

Le Brasseur's definition is based on the similarity of two French words, *grillot* and *grelot*. The pairing of *grillot* and *grelot* offers a fascinating linguistic similarity to *griot*, but unless we can find some use of these terms prior to *guiriot* a century and a half earlier, *grillot* or *grelot* does not appear to be a likely root. La Courbe's extensive use of *guiriot* in the late seventeenth century (see LaCourbe, 1913) suggests that Saint-Lô's adoption of the term was not an isolated case. *Grillot/grelot* do not appear to be likely roots for griot.

Wolof

In the nineteenth century, Bérenger-Féraud proposed an African origin: "The name Griot, which we have frenchified, belongs to the Wolof language; in the plural it becomes Gueroual or Guewoual in the idioms of Cayor and Walo [kingdoms on the coast of Senegal between Dakar and the Senegal River]" (1882, p. 266, cited in Charry, 1992, p. 60). Bérenger-Féraud's link of *griot* with Wolof is tempting, especially because of the first *gue* and *r* sounds, but as with *grillot*, one would need to assemble more linguistic evidence to make the shift from *guewel* and its dialectical variants in Cayor and Walo to *guiriot* and *griot*.

Fulbe

More recently, theories for sources in other sub-Saharan African languages have emerged. The Nigérien scholar Oumarou Watta suggested in his 1985 thesis on African epic that *griot* comes from a Fulbe term, *gawlo*. He proposed that *griot* is "a French rendering of a cluster of conceptual referents" rooted in the sound of *g* and a few other consonants (86). He may be right, but much more evidence is needed to confirm such a vague link.

Mande

The American linguist Charles Bird has suggested that *griot* comes from an early form of the Mande term for griot.

> "Griot" is a Frenchified African word. In the earliest references that I have found in French texts, the word is spelled "gueriau" or "guirot(e)." One does not have to go too far to see that *jeli* and *griot* are in fact derived from the same source. Velar consonants such as k and g palatalize in Bambara, so the original form geeli becomes jeeli. Similarly, in many dialects l after a long high vowel becomes r. *Geli* would thus become *geri*. (In northern and eastern dialects of Mandekan, one does in fact find these forms.) Lastly, all the dialects of Mandekan once had a definite article suffix, the form of which was -o. This suffix was always present in citation forms. Thus the early French explorers most likely heard a word something like *gerio*. (1971, p. 16)

The American historian David Conrad contests Bird's view by arguing that during the earliest period of French presence in Africa, there was relatively little contact with the Mande-speakers farther inland who use the term *jeli* (1981, pp. 8–9). He also cites numerous examples of usages by Europeans that were very close to local terminology.

Portuguese

For many researchers, Portuguese seemed to be a far more likely source of *griot* than African languages. Henri Labouret argued that

> griot does not seem to be borrowed from the local languages of West Africa, nor to derive from any of them. . . . One can only ask if this expression . . . comes from Negro-Portuguese. It would derive in this case from the verb *criar*: "to nurse, to nourish," by extension to "educate, to raise, to instruct," from which one can take *criador*, "nurse, patron"; *criado*, "who has been nourished, raised, educated, who lives in the house of the master"; and thus in a broader sense "domestic, dependent client, preferred client."

Labouret explains the transformation from *criado* to *griot* thus:

The transformation of the initial c into g is explained without difficulty, the two velar plosives being close and interchangeable. . . . The doubling of a syllable of the consonant-consonant-vowel type, and its passage to the consonant-vowel type is frequent in Negro-African, especially if it is a matter of borrowing from foreign languages. (1951, pp. 56–57)

Labouret's theory has some basis in the fact that the Portuguese arrived in West Africa long before the French, and Portuguese was spoken along the coast from Senegal southward for some distance. Another aspect of Labouret's hypothesis finds support in griot-patron relations: the griot is traditionally housed and provided for by his or her patron. But Sory Camara, in his summary of the discussion on the origin of the word *griot*, finds the reference to "Negro-African" in Labouret's definition too vague to be of any use. "Can we speak of Negro-African the way we speak of English?" he rightly asks (1976, p. 100).

Other possibilities in Portuguese appear to be more promising. For example, Saint-Lô and other travelers to the coast of West Africa emphasized the noise that these performers made. There is an obvious link between noise and a Portuguese family of words based on the verb *gritar*, "to shout." It includes *grito*, "a shout," *gritalhao*, "a person who shouts a lot," or *gritador*, "a person or place that is the source of much shouting or *gritaria* (many shouts at once)." On the basis of the similarity of the first three letters plus some sound shifts, one could build a case for *gritar* as the origin. Tempting as this theory may seem, it raises a perplexing question: if *gritar* is the source of griot, why would the French adopt a variant of that particular term from Portuguese and not *judeu*, the word used by Portuguese and Portuguese creole-speakers for five centuries in West Africa?

Judeu, Jew in Portuguese, predates by 130 years the 1637 use of *guiriot* by Saint-Lô. It is still employed in Guinea-Bissau in both standard Portuguese and in Portuguese creole, where it has become *jidiu* or *djidiu*. *Judeu/jidiu* could have evolved into the early French term *guiriot* by the beginning of the seventeenth century. From Fernandes in 1506 to Saint-Lô in 1637 is time enough for much linguistic change. The shift could well have occurred in Portuguese by mid-sixteenth century. When the French arrived in the early seventeenth century, *jidiu* could have shifted easily to *guiriot* as the process of communication between Portuguese creole-speaking Africans and French travelers developed. Fiona McLaughlin, an American linguist who has studied the languages of the region, suggested to me (1992) that the shift from the *j*, an alveo palatal stop, to *g*, a velar stop in the initial syllable, and the shift from *d* to *r* in the midsyllable, are quite common. She adds that there is no *g* plus *r* sound in Wolof, which would explain the early use of the term *guiriot* which later became *griot* in French.

Spanish

Spanish contacts predate the invasion of Spain in 711 by Arab and Berber armies. Throughout the Middle Ages, Africans came to Spain via several routes:

trade across the Sahara and the Mediterranean through Gilbraltar and other ports, direct importation by slavers who landed along the west and northwest coast, especially during the fifteenth and sixteenth centuries, and by way of the Canary Islands, which served as a transfer site between the two continents.

Africans were so well known in southern Spain in the sixteenth century that they appear often not only in the literature of the time but also in other cultural activities they brought with them. Their influence is evident in a variety of vocabulary, including the *guirigay*, a dance popular in Seville in the sixteenth century (Ortiz, 1924, p. 246). Researchers know little about the dance, but *guirigay*, a term whose first five letters match exactly the first five letters of the early French *guiriot*, entered Spanish from this time as meaning something else: "obscure language, language that is difficult to understand." Given the extent of Spanish contact with the Guinea coast from the late fifteenth to the late sixteenth century, it is quite possible that Spanish travelers invented this term to portray what they saw as the unintelligible song and bizarre dance of griots. It would then have been applied to the African-inspired dance in Seville.

Guirigaray appears in Spanish in a variety of forms (*guirigall* or *guirigai*, *guiriguirigay*) and is listed as an onomatopoeic word for "confused speech, obscure speech, speech difficult to understand." The echoes in Catalan are *guirolar* and *girgola*. The word for griot today in Spanish, *guiriote*, may well have been inspired either by the seventeenth-century French term *guiriot* or may have developed from *guirigaray*. To confirm a connection between *guirigaray* and *guiriot*, however, one would need to do considerable historical linguistic research in Spanish archives from the period.

Berber

Between West Africa and Europe, the Berber-speaking region marked by later Arabic influences constitutes a large zone of cultural diffusion spreading to neighboring peoples on both sides. The French Africanist Vincent Monteil suggested that *griot* was, in fact, of African origin, specifically Berber, and came from the Hassaniya Arabic dialect spoken in northwest Africa: "The griot is called *iggio*, or *iggiw* or *iggow*. . . . This word is Berber. Our French word griot would come then directly from *iggio* with a floating r—as the old form of griot shows, *guiriot*" (1968, p. 778).

If Monteil is correct, one would have to ask what the link is between Berber and sub-Saharan African languages. Did griots come from Mauritania or from farther south? H. T. Norris rejected Monteil's view of the origin of *iggiw* by arguing for a sub-Saharan origin of the Berber term:

> It is almost certain that a musician class, Soninké influenced, existed in Mauritania prior to the Hassānī invasion. The word īggīw (pl. īggāwen) is derived from Sudanic languages, but it also bears a Znāga stamp. As a musician class is endemic in Sudanic societies, and is absent from other Saharan communities, it is reasonable to assume that these people were an element in Southern Mauritania (Takrūr), and perhaps in the

Hawd. Both districts were at times subject to the Mali and Songhai monarchies. (1968, pp. 35–36)

Norris explains that the borrowing comes from "communities across the [Senegal] river. It is *gêwel* in Wolof and *gawlo* in Toucouleur." The Znaga stamp to which he refers stems from its feminine form, *tiggiwit* (pl. *tiggawaten*) (53).

Norris's view finds support in the research of Michel Guignard on the music of Moors. In *Musique, Honneur et Plaisir au Sahara* (1975), he reports that the Moors, in particular their musicians, trace at least part of their musical tradition to black Africans. In the Arab-Berber world, he explains, there are no performers who fulfill the many roles of the griot, although one does find musicians, singers, and poets, as well as people who do all of these activities. The same kinds of performers are found in Moor society, but they are distinct from the *iggawen*, who are the only ones who play the lute and carry out "the psychological and social functions" that set them apart from other musicians. Guignard suggests that the griots may have come from the south, adding that this hypothesis matches the belief of many Moors who trace the genealogies of their musicians either to black Africans or to Arabs. Black influence on Moor music is very ancient and, Guignard notes, continues today (178–79).

Arabic

Whatever the origin of *iggio*, North African or sub-Saharan West African, the link between the two regions is clear. One theory elaborated by the American ethnomusicologist Eric Charry suggests much earlier origins for *griot* in Arabic. He has proposed that it comes from the term *qawal*, or singer, via the Wolof *guewel*.

Charry sees a similarity between *qawal*, *griot* and *iggiw* (Hassaniya Arabic), *gewel* (Wolof), and *gaulo* (Fulbe): "The Arabic root q-w-l essentially concerns speech. Some of the definitions [of *qawal*] given in dictionaries of medieval Arabic are virtual job descriptions of griots" (68).

Charry quotes Lane's *Arabic-English Lexicon* (1956, supplement, 2995): "he spoke in verse . . . poeticized . . . good in speech . . . loquacious . . . copious in speech . . . eloquent . . . the man who talks too much." Charry also cites Dozy's *Supplément au dictionnaire arabe* (1881): "Man of the spoken word . . . singer . . . traveling poet . . . improviser . . . to recite verse that one has composed oneself" (Dozy, 1967 reprint, vol. 2, pp. 420–21). He explains that

> the use of the term *qawal* to refer to musicians is not unknown in the Moslem world. In Pakistan and India *qawwali* is a major musical genre associated with Sufism that is performed by professional musicians, known as *qawwals*, who are organized into endogamous patrilineal communities. (68, citing Qureshi, 1986, pp. xiii, 96–98)

Charry then proposes a set of sound changes that might account for the relationship between *qawal* and various West African languages. Reading Table 1 from top to bottom, one follows the hypothetical changes (69).

Table 1

Mande	Soninké	Wolof	Fula	Hassaniya
qawal	qawal	qawal	qawal	qawal
jawal	jawal	gawal	gawal	igawal
ja al	ja al	gewel	gaw l	igiw l
jaali	jaale		gawlo	igiw
	jaare			

Charry's tying of *qawal* to *gewel/gawlo/iggiw* is very convincing. The final link in his theory, however, is based on the relationship between *gewel* and *griot* proposed by Bérenger-Féraud a century ago. That relationship is much less persuasive than the *qawal/gewel* etymology. Charry's tantalizing hypothesis represents one of the best examples of historical linguistic research carried out on any aspect of griot-related etymology, but more research is needed.

Hale's Theory

My own theory—and it is in many ways no better than the others cited so far— takes the question of the origin of *griot* back as far as the Ghana empire by way of the slave trade through Spanish to Berber. Such a long itinerary, seven centuries old, requires a rather lengthy explanation, one which may interest researchers more than the generalist reader. But the explanation is crucial to my belief that *griot* originates not in Europe but in Africa and that the term griot deserves to be maintained today. The theory depends on two elements: a reinterpretation of the origin of the word *guinea*, which today is used to name several African countries and geographical features, and a sound shift in a variant of that term, *guineo*, that may have produced *guiriot*.

Edward Bovill (1958, 1995) provides the point of departure for this theory by arguing that *guinea* comes from Berber. In a long note in his study on the fourteenth-century kingdoms of the Moors, he states:

> The name Guinea is usually said to have been a corrupt form of the name Ghana, picked up by the Portuguese in the Maghrib. The present writer finds this unacceptable. The name Guinea has been in use both in the Maghrib and in Europe long before Prince Henry's time. For example, on a map dated about 1320 by the Genoese cartographer Giovanni di Carignano, who got his information about Africa from a fellow-countryman in Sijilmas [ancient trading city in North Africa], we find Gunuia, and in the Catalan atlas of 1375 as Ginyia. A passage in Leo [Africanus] (vol. III, 822) points to Guinea having been a corrupt form of Jenne [2,000-year-old city in central Mali on the Niger River], less famous than Ghana but neverthless for many centuries famed in the Maghrib as a great market and a seat of learning. The relevant passage reads: "The Kingdom of Ghinea . . . called by the merchants of our nation Gheneoa, by the natural inhabitants thereof Genni and by the Portugals and other people of Europe Ghinea." But it seems more probable that Guinea derives from *aguinaou*, the Berber for Negro. Marrakech [city in southern Morocco] has a gate, built in the twelfth century, called the Bab Aguinaou, the Gate of the Negro (Delafosse, *Haut-Sénégal-Niger*, II, 277–278).

The modern application of the name Guinea to the coast dates only from 1481. In that year the Portuguese built a fort, São de Mina (the Elmina of today) on the Gold Coast, and their king, John II, was permitted by the Pope to style himself Lord of Guinea, a title which survived until the recent extinction of the monarchy. (116)

Bovill's theory provides the link between Africa and Europe. The people who came from Guinea were called *guineos* in Spanish. In fact, during the sixteenth century, a period when Spain and its dependencies, especially the Canary Islands, had continuous contact with West Africa, the term *guineo* referred both to people from West Africa and to a dance in southern Spain that was inspired by Africans.

Agenaou, the current spelling for *aguinaou,* the Berber root proposed by Bovill for *guinea,* is close enough to *iggio* and *iggiw* to support the hypothesis that *griot* is of African, not European origin. Evidence from recent archaeological work in Mali, as well as studies of music in Morocco, supports the notion that the term came from south of the Sahara. That evidence requires a brief but key digression into the history of relations between North and sub-Saharan Africa.

Until relatively recently, scholars assumed that the cities of the Sahel were the product of trade between North Africa and the empires of the region during the Middle Ages. From the work of archaeologists, especially that of the Americans Roderick and Susan McIntosh in Mali in the late 1970s and early 1980s (1981, pp. 1–22) at the site of ancient Jenné, known as Jenné-Jeno, it appears now that at least one of the Sahelian cities has existed for over 2,000 years. Jenné-Jeno was founded in 250 B.C.E., and by 400–800 C.E. was a major trading center in the inland delta of the Niger River, upstream from Bamako, the modern capital of Mali. Jenné was a large city for its time. Archaeological evidence shows that Jenné-Jeno was surrounded by a two-kilometer walled perimeter. Traders there dealt in gold imported from sources 800 kilometers to the south; the gold was then exported along with other products—food, ivory, and slaves—northward by caravan and northeastward on the Niger River. As indicated by Bovill, it was not until the early fourteenth century that Jenné began to appear on European maps.

This trade expanded considerably in the eighth century with the introduction of the camel. The slaves and gold were particularly important for the dynasties that controlled North Africa and part of Spain during this period: the Almoravides from 1071 to 1147, the Almohads from 1147 to 1248. The slaves were especially valuable because of their use as both soldiers in the armies of the sultans and laborers for the building of cities and fortresses. One city in particular, Marrakesh in southeastern Morocco, assumed a dominant role as a major gateway to trade in sub-Saharan Africa and a powerful political center in the region. Youssef ben Tachfine, appointed by the Almoravid leader Abu Bekr in 1071 to command Marrakesh, assumed control there and began to build mosques and barracks for an army of 2,000 black slaves. It is not surprising that the importance of trade with sub-Saharan Africa and the presence of so many black Africans should prompt Sultan el Mansour, a later Almohad ruler, to order the Bab Agenaou, or Gate of Black Africans, to be built in 1185. It was the entrance through which flowed the slaves, gold, and other products from sub-Saharan Africa to the Kasbah, that part of the city containing the headquarters—palaces, mosques, and military barracks—of the vast Almohad empire. From that time on, the black African presence in Marrakesh has grown. The flow of slaves increased considerably after the Moroccan conquest of the Songhay empire in 1591, and by the time of Sultan Mouley Ishmael a century later (1672–1727), the regime depended upon not only Arab and Berber forces but to a much greater extent on what was viewed as a more reliable 150,000-man army of black Africans. Slaves continued to be bought and sold in Marrakesh until the early twentieth century.

The *agenaou*—the people from "Ghana" or black Africa—who passed through that gate to serve as soldiers, laborers, and servants were accompanied not only by gold and ivory but also by their living traditions, and they suffered less cultural loss in Morocco than other Africans during the later Atlantic slave trade. Evidence from the musical tradition of people of sub-Saharan African origin in Morocco supports the belief that the term *agenaou* comes from Ghana, the empire that was the source of much trade, especially in slaves, with Morocco. Any visitor to Marrakesh today quickly encounters a living remnant of the cultures of these slaves in a group of musicians known as *gnawa*.

The *gnawa* are not griots. But in both their own collective memory and in that of the people of Morocco, they are of sub-Saharan African origin. Their presence in Morocco probably precedes the sixteenth-century date most often given for the creation of the *gnawa*, but with the Moroccan conquest of Songhay in 1591, the flow of slaves across the desert increased dramatically and probably contributed greatly to the growth of what Viviana Pâques terms the "brotherhood of the slaves" in her monumental study of these performers (1991).

Gnawa musicians represent a blending of both the musical art of the griot (and other kinds of musicians) and the healing rituals of sub-Saharan Africa. Philip Schuyler (1981) describes them as a religious brotherhood that "claims spiritual descent from Bilal al Habashi, an Ethiopian who was the Prophet Mohammed's first muezzin," but adds that "most aspects of *Gnawa* ritual, however, clearly come from South of the Sahara" (5). Their ceremonies focus on placating spirits that may have brought illness or other problems or "to prolong a happy relationship with a spirit that has brought wealth, clairvoyance, or other blessings." They play a three-stringed instrument called the *gambere*, in some ways similar to the lutes common in Senegal, Mali, and Niger, as well as drums and metal castanets. They are best known for the lengthy and complex *derdeba* ceremony that leads to trances, spirit possession, dancing, and pantomime. Music and trance are not limited to sub-Saharan Africa; possession dance as part of the healing process has been practiced for many centuries in West Africa, especially among the Songhay, as documented by Paul Stoller in numerous studies of this people.

The music of the *gnawa* refers to languages and places in sub-Saharan Africa and often includes words that the singers do not understand today. The link between them and sub-Saharan Africa has therefore survived but in a syncretic form that contains traces of many cultural activites tied to blacksmiths, griots, and sorcerers. The *gnawa* I interviewed and saw performing in October 1992 in Marrakesh were clearly different from griots. Yet the sounds and rhythms of their music echoed much of what one can hear today on the other side of the Sahara. The *gnawa*, then, are the cultural descendants of the *agenaou* who migrated through slavery and trade to North Africa. Their survival today suggests that *agenaou* is not simply a Berber term for black African, but a descriptor that represents a significant and ancient link between North and West African cultures. *Agenaou*, so deeply embedded in the intertwined cultures of the North and West African regions, was most likely a step in the process of linguistic change that began with *Ghana* and went on to the people brought from that land, the *agenaou*, who became the *guineo* in Spanish, and, I believe, *guiriot* in French to designate the first Africans that French sailors encountered.

Two questions remain. What was the origin of *Ghana*, the name attributed to an empire that was also widely known as Wagadu, and how did *guineo* become *guiriot*? There is no clear answer to the first, though it is quite likely that Ghana, the name given by Arabs for the kingdom that was a great source of gold a millennium ago, was also the capital of the empire known by the Soninké as Wagadu. Today the ruins of a town called Ghanata exist ten kilometers north of Kumbi-Saleh, the name of the capital of the Soninké empire according to their oral traditions (Levtzion, 1980, p. 25). The origin of the term *Ghana* remains unclear, though it has served for the past 1,000 years as the word to designate the first great empire of the Sahel (Monteil, 1951b).

As for the second question, the answer is simpler but more speculative. I believe that *guiriot* resulted from contact with Portuguese, Spanish, or Arab navigators and seamen who knew the northwest coast of Africa. At the time the French began to explore the region, North and West Africa were marked by a complex cultural blend. In addition to people of diverse Berber, Arab, and sub-Saharan African origin, one could find Jews from both sides of the Mediterranean, Spaniards, Portuguese, and other Europeans. Some were slaves, while others were traders or professionals in other fields. For example, a Spanish soldier known as Pasha Judar commanded the Moroccan army that invaded the Songhay empire in 1591. His 3,000-man force was a mixture of adventurers from the entire region as well as Berber troops provided by the Sultan.

In the same way, it is highly probable that when crews were assembled by the French to sail south to what was for them the relatively unknown coast of North and West Africa, those in command made a point to include at least some experienced sailors and navigators who knew the region—most likely old hands from neighboring Spain who had lived in North Africa. When a French captain encountered a local ruler on the West African coast, the person who made the most noise and who walked before the ruler to announce him and praise him was always a griot. If a captain asked who was the man making such a racket, the response of those in the crew who had visited the coast before may well have been a condescending "he is just another *guineo.*" It is probable that in this way race became profession: the *guineo* became a *guiriot* through a slight but quite normal linguistic change — *n* to *r*.

The theory for the origin of *griot* that I propose is based on a series of plausibilities and probabilities that appear to me to add up to a more convincing hypothesis than any other suggested so far. But further research is needed to confirm the argument that *guineo* is the last link to *guiriot.* Evidence for this hypothesis, if it exists, is likely to emerge from unpublished logs of French ships of the early seventeenth century.

✳ Selected Bibliography ✳

Africanus, Leo. 1550. *The History and Description of Africa and the Notable Things Therein Contained.* English edition, 1660. Cited in Basil Davidson, ed., *The African Past*, p. 90. Boston: Little, Brown, 1964.

Al-Bakri, Abu Ubayd 'Abd Allah b. 'Abd al-'Aziz. 1911. *Kitab al-masālik wa-'l-mamālik.* Ed. Baron MacGuckin de Slane. *Description de l'Afrique septentrionale.* Algiers.

Alhassane, Sidi Ahmed Ag. 1992. Interview with the author, Bamako, Mali, February 10.

Al-Idrīssī. 1154. *Nuzhat al-mushtāq fī ikhtirāq al-āfāq.* In French as *Description de l'Afrique et de l'Espagne par Edrîsî*, ed. R. Dozy and M. J. De Goeje, Leiden, 1866. Excerpted in Levtzion and Hopkins (1981), pp. 104–31.

Alquier, Prosper. 1922. Report published in *Bulletin du Comité d'Etudes Historique et Scientifique de l'Afrique Occidentale Française*, vol. 2 (April-June), 277–320.

Al 'Umāri. 1337–38. *Masālik al absār fī mamālik al-amsar* (Pathways of vision in the realms of the metropolises). Excerpted in Levtzion and Hopkins (1981), pp. 252–78.

Alvares d'Almada, André. 1946. *Tratado Breve dos Rios de Guiné do Cabo-Verde.* Lisbon: Silveira, 1946.

Alvares, Manuel. 1616. "Etiopia Menor," unpublished manuscript, Biblioteca Sociedad de Geografia, Lisbon. Typescript established by P. E. H. Hair and Avelino Teixeira da Mota. Excerpt supplied to the author by John Thornton.

Ames, David W. 1973. "A Sociocultural View of Hausa Musical Activity." In Warren L. d'Azevedo, ed., *The Traditional Artist in African Societies*, pp. 128–61. Bloomington: Indiana University Press.

———, and Anthony V. King. 1971. *Glossary of Hausa Music and Its Social Contexts.* Evanston: Northwestern University Press.

Anderson, Ian. 1986. "The Original Journalist." *Folk Roots*, December 1986, 11, 41.

Andrews, William L., Frances Smith Foster, and Trudier Harris. 1997. *The Oxford Companion to African American Literature*. New York: Oxford University Press.

Anonymous. 1889. "Chronique de l'Exposition: L'Exposition coloniale." *Le Temps*, May 1, p. 2.

———. 1944. "Chronique de Oualo." *Sénégal Magazine*, vol. 60, pp. 23–27.

———. 1975. *Premier colloque international de Bamako, 27 janvier–1er février, 1975. Actes du Colloque. Histoire et Tradition Orale. Première année: L'Empire du Mali*. Paris: SCOA, 1975.

———. 1976. *Deuxième Colloque International de Bamako, 16 février–22 février, 1976. Actes du Colloque. Histoire et Tradition Orale. Projet Boucle du Niger. 2e année: L'Empire du Mali, l'empire du Ghana, l'empire du Songay*. Paris: SCOA, 1977.

———. 1977a. "Why *Roots* Hit Home." *Time*, February 14, pp. 68–71.

———. 1977b. *Troisième colloque international de l'Association SCOA, Niamey, 30 novembre–6 décembre, 1977. Actes du Colloque. Histoire et Tradition Orale. Projet Boucle du Niger. Troisième année: L'Empire du Mali, l'empire du Ghana, l'empire du Songhay*. Paris: SCOA, 1977.

———. 1984. "The Day Ndaga Came to Sweden." *The Gambia News-Letter*, June 1984, pp. 2–4.

———. 1984b. *Premier séminaire international de l'Association SCOA: Niamey, 14–21 janvier 1981. Actes du Séminaire. Rapport du Moyen Niger avec le Ghana Ancien*. Paris: SCOA, 1984.

———. 1992a. "Vexatious Vocabulary." *Time*, October 19, p. 13.

———. 1992b. "N'Dour Endures." *Time*, May 4, p. 83.

———. 1994. "La Semaine de la poésie dédiée à Glissant." *France-Antilles*, May 9.

———. 1997. "Businessman Pays for Band's Trip to Parade." *Centre Daily Times*, March 12.

Applebaum, Stuart. 1997. Personal communication, October 5.

Arcin, André. 1907. *La Guinée française*. Paris: Challamel.

Arnoldi, Mary Jo. 1995. *Playing with Time: Art and Performance in Central Mali*. Bloomington: Indiana University Press.

Arnston, Laura (listed originally as Laura Arnston Harris). 1992a. "The Play of Ambiguity in Praise-Song Performance: A Definition of the Genre Through an Examination of Its Practice in Northern Sierra Leone." Ph.D. diss., Indiana University.

———. 1992b. Interview with the author, Boston, November 23, 1992.

———. 1998. "Praise Singing in Northern Sierra Leone." In *Africa: The Garland Encyclopedia of World Music*. Ed. Ruth Stone. New York.

Austen, Ralph. 1999. *In Search of Sunjata: The Mande Oral Epic as History, Literature, and Performance*. Bloomington: Indiana University Press.

Bâ, Mariama. 1980. *Une si longue lettre*. Dakar: Nouvelles Editions Africaines. In English as *So Long a Letter*, trans. Modupé Bodé-Thomas. London: Heinemann, 1981.

———. 1981. *Un chant écarlate*. Dakar: Nouvelles Editions Africaines. In English as *Scarlet Song*, trans. Dorothy S. Blair. London: Longman, 1986.

Bâ, Tapo. 1992. Interview with the author, Bamako, Mali, February 21.

Ba Konaré, Adame. 1993. *Dictionnaire des femmes célèbres du Mali*. Bamako: Jamana.

Bachy, Victor, ed. 1989. *Tradition orale et nouveaux medias*. Bruxelles: Organisation Catholique Internationale du Cinéma et de l'Audiovisuel and Festival Panafricain du Cinéma de Ouagadougou.

Badié, Djeliba Djibo. 1980. Interview with the author, Niamey, Niger, November 24.

———. 1984. Cited in *Rapport du moyen Niger avec le Ghana ancien: Actes du séminaire international de l'Association SCOA, Niamey, January 14–21, 1981*, p. 13. Paris: Association SCOA.

Bagna, Garba. 1980. Interview with the author, Liboré, Niger, October 10.

Bailleul, Charles. 1981. *Petit Dictionnaire Bambara-Français Français-Bambara*. Amersham, England: Avebury.

Baraka, Amiri. 1995. *Wise Why's Y's: The Griot's Song: Djeli Ya*. Chicago: Third World Press.

Barber, Karin. 1990. *I Could Speak until Tomorrow: Oriki, Women, and the Past in a Yoruba Town*. Washington, D.C.: Smithsonian Institution Press.

Barbot, John. 1792. *A Description of the Coasts of North and South-Guinea, and of Ethiopia Inferior*. Paris.

Barlow, William. 1989. *"Looking Up at Down": The Emergence of Blues Culture*. Philadelphia: Temple University Press.

Barry, Boubacar. 1985. *Le Royaume du Waalo: Le Sénégal avant la conquête*. 2d ed. Paris: Karthala.

Barth, Heinrich. 1965. *Travels and Discoveries in North and Central Africa in the Years 1849–1855*. New York: Harper.

Bassett, Thomas. 1991. Conversation with the author, Archives d'Outre-Mer, Aix-en-Provence, France, June 27.

Bathily, Ibrahim. 1936. "Les Diawandos ou Diogoramés: Traditions orales receuillies à Djenné, Corientze, Ségou et Nioro." *Education Africaine*, vol. 25, pp. 173–93.

———, and Claude Meillassoux. 1976. *Lexique Soninké (Sarakolé)-Français*. Dakar: Centre de Linguistique Appliquée de Dakar.

Batoutah, Ibn. 1854. *Voyages d'Ibn Batoutah*. Ed. C. Defrémery and B. R. Sanguinetti. Paris.

Bazin, Jean. 1985. "A chacun son Bambara." In Jean-Loup Amselle and Elikia M'Bokolo, eds., *Au coeur de l'ethnie: Ethnie, tribalisme, et état en Afrique*, pp. 87–127. Paris: La Découverte.

Bebey, Francis. 1975. *African Music: A People's Art*. Westport: Lawrence Hill, trans. Josephine Bennett, 1975.

Belcher, Stephen. 1997. Personal communication.

——. 1999. *Epic Traditions of Africa*. Bloomington: Indiana University Press.

Bender, Wolfgang. 1991. *Sweet Mother: Modern African Music*. Chicago: University of Chicago Press.

Bérenger-Féraud, L. J. B. 1882. "Etude sur les griots des peuplades de la Sénégambie." *Revue d'Anthropologie*, vol. 50, pp. 266–79.

Bernard, Yves, and Mary White-Kaba. 1994. *Dictionnaire Zarma-Français (République du Niger)*. Paris: Agence de Coopération Culturelle et Technique.

Besmer, Fremont E. 1983. *Horses, Musicians, and Gods: The Hausa Cult of Possession-Trance*. Zaria: Ahmadu Bello University Press.

Bird, Charles S. 1971. "Oral Art in the Mande." In Carleton T. Hodge, *Papers on the Manding*, pp. 15–23. Research Center for the Language Sciences, Indiana University, Bloomington.

——. 1977. Review of *Sunjata: Three Mandinka Versions* by Gordon Innes. *Research in African Literatures*, vol. 9, no. 3, pp. 352–69.

——. 1978. Lecture at The Pennsylvania State University, December 6.

——. 1988. Interview with the author, Bloomington, Indiana, November 17.

——. 1992. Interview with the author, Evanston, Illinois, November 15.

——. 1997. "The Epic of Sara. Narrated by Sira Mori Jabaté." Trans. and transcription by Charles Bird and Kassim Koné. In Johnson, Hale, and Belcher (1997), pp. 114–23.

——, and Martha B. Kendall. 1980. "The Mande Hero: Text and Context." In Ivan Karp and Charles Bird, eds., *Explorations in African Systems of Thought*, pp. 13–26. Bloomington: Indiana University Press.

——, and Martha B. Kendall. 1988. Interview with the author, Bloomington, Indiana, November 16.

Bisilliat, Jeanne, and Diouldé Laya. 1972. *Les Zamu ou poèmes sur les noms*. Niamey: Centre Nigérien de Recherche en Sciences Humaines.

Boilat, David. 1853. *Esquisses sénégalaises*. Paris: Bertrand.

Bourgault, Louise M. 1995. *Mass Media in Sub-Saharan Africa*. Bloomington: Indiana University Press.

Bovill, Edward William. 1958. *The Golden Trade of the Moors: West African Kingdoms in the Fourteenth Century*. Oxford: Oxford University Press; 2d ed. Princeton: Wiener, 1995.

Bowles, Brett, and Thomas A. Hale. 1996. "Piloting through Turbulence: Griots, Islam, and the French Encounter in Four Epics about 19th Century West African Heroes." In Kenneth Harrow, ed., *The Marabout and the Muse: New Approaches to Islam in African Literature*, pp. 77–91. Portsmouth: Heinemann.

Brenner, Louis. 1973. *The Shehus of Kukawa*. Oxford: Clarendon Press.

Brévié, Jules. 1935. "Documents et recherches historiques en A.O.F. (circulaire numéro 175 du 2 mai 1935 de M. le Gouverneur-Général Brévié)." *L'Education en Afrique*, vols. 90–91 (April-September 1935), pp. 131–33.

Brisson, M. de. 1984. *Histoire du naufrage et de la captivité de Monsieur de Brisson en 1785*. Ed. Attilio Gaudio. Paris: Nouvelles Editions Latines.

Broughton, Simon, Mark Ellingham, David Muddyman, and Richard Trillo. 1994. *World Music: The Rough Guide*. London: Rough Guides.

Caillié, René. 1830. *Journal d'un voyage à Tombouctou et à Jenné, précédé d'observations faites chez les Maures, Braknas, les Nalous et autres peuples, pendants les années 1824, 1825, 1826, 1827, 1828*. 2 vols. Paris: Imprimerie Royale; reprint, La Découverte, 1989.

Calame-Griaule, Geneviève. 1987. *Ethnologie et langage: La parole chez les Dogon*. Paris: Institut d'Ethnologie.

Camara, Dansy. 1967. "L'Ecole des Arts: Un établissement polytechnique d'education artistique." *Sénégal*, no. 1, January, pp. 31–37.

Camara, Pathé. 1991. Interview with the author, Dakar, Senegal, October 9.

Camara, Seydou. 1990. "La tradition orale en question: conservation et transmission des traditions historiques au Manden: Le centre de Kéla et l'histoire de Mininjan." Doctoral diss., Ecole des Hautes Etudes en Sciences Sociales, Université de Paris.

Camara, Sory. 1976. *Gens de la parole: Essai sur la condition et le rôle des griots dans la société malinké*. Paris: Mouton.

Capaccio, George. 1993. "The Griots of Roxbury." *Peacework*, October, pp. 8–9.

Carreira, Antonio. 1964. "Aspectos da influência da cultura portuguesa na área compreendida entre o rio Senegal e o norte de Serra Leoa." *Boletim Cultural da Guiné Portuguesa*, October, pp. 373–416.

Césaire, Aimé. 1960. In "Aimé Césaire et les nègres sauvages," interview with Jeanine Cahen. *Afrique action*, November 21, p. 23.

Charry, Eric. 1992. "Musical Thought, History, and Practice among the Mande of West Africa." Ph.D. diss., Princeton University. Forthcoming as *Mande Music*, University of Chicago Press, 1999.

——. 1993a. Interview with the author, Boston, October 5.

——. 1993b. "When a Griot Modernizes: A View from the Recording Studio." Paper presented at the African Studies Association meeting, Boston, October 6.

——. 1994a. Conversation with the author, February 7.

——. 1994b. "The Grand Mande Guitar Tradition of the Western Sahel and Savannah." *The World of Music*, vol. 36, no. 2, pp. 21–61.

——. 1996a. "A Guide to the Jembe." *Percussive Notes*, vol. 34, no. 2, April, pp. 66–73.

——. 1996b. "Plucked Lutes in West Africa: An Historical Overview." *Galpin Society Journal*, March, pp. 3–37.

——. 1996c. Personal communication, July 25.

Charters, Sam. 1981. *The Roots of the Blues: An African Search*. New York: Putnam.

Chernoff, Joel Miller. 1979. *African Rhythm and African Sensibility*. Chicago: University of Chicago Press.

Chester, Galina, and Tunde Jegede. 1987. *The Silenced Voice: Hidden Music of the Kora*. London: Diabaté Kora Arts.

Chilson, Peter. 1994. "The Fickle God: Stories from the African Road." Master's thesis, The Pennsylvania State University.

Chinosole. 1995. "Maryse Condé as Contemporary Griot in *Segu.*" *Callaloo*, vol. 18, no. 3, pp. 593–601.

Chouraqui, André. 1985. *Histoire des Juifs en Afrique du Nord*. Paris: Hachette.

Cimbala, Paul A. 1995. "Black Musicians from Slavery to Freedom: An Exploration of an African-American Folk Elite and Cultural Continuity in the Nineteenth-Century Rural South." *Journal of Negro History*, vol. 80, no. 1, Winter, pp. 15–29.

Cissé, Diango. 1970. *Structures des Malinké de Kita*. Bamako: Editions Populaires.

Cissé, Youssouf Tata. 1994. *La Confrérie des chasseurs malinké et bambara: Mythes, rites et récits initiatiques*. Ivry: Nouvelles du Sud.

———, and Wâ Kamissoko. 1988. *La Grande geste du Mali, des origines à la fondation de l'Empire*. Paris: Karthala and Association pour la Promotion de la Recherche Scientifique en Afrique Noire.

Cissoko, Baba. 1991. Interview with the author, Bamako, Mali, February 7.

Cissoko, Sékéné-Mody. 1986. *Contribution à l'histoire politique du Khasso dans le Haut-Sénégal des origines à 1854*. Paris: Harmattan.

Cissoko, Tiémoko (known as Soundioulou). 1991. Interview with the author, Dakar, Senegal, October 14.

Colin, Roland. 1957. *Les Contes noirs de l'Ouest Africain: Témoins majeurs d'un humanisme*. Paris: Présence Africaine.

Collins, John. *West African Pop Roots*. Philadelphia: Temple University Press, 1992.

Conrad, David C. 1981. "The Role of Oral Artists in the History of Mali." Ph.D. diss., University of London.

———. 1985. "Islam in the Oral Traditions of Mali: Bilali and Surakata." *Journal of African History*, no. 26, pp. 33–49.

———. 1990. A *State of Intrigue: The Epic of Bamana Segu according to Tayiru Banbera*. Oxford: Oxford University Press.

———. 1992. "Burying Bards in Baobabs: Early European Impressions of Griot Status and Identity." Paper presented at the annual meeting of the African Studies Association, Seattle, Washington.

———. 1994. Interview with the author, Toronto, November 6.

———. 1995. Personal communication, December 20.

———. 1996. Personal communication, September 12.

———, and Barbara E. Frank. 1995. *Status and Identity in West Africa: Nyamakalaw of Mande*. Bloomington: Indiana University Press.

———, and Sory Fina Kamara. 1997. Excerpts from *The Epic of Almami Samori Touré*. In Johnson, Hale, and Belcher (1997), pp. 68–79.

Conway, Cecilia. 1995. *African Banjo Echoes in Appalachia*. Knoxville: University of Tennessee Press.

Coolen, Michael T. "Senegambian Influences on Afro-American Musical

Culture." *Black Music Research Journal*, vol. 11, no. 1, Spring 1991, pp. 1–18.

Coulibaly, Aly. 1990 "I. Quand l'égalité devient fiction" and "Le bons sens déserte." *Sud Hebdo*, March 1 and 8.

Coulibaly, Dramane. 1992. Interview with the author, Bamako, Mali, February 21.

Coulibaly, Fernand. 1992. Interview with the author, Bamako, Mali, February 21.

Coxson, Sarah. "The Complete Set." *Folk Roots*, no. 89, November, pp. 13, 15.

Cremer, Jean Henri. 1923. *Matériaux d'ethnographie et de linguistique soudanaises.* vol. I: *Dictionnaire français-peul.* Paris: Geuthner.

Cuoq, Joseph. 1985. *Receuil des sources arabes concernant l'Afrique occidentale du 8e au 16e siècle.* Paris: Centre National de la Recherche Scientifique.

Cutter, Charles H. "The Politics of Music in Mali." *African Arts / Arts d'Afrique.* 1:3 (Spring 1968): 38–39, 74–77.

Dalby, David. 1972. *Report of the International Conference on Manding Studies.* London: School of Oriental and African Studies.

Daniels, Geraldine. 1990. "Harlem Renaissance Gave Us 'Big Apple.'" *New York Times*, August 26.

Dapper, D. M. 1686. *Description de l'Afrique.* Amsterdam.

Davies, Carole Boyce, and Anne Adams Graves. 1986. *Ngambika: Studies of Women in African Literature.* Trenton, N.J.: African World Press.

De Jorio, Rosa. 1995. "Competing Models and Individual Strategies for Marriage in Contemporary Mali." Paper presented at the African Studies Association annual meeting, Orlando, November 6.

Delafosse, Maurice. 1912. *Haut-Sénégal-Niger.* Paris: Larose.

De Lajaille. 1802. *Voyage au Sénégal pendant les années 1784 et 1785, d'après les mémoires De Lajaille, ancien officier de la Marine française; Contenant des recherches sur la Géographie, la Navigation et le Commerce de la côte occidentale d'Afrique, depuis le cap Blanc jusqu'à la rivière de Serralione* [sic]; *avec des notes sur la situation de cette partie de l'Afrique jusqu'en l'an x (1801 et 1802) par P. Labarthe.* Paris: Dentu.

Dembélé, Dramane. 1992. Research report to the author, March 10.

Derrien, Isidore. 1882. "Le Haut Sénégal: Mission topographique du Commandant Derrien, 1880–81. Extraits de rapport d'ensemble." *Bulletin de la Société de Géographie et d'Archéologie de la Province d'Oran*, vol. 12, pp. 141–216.

DeVale, Sue Carole. 1989. "African Harps: Construction, Decoration, and Sound." In *Sounding Forms: African Musical Instruments.* Ed. Marie-Thérèse Brincard. New York: American Federation of the Arts.

Diabaté, Bala. 1992. Interview with the author, Kéla, Mali, February 22.

Diabaté, Massa Makan. 1985. *L'Assemblée des djinns.* Paris: Présence Africaine.

Diabaté, Sidiki. 1992. Interview with the author, Bamako, Mali, February 21.

Diabaté, Toumani. 1992. Interview with the author, Bamako, Mali, February 17.

Diagne, Ahmadou Mapaté. 1916. "Folklore: Origine des Griots." *Bulletin de l'Association de l'Enseignement de l'Afrique Occidentale Française*, June, pp. 275–78.

Diakité, Fatoumata Siré. 1977. "The Oral Tradition of the Geseres in Mali." Diss., Ecole Normale Supérieure, Bamako.

Diallo, Lamine. 1991. Interview with the author, Dakar, Senegal, October 15.

Diallo, Nafissatou. 1975. *De Tilène au Plateau: Une enfance dakaroise.* Dakar: Nouvelles Editions Africaines.

——. *La Princesse de Tiali.* 1987. Dakar: Nouvelles Editions Africaines. In English as *Fary, Princess of Tiali*, 1987. Trans. Ann Woollcombe. Washington, D.C.: Three Continents Press.

Diarra, Agnès-Fatoumata. 1971. *Femmes africaines en devenir: Les femmes zarma du Niger.* Paris: Anthropos.

Diawara, Mamadou. 1989. "Women, Servitude, and History: The Oral Historical Traditions of Women of Servile Condition in the Kingdom of Jaara (Mali) from the Fifteenth to the Mid-Nineteenth Century." In Karin Barber and P. F. de Moraes Farias, eds., *Discourse and Its Disguises: The Interpretation of African Oral Texts*, pp. 109–37. Center of West African Studies, University of Birmingham.

——. 1990. *La Graine de la parole.* Stuttgart: Steiner.

——. 1992. Interview with the author, Evanston, Illinois, November 16.

——. 1997. "Mande Oral Popular Culture Revisited by the Electronic Media." In *Readings in African Popular Culture.* Ed. Karin Barber. London: International African Institute; Oxford: James Currey; Bloomington: Indiana University Press.

Dieng, Bassirou. 1991. Interview with the author, Dakar, Senegal, October 14.

——. 1992. "La Figure du pouvoir et la figure de la parole dans les mythes et épopées soudaniens." Paper presented at the annual meeting of the African Studies Association, Seattle, December 6.

——. 1993. *L'Epopée du Kajoor.* Dakar: Centre Africain d'Animation et d'Echanges Culturels, Editions Khoudia, and Agence de Coopération Culturelle et Technique.

——, and Thomas A. Hale. 1994. Project proposal.

Dieterlen, Germaine. 1956. "Mythe et organisation sociale au Soudan français." *Journal de la Société des Africanistes*, vol. 25, nos. 1 and 2.

Diop, Abdoulaye-Bara. 1981. *La Société wolof: Tradition et changement.* Paris: Karthala.

Diop, Birago. 1947. *Les Contes d'Amadou Koumba.* Paris: Fasquelle.

——. 1958. *Les nouveaux contes d'Amadou Koumba.* Paris: Présence Africaine.

Diouf, Ibrahima. 1944. "Légende autour d'une dynastie par l'instituteur Diouf Ibrahima en service à l'Ecole primaire Blanchot à Saint-Louis." *Sénégal Magazine*, no. 62, April, pp. 177–83.

DjeDje, Jacqueline Cogdell. 1985. "Women and Music in Sudanic Africa." In *More Than Drumming: Essays on African and Afro-Latin American Music and Musicians.* Ed. Irene V. Jackson. Westport: Greenwood.

Dowd, Maureen. 1986. "For Many Cabbies Today, It's Not Noo Yawk." *New York Times*, January 23.

Dozy, R. 1881. *Supplément aux dictionnaires arabes*. Paris: Maisonneuve et Larose. Reprinted 1967.

Dramé, Adama, and Arlette Senn-Borloz. 1992. *Jeliya: Etre griot et musicien aujourd'hui*. Paris: Harmattan.

Dramé, Jali Muso. 1991. Interview with the author, Serrekunda, The Gambia, September 28.

Dubois, Félix. 1893. *La Vie au continent noir*. Paris: Bibliothèque d'Education et de Recréation.

Dumestre, Gérard. 1990. Conversation in Paris, June 30.

Dunn, Ross E. 1986. *The Adventures of Ibn Battuta: A Muslim Traveler of the 14th Century*. Berkeley: University of California Press.

Dupire, Marguerite. 1970. *Organisation sociale des Peul*. Paris: Plon.

Durán, Lucy. 1978. *Recorded Sound*, no. 69, January, pp. 754–57.

———. 1981. "A Preliminary Study of the Wolof Xalam (with a list of recordings at the British Institute of Record Sound)." *Recorded Sound*, no. 79 (January), pp. 29–50.

———. 1987. In "On Music in Contemporary West Africa." Kwabena Fosu-Mensah, Lucy Durán, and Chris Stapleton. *African Affairs*, vol. 86, no. 343 (April), pp. 227–40.

———. 1988. "Key to N'Dour." *Folk Roots*, October, pp. 33–35, 37.

———. 1989a. "Djely Mousso—Women of Mali." *Folk Roots*, vol. 11, no. 3 (September), pp. 34–39.

———. 1989b. Liner notes to "Jatigui," CD recording by Tata Bambo Kouyaté, Globestyle Records CDORB 042.

———. 1992. "Djinnius of the River." *Folk Roots*, November, pp. 38–41.

———. 1993a. Interviews with the author in London, June 12 and 17.

———. 1993b. "Savannah Sex Wars," *Wire*, no. 114 (August), pp. 42–44.

———. 1994. Conversation with the author, January 29.

———. 1995a. "Birds of the Mande—Freedom of Expression and Expressions of Freedom in the Popular Music of Southern Mali." *British Journal of Ethnomusicology*, vol. 4, pp. 101–34.

———. 1995b. "Jelimusow: The Superwomen of Malian Music." In Graham Furniss and Liz Gunner, eds., *Power, Marginality, and African Oral Literature*, pp. 197–207. Cambridge: Cambridge University Press.

———. 1995c. "'Musical Bargaining': Recordings and Musical Creativity in the Mande Jeli Tradition." Paper presented at the annual meeting of the African Studies Association, Orlando, November 4.

———. 1996. Personal communication, July.

Dyan, Brigitte, and Jean-Jacques Mandel, eds. 1984. *L'Afrique à Paris*. Paris: Rochevignes.

Ebron, Paulla. 1993. "Negotiating the Meaning of Africa: Mandinka Praisesingers in Transnational Context." Ph.D. diss., University of Massachusetts.

Es-Sa'di, Abderrahman ben Abdallah ben 'Imran ben 'Amir. 1898–1900. *Tarîkh es-Soudan*. Trans. Octave Houdas. Paris: Ecole des Langues Orientales Vivantes, 1898–1900. 2d ed., Paris: Adrien-Maisonnneuve, 1964.

Ewens, Graeme. 1991. *Africa O-Ye! A Celebration of African Music*. Enfield, Middlesex: Guinness.

Eyre, Banning. 1996. Report on "All Things Considered," National Public Radio, October 17.

Fadiga, Bouillagui. 1934. "Une circoncision chez les Markas du Soudan." *Bulletin du Comité d'Etudes Historiques et Scientifiques de l'Afrique Occidentale Française*, no. 18 (October-December), pp. 568–69.

Farmer, Henry George. 1928. "A North African Folk Instrument." *Journal of the Royal Asiatic Society*. lst quarter, pp. 25–34.

Faye, Louis Diène. 1983. *Mort et Naissance: Le monde sereer*. Dakar: Nouvelles Editions Africaines.

Fernandes, Valentim. 1938. *Description de la Côte d'Afrique de Ceuta au Sénégal (1506–1507)*. Ed. and trans. P. de Cenival and Théodore Monod. Paris: Larose.

———. 1951. *Description de la Côte Occidentale d'Afrique (Sénégal au Cap de Monte Archipels) (1506–1510)*. Ed. and trans. Théodore Monod, A. Teixeira da Mota, and Raymond Mauny. Bissau: Mémoria no. 11, Centro de Estudios Guiné Portuguesa.

Finnegan, Ruth. 1970. *Oral Literature in Africa*. Oxford: Clarendon Press.

Flutre, L.-F. 1956. "Sur deux mots qui viennent d'Afrique: baobab et griot." *Studia Neophilologica*, vol. 28, no. 2, pp. 218–25.

Freydberg, Malika Hadley. 1993. "The Griots of Roxbury: Continuing an African Tradition." *United Youth of Boston*, Summer, p. 8.

Frobenius, Leo. 1921. *Spielmannsgeschichten der Sahel*. Jena: Diederichs. English trans. in Frobenius and Douglas C. Fox, *African Genesis*. New York: Stackpole, 1937.

———. 1925. *Dichten und Demken im Sudan*. Jena, Atlantis V.

Furniss, Graham. 1995. "The Power of Words and the Relation between Hausa Genres." In *Power, Marginality, and African Oral Literature*. Ed. Graham Furniss and Liz Gunner. Cambridge: Cambridge University Press, pp. 130–44.

———. 1996. *Poetry, Prose, and Popular Culture in Hausa*. Edinburgh: Edinburgh University Press.

Gaby, Jean-Baptiste. 1689. *Relation de la Nigritie*. Paris: Edme Couterot.

Gaden, Henri. 1931. *Proverbes et maximes Peuls et Toucouleurs*. Paris: Institut d'Ethnologie, 1931.

Galliéni, Joseph Simon. 1885. *Un voyage au Soudan français (Haut-Niger et pays de Ségou. 1879–1881)*. Paris: Hachette.

———. 1891. *Deux campagnes au Soudan français. 1886–1888*. Paris: Hachette.

Gaudio, Attilio. 1993. *Les Populations du Sahara occidental*. Paris: Karthala.

Gerteiny, Alfred G. 1967. *Mauritania*. New York: Praeger.

Gleason, Judith. 1980. *Leaf and Bone: African Praise Poems*. New York: Viking.

Golberry, Silvestre Meinrad Xavier. 1802. *Fragmens* [sic] *d'un voyage en Afrique fait pendant les années 1785, 1786 et 1787, dans les Contrées occidentales de ce continent, comprises entre le cap Blanc de Barbarie, par 20 degrés, 47 minutes, et le cap de Palmes, par 4 degrées, 30 minutes latitude boréale.* Paris. In English as *Travels in Africa,* trans. William Mudford. London, 1808.

Gold, Nicholas. 1993. Interview with the author, London, June 23.

Goldstein, Kenneth. 1964. *A Guide for Fieldworkers in Folklore.* Hatboro, PA. Folklore Associates.

Gomes, Aldonía, and Fernanda Cavacos. 1993. "La Littérature du savoir traditionel." Trans. Michel Laban. *Notre Librairie,* no. 112 (January-March), pp. 93–97.

Gomez, Michael A. 1998. *Exchanging our Country Marks: The Transformation of African Identities in the Colonial and Antebellum South.* Chapel Hill: University of North Carolina Press.

Gonzalez, Fernando. 1992. "Out of Africa: New Visions of Pop Possibilities." *Boston Globe,* July 12, 1992, pp. B25, B27.

Gorer, Geoffrey. 1962. *Africa Dances.* New York: Norton.

Graham, Ronnie. 1988. *The Da Capo Guide to Contemporary African Music.* New York: Da Capo.

Gravrand, Henry. 1983. *La civilisation sereer: Cosaan.* Dakar: Nouvelles Editions Africaines.

Gray, John M. 1940. *A History of The Gambia.* London: Cass

Gray, John. 1991. *African Music: A Bibliographical Guide to the Traditional, Popular, Art, and Liturgical Musics of Sub-Saharan Africa.* New York: Greenwood.

Gray, William. 1825. *Travels in Western Africa, in the years 1818, 19, 20, and 21, from the River Gambia, through Woolli, Bondoo, Galam, Kasson, Kaarta, and Foolidoo, to the River Niger.* London: John Murray.

Grégoire, Abbé. 1808. *De la littérature des nègres.* Paris. Reprint, Paris: Perrin, 1991.

Griaule, Marcel. Cited in Linda Makarius, "Observations sur la légende des griots malinké," *Cahiers d'Études Africaines,* vol. 9, no. 4, p. 633.

Guignard, Michel. 1975. *Musique, honneur, et plaisir au Sahara.* Paris: Geuthner.

Hale, Thomas A. 1984. "Kings, Scribes, and Bards: A Look at Signs of Survival for Keepers of the Oral Tradition among the Songhay-Speaking Peoples of Niger." *Artes Populares,* vol. 10–11, pp. 207–10.

———. 1985. "Islam and the Griots in West Africa: Bridging the Gap between Two Traditions." *Africana Journal,* vol. 13, nos. 1–4, pp. 84–90.

———. 1990a. *Scribe, Griot and Novelist: Narrative Interpreters of the Songhay Empire. Followed by The Epic of Askia Mohammed Recounted by Nouhou Malio.* Gainesville: University of Florida Press and Center for African Studies.

———. 1990b. *Griottes of the Sahel: Female Keepers of the Songhay Oral Tradition in Niger*. An eleven-minute video distributed by Audio-Visual Services, The Pennsylvania State University.

———. 1994. "Griottes of the Sahel: Female Voices from West Africa," *Research in African Literatures*, vol. 25, no. 3, pp. 71–91.

———. 1996a. "Misrepresenting and Misreading *The Epic of Askia Mohammed*." *Research in African Literatures*, vol. 27, no. 3, pp. 128–35.

———. 1997a. "From the Griot of *Roots* to the Roots of *Griot*: A New Look at the Origins of a Controversial African Term for Bard." *Oral Tradition*, October 1997.

———. 1997b. "The Epic of Mali Bero. Narrated by Djibo Badié, known as Djeliba." In Johnson, Hale, and Belcher (1997), pp. 133–39.

———, and Paul Stoller. 1985. "Oral Art, Society, and Survival in the Sahel Zone." In Stephen Arnold, ed., *African Literature Studies: The Present State / L'Etat présent*, 163–69. Washington and Edmonton: Three Continents Press, African Literature Association, and Institute for Research in Comparative Literature.

———, and Nouhou Malio. 1996. *The Epic of Askia Mohammed*. Bloomington: Indiana University Press.

Haley, Alex. 1976. *Roots: The Saga of an American Family*. New York: Doubleday, 1976.

———. 1991. Interview with the author, State College, Pennsylvania, November 7.

Hama, Boubou. 1980. Interview with the author, Niamey, Niger, December 9.

Hamdun, Said, and Noël King. 1975. *Ibn Battuta in Black Africa*. London: Rex Collings.

Harris, Jessica B. 1995. *A Kwanzaa Keepsake: Celebrating the Holiday with New Traditions and Feasts*. New York: Simon and Schuster.

Harris, Laura Arnston. See Arnston, Laura.

Ibn Hawqal, Abu 'l-Qasim al-Nusaybi. *Kitab Surat al-ard*. Ed. J. H. Kramers. Leiden: 1938–39. Excerpted in Nehemiah Levtzion and J. F. P. Hopkins, eds., *Corpus of Early African Sources for West African History*, pp. 43–52. Cambridge: Cambridge University Press, 1981.

Haydon, Geoffrey. 1985. Introduction to *Repercussions: A Celebration of African-American Music*, ed. Haydon and Dennis Marks, pp. 9–13. London: Century.

Héricé, M. 1847. *Mémoire presenté à M. le Ministre de la Marine et des colonies, relativement à quelques améliorations à porter à la colonie du Sénégal*. Paris: Plon.

Hill, Patricia Liggins, ed. 1988. *Call and Response: The Riverside Anthology of the African American Literary Tradition*. Boston: Houghton Mifflin.

Hoffman, Barbara. 1990a. "The Power of Speech: Language and Social Status among Mande Griots and Nobles." Ph.D. diss., Indiana University.

———. 1990b. Interview with the author, Baltimore, November 2.

———. 1994. Conversation with the author, January 25.

———. 1995a. "Power, Structure, and Mande *Jeliw*." In Conrad and Frank (1995), pp. 36–57.

——. 1995b. "Technology and 'Tradition': Television and Jeliya." Paper presented at the annual meeting of the African Studies Association, Orlando, November 4.

——. 1995c. Personal communication cited in Arnoldi, p. 82.

——. 1996. Personal communication, August 20.

——. 1997. "Mande Social Structure and the Roles of the Griot." Paper presented March 21 at the Conference on Antebellum Culture and the Banjo, University of Virginia.

Hopkins, Nicholas. 1972. *Popular Government in an African Town: Kita, Mali.* Chicago: University of Chicago Press.

Hudson, Mark. 1989. *Our Grandmothers' Drums.* New York: Grove Weidenfeld.

Hugo, Victor. 1818, 1826. *Bug-Jargal ou la révolution haitienne.* Critical edition, ed. Roger Toumson. Fort-de-France, Martinique: Désormeaux, 1979.

Hunwick, John. 1985. *Sharī'a in Songhay: The Replies of al-Maghīlī to the Questions of Askia al-Hājj Muhammad.* New York: Oxford University Press.

——. 1996. Personal communication, January 30.

Hutchinson, John, and Kassim Kone. 1994. Project proposal.

Innes, Gordon. 1974. *Sunjata: Three Mandinka Versions.* London: School of Oriental and African Studies.

——. 1976. *Kaabu and Fuladu: Historical Narratives of the Gambian Mandinka.* London: School of Oriental and African Studies, 1976.

——. 1978. *Kelefa Saane: His Career Recounted by Two Mandinka Bards.* London: School of Oriental and African Studies.

Irvine, Judith Tempkin. 1973. "Caste and Communication in a Wolof Village." Ph.D. diss., University of Pennsylvania.

Irwin, Paul. 1981. *Liptako Speaks: History from Oral Tradition in Africa.* Princeton: Princeton University Press.

Jablow, Alta. 1971. *Gassire's Lute.* New York: Dutton; Prospect Heights: Waveland, 1991.

Jacquey, Marie-Clotilde. 1984. "Etre griot aujourd'hui: Entretien avec Massa Makan Diabaté." *Notre Librairie,* nos. 75–76 (July-October), pp. 114–19.

Jansen, Jan. 1994. "The Secret of the Dog That Seized the Soap: Some Observations on Mande Oral Tradition." *St. Petersburg Journal of African Studies,* no. 3, pp. 120–29.

——. 1996a. "'Elle connâit tout le Mande: A Tribute to the Griotte Siramori Diabate." *Research in African Literatures,* vol. 27, no. 4, pp. 180–97.

——. 1996b. Interview with the author, San Francisco, November 24.

——. 1997. "The Mande School of Oral Tradition as a Total Institution: The Case of Kéla." Paper presented at the African Studies Association meeting, Columbus, Ohio, November 13–16.

——. 1999. "An Ethnography of the Epic of Sunjata in Kela." In *In Search of Sunjata: The Mande Oral Epic as History, Literature, and Performance.* Ed. Ralph A. Austen. Bloomington: Indiana University Press.

———, and Cemako Kanté. 1991. *Siramuri Diabaté et ses enfants: une étude sur deux générations des griots malinké*. Utrecht and Bamako: University of Utrecht and Institut des Sciences Humaines.

———, Esger Duintjer, and Boubacar Tamboura, eds. 1995. *L'Epopée de Sunjata d'après Lansine Diabaté de Kéla*. Leiden: Research School CNSW.

———, and Clemens Zobel, eds. 1996. *The Younger Brother in Mande: Kinship and Politics in West Africa*. Leiden: Research School CNSW, Leiden University.

Jatta, Sidia. 1985. "Born Musicians: Traditional Music from The Gambia." In *Repercussions: A Celebration of African-American Music*, ed. Geoffrey Haydon and Dennis Marks, pp. 14–29. London: Century.

Jessup, Lynne. 1983. *The Mandinka Balafon: An Introduction with Notation for Teaching*. La Mesa, Calif: Xylo.

Jewsiewicki, Bogumil. 1987. "African Historical Studies: Academic Knowledge as 'Usable Past,' and Radical Scholarship." Paper presented at the annual meeting of the African Studies Association, Denver, November 19–23.

Jobson, Richard. 1623. *The Golden Trade*. London.

Johnson, John William. 1980. "Yes, Virginia, There is an Epic in Africa." *Research in African Literatures*, vol. 11, no. 3, 308–26.

———. 1988. Interview with the author, Bloomington, Indiana, November 17.

———. 1989. "Historicity and the Oral Epic: The Case of Sun-Jata Keita." In Robert E. Walls and George H. Shoemaker, eds., *The Old Traditional Way of Life: Essays in Honor of Warren E. Roberts*, pp. 251–61. Bloomington, Indiana: Trickster Press.

———. 1995. Personal communication, December 18.

———. 1996a. Conversation with the author, August 21.

———. 1996b. Conversation with the author, September 7.

———. 1996c. "Authenticity and Oral Performance: Textualizing the Epics of Africa for Western Audiences." Paper presented at the annual meeting of the African Studies Association, San Francisco, November 23–26.

———, and Fa-Digi Sisòkò. 1992. *The Epic of Son-Jara, A West African Tradition*. 2d ed. 1st ed., Bloomington: Indiana University Press, 1986.

———, Thomas A. Hale, and Stephen Belcher. 1997. *Oral Epics from Africa: Vibrant Voices from a Vast Continent*. Bloomington: Indiana University Press.

Johnston, H. A. S., and D. J. M. Muffett. 1973. *Denham in Bornu*. Pittsburgh: Dusquesne University Press.

Joseph, George. 1977. "The Wolof Oral Praise Song for Sému Coro Wende." In *Artist and Audience: African Literature as a Shared Experience*. Ed. Richard K. Priebe and Thomas A. Hale. Washington: Three Continents.

Ka, Abdou Anta. 1959. "Les Griots sont-ils condamnés à disparaître?" *Bingo*, no. 83, pp. 30–32.

Kabinè, Sissoko, Lilyan Kesteloot, Gérard Dumestre, and J.-B. Traoré. 1975. *La Prise de Dionkoloni*. Paris: Colin.

Kalissi, Fodé. 1993. Interviews with the author, Fort-de-France, Martinique, June 30, and State College, Pennsylvania, October 7.

Kamissoko, Nantenegwe. 1992. Interview with the author, Bamako, Mali, February 9.

Kane, Mohamadou. 1971. *Birago Diop.* Paris: Présence Africaine.

Kanuteh, Haja Nuse. 1991. Interview with the author, Serrekunda, The Gambia, September 29.

Kanuteh, Hawa. 1991. Interview with the author, Serrekunda, The Gambia, September 29.

Kanuteh, Jali Madi. 1991. Interview with the author, Serrekunda, The Gambia, September 29.

Karma, Weybi. 1989. Interview with the author and Aissata Niandou, Niamey, Niger.

Kâti, Mahmoud. 1913. *Tarîkh el-Fettâch ou chronique du chercheur pour servir à l'histoire des villes, des armées et des principaux personnages du Tekrour.* Trans. Octave Houdas and Maurice Delafosse. Paris: Ernest Leroux.

Keita, Cheick M. Chérif. 1995a. *Massa Makan Diabaté: un griot mandingue à la rencontre de l'écriture.* Paris: Harmattan.

———. 1995b. "Jaliya in the Modern World: A Tribute to Banzumana Sissoko and Massa Makan Diabaté." In Conrad and Frank (1995), 182–96.

Kendall, Martha B. 1982. "Getting to Know You." In David Parkin, ed., *Semantic Anthropology,* pp. 197–209. New York: Academic Press.

Kesteloot, Lilyan. 1991. "Power and Its Portrayal in Royal Mande Narratives." Trans. Thomas A. Hale and Richard Bjornson. *Research in African Literatures,* vol. 22, no. 1, pp. 17–26.

———, and Bassirou Dieng. 1989. *Du Tieddo au Talibé: Contes et mythes wolof II.* Paris: Présence Africaine, Agence de Coopération Culturelle et Technique, and Institut Fondamental d'Afrique Noire.

———, and Bassirou Dieng. 1997. *Les Epopées d'Afrique noire.* Paris: Karthala/UNESCO.

———, Amadou Traoré, Jean Baptiste Traoré, and Amadou Hampaté Bâ. 1992. *L'Epopée Bambara de Ségou.* Paris: Harmattan.

Kinte, Binta. 1991. Interview with the author, Juffure, The Gambia, October 5.

Knight, Roderic. 1971. "Towards a Notation and Tablature for the Kora, and Its Application to Other Instruments." *African Music,* vol. 5, no. 1, pp. 23–36.

———. 1973. "Mandinka Jaliya: Professional Music of The Gambia." Ph.D. diss., University of California at Los Angeles.

———. 1987. "Women as Musicians and Patrons of Music in Mande Society." Paper presented at the African Studies Association annual meeting, Denver, November 19–23.

———. 1991. "Music Out of Africa: Mande Jaliya in Paris." *The World of Music,* vol. 33, no. 1, pp. 52–68.

——. 1994. Conversation with the author, February 9.

——. 1996. Personal communication, July 1.

Koné, Kassim. 1995. Personal communication, December 21.

Konte, Dembo. 1991. Interview with the author, Brikama, The Gambia, October 1.

Korzybski, Alfred. 1933. *Science and Sanity: An Introduction to Non-Aristotelian Systems and General Semantics*. Lakeville, Conn.: International Non-Aristotelian Library.

Kourouma, Ahmadou. 1968. *Les Soleils des indépendances*. Paris: Seuil. In English as *The Suns of Independence*, trans. Adrian Adams. New York: Africana, 1981.

Kouyaté, Assa. 1992. Interview with the author, Bamako, Mali, February 16.

Kouyaté, Beya. 1991. Interview with the author, Lewisburg, Pennsylvania, April 14.

Kouyaté, Batourou Sékou. 1992. Interview with the author, Bamako, Mali, February 9.

Kouyaté, Djimo. 1997. Interview with the author, Charlottesville, Virginia, March 21.

Kouyaté, Kaba. 1995. Interview with the author, Bamako, Mali, February 10.

Kouyaté, Lamine. 1992. Interview with the author, Bamako, Mali, February 16.

Kouyaté, Mariam. 1992. Interview with the author, Bamako, Mali, February 21.

Kouyaté, Sékou. 1991. Interview with the author, Villepinte, France, July 6.

Kouyaté, Sidiki. 1992. Interview with the author, Bamako, Mali, February 21.

Kuyate, Aja Nafi. 1991. Interview with the author, Brikama, The Gambia, October 1.

Kuyate, Joma. 1991. Interview with the author, Serrekunda, The Gambia, September 29.

La Courbe, Michel Jajolet de. 1913. *Premier voyage du Sieur de La Courbe fait à la Coste d'Afrique en 1685*. Ed. Pierre Cultru. Paris: Champion.

Labouret, Henri. 1951. "A Propos du mot griot." *Notes Africaines*, no. 50, p. 56.

Laing, Alexander Gordon. 1825. *Travels in the Timannee, Kooranko, and Soolima Countries, in Western Africa*. London: John Murray.

Lambert, Pam. 1986. "Out of Africa: A Senegalese Superstar." *Wall Street Journal*, December 10, p. 28.

Lamiral, M. 1789. *L'Affrique* [sic] *et le peuple affriquain* [sic]. Paris: Dessenne.

Lane, Edward William. 1956. *Arabic-English Lexicon*. New York: Ungar.

Lavallière, H. de. 1911. "Cercle de Siguiri: Historique, notes, renseignements divers d'après les archives du poste." Report dated February 12, 1911, archived in the Fonds Terrien, no. 5928, Guinée française, vol. 1., Institut de France, Paris.

Laye, Camara. 1953. *L'Enfant noir*. Paris: Plon. In English as *The Dark Child*, trans. James Kirkup and Ernest Jones. New York: Farrar, Straus and Giroux, 1954.

——. 1978. *Le Maître de la parole: kouma lafôlô kouma*. Paris: Plon. In English as *The Guardian of the Word*, trans. James Kirkup. London: Collins, 1980.

Le Brasseur. 1778. "Détails historiques et politiques sur la religion, les moeurs et le commerce des peuples qui habitent la côte occidentale d'Affrique [sic] depuis l'Empire du Maroc jusqu'aux rivières de Casamance et de Gambie. Redigés et presentés à Son Altesse Sérénissime Monsieur le Duc de Penthièvre Amiral de France par M. Le Brasseur Commissaire ordonnateur Ancien Commandant pour le Roi et administrateur Général des possessions françaises à la Côte occidentale d'Affrique au mois de juin 1778 à Rambouillet." MS., Ancien Fonds, Salle de Réserve, Bibliothèque Nationale de France.

Le Maire. 1695. *Les voyages du Sieur Le Maire aux Isles Canaries, Cap-Verd, Senegal, et Gambie*. Paris: Collombat.

Lee, Hélène. 1988. *Rockers d'Afrique*. Paris: Albin Michel.

Ledger, Fiona. 1992. Conversation, World Service, British Broadcasting Corporation, London, June 15.

Leland, John. 1992. "You Gotta Pay Respect." *Newsweek*, January 6, p. 50.

Levtzion, Nehemia. 1980. *Ancient Ghana and Mali*. 2d ed. New York: Africana.

——, and J. F. P. Hopkins. 1981. *Corpus of Early Arabic Sources for West African History*. Cambridge: Cambridge University Press.

Leymarie, Isabelle. 1978. "The Role and Function of the Griots among the Wolof of Senegal." Ph.D. diss., Columbia University.

Limbo, Ibrahim. 1992. Interview with the author, Timbuktu, Mali, February 14.

Lindfors, Bernth. 1968. "The Palm Oil with Which Achebe's Words Are Eaten." *African Literature Today*, no. 1, pp. 2–18.

Locke, David. *Drum Damba: Talking Drum Lessons*. Crown Point, Ind.: White Cliffs, 1990.

Lombard, Jacques. 1965. *Structures de type "féodal" en Afrique noire: Etude des dynamismes internes et des relations sociales chez les Bariba du Dahomey*. Paris and La Haye: Mouton.

Lord, Albert. 1960. *The Singer of Tales*. Cambridge: Harvard University Press.

Lovejoy, Paul. 1986. *Salt of the Desert Sun*. Cambridge: Cambridge University Press.

Ly, Amadou. 1991. *L'Epopée de Samba Guéladiégui*. Dakar: Institut Fondamental d'Afrique Noire/UNESCO.

McGill, Alice, Mary Carter Smith, and Elmira M. Washington. 1985. *The Griots' Cookbook: Rare and Well-Done*. Columbia, Md.: Fairfax.

McIntosh, Roderick, and Susan Keech McIntosh. 1981. "The Inland Niger Delta before the Empire of Mali: Evidence from Jenne-Jeno." *Journal of African History*, no. 22, pp. 1–22.

McLaughlin, Fiona. 1992. Conversation with the author, November 22.

——. 1998. "Islam and Popular Music in Senegal: The Emergence of a 'New Tradition.'" *Africa: Journal of the International African Institute*, vol. 67, no. 4, pp. 560–81.

McNaughton, Patrick R. 1988. *The Mande Blacksmiths: Knowledge, Power, and Art in West Africa*. Bloomington: Indiana University Press.

Mack, Beverly. 1981. "Wakokin Mata: Hausa Women's Oral Poetry." Ph.D. diss., University of Wisconsin.

Mage, Eugène. 1868. *Voyage au Soudan Occidental (1863–1866)*. Paris: Hachette. 1980. Paris: Karthala.

Magel, Emil. 1981. "Caste Identification of the Hare in Wolof Oral Narratives." *Research in African Literatures*, vol. 12, no. 2, pp. 185–202.

———. 1984. *Folktales from the Gambia: Wolof Fictional Narratives*. Washington, D.C.: Three Continents Press.

Makarius, Laura. 1969. "Observations sur la légende des griots malinké." *Cahiers d'Etudes Africaines*, vol. 9, no. 4, pp. 626–40.

Makward, Edris. 1990. "Two Griots of Contemporary Senegambia." In Isidore Okpewho, ed., *The Oral Performance in Africa*, pp. 23–41. Ibadan: Spectrum.

Malio, Nouhou. 1981. Interview with the author, Saga, Niger, January 26.

Mane, Ismaila. 1991. Interview with the author, Serrekunda, The Gambia, October 4.

Mane, Nyuma. 1991. Interview with the author, Serrekunda, The Gambia, September 28.

Manniche, Lise. 1991. *Music and Musicians in Ancient Egypt*. London: British Museum Press.

Mariko, Keletigui. 1989. Interview with the author, Niamey, Niger, February 20.

Marty, Martin E. 1995. "Faithful Griots: Storytellers in West Africa." *Christian Century*, vol. 112, no. 9, p. 311.

Meillassoux, Claude. 1964. "Histoire et institutions du *kafo* de Bamako d'après la tradition des Niaré." *Cahiers d'Etudes Africaines*, vol. 4, no. 14, pp. 186–227.

———, Lassana Doucouré, and Diaowé Simagha. 1967. *La Légende de la dispersion des Kusa*. Dakar: Institut Fondamental d'Afrique Noire.

Miles, Milo. 1994. "Sinewy Sweetness from Mali." *New York Times*, February 2, section H, p. 30.

Miller, Christopher L. 1990. *Theories of Africans*. Chicago: University of Chicago Press.

Miller, Joseph C. 1980. "Listening for the African Past." In J. C. Miller, ed., *The African Past Speaks: Essays on Oral Tradition and History*. Folkestone: William Dawson.

Mo., V. 1995. "Youssou N'Dour." *Le Monde*, January 14.

Modic, Kate. 1993. "Bamana Women Drummers." In Esther Dagan, ed., *Drums: The Heartland of Africa*, pp. 78–79. Montreal: Galerie Amrad/African Arts.

———. 1996. "Song, Performance, and Power: The Ben Ka Di Women's Association in Bamako, Mali." Ph.D. diss., Indiana University.

Monteil, Charles. 1951a. "Problèmes du Soudan occidental: Juifs et judaïsés." *Hespéris. Archives Berbères et Bulletin de l'Institut des Hautes Etudes Marocaines*, no. 59, pp. 265–98.

——. 1951b. "Les 'Ghâna' des géographes arabes et des Européens." *Hespéris*, pp. 441–52.

——. 1953. "La Légende de Ouagadou et l'origine des Soninké." In *Mélanges Ethnologiques*, Mémoire 23, pp. 359–408. Dakar: Institut Fondamental d'Afrique Noire.

Monteil, Vincent. 1968. "Un cas d'économie ostentatoire: Les griots d'Afrique noire." *Economies et Sociétés*, vol. 2, no. 4 (April), pp. 773–91.

Moore, David Chioni. 1994. "Routes: Alex Haley's *Roots* and the Rhetoric of Genealogy." *Transition*, no. 64, pp. 4–21.

——. 1996. "Revisiting a Silenced Giant: Alex Haley's Roots—A Bibliographic Essay, and a Research Report on the Haley Archives at the University of Tennessee, Knoxville." *Resources for American Literary Study*, vol. 22, no. 2, pp. 195–249.

Moore, Francis. 1740. *Travels into the Inland Parts of Africa*. London: Cane.

Moraes Farias, Paulo de. 1992. "Praise as Intrusion and as Foreign Language: A Sunjata Paradigm Seen from the Gesere Diaspora in Béninois Borgu." Paper presented at the Sunjata Conference, Northwestern University, Evanston, Illinois, November 15.

——. 1993a. Interview with the author, Birmingham, England, June 18.

——. 1993b. "The Oral Traditionist as Critic and Intellectual Producer: An Example from Contemporary Mali." In Toyin Falola, ed., *African Historiography: Essays in Honor of Jacob Ajayi*. London: Longman.

——. 1995. "Praise Splits the Subject of Speech: Constructions of Kinship in the Manden and Borgu." In Graham Furniss and Liz Gunner, eds., *Power, Marginality, and African Oral Literature*, pp. 225–43. Cambridge: Cambridge University Press.

Moreau, J. L. M. 1897. "Notice générale sur le Soudan: 2ème partie, ethnologie." Archives Nationales du Mali, ID-91.

Morrow, Lance. 1992. "Folklore in a Box." *Time*, September 21, pp. 51–52.

Mounkaila, Fatima. 1989. Interview with the author, State College, Pennsylvania, September 11.

Muhammed, Dalhatu. 1981. "The Tabuka Epic in Hausa: An Exercise in Narratology." *Proceedings of the Hausa Conference at Bayero University*, Kano, April 2–5.

Ndao, Cheik. 1967. *L'exil d'Albouri*. Paris: Oswald.

N'diaye. 1959. "Triomphe à New York des Ballets Africains de Keita Fodeba." *Bingo*, no. 77, pp. 18–20.

Ndiaye, A. Raphaël. 1986. *La Place de la femme dans les rites au Sénégal*. Dakar: Nouvelles Editions Africaines.

N'diaye, Diana. 1991. "Senegal at the 1990 Festival of American Folklife." *Smithsonian Folklife News*, January, p. 3.

N'diaye, Michèle. 1991. Interview with the author in Dakar, Senegal, October 12.

N'diaye, Moussa. 1991. Interview with the author, Dakar, Senegal, October 15.

Newman, Paul, and Roxana Ma Newman. 1979. *Modern Hausa-English Dictionary*. Ibadan: University Press Limited.

Newton, Robert C. 1994. Paper presented at the annual meeting of the African Studies Association, Toronto, November 3–6.

———. 1995. "Epic Proportions: Jeliya in the Big Band Era." Paper presented at the annual meeting of the African Studies Association, Orlando, November 6.

———. 1997. "The Epic Cassette: Technology, Tradition and Imagination in Contemporary Bamana Segou." Ph.D. diss., University of Wisconsin.

Niandou, Ramatou. 1989. Interview with the author, Niamey, Niger, February 15.

Niane, Djibril Tamsir. 1960. *Soundjata, ou l'épopée mandingue*. Paris: Présence Africaine. In English as *Sundiata: An Epic of Old Mali*, trans. G. D. Pickett. London: Longman, 1965.

———. 1971. *Sikasso ou la dernière citadelle*. Honfleur: Oswald.

———. 1998. Interview with the author, Medford, Massachusetts, May 21.

Nicolas, Guy. 1968. "Processus oblatifs à l'occasion de l'intronisation de chefs traditionelles en pays hausa (République du Niger)." *Revue du Tiers-Monde*, vol. 9, no. 33 (January-March), pp. 43–93.

Nobile, Philip. 1993. "Alex Haley's Hoax: Secret Tapes & Private Papers Reveal How the Celebrated Author Faked the Pulitzer Prize–Winning *Roots*." *Village Voice*, February 23, pp. 31–38.

Norris, H. T. 1968. *Shīnqītī Folk Literature and Song*. Oxford: Clarendon Press.

Okpewho, Isidore. 1979. *The Epic in Africa: Toward a Poetics of the Oral Performance*. New York: Columbia University Press.

———. 1996. "How Not to Treat African Folklore." *Research in African Literatures*, vol. 27, no. 3, pp. 119–28.

Oliver, Paul. 1970. *Savannah Syncopators: African Retentions in the Blues*. New York: Stein and Day.

Olivier de Sardan, Jean Pierre. 1982. *Concepts et conceptions songhay-zarma*. Paris: Nubia.

Ortiz, Fernando. 1924. *Glosario de Afronegrismos*. Habana: El Siglo XX.

Ottaway, Mark. 1977. "Doubts Raised Over Story of the Big TV Slave Saga." *The Sunday Times*, London, April 10, pp. 1, 17–18, 21.

Oumar, Sidi Ali. 1992. Interview with the author, Timbuktu, Mali, February 14.

Owusu, Kwesi. 1986. *The Struggle for Black Arts in Britain*. London: Comedia.

Pageard, Robert. 1959. "Note sur les Diawambé ou Diokoramé." *Journal de la Société des Africanistes*, no. 29, pp. 239–60.

Palmer, Richard. 1936. *The Bornu Sahara and Sudan*. London: John Murray; New York: Negro Universities Press, 1970.

Panzacchi, Cornelia. 1994. "The Livelihoods of Traditional Griots in Modern Senegal." *Africa*, vol. 64, no. 2, pp. 190–210.

Pâques, Viviana. 1991. *La Religion des esclaves: Recherches sur la confrérie marocaine des Gnawa*. Bergamo: Moretti and Vitali.

Pareles, John. 1989. "Africa's Vast Variety, in Sights and Sounds." *New York Times*, May 13, pp. 12–13.

———. 1990. "A New Respect for Folk—But Black Tie Optional." *New York Times*, October 28, p. 32.

———. 1992. "A Singer from Senegal by Way of the World." *New York Times*, November 9.

Park, Mungo. 1799. *Travels in the Interior Districts of Africa*. London: 1799. Reprint, London: Eland, 1983.

Paul, Sigrid. 1987. "The Wrestling Tradition and Its Social Functions." In William J. Baker and James A. Mangan, eds., *Sport in Africa: Essays in Social History*, pp. 23–46. New York: Africana.

Person, Yves. 1968. *Samori: Une révolution dyula*. vols. I, II, III. Dakar: IFAN, 1968–1975.

Peterson, Hannibal. 1993. *African Portraits*. Austin: Hannibal Lokombe Music.

Pevar, Marc, and Oliver Franklin. 1979. *Al Haji Bai Konte*. A twelve-minute film distributed by Cultural Encounters, Inc., c/o Marc Pevar, 606 Ridge Avenue, Kennett Square, PA 19348.

Pevar, Susan Gunn. 1977. "Teach-In: The Gambian Kora." *Sing Out!*, vol. 25, no. 6, pp. 15–17.

———. 1978. "The Construction of a Kora." *African Arts*, vol. 11, no. 4, pp. 66–73.

Pfaff, Françoise. 1984. *The Cinema of Ousmane Sembène*. Westport: Greenwood.

P.H.S. 1977. "The *Times* Diary: Sticking Pins into a Best-Seller." *The Times*, London, April 12, p. 12.

Pollet, Eric, and Grace Winter. 1971. *La Société soninké*. Brussels: Institut de Sociologie, Université Libre de Bruxelles.

Porquet, Niangoranh. 1989. "La Griologie: combinatoire multimédia et impac-togénèse de la tradition orale." In Victor Bachy, ed., *Tradition orale et nouveaux medias*, pp. 55–67. Brussels: Organisation Catholique Internationale du Ciné-ma et de l'Audiovisuel and Festival Panafricain du Cinéma de Ouagadougou.

Prédal, René, ed. 1982. *Jean Rouch: un griot gaulois*. Special issue of *Ciném-Action*, no. 17.

Priebe, Richard K., and Thomas A. Hale. 1979. *Artist and Audience: African Literature as a Shared Experience*. Washington, D.C.: Three Continents Press and African Literature Association.

Puigadeau, Odette. 1936. *Pieds nus à travers la Mauritanie*. Paris: Plon.

Quillian, Linda. 1996. "River Deep, Mountains High: Modern-Day Griots Pass on Ways to Hurdle Racism." *Black Issues in Higher Education*, January 25, pp. 24–25.

Quiquandon, F. 1892. "Histoire de la puissance mandingue." *Bulletin de la Société de Géographie Commerciale de Bordeaux*, June 6, pp. 305–429.

Qureshi, Regula Burckhardt. 1986. *Sufi Music of India and Pakistan: Sound, Context, and Meaning in Qawwali*. Cambridge: Cambridge University Press.

Raffenel, Anne. 1846. *Voyage dans l'Afrique Occidentale*. 2 vols. Paris: Bertrand.

Rasmussen, Susan J. 1995. "Between Ritual, Theatre, and Play: Blacksmith Praise at Tuareg Marriage." Paper presented at the African Studies Association Meeting, Orlando, November 3–6.

———. 1997. *The Poetics and Politics of Tuareg Aging: Life Course and Personal Destiny in Niger.* DeKalb, Ill.: Northern Illinois University Press.

Reid, Calvin. 1997. "Fact or Fiction? Hoax Charges Still Dog *Roots* 20 Years On." *Publishers Weekly*, October 6.

Riley, Dorothy Winbush. 1995. *The Complete Kwanzaa: Celebrating Our Cultural Harvest.* New York, HarperCollins.

Rouch, Jean. 1990. Interviews with the author, Paris, June 27 and 28.

Rousseau, Raymond. 1929. "Le Sénégal d'autrefois. Etude sur le Oualo." *Cahiers de Yoro Dyâo, Bulletin de Commerce, d'Etudes, d'Histoire et de Science en Afrique Occidentale Française,* nos. 1–2, pp. 133–211.

Rule, Sheila. 1992. "An African Superstar Sings Out to the World." *New York Times,* September 5, p. 11.

Sagado, Gitu. 1989. Interview with the author, Yatakala, Niger, February 18.

Saint-Lô, Alexis de. 1637. *Relation du voyage du Cap-Verd.* Paris: Targa.

Sangaré, Oumou. 1993. *Ko Sira.* CD, World Circuit WCD 036.

Schultze, A. *The Sultanate of Bornu.* 1968 (1913). Trans. and ed. P. A. Benton. London: Cass.

Schuyler, Phillip D. 1981. "Music and Meaning among the Gnawa Religious Brotherhood of Morocco." *The World of Music,* vol. 23, no. 1, pp. 3–11.

Seck, E. Nago, and Sylvie Clerfeuille. 1986. *Musiciens africains des années 80: Guide.* Paris: Harmattan.

Sembène, Ousmane. 1973. *Xala.* Paris: Présence Africaine.

Seydou, Christiane. 1972. *Silâmaka et Poullôri: récit épique peul raconté par Tinguidji.* Paris: Colin.

———. 1997. "The Epic of Hambodedio and Saïgalare. Narrated by Hamma Diam Bouraima." In Johnson, Hale, and Belcher (1997), pp. 149–61.

Sherman, Tony. 1994. "A Jazz Griot with a Sense of Civility." *New York Times,* January 23, p. 28.

Sidibe, Bakari. 1991. Interview with the author, Banjul, The Gambia, October 3.

Sidibé, Mamby. 1959. "Les gens de caste ou nyamakala au Soudan français." *Notes Africaines,* no. 81, pp. 13–17.

Sidikou, Aïssata. 1997. "Recreating Words, Reshaping Worlds: The Verbal Art of Women from Niger, Mali, and Senegal." Ph.D. diss., The Pennsylvania State University.

Silla, Ousmane. 1966. "Persistance des castes dans la société wolof contemporaine." *Bulletin de l'Institut Fondamental d'Afrique Noire,* vol. 28, series B, no. 34, pp. 731–70.

Skinner, Elliott P. 1989. *The Mossi of Burkina Faso: Chiefs, Politicians and Soldiers.* 2nd ed. Prospect Heights, Ill.: Waveland.

Smith, Mary Carter. 1996. Conversation with the author, January 4.

Sow Fall, Aminata. 1982. *L'Appel des arènes*. Dakar: Nouvelles Éditions Africaines.

Stapleton, Chris, and Chris May. 1990. *African Rock: The Pop Music of a Continent*. New York: Dutton.

Stoller, Paul. 1989. *The Fusion of the Worlds: An Ethnography of Possession among the Songhay of Niger*. Chicago: University of Chicago Press.

——. 1992. *The Cinematic Griot: The Ethnography of Jean Rouch*. Chicago: University of Chicago Press.

——. 1997. *Sensuous Scholarship*. Philadelphia: University of Pennsylvania Press.

——, and Cheryl Olkes. 1987. *In Sorcery's Shadow: A Memoir of an Apprenticeship among the Songhay of Niger*. Chicago: University of Chicago Press.

Stone, Ruth. 1998. *Africa: The Garland Encyclopedia of World Music*. vol. 1. New York: Garland.

Street, Brian V. 1984. *Literacy in Theory and Practice*. Cambridge: Cambridge University Press.

Suso, Aja Mariam. 1991. Interview with the author, Serrekunda, The Gambia, September 28.

Suso, Bofi. 1991. Interview with the author, Serrekunda, The Gambia, September 28.

Suso, Foday Musa. 1991. Interview with the author, Serrekunda, The Gambia, September 29.

Suso, Mohammed Manjako. 1991. Interview with the author, Serrekunda, The Gambia, September 28.

Suso, Nakoyo. 1994. Interview with the author, State College, Pennsylvania, October 7.

Suso, Sayendeng. 1991. Interview with the author, Serrekunda, The Gambia, September 28.

Susso, Papa Bunka. 1988. Interview with the author, State College, Pennsylvania, February 17.

——. 1993. Comments during discussion on griots, African Studies Association meeting, Boston, December 6.

Sylla, Assane. 1978. *La Philosophie morale des Wolofs*. Dakar: Sankoré.

Tamari, Tal. 1987. "Les Castes au Soudan Occidental: Etude anthropologique et historique." Ph.D. diss., University of Paris X.

——. 1991. "The Development of Caste Systems in West Africa." *Journal of African History*, no. 32, pp. 221–50.

——. 1995. "Linguistic Evidence for the Existence of West African 'Castes.'" In Conrad and Frank (1995), pp. 61–85.

Tandina, Ousmane Mahamane. 1997. "Gama Gari Kanta et Agabba, épopée haoussa." Narrated by Adam Toudou. In *Les Epopées d'Afrique noire*, ed. Lilyan Kesteloot and Bassirou Dieng, pp. 392–99. Paris: Karthala/UNESCO.

Tauxier, Louis. 1927. *La Religion des Bambara*. Paris: Geuthner.

Télémaque, Hamet Sow. 1916. "Folklore: Origine des griots." *Bulletin de l'Association de l'Enseignement de l'Afrique Occidentale Française*, no. 25 (June), pp. 275–78.

Téra, Kalilou. 1974. "Kore Dugakoro: Epopée bambara de Baba Sissoko." Mémoire, Ecole Normale Supérieure, Bamako, pp. 5–6.

Terkel, Studs. 1995a. *Coming of Age: The Story of Our Country by Those Who've Lived It*. New York: New Press.

———. 1995b. In Sonia Csencsits, "Unforgettable Gertie Fox Recalled in Terkel Book." *The Morning Call* [Allentown, PA], September 17, p. B3.

———. 1995c. In Tom Heinen, "Unrestrained: Terkel Tells It As He Sees It." *Milwaukee Journal Sentinal*, October 21, p. 1.

Tessa, Ayouba. 1981. Interview with the author, Garbey Kourou, Niger, April 17.

Thoyer-Rozat, Annik. 1981. *Le riche et le pauvre: Conte bambara du Mali par Tayiru Banbera*. Paris: By the author.

Toop, David. 1991. *Rap Attack 2: African Rap to Global Hip Hop*. London: Serpent's Tail.

Touré, Ali Farka. 1993. Interview with the author, London, England, June 19.

Traoré, Sékou. 1989. *Questions africaines: francophonie, langues nationales, prix littéraires, O.U.A.* Paris: Harmattan.

Urvoy, Yves. 1942. *Petit Atlas ethno-démographique du Soudan*. Paris: Larose.

Van Natta, Jr., Don. 1997. "An R.S.V.P. to the President: Deep Regrets. I'm in Custody." *New York Times*, March 22, pp. 1, 12.

Verneuil, Victor. 1858. *Mes aventures au Sénégal: Souvenirs de voyage*. Paris: Librairie Nouvelle.

Villalón, Leonardo. 1995. *Islamic Society and State Power in Senegal: Disciples and Citizens in Fatick*. Cambridge: Cambridge University Press.

Wane, Yaya. 1969. *Les Toucouleurs du Fouta Tooro (Sénégal): Stratification sociale et structure familiale*. Dakar: Institut Fondamental de L'Afrique Noire.

Warms, Richard. 1992. Interview with Zoumana Kouyaté, in Bougouni, Mali, January 7.

Watkins, Mel. 1976. "A Talk with Alex Haley." *New York Times Book Review*, September 26, pp. 2, 10, 12.

Watrous, Peter. 1989a. "Continent of Music: Africa on Stage." *New York Times*, May 12, pp. C1, C22.

———. 1989b. "Youssou N'Dour Finds His International Groove." *New York Times*, May 15, p. C17.

Watta, Oumarou. "The Human Thesis: A Quest for Meaning in African Epic." Ph.D. diss., University of Buffalo, 1985.

———. 1993. *Rosary, Mat and Molo: A Study in the Spiritual Epic of Omar Seku Tal*. New York: Lang.

Wickham, DeWayne. 1994. "The Many Persona of Speaker Gingrich." Gannett News Service, December 30.

Wisniewski, David. 1992. *Sundiata: Lion King of Mali*. New York: Clarion Books.

Wright, Bonnie L. 1989. "The Power of Articulation." In William Arens and Ivan Karp, eds., *Creativity of Power: Cosmology and Action in African Societies*, pp. 39–57. Washington, D.C.: Smithsonian Institution Press.

Wright, Donald R. 1981. "Uprooting Kunta Kinte: On The Perils of Relying on Encyclopedic Informants." *History in Africa*, no. 8, pp. 205–17.

———. 1997. *The World and a Very Small Place in Africa*. Armonk, N.Y.: Sharpe.

Zahan, Dominique. 1963. *La Dialectique du verbe chez les Bambara*. Paris: Mouton.

Zemp, Hugo. 1968. "La Légende des griots malinké." *Cahiers d'Etudes Africaines*, vol. 6, no. 4, pp. 611–42.

Zobel, Clemens. 1996. "The Noble Griot—The Construction of Mande *Jeliw*-Identities and Political Leadership as Interplay of Alternate Values." In Jan Jansen and Clemens Zobel, eds. (1996), pp. 35–47.

❊ Index ❊

THOMAS A. HALE is Professor of African, French, and comparative literature at The Pennsylvania State University. He is the author of *Les Ecrits d'Aimé Césaire* (Montreal, 1978) and *Scribe, Griot and Novelist* (Florida, 1990). He collected, translated, and edited *The Epic of Askia Mohammed* (Indiana, 1996). He has co-edited, with Richard Priebe, *The Teaching of African Literature* (Texas, 1977; Three Continents, 1989), and *Artist and Audience: African Literature as a Shared Audience* (Three Continents, 1979). With John Johnson and Stephen Belcher, he recently co-edited and contributed texts to *Oral Epics from Africa* (Indiana, 1997).